The Adobe Illustrator

WOW!

Book

tips, tricks, and techniques from 100 top Illustrator artists

SHARON STEUER

Adobe

Peachpit
Press

The Adobe Illustrator CS2 Wow! Book

Sharon Steuer

Peachpit Press

1249 Eighth Street

Berkeley, CA 94710

510/524-2178, 510/524-2221 (fax)

Find us on the World Wide Web at: www.peachpit.com

To report errors, please send a note to errata@peachpit.com

Peachpit Press is a division of Pearson Education

The Adobe Illustrator CS2 Wow! Book is published in association with Adobe Press

Real World Adobe Illustrator CS2 excerpted content is ©2006 Mordy Golding

Contributing writers to this edition: Dave Awl, Conrad Chavez, Steven H. Gordon, Lisa Jackmore, Gabriel Powell
Wow! Series editor: Linnea Dayton
Copy editor: Mark Stricker
First edition Illustrator Wow! Book design: Barbara Sudick
Tech editors: Vicki Loader, Jean-Claude Tremblay
Cover Illustration: Russell Benfanti
Indexer: Karin Arrigoni

ISBN 0-321-32046-8

9 8 7 6 5 4 3 2 1

Printed and bound in the United States of America.

The Adobe Illustrator CS2

WOW!
Book

The Adobe Illustrator CS2 Wow! Book
Team of Contributing Writers and Editors

Sharon Steuer is the originator of *The Illustrator Wow! Books,* and author of *Creative Thinking in Photoshop: A New Approach to Digital Art.* Sharon has worked in the field of digital art since 1983; teaching, exhibiting, and writing. In between *Wow!* books, Sharon is a full-time artist working in traditional and digital media (www.ssteuer.com). She lives with her cats, Puma and Bear, and radio star husband, the real Jeff Jacoby. She is extremely grateful to her co-authors, editors, testers, *Wow!* team members (past and present), Adobe, Peachpit, and of course the *Wow!* artists for making this book possible.

Dave Awl is a Chicago-based writer and editor. Returning to the *Wow!* team, he revised many of the chapter Introductions, as well as Chapter 1. Dave is also a poet, performer, and alumnus of Chicago's Neo-Futurists theater company. His work is collected in the book *What the Sea Means: Poems, Stories & Monologues 1987-2002.* You can find out more about his various projects at his Web site: Ocelot Factory (www.ocelotfactory.com).

Conrad Chavez is new to the *Wow!* team. Conrad's long relationship with the Pen tool begun during his days as the support lead for Aldus (later Macromedia) FreeHand 1.0-4.0, and continued throughout the 1990s when he documented Adobe's print, Web, and video products. Now a Seattle-based writer and editor, Conrad also works the bitmap side of digital graphics as a fine-art photographer. You can check out his work at www.conradchavez.com. Conrad is co-author of the third edition of *Real World Scanning and Halftones* (Peachpit Press).

Steven H. Gordon is a returning co-author for Step-by-Steps and Galleries. Steven has been an ace member of the team since the *Illustrator 9 Wow! Book.* He has too many boys to stay sane. If only they wouldn't fall off cliffs in Bryce—the National Park, not the software. Steven runs Cartagram (www.cartagram.com), a custom mapmaking company located in Madison, Alabama. He thanks Monette and his mom for their encouragement, and the boys for their cessation of hostilities.

Lisa Jackmore has returned as a contributing writer for Galleries, and the *Illustrator Wow! Course Outline.* She is a wonderful artist, both on and off the computer, creating miniatures to murals. By day, she wields a crayon and defends herself against shark-jets and galactic zappers with her son, Sam. Using her digital pen, she works on illustrations that we should all see some day in story books and in the Pottery Barn catalog above that leather club chair.

Vicki Loader has moved from tester to tech editor and consultant for the *Wow! Team*, where her role has included reworking the *Illustrator Wow!* style guide, the templates, and styles. During the week, she works in London as an independent consultant and trainer. Weather permitting, the weekends finds her in her little yellow convertible, blowing the dust of London from her mind by getting lost on English country lanes; she calls it having a sense of adventure; her friends put it down to lacking any sense of direction.

Gabriel Powell has joined the team, writing some critical lessons and Galleries, and working on chapter intros. He is an Adobe Certified Instructor and Senior Training Director for Metafusion Training. His passion is to help people learn and find success in what they do. Those who discover his classes rave about how easy and fun it is to learn from him—we hope he'll be back next edition!

Jean-Claude Tremblay has been an Illustrator output expert for many years. After serving as a magnificent *Wow!* Tester for the past few editions of the book, Jean-Claude worked on this edition as our last-phase tech editor and resident magician, rescuing corrupt files. He lives in Montreal, Quebec, Canada with his wife Suzanne and 2-year old daughter Judith; watching her growth is the most beautiful and amazing "art" experience he has ever seen.

Mordy Golding has been a contributor to the *Illustrator Wow! Books* from the beginning, and was the primary co-author on the second edition of the *Wow!* book. Since then, Mordy has been busy writing his own books and, for a stint, working as product manager for Adobe Illustrator. Mordy is now the author of *Real World Adobe Illustrator CS2*, in addition to continuing as a *Wow!* technical consultant; *Real World Adobe Illustrator* and *Adobe Illustrator Wow!* have now joined into a partnership. While *Real World* will print a full-color insert highlighting some of our lessons and Galleries, *Illustrator Wow!* will be excerpting and adapting passages from *Real World* where we feel Mordy's insider's perspective of new and cryptic features of Illustrator will be helpful to readers.

Additional contributing writers and editors: **Victor von Salza** led the update team for the CS edition of *Wow!* and was instrumental in our moving the book from Quark to InDesign. **Mark Stricker** is a writer and editor who lives in Hamden, CT; he is co-curator of a reading series at the Arts + Literature Laboratory Gallery in New Haven, CT. **Sandee Cohen,** a.k.a. vectorbabe.com, was our emergency technical consultant. **Peg Maskell Korn** is a woman of many hats. Sharon's savior in the last hours of the first edition, Peg has only missed working on one edition of the book. Besides being master tweaker of the book, Peg updated screenshots and proofread this edition. Please see the Acknowledgments for a thorough listing of the *Wow!* team contributors.

The Wow! CD: **Jay Nelson** and **Design Tools Monthly** have joined *Wow!* in a partnership; **Design Tools Monthly** is contributing the list of Illustrator plug-ins and resources as a *Wow! Appendix* and PDF on the *Wow! CD*. Victor Gavenda from Peachpit did a great job mastering the *Wow! CD*.

Contents

Live Effects & Graphic Styles

11 Live 3D Effects

12

13

Important: Read me first!

Where's the AICS2 User Guide?

Once upon a time, buying software meant getting a big, thick, printed user guide. Not any more. Adobe Illustrator CS2 (AICS2) is sold in a number of different configurations (alone, and with various combinations of the Creative Suite), and not all versions include a printed *User Guide*. Therefore, when needed, we will refer you to *Illustrator Help* (it's part of the "Adobe Help Center"). Choose Help > Illustrator Help to access this convenient searchable version of the *User Guide*. CS2 Standard and Premium edition owners can find a PDF version of the *User Guide* on the "Resources and extras" CD. You can purchase a printed copy from adobe.com.

Design Tools Monthly on *Wow!*

When it came time to decide which Illustrator plug-ins we should tell you about, we went to the source. Every month *Design Tools Monthly* compiles and summarizes all the newest trends in graphic software and hardware. At the back of the book you'll find a *Wow!* Appendix compiled by Jay Nelson, editor of *Design Tools Monthly*, especially for *Wow!* In addition, on the *Wow! CD* you'll find a PDF version of this special appendix with clickable links to the products' websites.

We had a lot of decisions to make with this 8th edition of *The Illustrator Wow! Book*. Back in 1994 when I embarked on the creation of the original *Illustrator Wow! Book* (with no version number!), Adobe Illustrator was still a fairly simple program. Even though the first edition was only 224 pages, it was packed with almost every detail found in the longer "bible" type books at the time.

First, I want readers to know is that this is no longer a solo project. In order to provide you with the most thoroughly updated book possible in a timely manner (as close as possible to the shipping of the new version of the program), this book now requires a large team of experts working simultaneously. I'm immensely proud of and grateful for everyone who works so hard to deliver the best book possible to you, the reader.

In addition, Adobe Illustrator CS2 can no longer be considered a simple program. And as this book grew to double the size of the original, we were faced with a decision: Do we keep writing bigger and denser books with technical information (with a higher cover price for readers to bear), or do we concentrate on being the full-color book for designers and illustrators like we did in the beginning? We chose the latter, so you'll see a renewed focus on the *Wow!* aspects of how to create art and design using Adobe Illustrator. We'll leave the more technical aspects of the program to the more comprehensive technical books, such as *Real World Adobe Illustrator CS2*.

And speaking of *Real World Adobe Illustrator CS2*, we've now engaged in an exclusive partnership with this author Mordy Golding. We are honored to have been granted permission to adapt the "Special Section: Working with Live Paint and Group Isolation Mode," from Golding's book *Real World Adobe Illustrator CS2* (also Peachpit Press). You'll also find additional technical information, excerpted in full from *Real World Adobe Illustrator CS2*, presented on *Wow! CD* in PDF format.

In order to provide you with lots of new work In this fully updated, reworked, and expanded edition of *Illustrator Wow!*, we have also retired many wonderful artworks that have been in this book for over a decade. As always you'll find hundreds of essential production techniques, timesaving tips, and beautiful art generously shared by *Illustrator Wow!* artists worldwide. In addition to the wonderful contributing artists, and contributing writers, our amazing team of *Wow! testers* sets this book apart from all others. This team thoroughly tests every lesson and gallery to make sure it actually works. We deliberately keep all lessons short to allow you to squeeze in a lesson or two between clients, and to encourage the use of this book within the confines of supervised classrooms.

In order to keep the content in this book tantalizing to everyone, I've assumed the reader has a reasonable level of competence with basic Mac and Windows concepts, such as opening and saving files, launching applications, copying objects to the clipboard, and performing mouse operations. I've also assumed that you understand the basic functionality of most of the tools.

I'd love to tell you that you can learn Adobe Illustrator just by flipping through the pages of this book, but the reality is that there is no substitute for practice. The good news is, the more you work with Illustrator, the more techniques you'll be able to integrate into your creative process.

Use this book as a reference, a guide for specific techniques, or simply as a source of inspiration. After you've read this book, read it again, and you'll undoubtedly learn something you missed the first time. As I hope you'll discover, the more experienced you become with Adobe Illustrator, the easier it will be to assimilate all the new information and inspiration you'll find in this book. Happy Illustrating!

Sharon Steuer

Where's Live Paint & Live Trace?

Find new Live Paint lesson in the *Zen of Illustrator* chapter, and Live Paint and Live Trace in the *Beyond Basic Drawing & Coloring* chapter.

Lots of artwork on the CD!

Now we put even more of our *Wow!* artists' artwork on the *Wow! CD* so you can follow along, or simply pick the art apart to see how it was constructed.

Additional Illustrator training

You'll find additional lessons in the "Ch02-zen_lessons" folder on the *Wow! CD*. Included in that folder are the *Zen Lessons* (which supplement *The Zen of Illustrator* chapter). These lessons walk you through some basics of working with the Pen tool, Bézier curves, layers, and stacking order. And also starting in this edition, you'll find the "Zen of the Pen" commercial edition (by Sharon Steuer and Pattie Belle Hastings) in the Ch02-zen_lessons folder; these lessons include QuickTime movies to help you learn to work with the Pen tool and Bézier curves in Illustrator, Photoshop and InDesign. If you're new to Illustrator, you may even want to begin by taking a class. If you're teaching a class in Illustrator, download the *IllustratorCS2 Wow! Course Outline* (by Sharon Steuer and Lisa Jackmore) from: www.ssteuer.com/edu

How to use this book...

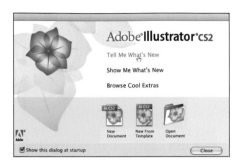

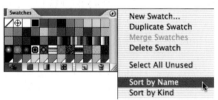

With the All Swatches icon selected choose "Sort by Name" then "List View" from the pop-up menu

The Swatches palette viewed with "Sort by Name" selected

Before you do anything else, read the *Wow! Glossary* on the pull-out quick reference card at the back of the book. The Glossary provides definitions for the terms used throughout *The Illustrator CS2 Wow! Book* (for example, ⌘ is the Command or Apple key for Mac).

WELCOME TO *WOW!* FOR WINDOWS AND MAC

If you already use Adobe Photoshop or InDesign you'll see many interface similarities to Illustrator CS2. The similarities should make the time you spend learning each program much shorter. Your productivity should also increase across the board once you adjust to the new shortcuts and methodologies (see "Shortcuts and keystrokes" following, and the *Illustrator Basics* chapter).

Shortcuts and keystrokes

Because you can now customize keyboard shortcuts, we're restricting the keystrokes references in the book to those instances when it's so standard that we assume you'll keep the default, or when there is no other way to achieve that function (such as Lock All Unselected Objects). We'll always give you Macintosh shortcuts first, then the Windows equivalent (⌘-Z/Ctrl-Z). For help with customization of keyboard shortcuts, and tool and menu navigation (such as single key tool access and Tab to hide palettes), see the *Illustrator Basics* chapter.

Setting up your palettes

In terms of following along with the lessons in this book, you'll probably want to enable the "Type Object Selection by Path Only" option (see Tip "Selecting type by accident" in the *Type* chapter). Next, if you want your palettes to look like our palettes, you'll need to sort swatches by name. Choose "Sort by Name" and "List View" from the Swatches pop-up menu. (Hold Option/Alt when you choose a view to set this as the default for all swatches.)

Illustrator CS2 sets an application default that could inhibit the way Illustrator experts work. In order for your currently selected object to set all the styling attributes for the next object you draw (including brush strokes, live effects, transparency, etc.), you must open the Appearance palette (Window menu) and disable New Art Has Basic Appearance. You can disable (and re-enable) this default either by: 1) clicking on the bottom left icon in the Appearance palette (dark shows that it's enabled; see Tip at right), *or* 2) choosing New Art Has Basic Appearance from the Appearance palette pop-up menu (✓ shows it's enabled). Your new setting sticks even after you've quit.

HOW THIS BOOK IS ORGANIZED...

You'll find six kinds of information woven throughout this book—all of it up to date for Illustrator CS2: **Basics, Tips, Exercises, Techniques, Galleries, and References.**

1 Basics. *Illustrator Basics* and *The Zen of Illustrator* qualify as full-blown chapters on basics and are packed with information that distills and supplements your Adobe Illustrator manual and disk. Every chapter starts with a general overview of the basics. These sections are designed so advanced Illustrator users can move quickly through them, but I strongly suggest that novices and intermediate users read them very carefully. This book supplements the tutorials that ship with Illustrator.

2 Tips. When you see this icon ⊙, you'll find related artwork on the *Illustrator CS2Wow!CD* (referred to hereafter as the *Wow! CD*) within that chapter's folder. Look to the information in the gray and red boxes for hands-on Tips that can help you work more efficiently. Usually you can find tips alongside related textual information, but if you're in an impatient mood, you might just want to flip through, looking for interesting or relevant tips. The red arrows ⟶, red outlines and **red text** found in tips (and sometimes with artwork) have been added to emphasize or further explain a concept or technique.

Disable Appearance default

If you want your currently selected object to set *all* styling attributes for the next object, disable New Art Has Basic Appearance in the Appearance palette (see at right).

Default   Disabled

1

2 ⊙ *The CD icon indicates that related artwork is on the* Illustrator CS2Wow!CD

Tip boxes

Look for these gray boxes to find Tips about Adobe Illustrator.

Red Tip boxes

Red Tip boxes contain warnings or other essential information.

3
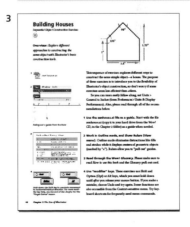

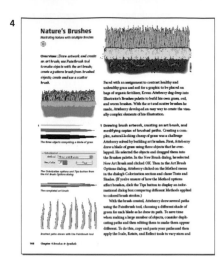

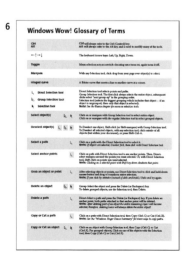

3 Exercises. (Not for the faint of heart.) We have included step-by-step exercises to help you make the transition to Illustrator technician extraordinaire. *The Zen of Illustrator* chapter and the *Zen Lessons* on the *Wow! CD* are dedicated to helping you master the mechanics (and the soul) of Illustrator. Take these lessons in small doses, in order, and at a relaxed pace. All of the Finger Dances are customized for Mac and Windows.

4 Techniques. In these sections, you'll find step-by-step techniques gathered from almost one hundred *Illustrator Wow!* artists. Most *Wow!* techniques focus on one aspect of how an image was created, though we'll often refer you to different *Wow!* chapters (or to a specific step-by-step technique, Tip, or Gallery where a technique is introduced) to give you the opportunity to explore a briefly-covered feature more thoroughly. Feel free to start with almost any chapter, but each technique builds on those previously explained, so you should try to follow the techniques within each chapter sequentially. Some chapters include **Advanced Technique** lessons, which assume that you have assimilated all of the techniques found throughout the chapter. *Advanced Techniques* is an entire chapter dedicated to advanced tips, tricks, and techniques.

5 Galleries. The Gallery pages consist of images related to techniques demonstrated nearby. Each Gallery piece is accompanied by a description of how the artist created that image, and may include steps showing the progression of a technique detailed elsewhere. *Illustrator & Other Programs* consists almost entirely of Gallery pages to give you a sense of Illustrator's flexibility.

6 References. *Resources* and *Artists* appendixes, *Glossaries*, and *General Index* can be found in the back of this book and on the pull-out card. In addition, we will occasionally direct you to *Illustrator Help* when referring to specific information that's well-documented in the Adobe Help Center. To access this choose Help > Illustrator Help.

Acknowledgments

As always, my most heartfelt gratitude goes to the more than 100 artists and Illustrator experts who generously allowed us to include their work and divulge their techniques.

First thanks must go to Mordy Golding, who, as former Adobe Illustrator product manager, and now author of *Real World Adobe Illustrator CS2,* continues to champion this book, and to share his expertise with the *Wow!* team. And thanks to all at Adobe, including Philip Guindi, Marcus Chang, Teri Pettit, Brenda Sutherland, Julie Meridian, Ian Giblin, and Jill Merlin who answered our zillions of questions, and came through with our special requests. Thank you John Nack for Photoshop help with understanding Smart Objects and Chad Seigel for help with InDeisgn.

This revision required a major team effort, and would not have happened without an amazing group of people. Thankfully, Steven Gordon agreed to return to the team to tackle a batch of new Step-by-Steps and Galleries—Steven always adds a dose of humor to his incredible resourcefulness, for which we're all exceedingly grateful. Steven also manages the artist releases and shares with me the job of curating the art. Thank you, Dave Awl for all your hard work and dedication on revisions to *Chapter 1* and many of the chapter introductions. Thank you Lisa Jackmore for doing such a great job with Galleries and the *Illustrator CS2 Wow! Course Outline* (from www.ssteuer.com/edu). Thank you to Conrad Chavez who joined us as a heavy-hitting *Wow!* writer of the first order. And thanks to Gabriel Powell for learning the ropes so quickly and helping us make our deadlines by contributing key writing. Thanks to Mark Stricker for working at all hours while mastering the job of *Wow!* copyediting. Thank you to Peg Maskell Korn for being involved since the beginning, putting up with me on a moment-to-moment basis. Thank you Vicki Loader and Jean-Claude Tremblay for doing extraordinary jobs as technical editors and technical consultants; we could not have completed this edition without your incredible dedication! As always, thanks also go to our stellar team of testers and consultants, especially Adam Z Lein, Jean-Claude Tremblay, Bob Geib, Vicki Loader, Federico Platón, Gary Newman, Chuck Sholdt, Nini Tjäder, and Mike Schwabauer. Thank you Victor von Salza for all the advance work on this edition. Thanks to Cynthia Baron for offering to help, and Laura Mucci for helping with *Wow!* clean-up tasks. Thank you Leonard Rosenthol of Apago for helping us make some of our PDFs smaller. Thank you to Sandee Cohen who continues as our official kibbitzer. And thanks to Karin Arrigoni for being so flexible with the index! Thank you Adam Z Lein for the fabulous updated online database wo we can track who's doing what. Thank you Jay Nelson for the partnership between *Wow!* and *Design Tools Monthly.*

Thank you to all the folks at Commercial Document Services for the fabulous printing job. And thanks to everyone at Peachpit Press for all the things you do to make sure this book happens. Thanks *especially* Nancy Davis, Connie Jeung-Mills, Nancy Ruenzel, Kelly Ryer, and Rebecca Ross. And of course thanks also to Gary-Paul Prince, Zigi Lowenberg, Lisa Brazieal, Hannah Onstad-Latham, and Kim Lombardi. And a final very special thank you to Victor Gavenda for coming out of CD retirement to work at all hours to master our *Wow!* CD, and Eric Geoffroy as our media producer. Last, but not least, thanks to Linnea Dayton for being the *Wow!* series editor.

Illustrator Basics

1

Illustrator Basics

Don't start yet!

Before you begin this book, make sure you read both the "How to Use This Book" section in the front of the book, and the pullout *Glossary* at the back.

Minimum system requirements

Macintosh:
- G4 or G5 processor
- Mac OS X version 10.2.8 or later

Windows:
- Intel Pentium 3 or higher processor
- Windows 2000 (SP3 or SP4), or Windows XP (SP1 or SP2)

Both systems:
- 256 MB of RAM installed
- 820 MB (Win) or 960 MB (Mac) of available hard drive space
- If using Adobe PostScript Printers: Adobe PostScript Level 2 or Adobe PostScript 3
- 1024 x 768 or better monitor resolution recommended
- CD-ROM drive for installation

AICS2 images & files cropped!

Unlike previous versions of Illustrator, when you place or open an AICS2 image in another application (PS, ID, or a previous version of AI), art extending beyond the paper size will be cropped. To avoid this, choose a larger paper size before saving as a CS2 file.

This chapter is packed with tips and techniques chosen to help you use Adobe Illustrator with optimal ease and efficiency. Whether you're a veteran of Illustrator or a relative newcomer, you're likely to find information here that will greatly increase your productivity and help you get up to speed on the latest features. Be sure to heed the advice of the "Don't start yet!" Tip at left.

COMPUTER & SYSTEM REQUIREMENTS

Creating artwork on the computer is as rewarding as it is challenging. Computer art tools, including Adobe Illustrator, have undergone great improvements in the past few years. In order to accommodate demands for faster and more powerful software, the more powerful upgrades might not run on older computers. For example, the minimum requirement is now at least 256 MB of RAM available to run Illustrator. You'll also need more hard disk space than ever before: at least 1.2 GB and probably much more, because Illustrator files containing live blends, brushes, raster images, gradient meshes, live effects, and transparency can be quite large. (Not to mention that the Adobe Illustrator CS2 CD contains lots of bonus content you'll want room for, including templates, libraries, and fonts.) Illustrator doesn't require a large monitor, but your monitor should be able to accommodate a resolution of at least 1024 x 768 so that you don't feel cramped. The best solution is to use two monitors; keep your palettes on one monitor and create your artwork on the other.

SETTING UP YOUR PAGE
New Document

When you first launch Illustrator, you'll be greeted by a Welcome screen that allows you to choose one of three possible options for getting started: New document (which simply opens a new blank document), New from Template (which allows you to select a template file on which to base your document), and Open Document (while lets you choose a pre-existing file to open). After startup, New, New from Template, and Open are accessible from the File menu, and the Welcome screen remains available from the Help menu.

To create a new blank document, select New from the File menu or the Welcome screen. In the dialog box, select the Artboard Setup (the document dimensions and orientation) and the Color Mode (CMYK or RGB). For dimensions, the default page size is 612 pt x 792 pt, which is equivalent to 8.5" x 11". You can choose different page sizes from the pop-up menu (including common paper sizes for print purposes, and several common Web page sizes in pixels), and you can also choose your preferred measurement system. Pages can be as small as 1 pixel x 1 pixel, or as large as 227.5" x 227.5". For orientation, choose either the Portrait or Landscape button. For color mode, Illustrator doesn't allow you to create new art that uses both CMYK and RGB colors in the same document, so you'll need to pick one or the other.

Templates

Template files make it easy for you to save finished designs that can be used as the basis for new work. This comes in handy when you need to create a number of documents or pages with both common design elements and specific content that changes.

Illustrator's templates are actually a special file format (ending in .ait). When you choose New from Template (from the File menu or the Welcome screen), Illustrator creates a regular Illustrator document (ending in .ai) based on the template, while the original .ait template file remains unchanged, ready for the next time you need it, no matter what changes you make to your new document.

When you create a new file from a template, Illustrator automatically loads the various settings associated with the template file (including details such as Artboard dimensions, swatches, type styles, symbols, and guides), as well as any content the template contains.

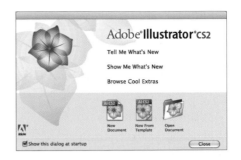

The Welcome screen offers you a number of options for starting your session, as well as convenient access to information and extras

If Welcome isn't welcome

If you don't want the Welcome screen to appear every time you launch Illustrator, don't worry. Just uncheck the "Show this dialog at startup" box in the Welcome screen's lower left corner and it will no longer appear automatically. (But it will remain available via the Help menu if you change your mind.)

Preferences in Mac & Windows

Illustrator Preferences are located under different menus in Mac and Windows. In Mac, Preferences are accessed via the Illustrator menu (or ⌘-K), whereas in Windows, Preferences are accessed via the Edit menu (or Ctrl-K).

Note: *If things ever go terribly wrong with Illustrator, search for the folder "Adobe Illustrator CS2 Settings" where you'll find "AIPrefs" (Win) or "Adobe Illustrator Prefs" (Mac); delete this file. Illustrator will create brand-new preferences when you restart the program.*

One of the free templates that ships with Illustrator CS2—this one is a CD traycard. (Come to think of it, Lorem Ipsum is a pretty good name for a band.)

You can create as many original templates as you need or want, and you can also take advantage of the more than 200 professionally designed templates included with Illustrator—everything from business cards to Web pages to restaurant menus.

The Artboard

A box with a solid black outline defines the Artboard dimensions and the final document size. Double-click the Hand tool to fit your image to the current window. One change you may notice from previous versions of Illustrator is that the dotted line indicating page tiling (and showing the current printable area) no longer displays on the Artboard by default. That's because page tiling is now displayed and controlled from the preview in the Print dialog box (as discussed below), so most users will never need to view page tiling on the Artboard. (That said, you can still use View > Show Page Tiling to display dotted lines if you want them, and View > Hide Page Tiling to conceal them. Use the Page tool to click-drag the dotted-line page parameters around the Artboard.)

With Illustrator's sophisticated print controls, you can make very precise choices about what to print. From the Crop to Artboard pop-up, you can choose Artboard, Artwork Bounding Box, or Crop. Artboard uses the dimensions of your Illustrator page size to determine what gets printed. Artwork Bounding Box uses the artwork bounding box. And Crop allows you to define a crop area.

The One-Stop Print Dialog Box

Thanks to Illustrator's full-service Print dialog box, it's no longer necessary to use a Page Setup dialog box to change things like page size and orientation. You can control all those settings and more from within the Print dialog box. (In fact, the Mac version still has a Page Setup button, but if you click on it you'll get a warning that the Page Setup dialog box is provided by the OS, and for best results you should set all options from within Illustrator's Print dialog box.)

As previously mentioned, the preview area in the Print dialog box shows you the page's printable area. It also lets you scale artwork to order as you go to print it, while choosing exactly which artwork in the document you want to print. So you don't have to worry about changing the size of the Artboard itself in order to print things at a different scale.

Illustrator also lets you save your Print settings as time-saving presets, so if you're designing billboards or other very large media sizes, you can set the appropriate scale and then save it as a Print preset for easy access.

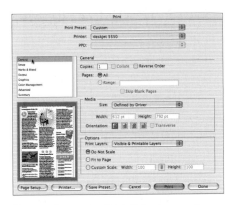

Illustrator's one-stop Print dialog box—note the preview area in the lower left corner, which shows you the printable area of the page, and lets you adjust and scale your artwork to print

MAKING YOUR MOVES EASIER

Look over this section to make sure you're aware of the many ways to select tools and access features. Learning these simple techniques will free you from mousing to the toolbox or depending on the pull-down menus.

Keyboard shortcuts for tools and navigation

Need to access a tool? Press a key. Press "T" to choose the Type tool, "P" for the Pen tool, and so on. Choose any tool in the toolbox by pressing its keyboard shortcut. (Each shortcut used to be a single key, but there are now so many tools that a few of them have double-key shortcuts.) To learn the default keyboard shortcuts for your tools, with Show Tool Tips enabled (this is on by default), hold the cursor over any tool in the toolbox, and its keyboard shortcut will appear in parentheses next to the tool name (toggle the Tool Tips option in General Preferences). **Note:** *Keyboard shortcuts won't work while you're in text editing mode. Press Escape to leave text editing mode and use a keyboard shortcut. Your text will remain unchanged, with edits preserved.*

Changing keyboard shortcuts

To change a shortcut for a tool or menu item, open the Keyboard Shortcut dialog box (Edit > Keyboard Shortcuts). Making a change to a shortcut will change the set name to "Custom." When you're finished making changes

Mac users: It's recommended that you set all your options in Illustrator's Print dialog box, rather than through the OS-provided Page Setup dialog box. If you forget, Illustrator will remind you with the message shown above

Custom keyboard shortcuts

To assign a shortcut to a menu item or tool, select Edit > Keyboard Shortcuts. Making any changes will rename the set "Custom." If you choose a shortcut already in use, you will get a warning that it is currently being used and that reassigning it will remove it from the item to which it is currently assigned. When you exit the dialog box you will be asked to save your custom set. You can't overwrite a *preset*.

If you double-click the Scale tool, you can resize your selection with or without altering line weights:

- To scale a selection, while also scaling line weights, make sure to enable the Scale Strokes & Effects checkbox.
- To scale a selection while maintaining your line weights, disable Scale Strokes & Effects.
- To decrease line weights (50%) without scaling objects, first scale the selection (200%) with Scale Strokes & Effects disabled. Then scale (50%) with it enabled. Reverse these steps to increase line weights.

PAPCIAK-ROSE

Various options displayed in the Control palette when a (non-text) vector object is selected

Various options displayed in the Control palette when a Type object is selected

Various options displayed in the Control palette when a Live Paint group is selected (Live Paint is discussed in the Beyond Basic Drawing & Coloring *chapter)*

and want to exit the dialog box, you will be asked to save your shortcuts to a new file. This custom file will be saved in the Adobe Illustrator CS2 Settings folder and will end in ".kys." If you move your .kys file to the appropriate Presets folder (inside the Illustrator application folder), it will be available to all users on that computer. In addition, every time you make any changes to a saved set (not a default preset), you'll be asked if you want to overwrite that set. You can also use the Save button to create a new keyboard shortcut file. Click the Export Text button if you need a text file as a reference for a specific set of shortcuts, or if need to print them.

Note: *You can't change most palette items, but the few you can change are found at the bottom of the menu commands list in the Edit > Keyboard Shortcuts dialog box.*

The new Control palette

One of the handiest features introduced in Illustrator CS2 is the new Control palette, which by default is docked at the top of the working area, and which changes contextually to display different tools and controls depending on the type of object currently selected. If you select a text object, for example, the palette will display text-formatting controls; whereas selecting a path will display options such as Brush and Style, or Expand and Release buttons, depending on the kind of path. If you have multiple kinds of objects selected, the Control palette displays alignment controls in addition to allowing you to set options for all those selected objects.

You can customize the Control palette by clicking on its menu button. You can choose to dock the Control palette to the bottom of your working area rather than the top, and select or deselect various types of controls that can be displayed in the palette.

When you see underlined words in the Control palette, you can click them to display a relevant palette. For instance, clicking on the word Stroke will display a Stroke palette. Clicking on the word Opacity opens a pop-up Transparency palette. Clicking on the arrows reveals mini pop-ups, such as the arrow to the right of Opacity, which reveals a handy pop-up Opacity slider!

Context-sensitive menus

If you're not already familiar with context-sensitive menus, you might find them to be a great time saver. Windows users merely click the right mouse button. If you're on a Mac with a single-button mouse, press the Control key while you click and hold the mouse button. In both cases a menu pops up (specific to the tool or item you are working with), providing you with an alternative to the regular pull-down menus.

Tear off palettes

The Illustrator Toolbox lets you tear *off* subsets of tools so you can move the entire set to another location. Click on a tool with a pop-up menu, drag the cursor to the arrow end of the pop-up, and release the mouse.

WORKING WITH OBJECTS
Anchor points, lines, and Bézier curves

Instead of using pixels to draw shapes, Illustrator creates objects made up of points, called "anchor points." They are connected by curved or straight outlines called "paths" and are visible if you work in Outline mode. (Choose View > Outline to enter Outline mode, and View > Preview to change back.) Illustrator describes information about the location and size of each path, as well as its dozen or so attributes, such as its fill color and stroke weight and color. Because you are creating objects, you'll be able to change the order in which they stack. You'll also be able to group objects together so you can select them as if they were one object. You can even ungroup them later, if you wish.

If you took geometry in your school days, you probably remember that the shortest distance between two points is a straight line. In Illustrator, this rule translates into each line being defined by two anchor points that

An example of a clickable underlined word in the Control palette. If you click on the word Stroke, a dropdown version of the Stroke palette will open

Flotation device

You can "float" the Control palette and position it anywhere you like just by dragging its gripper bar (at the left edge of the palette). To redock the palette, just drag it back to the top or bottom of your working area, where it will snap back into place.

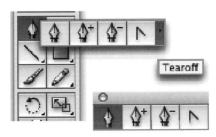

Tear off tool palettes

Changing measurement units

To set units of measurement for rulers, palettes, and some dialog boxes or filters, as well as units for measuring strokes and text, use the Units & Display Performance area of Preferences.
Note: *Control-click (Mac) or right mouse-click (Win) on the rulers to select different units.*

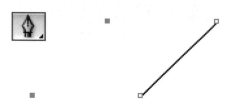

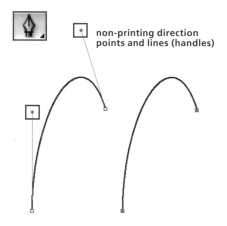

Clicking with the Pen tool to create anchor points for straight lines

non-printing direction points and lines (handles)

Click-dragging with the Pen tool to create anchor points and pulling out direction lines for curves

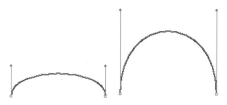

When direction handles are short, curves are shallow; when handles are long, curves are deep

The length and angle of the handles determine the "gesture" of the curves

you create by either clicking with the Pen tool or drawing with the Line Segment tool.

In mathematically describing rectangles and ellipses, Illustrator computes the center, the length of the sides, or the radius, based on the total width and height you specify.

For more complex shapes involving free-form curves, Adobe Illustrator allows you to use the Pen tool to create Bézier curves, defined by non-printing anchor points (which literally anchor the path at those points), and direction points (which define the angle and depth of the curve). To make these direction points easier to see and manipulate, each one is connected to its anchor point with a non-printing direction line, also called a "handle." The direction points and handles are visible when you're creating a path with the Pen tool or editing the path with the Direct Selection tool. While all of this might sound complicated, manipulating Bézier curves can become intuitive. Mastering these curves, though initially awkward, is the heart and soul of using Illustrator.

More about Bézier curves

If you're new to using Bézier curves, take some time to go through the Adobe training materials. The "Ch02-zen_lessons" folder on the *Wow! CD* includes several "Zen" practice lessons that will help you fine-tune your Bézier capabilities (such as the "Zen of the Pen" Bézier lessons, which include QuickTime demonstrations on drawing and editing paths and curves).

Many graphics programs include Béziers, so mastering the Pen tool, though challenging at first, is very important. Friskets in Corel Painter, paths in Photoshop and InDesign, and the outline and extrusion curves of many 3D programs all use the Bézier curve.

The key to learning Béziers is to take your initial lessons in short doses and to stop if you get frustrated. Designer Kathleen Tinkel describes Bézier direction lines as "following the gesture of the curve." This artistic view should help you to create fluid Bézier curves.

Some final rules about Bézier curves

- The length and angle of the handles "anticipate" the curves that will follow.
- To ensure that the curve is smooth, place anchor points on either side of an arc, not in between.
- The fewer the anchor points, the smoother the curve will look and the faster it will print.
- Adjust a curve's height and angle by dragging the direction points, or grab the curve itself to adjust its height.

WATCH YOUR CURSOR!

Illustrator's cursors change to indicate not only what tool you have selected, but also which function you are about to perform. If you watch your cursor, you will avoid the most common Illustrator mistakes.

If you choose the Pen tool:

- **Before you start,** your cursor displays as the Pen tool with "×" indicating that you're starting a new object.

- **Once you've begun your object,** your cursor changes to a regular Pen. This indicates that you're about to add to an existing object.

- **If your cursor gets close to an existing anchor point,** it will change to a Pen with "–" indicating that you're about to delete the last anchor point! If you click-drag on top of that anchor point, you'll redraw that curve. If you hold the Option (Mac)/Alt (Win) key while you click-drag on top of the point, you'll pull out a new direction line, creating a corner (as in the petals of a flower). If you click on top of the point, you'll collapse the outgoing direction line, allowing you to attach a straight line to the curve.

- **If your cursor gets close to an end anchor point of an object,** it will change to a Pen with "o" to indicate that you're about to "close" the path. If you do close the path, then your cursor will change back to a Pen with "×" to indicate that you're beginning a new object.

Quick selection tool switch

You can switch from the Selection tool to the Direct Selection tool on the fly by holding down the ⌘/Ctrl key. ⌘-Option/Ctrl-Alt will get you the Group selection tool.

 Starting an object

 Adding a point

 Removing a point

 Creating a corner (when over an existing point)

 Continuing from an anchor point

 Joining two line segments

 Closing an object

Basic cursor feedback for the Pen tool

The hollow snap-to arrow

As long as Snap to Point is enabled (in the View menu) and your object is selected, with your Direct Selection tool you can grab objects from any path or point and drag until they snap to a guide or another anchor point. Watch for the cursor to change to a hollow (white) arrow.

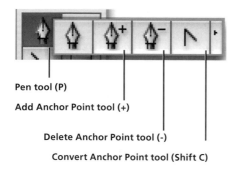

Pen tool (P)

Add Anchor Point tool (+)

Delete Anchor Point tool (-)

Convert Anchor Point tool (Shift C)

- **If you use the Direct Selection tool to adjust the object as you go,** be sure to look at your cursor when you're ready to continue your object. If it's still a regular Pen, then continue to place the next point, adding to your object. If the Pen tool has "×" (indicating that you are about to start a new object), then you must redraw your last point. As you approach this last anchor point, your cursor will change to a Pen with "/"; click and drag over this last point to redraw the last curve.

  To form a hinged corner on a point *as you draw*, hold down Option (Mac)/Alt (Win) as you click-drag out a new direction line.

BÉZIER-EDITING TOOLS

Bézier-editing tools are the group of tools you can use to edit Illustrator paths. To access them, click and hold the Pen, Pencil, or Scissors tool and drag to select one of the other tools. You can also tear off this palette. (To learn how to combine paths into new objects, read about the Pathfinder palette in the *Beyond Basic Drawing & Coloring* chapter.)

- **The Pen tool** and **Auto Add/Delete** can perform a variety of functions. Auto Add/Delete (which is on by default, but can be disabled in General Preferences) allows the Pen tool to change automatically to the Add Anchor Point tool when the tool is over a selected path segment, or to the Delete Anchor Point tool when over an anchor point. To temporarily disable the Auto Add/Delete function of the Pen tool, hold down the Shift key. If you don't want the path to constrain to an angle, release the Shift key prior to releasing the mouse.

- **The Convert Anchor Point tool,** hidden within the Pen tool (default is Shift-C), converts an anchor point from a smooth curve to a corner point when you click on it. To convert a corner point to a smooth curve, click-drag on the anchor point counterclockwise to pull out a new direction handle (or twirl the point until it straightens out the curve). To convert a smooth curve to a hinged curve (two curves hinged at a point), grab the direction point and hold Option/Alt as you drag out to the new position. With the Pen tool selected, you can temporarily access the Convert Anchor Point tool by pressing Option/Alt.

- **The Add Anchor Point tool,** accessible from the Pen pop-up menu or by pressing the + (plus) key, adds an anchor point to a path at the location where you click.

- **The Delete Anchor Point tool,** accessible from the Pen pop-up menu or by pressing – (minus), deletes an anchor point when you click directly on the point.
  Note: *If you select the Add/Delete Anchor Point tools by pressing + or –, press P to get back to the Pen tool.*

- **The Pencil tool** reshapes a selected path when Edit selected paths is checked in the tools preferences. Select a path and draw on or near the path to reshape it.

- **The Smooth tool** smooths the points on already-drawn paths by smoothing corners and deleting points. As you move the Smooth tool over your path, it attempts to keep the original shape of the path as intact as possible.

- **The Erase tool** removes sections of a selected path. By dragging along the path you can erase or remove portions of it. You must drag along the path—drawing perpendicular to the path will result in unexpected effects. This tool adds a pair of anchor points to the remaining path, on either side of the erased section of the path.

- **The Scissors tool** cuts a path where you click by adding two disconnected, selected anchor points exactly on top of each other. To select just one of the points, deselect the object, then click with the Direct Selection tool on the spot where you cut. This will allow you to select the upper anchor point and drag it to the side in order to see the two points better.

Correcting common mistakes

Avoid these common mistakes:

- If you try to deselect by clicking outside your object while you still have the Pen tool chosen, you'll scatter extra points throughout your image, causing possible problems later. If you're aware that you clicked by mistake, Undo. To remove stray points, choose Edit > Select > Stray Points and then press Delete. (Or, alternatively, you can choose Object > Path > Clean Up.) The best solution is to remember to hold down the ⌘ (Mac) or Ctrl (Win) key when you click; the cursor will temporarily toggle to the Selection tool. Then you can safely click to deselect.

- If you try to delete an object that you selected with the Direct Selection tool, you'll delete only the selected points or paths. What remains of the object will now be fully selected. Delete again to remove the remaining portions of the object.

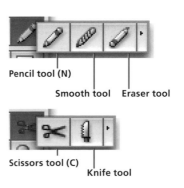

Pencil tool (N)

Smooth tool   Eraser tool

Scissors tool (C)

Knife tool

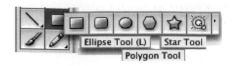

- **The Knife tool** slices through all unlocked visible objects and closed paths. Simply drag the Knife tool across the object you want to slice, then select the object(s) you want to move or delete. Hold down the Option (Mac)/Alt (Win) key to constrain the cut to a straight line.

GEOMETRIC OBJECTS

The Ellipse, Rounded Rectangle, Polygon, and Star tools create objects called "geometric primitives." These objects are mathematically-described symmetrical paths grouped with a non-printing anchor point, which indicates the center. (In order for the center of a star or polygon to be visible, you'll need to click the Show Center checkbox on the Attributes palette.) Use the centers of the geometric objects to snap-align them with each other, or with other objects and guides. You can create these geometric objects numerically or manually. Access the tools in the pop-up palette from the Rectangle tool in the Toolbox. (See the *Zen of Illustrator* chapter for exercises in creating and manipulating geometric objects, and Tip at right.)

- **To create a geometric shape manually,** select the desired geometric tool, and click-drag to form the object from one corner to the other. To create the object from the center, hold down the Option (Mac)/Alt (Win) key and drag from the center outward (keep the Option/Alt key down until you release the mouse button to ensure that it draws from the center). Once you have drawn the geometric objects, you can edit them exactly as you do other paths.
- **To create a geometric object with numeric input,** select a geometric tool and click on the Artboard to estab-lish the upper left corner of your object. Enter the desired dimensions in the dialog box and click OK. To create the object numerically from the object's center, Option-click (Mac)/Alt-click (Win) on the Artboard.

   To draw an arc, select the Arc tool and then click and drag to start drawing the arc. Press the "F" key to flip the arc from convex to concave, and use the up and down

Arrow keys to adjust the radius of the arc. Pressing the "C" key will "close" the arc by drawing the perpendicular lines that form the axes, and pressing the "X" key will flip the arc without moving these axes ("F" flips both the arc and the axes). Release the mouse to finish the arc.

To draw a grid, select either the Rectangular Grid tool or the Polar Grid tool and click-drag to start drawing the grid. You can control the shape of the grid by pressing various keys as you draw (see *Illustrator Help* for details). Release the mouse to finish the grid.

SELECTING & GROUPING OBJECTS
Selecting

The Select menu gives you easy access to basic selection commands, including the ability to select specific types of objects and attributes. You can use the Selection tools to select individual or multiple objects. You can use the target indicators in the Layers palette to select and target objects, groups, and layers. Targeting a group or layer selects everything contained within it, and makes the group or layer the focus of the Appearance and Graphic Styles palettes. (For more on targeting and selecting via the Layers palette, see the *Layers & Appearances* chapter.)

Use the Lasso tool to select an entire path or multiple paths by encircling them. Combining Option/Alt with the Lasso tool subtracts entire paths from a selection (though this may require a certain amount of finesse). Combining Shift with the Lasso tool adds entire paths to a selection.

You can also use the Lasso tool to select individual anchor points or path segments by encircling them with the tool. Combining Option/Alt with the Lasso tool subtracts anchor points from a selection; Shift with the Lasso tool adds anchor points to a selection.

Grouping and selecting

Many programs provide you with a grouping function so you can treat multiple objects as one unit. In Illustrator, grouping objects places all the objects on the same layer and creates a <group> container in the Layers palette;

Tool tolerance options

Drawing freehand while holding a mouse, or even a digital pen, can be less than elegant. The Pencil, Smooth, and Brush tools contain options that can help you to create more types of paths, ranging from very realistic to more shapely and graceful, without the constant need to adjust anchor points. Double-click on the tool to view the options.

- **Fidelity** increases or decreases the distance between anchor points on the path created or edited. The smaller the number, the more points that will make up the path, and vice versa.
- **Smoothness** varies the percentage of smoothness you'll see as you create and edit paths. Use a lower percentage of smoothness for more realistic lines and brush strokes, and a higher percentage for less realistic but more elegant lines.

Note: *Closing Pencil and Brush tool paths is a bit awkward. If you hold down the Option/Alt key when you are ready to close a path, a straight line segment will be drawn between the first and last anchor points. If you hold down the Option/Alt key and extend slightly past the first anchor point, the path will close automatically. Set the tool preferences to low numbers to make closing easier.*
— Sandee Cohen

| Selection tool | Direct Selection tool | Group Selection tool |

remember don't choose Group if you want your objects on different layers. (For more on layers and objects, see the *Layers & Appearances* chapter.) So, when *do* you want to group objects? Group objects when you need to select them *repeatedly* as a unit or when you want to apply an appearance to the entire group. Take an illustration of a bicycle as an example. Use the Group function to group the spokes of a wheel. Next, group the two wheels of the bicycle, then group the wheels with the frame. We will continue to refer to this bicycle below.

- **With the Direct Selection tool.** Click on a point or path with the Direct Selection tool to select that point or portion of the path. If you click on a spoke of a wheel, you'll select the portion of the spoke's path you clicked.

- **With the Selection tool.** Click on an object with the Selection tool to select the largest group containing that object. In our example, this would be the entire bicycle.

- **With the Group Selection tool.** Use the Group Selection tool to select sub-groupings progressively. The first click with the Group Selection tool selects a single spoke. The next click selects all of the spokes. The third click selects the entire wheel; the fourth selects both wheels, and the fifth, the entire bicycle. (Or, marquee part of the objects to select all of them.) To move objects selected with the Group Selection tool, drag without releasing the mouse. If you continually click with the Group Selection tool, you're always selecting additional groups.

- **See the "Finger Dance" lessons in the *Zen* chapter.** This section includes a variety of selection exercises.

USING THE ALIGN PALETTE

The Align palette (Window > Align) contains a highly useful set of tools that allow you to control how objects are aligned or distributed. Although most of its controls appear in the Control palette as well, there are a few very powerful controls that only show up in the Align palette itself. So if you're aligning or distributing objects via the Control palette, you might need to open the Align palette to access some of its advanced functions, such as Cancel Key Object or the Distribute Spacing controls.

To make sure all of the Align palette's options are showing, click the double triangle on the Align palette tab or choose Show Options from the palette's menu.

The Align palette lets you align objects along a specified axis, according to either the edges or the anchor points of objects. Begin by selecting the objects that you want to align or distribute. If you want to align or distribute relative to the bounding box of all the objects you have selected, just click whichever button on the Align palette reflects the arrangement you want.

On the other hand, if you want to align or distribute relative to a specific object, click that object first and then click the appropriate button on the Align palette. (You can choose Cancel Key Object from the palette menu at any time while the original set is still selected to "reset" the controls so they no longer align or distribute relative to the object you previously clicked.)

Here's an especially handy feature: You can align objects relative to the Artboard by choosing the Align to Artboard command from the palette menu, and then clicking the appropriate button on the palette itself.

Note that by default, Illustrator uses the paths of objects to determine how the objects will be aligned and distributed. But you can also use the edge of the stroke to determine alignment and distribution, by choosing Use Preview Bounds from the palette menu. (This is useful for objects with differing stroke weights.) But keep in mind that Adobe's definition of "the edge of the stroke" includes any effects applied to that object, including things that extend well beyond the visible edge of the stroke, such as drop shadows.

The Align palette even lets you specify exact distances by which objects should be distributed. First, select the objects you want to distribute; then, in the Distribute

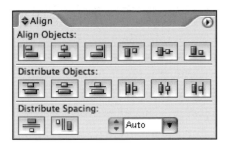

The Align palette with all of its options displayed

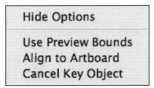

The Align palette's Options menu

Align warning

Once you specify a value in the Align palette Options section for Distribute, you have to choose a key object every time. If you get this dialog warning, reset the value to Auto. —*Mordy Golding*

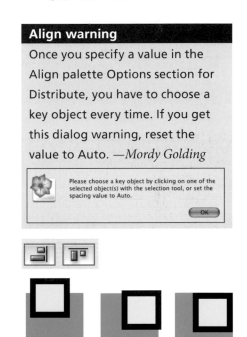

Use Preview Bounds helps visually align stroked objects, but yields mysterious results with live graphic effects such as drop shadows: The left rectangles are unaligned; at center are the same rectangles, each pair having been aligned top and right; at right the pairs are aligned top/right with "Use Preview Bounds" enabled

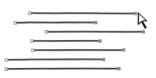

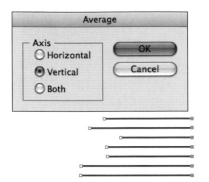

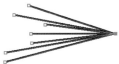

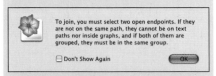

Using the Average command to align selected endpoints vertically, then choosing Both

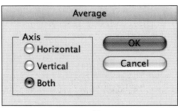

Joining warning

If you get an error message that you can't join points, do the following—in addition to the conditions in the warning:

> To join, you must select two open endpoints. If they are not on the same path, they cannot be on text paths nor inside graphs, and if both of them are grouped, they must be in the same group.
>
> ☐ Don't Show Again   OK

- Make sure you've selected only two points (and no third stray point selected by mistake).
- Make sure you've selected *endpoints*, not midpoints.

Spacing field of the Align palette, enter the amount of space by which the objects should be separated. (Remember, you may need to choose Show Options in order for the Distribute Spacing field to be visible in the Align palette; these controls don't appear in the Control palette.) Using the Selection tool, click on the path of the object you want to remain fixed, while the other objects distribute themselves relative to it. Then click either the Vertical or Horizontal Distribute Space button. (Choose Auto from the pop-up menu to cancel this option.)

JOINING & AVERAGING

Two of Illustrator's most useful functions are Average and Join (both found under the Object > Path menu or in the Context-sensitive menu). Whereas the Align palette allows you to align selected *objects* (see previous section), averaging allows you to align selected *points*.

Use the Average function to sandwich two endpoints on top of each other. Use the Join function to join two endpoints. The Join function will operate differently depending on the objects.

To average, use the Direct Selection tool or Lasso tool to marquee-select or Shift-select any number of points belonging to any number of objects. Then use the Context-sensitive menu (hold the Control key for the Mac; use the right mouse button for Windows) to average, aligning the selected points horizontally, vertically, or along both axes.

- **If the two open endpoints are exactly on top of each other,** then Join opens a dialog box asking if the join should be a smooth point or a corner. A smooth point is a curved Bézier anchor that smoothly joins two curves, with direction handles that always move together; a corner point is any other point connecting two paths. Once you've clicked OK in the dialog box, both points will fuse into a single point. However, keep in mind that a true smooth point will only result if the proper conditions exist: namely, that the two curves that you are trying to join have the potential to join together into a smooth curve. Otherwise, you'll get a corner point, even if you chose Smooth in the dialog box.

- **If the two open endpoints are not exactly on top of each other,** then Join will connect the two points with a line. If you try to Join two points to fuse as one but don't get a dialog box, then you've merely connected your points with a line! Undo (⌘-Z for Mac/Ctrl-Z for Windows) and see "To Average & Join in one step" below.

- **If you select an open path** (in this case, you don't need to select the endpoints), then Join closes the path.

- **If the two open endpoints are on different objects,** then Join connects the two paths into one.

- **To Average & Join in one step,** use the following keyboard command: ⌘-Option-Shift-J (Mac)/Ctrl-Alt-Shift-J (Win); there is no menu equivalent! This command forms a corner when joining two lines, or a hinged corner when joining a line or curve to a curve.

WORKING WITH PALETTES

Most of Illustrator's palettes are accessible via the Window menu. Each palette is unique, but all palettes share common features:

- **You can regroup tabbed palettes to save desktop space.** Reduce the space that palettes require by nesting them together into smaller groups. Grab a palette's tab and drag it to another palette group to nest it. You can also drag a tab to the *bottom* of a palette to dock the palettes on top of one another.

- **You can make most palettes smaller or larger.** If there's a sizing icon in the lower right corner, click and drag it to shrink or expand the palette. Palettes also have pop-up menus offering additional options. If a palette

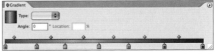

The top grouping shows various modes of expansion for docked palettes; middle figure shows the Gradient palette, alone and expanded; directly above are palettes tabbed together

Typing units into palettes

To use the current unit of measurement, type the number, then Tab to the next text field or press Return/Enter. To use another unit of measurement, *follow* the number with "in" or " (for inch), "pt" (point), "p" (pica), or "mm" (millimeter) and press Return/Enter. To resume typing into an image text block, press Shift-Return. You can also enter *calculations* in palettes. For example, if you were specifying the size of a rectangle, you could type 72 pt + 2 mm for the height. Illustrator would then perform the calculation and apply the result. Partial calculations work as well; if you type + 2, Illustrator will add two of whatever unit you're currently using. Try it!

The original objects

Objects selected (the bottom of the Toolbox indicates different strokes and fills are selected)

contains more options, it will have a double arrow to the left of the palette name. Click on the arrows to cycle through the various options. Click the square (minimize box), on the top of the title bar to shrink all palettes docked or nested together down to just title bars and tabs. Click the right square again, and the palettes will re-expand. Double-click the title bar to cycle through the states, from maximum to collapsed.

- **Reset palettes easily.** Certain palettes (including the Character, Paragraph and OpenType palettes) contain a Reset Palette command that allows you to easily restore the palette's default settings.

- **You must select your object(s) before you can make changes.** With your objects selected, you can click on the label or inside any edit box in the palette containing text and begin typing. If you're typing something that has limited choices (such as a font or type style), Illustrator will attempt to complete your word; just keep typing until your choice is visible. If you're typing into a text field, use the Tab key to move to other text fields within the palette. **IMPORTANT:** *When you've finished typing into palette text fields, you must press Return/Enter. This action tells the application that you are ready to enter text somewhere else or to resume manipulating your artwork.*

- **There are many ways to fill or stroke an object.** Focus on a selected object's fill or stroke by clicking on the Fill or Stroke icon near the bottom of the Toolbox, or toggle between them with the "X" key. To set the stroke or fill to None, use the / (slash) key. Set your color by: 1) adjusting the sliders or sampling a color from the color ramp in the Color palette, 2) clicking on a swatch in the Swatches palette, 3) sampling colors from the color picker, or 4) using the Eyedropper to sample from other objects in your file. In addition, you can drag color swatches from palettes to selected objects or to the Fill/Stroke icon in the Toolbox.

- **You can associate appearances with objects, groups of objects, or layers.** *Appearance attributes* are properties that affect the look of an object without affecting its underlying structure—such as strokes, fills, transparencies and effects. The term *appearance* is used in this book to refer to an object's collective appearance attributes. All objects have an appearance, even if that appearance is "no stroke and no fill."

- **You can apply a graphic style to an object, group of objects, or a layer.** The total sum of applied characteristics can be saved as a style in the Graphic Styles palette. *Graphic styles* are "live" (updatable) combinations of fills, strokes, blending modes, opacities, and effects. For details about working with combinations of effects and the Graphic Styles palette, see the *Live Effects & Graphic Styles* chapter, especially the chapter introduction and the "Scratchboard Art" lesson.

WORKSPACES: MANAGING YOUR WORKING AREA

Speaking of palettes—once you've arranged your palettes and the other features of your working area to your liking, Illustrator CS2's new Workspaces feature allows you to save that arrangement as a custom workspace. If you like to have different arrangements of palettes for different kinds of tasks, you can save multiple workspaces and then easily switch back and forth between them as you're working. Multiple users who share a computer setup can each create their own saved workspaces.

To save a custom workspace, once you've got everything arranged on your screen, just choose Workspace > Save Workspace from the Window menu. Enter a name for your custom workspace in the Name field, and click the OK button. Once you've created and saved a custom workspace, its name will show up in the Window > Workspace submenu, so you can easily switch between different workspaces just by clicking on their names. And you can always click on [Default] in the Workspace submenu to restore the default Illustrator workspace.

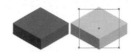

To update or replace a graphic style throughout the entire document, select an object and apply the style you want to modify and update. With the object selected, make changes to its appearance and choose Replace Graphic Style from the Appearance palette menu. The name of the style will display next to the replace command. This will globally update all objects using this named graphic style. To change the name of the style, double-click on the proxy in the Graphic Styles palette and rename it.

The Manage Workspaces dialog showing a number of custom workspaces

As of this writing, Illustrator CS2 has a nasty bug that can occur if you use the Tab key to hide your palettes, and then quit Illustrator before displaying them again. The next time you launch Illustrator, you may find that you can't get your palettes to appear again with the Tab key. Fortunately, workspaces can chase this bug away. If it happens to you, just choose any of your custom workspaces to get your palettes back (and if you don't have any custom ones set up, choose the [Default] workspace).

Scaling objects to an exact size

- *The Control or Transform palette way:* Type the new width or height in the palette and press ⌘-Return/Ctrl-Return. (Or click the lock icon in that palette to scale proportionately.)
- *The proxy way:* Create a proxy rectangle the size of your image, then from the upper left corner of the proxy, Option/Alt-click to create another rectangle in the target dimensions. With your proxy selected, click with the Scale tool in the upper left and grab-drag the lower right to match the target. (Hold Shift to scale in only one dimension.) Delete these rectangles, select your objects, double-click the Scale tool, and apply settings.

The Manage Workspaces dialog box allows you to delete, duplicate, or rename your custom workspaces at any time. Choose Window > Workspace > Manage Workspaces, and select the name of an existing custom workspace in the dialog box. Rename it by changing the text in the Name field, click the New button to create a duplicate of the current one, or Click the trash icon to delete.

TRANSFORMATIONS

Moving, scaling, rotating, reflecting, and shearing are all operations that transform selected objects. Since this chapter is devoted to Illustrator basics, this section will concentrate on the tools and palettes that help you to perform transformations. (To learn about live effects that perform transformations, see the *Live Effects & Graphic Styles* chapter.) Begin by selecting what you wish to transform. If you don't like a transformation you've just applied, use Undo before applying a new transformation—or you'll end up applying the new transformation on top of the previous one. In Illustrator, you can perform most transformations manually (see the *Zen of Illustrator* chapter for exercises), using a dialog box for numeric accuracy. Illustrator remembers the last transformation you performed, storing those numbers in the appropriate dialog box until you enter a new transform value or restart the program. (See the Tip "Transform again" in this section for how to repeat transformations.) For example, if you previously scaled an image and disabled Scale Strokes & Effects, the next time you scale (manually or numerically), your strokes and effects won't scale.

The bounding box

The bounding box should not be confused with the Free Transform tool (which allows you to perform additional functions; see discussion of the Free Transform tool below). The bounding box appears around selected objects when you are using the Selection tool (solid arrow), and can be useful for quickly moving, scaling, rotating, or duplicating objects. With the bounding box, you can easily scale several objects at once. Select the objects, click on a corner of the bounding box, and drag. To constrain proportionally while scaling, hold down the Shift key and drag a corner. By default, the bounding box is on. Toggle it off and on via the View > Hide/Show Bounding Box, or switch to the Direct Selection tool to temporarily hide it. To reset the bounding box after performing a transformation so it's once again square to the page, choose Object > Transform > Reset Bounding Box. **Note:** *As long as one of the bounding box handles is selected, holding down the Option/Alt key when you transform with the bounding box will not create a duplicate, but will instead transform from the center.*

Moving

In addition to grabbing and dragging objects manually, you can specify a new location numerically: Double-click the Selection arrow in the Toolbox or use the Context-sensitive menu to bring up the Move dialog box (select the Preview option). For help determining the distance you wish to move, click-drag with the Measure tool the distance you wish to calculate. Then *immediately* open the Move dialog box to see the measured distance loaded automatically, and click OK (or press Return/Enter).

The Free Transform tool

The Free Transform tool can be an easy way to transform objects once you learn numerous keyboard combinations to take advantage of its functions. In addition to performing simple transformations that can be performed with the bounding box (such as rotate and scale), you can also shear, and create perspective and distortions (see the Tip "Free Transform variations" at right, and the "Distort Dynamics" lesson in the *Drawing & Coloring* chapter). Bear in mind that the Free Transform tool bases its transformations on a fixed center point that cannot be relocated. If you need to transform from a different location, use the individual transformation tools, Transformation palette, or the Transform Each command.

Transform again

Illustrator remembers your last transformation—from simple moves to rotating a *copy* of an object. Use the Context-sensitive menu to repeat the effect (Transform Again), or ⌘-D/Ctrl-D.

Palette be gone!

To get rid of the various palettes on your screen temporarily, just press Tab to hide the palettes and Toolbox; then press Tab when you want to toggle them into view again. If you'd rather keep the Toolbox visible and just hide the other palettes, use Shift-Tab.

Free Transform variations

With the Free Transform tool, you can apply the following transformations to selected objects:

- **Rotate**—Click outside the bounding box and drag.
- **Scale**—Click on a corner of the bounding box and drag. Option-drag/Alt-drag to scale from the center and Shift-drag to scale proportionally.
- **Distort**—Click on a corner handle of the bounding box and ⌘-drag/Ctrl-drag.
- **Shear**—Click on a side handle of the bounding box and ⌘-drag/Ctrl-drag the handle.
- **Perspective**—Click on a corner handle of the bounding box and ⌘-Option-Shift-drag/Ctrl-Alt-Shift-drag.

The Transform palette

From this palette, you can determine numeric transformations that specify an object's width, height, and location on the document, as well as how much to rotate or shear it. You can also access a palette pop-up menu that offers options to Flip Horizontal and Vertical; Transform Object, Pattern, or Both; and to enable Scale Strokes & Effects. The current Transform palette is a bit odd: You can Transform Again once you've applied a transformation, but the information in the text fields is not always retained. To maintain your numeric input, apply transformations through the transformation tool's dialog box, discussed in the next section.

Individual transformation tools

For the scaling, rotation, reflection, and shearing of objects with adjustable center points, you can click (to manually specify the center about which the transformation will occur), then grab your object to transform it. For practice with manual transformations see the *Zen* chapter. Each transformation tool has a dialog box where you can specify the parameters for the tool, whether to transform the object or make a copy with the specified transform applied, and whether to transform just the objects and/or any patterns they may be filled with. (For more on transforming patterns see the *Drawing & Coloring* chapter.)

Here are three additional methods you can use to apply the individual transformation tools to objects:

• **Double-click on a transformation tool** to access the dialog box. (Or press Return/Enter with a transformation tool already selected.) This allows you to transform objects numerically, originating from an object's center.

• **Option-click/Alt-click on your image with a transformation tool** to access the dialog box that allows you to transform your objects numerically, originating from where you clicked.

- **Click-drag on your image with a transformation tool** to transform the selected objects, originating from the center of the group of selected objects.

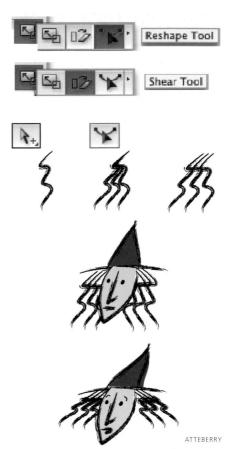

Reshape & Shear

The Reshape tool is different from the other transformation tools. Start by selecting all the points in the paths you wish to reshape (use the Group Selection or Selection tool). Next, choose the Reshape tool (hidden under the Scale tool) and marquee or Shift-select all points you wish to affect, then drag the points to reshape the path. The selected points move as a unit, but rather than move the same distance, as they would if you dragged with the Direct Selection tool, the points nearer to the cursor move more, and the ones farther away move less.

You will also find the Shear tool hidden within the Scale tool. Use the Shear tool to slant objects.

Transform Each

To perform multiple transformations at once, open the Transform Each dialog box (Object > Transform > Transform Each). You can perform the transformations on one or more objects. Additions to this dialog box include the ability to reflect objects over the X and Y axes, and to change the point of origin. If you want to apply a transformation, but you think you might want to change it later, try a Transformation Effect (see the *Live Effects & Graphic Styles* chapter).

ATTEBERRY

Kevan Atteberry drew one squiggle of hair with a chalk art brush, and then used the Reshape tool to reshape it, holding Option (Alt) when he dragged to make copies), he reshaped the triple strands to shape the witch's hair (he selected all of the three strands with the Selection tool, then with the Reshape tool he selected only the top anchor on each strand to reshape all three together), and then reshaped again to form the surprised witch's hair, and hat

WORKING SMART
Saving strategies

Probably the most important advice you'll ever get is to save every few minutes. Whenever you make a substantial change to your image, use File > Save As and give your image a new name.

It's much more time-efficient to save incremental versions of your image than it is to reconstruct an earlier version. Back up your work at least once a day before you shut down. Just think to yourself, "If this computer never

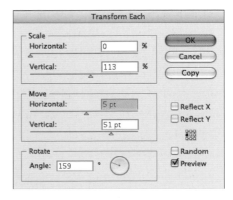

The Transform Each dialog box (Object > Transform > Transform Each)

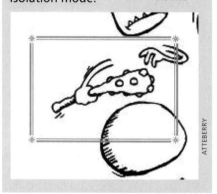

ATTEBERRY

starts up again, what will I need?" Develop a backup system using CDs, DVDs, external storage drives, DATs (digital audio tapes), or opticals so you can archive all of your work. Use a program such as Dantz's Retrospect to automatically add new and changed files to your archives.

Get in the habit of archiving virtually everything, and develop a file-naming system that actually helps you keep track of your work in progress—simplifying your recovery of a working version if necessary. Also, make sure that you keep all files in a named and dated folder that distinguishes them from other projects. (For saving in other formats see "Image Formats" later in this chapter.)

Multiple Undos

Some programs give you only one chance to undo your last move. Illustrator allows "unlimited undos," which, practically speaking, means that the number of undos you can perform is limited only by how much memory you have available.

Even *after* you save a file, your Undos (and Redos) will still be available (as long as you haven't closed and reopened the file), making it possible for you to save the current version, undo it to a previous stage and save it again, or as a different name, or continue working from an earlier state. But once you close your file, your undos are cleared from memory, so they won't be available the next time you open the file.

You can also revert the file to the most recently saved version by choosing File > Revert, but you can't undo a revert, so you'll want to be careful.

Note: *Not all operations are undoable. For example, changes to Preferences aren't affected by Undo, and neither are screen zooms.*

CHANGING YOUR VIEWS

From the View menu, you can show and hide several items, such as grids, guides, smart guides, transparency grids, edges, Artboards, and page tilings.

Preview and Outline

To control the speed of your screen redraw, learn to make use of the Preview mode and the Outline mode, which can be toggled in the View menu. In Preview mode, you view the document in full color; in Outline mode, you see only the wire frames of the objects.

Illustrator also offers a great way to control the speed and quality of your screen redraws when using the Hand Tool. In the Units & Display Performance area of Preferences, there's a Display Performance slider for the Hand Tool that lets you set your own preferred balance between the speed and quality of redraws.

New View

New View (View > New View) allows you to save your current window viewpoint, remembering also your zoom level and which layers are hidden, locked, or in Preview mode. Custom views are added to the bottom of the View menu to let you easily recall a saved view. You can rename a view, but the views themselves are not editable—if you need to make a change to a view, you'll have to make a New View.

New Window

Illustrator gives you the ability to display different aspects of your current image simultaneously. This allows you to separately view different Proof Setups, Overprint or Pixel Previews, and zoom levels. You can resize each window separately, and fore each window you can make edges hidden or visible, or hide or lock different *layers* in Preview or Outline (see the *Layers & Appearances* chapter and "Hide/Show Edges" later in this chapter). For instance, using multiple windows of the same file, you can view the full image in Preview and simultaneously work on close detail in Outline mode. This can be useful if you are using a large monitor or multiple monitors. Most window configurations are saved with with your file when you save.

Interrupting Preview

You don't have to wait for Illustrator to finish redrawing the Preview before you pull down the next menu or perform another task. You can interrupt redrawing the preview and go to Outline mode by typing ⌘-./Ctrl-. (period), or the Esc key for Windows.

Two views

Illustrator allows you to preview precise anti-aliasing in Pixel Preview mode, and allows you to preview overprints and traps in Overprint Preview mode.

Zoom shortcuts while typing

Press ⌘/Ctrl with the spacebar to zoom in or ⌘-Option/Ctrl-Alt with the spacebar to zoom out. As long as you press the ⌘/Ctrl first, this works even while you're typing in text-entry mode with the Type tool. (If you then let go of the Spacebar, you'll have the Hand tool.)

Don't forget about your edges!

Once you hide your edges in Illustrator (View > Hide Edges or ⌘-H/Ctrl-H), they stay hidden for all subsequent paths and selections. If you are trying to select a path or draw a new object, but the anchor points and path are not visible, try toggling to Show Edges.

The Navigator palette (always in Preview mode) offers many ways to zoom in and out of documents:

- Double-click the mountain icons along the bottom edge of the palette window to increase or decrease the amount of zoom in 200% increments.
- Hold the ⌘/Ctrl key and drag to marquee the area in the palette thumbnail that you want to zoom into or out from.
- Enable View Artboard Only to keep your view limited to the Artboard area. This is helpful if you are working on a document with objects on the pasteboard (outside the page margins) that are distracting your focus.

You can change the color of the border around the thumbnail in the View Options dialog box (in the Navigator palette pop-up).

Note: *Navigator might slow you down if your file contains a lot of text objects. The Navigator creates a thumbnail view of the document; every time you zoom or scroll, the Navigator must redraw its thumbnail. Unless you need to view the Navigator palette, close it.*

Where did the window go?

If you have many file windows open, simply select the file you want to bring to the front from the list of files at the bottom of the Window menu.

Window controls

There are three small icons at the very bottom of the Toolbox. One is always selected; this is the default in which Illustrator displays your file window. Starting at the far left, choose from Standard Screen mode (desktop showing around the edges of your file), Full Screen mode with menu bar (file window visible, but confined to the center of the screen with no desktop showing; you can access your menu bar), and Full Screen mode (same as above, but you cannot access your menu bar). You can toggle among the views by pressing the "F" key.

Zooming in & out

Illustrator provides many ways to zoom in and out.

- **From the View menu.** Choose Zoom In/Out, Actual Size, or Fit in Window.

- **With the Zoom tool.** Click to zoom in one level of magnification; hold down the Option/Alt key and click to zoom out one level. You can also click-drag to define an area, and Illustrator will attempt to fill the current window with the area that you defined.

- **Use the ⌘/Ctrl keys for Zoom.** With any tool selected, use ⌘-hyphen/Ctrl-hyphen (minus sign)—think "minus to zoom out"—and ⌘+/Ctrl+ (plus sign)—think "plus to zoom in." Or, you can hold ⌘-spacebar/Ctrl-spacebar and click-drag to zoom in; add Option/Alt to zoom out.

- **Use Context-sensitive menus.** With nothing selected, Control-click (Mac)/right mouse button (Win) to access a pop-up menu so you can zoom in and out, change views, undo, and show or hide guides, rulers, and grids.

- **Navigator palette.** With the Navigator palette, you can quickly zoom in or out and change the viewing area with the help of the palette thumbnail (see Tip "The Navigator palette & views" at left).

Rulers, Guides, Smart Guides, and Grids

Toggle Illustrator's Show/Hide Rulers, or use the ⌘-R/Crtl-R shortcut, or use the Context-sensitive menu (as long as nothing in your document is selected). The per-document ruler units are set in Document Setup. If you want all new documents to use a specific unit of measurement, change your preferences for Units (Preferences > Units & Display Performance).

Even though the ruler sits in the upper left-hand corner of the page, the location of the ruler origin (0,0) is in the lower left corner of the page. To change the ruler origin, grab the upper left corner (where the vertical and horizontal rulers meet) and drag the crosshair to the desired location. The zeros of the rulers will reset to the point where you release your mouse (to reset the rulers to the default location, double-click the upper left corner). But beware—resetting your ruler origin will realign all patterns and affect alignment of Paste in Front/Back between documents (see the *Layers & Appearances* chapter for more on Paste in Front/Back).

To create simple vertical or horizontal ruler guides, click-drag from one of the rulers into your image. A guide appears where you release your mouse. You can define guide color and style in General Preferences. Guides automatically lock after you create them. To release a guide quickly, ⌘-Shift-double-click (Mac)/Ctrl-Shift-double-click (Win) on the guide. You can lock and unlock guides with the Context-sensitive menu in Preview mode. You should note that locking or unlocking guides affects *every* open document. If you have too many guides visible in your document, simply choose View > Guides > Hide Guides. To make them visible again choose View > Guides > Show Guides. If you want to delete them all permanently, choose View > Guides > Clear Guides. This only works on guides that are on visible, unlocked layers. Hiding or locking layers retains any guides you have created. To learn how to create custom guides from objects or paths, see the "Varied Perspective" lesson in the *Layers & Appearances* chapter.

Zippy zooming

Current magnification is displayed in the bottom left corner of your document. Access a list of percentages (3.13% to 6400%) or Fit on Screen from the pop-up, or simply select the text and enter any percentage within the limit.

Glorious grids

Customize your grids in Illustrator. Select a grid style and color.

- View > Show Grid, use the Context-sensitive menu or ⌘-'(Mac)/Ctrl -'(Win) (apostrophe).
- Toggle Snap to Grid on and off from the View menu or use the shortcut ⌘-Shift-'(Mac)/Ctrl-Shift-'(Win) (apostrophe).
- Set the division and subdivision for your grid in Preferences > Guides & Grid and choose either dotted divisions or lines and the color of those lines.
- To toggle the grid display in front or in back of your artwork, check or uncheck the Grids In Back checkbox (Preferences > Guides & Grid).
- Tilt the grid on an angle by choosing Preferences > General and then changing the Constrain Angle value.

Note: *The Constrain Angle affects the angle at which objects are drawn and moved. (See the* Drawing & Coloring *chapter on how to adjust it for creating isometrics.)*

Understanding Smart Guides

There are a multitude of Smart Guide preferences. Here's what each one does:

- Text Label Hints provide information about an object when the cursor passes over it—helpful for identifying a specific object within complicated artwork.
- Construction Guides are the temporary guidelines that help you align between objects and anchor points.
- Transform Tools help with transformations.
- Object Highlighting enables the anchor point, center point, and path of a deselected object to appear as your cursor passes within a specified tolerance from the object. This can be very useful for aligning objects. For best alignment results, select an object's anchor point or center point.

Note: *Smart Guides will slow you down when working on very large files. Also, you can't align using Smart Guides if View > Snap to Grid is enabled.*

Bounding Box and Hide Edges

When you toggle to Hide Edges and have Show Bounding Box enabled (both in the View menu), the bounding box will remain visible while the anchor points and paths of objects will be hidden.

Smart Guides can be somewhat unnerving when you see them flash on and off as you work. However, with practice and understanding, you'll be able to refine how to incorporate them into your work flow (see Tip at left). Illustrator also has automatic grids. To view grids, select View > Show Grid, or use the Context-sensitive menu. You can adjust the color, style of line (dots or solid), and size of the grid's subdivisions from Preferences > Guides & Grid. You can also enable a snap-to grid function. Toggle Snap to Grid on and off by choosing View > Snap to Grid (see Tip "Glorious grids" on the previous page).

IMPORTANT: *If you adjust the X and Y axes in Preferences > General > Constrain Angle, it will affect the drawn objects and transformations of your grid, as they will follow the adjusted angle when you create a new object. This works out well if you happen to be doing a complicated layout requiring alignment of objects at an angle.*

Transparency Grid & Simulate Color Paper

Given Illustrator's transparency capabilities, you might want to change the background of the Artboard to the transparency grid, or to a color. Both the transparency grid and simulated color paper are non-printable attributes.

To view the transparency grid, select View > Show Transparency Grid. Change the grid colors in the Transparency panel of the Document Setup dialog box. If you change both grid colors to the same color, you can change the white background to a color (see the *Transparency* chapter).

Hide/Show Edges

If looking at all those anchor points and colored paths distracts you from figuring out what to do with selected objects in your current window, choose View > Hide/Show Edges to toggle them on or off (or use the shortcut: ⌘-H/Crtl-H). Once you hide the edges, all subsequent path edges will be hidden until you show them again. Hide/Show Edges is saved with your file.

COLOR IN ILLUSTRATOR

Consumer-level monitors, which display color in red, green, and blue lights (RGB), cannot yet match four-color CMYK (cyan, magenta, yellow, black) inks printed onto paper. Therefore, you must retrofit the current technology with partial solutions, such as calibrating your monitor.

Working in RGB or CMYK

Illustrator offers you the flexibility of working and printing in either RGB or CMYK color. This is a mixed blessing, because the printing environment cannot accurately capture vibrant RGB colors. As a result, the RGB colors are usually muddy or muted when printed. If your final artwork is going to be printed, work in CMYK!

Work in an RGB color space when creating artwork that will be displayed on-screen, or to simulate a spot color (such as a day-glo color) on your printer. (For more on working in RGB, see the *Web & Animation* chapter.)

Single color space

When you open a new document, you select a color model (or color space). Illustrator no longer allows you to work in multiple color spaces at the same time. If you work in print, always check your files to make certain they are in the appropriate color model before you output. The document's color model is always displayed next to the file name, on the title bar. You can change the document's color mode at any time by choosing File > Document Color Mode > CMYK Color or RGB Color.

Opening legacy documents (documents created with older versions of Illustrator) with objects containing mixed color spaces will invoke a warning asking you to decide in which color space (RGB or CMYK) the document should open. Currently, linked images are not converted to the document's color space. If you open the Document Info palette and select Linked Images, the "Type" info is misleading. For example, if you have a CMYK document with a linked RGB image, the linked image type is Transparent CMYK. The linked image has

CMY Color Model   *RGB Color Model*

CMY (Cyan, Magenta, Yellow) **subtractive** *colors get darker when mixed; RGB (Red, Green, Blue)* **additive** *colors combine to make white*

Converting RGB to CMYK

Although Illustrator can make conversions from RGB to CMYK (and vice versa), using File > Document Color Mode > CMYK/RGB, such conversions may result in undesirable color shifts. Consult *Illustrator Help,* your service bureau, and/or your commercial printer for detailed directions based on your job specifications.

Prepress and printing

For more about color and printing issues, be sure to see the "Prepress and Printing" PDF on the *Wow! CD.* This excerpt from Mordy Golding's *Real World Adobe Illustrator CS2* book provides expert real world advice about output from Illustrator.

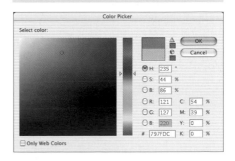

Adobe Color Picker

Appearance of black...

In an effort to display on-screen or proof graphics which more closely match what you will see on an actual printed sheet, Illustrator includes a setting specifically for how the color black is displayed or printed. You can choose to have your blacks display accurately, in which case black will appear closer to a dark gray color (closer to what you might see on press), or you can choose to display rich blacks, in which case your blacks will be much darker. Note that these settings are not color management settings and they don't affect your final separated output. These settings only affect your screen display or output to an RGB device.—*Mordy Golding, Real World Adobe Illustrator CS2*

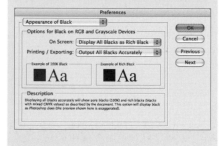

Exchange swatches

Save Swatches for Exchange feature lets you share swatches between CS2 applications. So swatches you create in Illustrator can be saved for use in Photoshop or InDesign, and vice versa. See the *Drawing & Coloring* chapter for more about this new feature.

not been converted, but the image preview has been converted to CMYK.

There are some effects (and graphic styles that use them) that work only in RGB mode. If you start off in RGB mode and use some of the default RGB graphic styles, they won't be rendered correctly if you then convert your document to CMYK mode.

Color systems and libraries

While your documents can be in RGB or CMYK, you can also mix colors with HSB sliders (Hue, Saturation and Brightness). You can also select colors from other color matching systems, such as the 216-color Web color palette or the color picker. You can access Focoltone, DIC Color, Toyo, Trumatch, and Pantone libraries or the Web palette by choosing Swatch Libraries from the Swatches pop-up menu, from the pop-up menus accessed from the Control palette (by clicking fill or stroke color or arrow), or from the Windows menu. Keep in mind that color libraries open as separate uneditable palettes, but once you use a color swatch, it will automatically load into your Swatches palette, where you can then edit it. The default for the Swatches palette is to open with swatches—not view by name. Use the palette menu to change to List View if you want your palettes to match ours. If you hold Option/Alt when you choose a view, such as List View, then all swatches will switch to the view you chose. To access styles, brushes, or swatches in other documents, either choose Window > Graphic Style, Brush, Symbol, or Swatch Libraries > Other Library. You can also use the new Open Library command in the Graphic Styles, Brushes, Symbols or Swatches palettes. Then select the file that contains the item you want. This opens a new palette with that document's components. To automatically store a component from an open library in your current document, just use the graphic style, brush, symbol, or swatch—or drag the swatch from its library palette to the document's palette. (For more about Swatches see the *Drawing & Coloring* chapter intro.)

SAVING AS PDF

Although you may be used to thinking of PDFs and Illustrator files as two different animals, underneath their hides they have a lot in common. In fact, as long as you save your Illustrator file (.ai) with "Create PDF Compatible File" enabled in the Illustrator Options dialog box, for all intents and purposes it *is* a PDF, and can be viewed in Adobe Acrobat Reader and other PDF viewers.

However, if you want more control over the final PDF product you create, Illustrator makes it easy, letting you choose what version of PDF you'd like to save as, while providing handy PDF presets that let you quickly save PDFs with different settings for different circumstances.

To save a document as a PDF, choose File > Save or File > Save As, and choose Illustrator PDF from the Format menu. After you click Save, you'll be presented with the Adobe PDF Options dialog box, where you can choose from a variety of options and settings, including compatibility (PDF version), compression, printer's marks and bleeds, security settings, and more.

The Compatibility menu lets you choose from a number of versions of PDF. Illustrator CS2's default is PDF 1.4, which is compatible with Acrobat 5. You can also choose to save in the newer PDF 1.5 and 1.6 formats, which are compatible with Acrobat 6 and 7 respectively, and which preserve advanced features, such as PDF layers. However, these files may not be compatible with earlier versions of Acrobat, so if you're going to be distributing the file widely, you may want to save as PDF 1.4 or even 1.3 to maximize compatibility. PDF 1.3 is compatible with Acrobat 4 and will be viewable and printable by the widest range of users, but it doesn't support transparency. (There are times when that may be exactly what you want—for example, when you want to flatten the file for sending to a commercial printer).

You can quickly access frequently used preset PDF settings from the Preset menu. You can create your own custom presets by choosing Custom from the menu, adjusting your settings, and then clicking the Save Preset

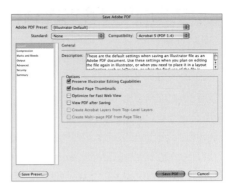

The Adobe PDF Options dialog box (choose Illustrator PDF in the Format menu of the File > Save or File > Save As dialog box)

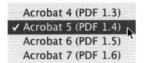

The Compatibility menu in the Adobe PDF Options dialog box

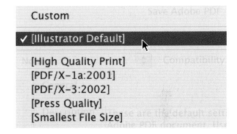

The Preset menu in the Adobe PDF Options dialog box

Verify PDF settings

When preparing a PDF file for a commercial printer or service provider, remember to check with the provider to find out what the final output resolution and other settings should be. It may be necessary to customize the settings for a particular provider, in which case you may find it helpful to create a custom preset.

The Links palette keeps a running (and updatable) list of all images in your document, whether they are linked or embedded. The key features of this palette are:

- You can quickly find out if you are missing a link (stop sign icon on the link layer) or need to update a link (exclamation icon).
- You can replace a link, update a link, go to a link, or edit a link with the click on an icon.
- You can change a linked image into an embedded image through the pop-up menu.
- You can find out information about the link (file name, location, size, kind, date modified, and transformations made) by double-clicking on a link layer to open the Link information dialog box (not all information is available for all formats).

Note: *Until the Links palette provides information on the color mode (RGB, CMYK, Grayscale, or raster images), be careful to check your links manually!*

Want the best on-screen preview for your art? Choose View > Overprint Preview for the best way to proof color on your screen and to see how your art will look when printed.

button at the bottom of the dialog box. Additionally, Illustrator ships with a number of predefined presets for experimenting. PDF settings can also be shared among different applications within the Creative Suite.

IMAGE FORMATS

You might need to open a document created in an earlier version of Illustrator (FreeHand, CorelDraw, and some 3D programs allow you to save images in older Illustrator formats). To open any file saved in an earlier version (known as a *legacy file*), drag it onto an Illustrator alias, or open the older formatted file from within Illustrator by choosing File > Open and selecting the document you want to open. Your document will be converted to Illustrator CS2 format, and [Converted] will be added to the file name. If you want to save it in any pre-Illustrator CS2 format, you can do so by choosing File > Save As and then choosing Adobe Illustrator Document from the Format menu in the dialog box. After you name your file and click Save, you'll be presented with the Illustrator Options dialog box, with a pop-up Version menu that lets you choose from a number of earlier AI versions.

If you open any legacy file containing type, you'll get a dialog box asking you how to handle the conversion, because Illustrator's current type engine handles type very differently from the way engines did in versions prior to CS. See the *Type* chapter (as well as *Illustrator Help*) for details on working with legacy type.

EPS (Encapsulated PostScript)

EPS is a universal format, which means that a wide variety of programs support importing and exporting EPS images for printing to PostScript printers. As in most programs, when saving an image in EPS format, you can choose to include a Preview. This preview is an on-screen PICT or TIFF representation of your image. When an EPS image is placed into another program without a preview, it will print properly, but it cannot be viewed. In order to import an EPS image into Illustrator, choose File > Place (see the *Layers* and *Illustrator & Other Programs* chapters to learn more about EPS).

Other image formats

Illustrator supports many file formats (such as SWF, SVG, GIF, JPEG, TIFF, PICT, PCX, Pixar, and Photoshop). You can also open and edit PDF documents, and even "raw" PostScript files, directly from within Illustrator. If you place images into a document, you can choose whether these files will remain *linked* (see Tip "Links are manageable" opposite) or will become *embedded* image objects (see the *Illustrator & Other Programs* chapter for specifics on embedding, and the *Web & Animation* chapter for details on Web-related formats). If you use File > Open, then images become embedded. (See *Illustrator Help* and *Read Me* files for lists of supported formats that shipped with this version.) Check Adobe's Web site (www.adobe. com) for the latest information on supported formats, as well as other file format plug-ins. (For more on file format issues, see the *Other Programs* chapter.)

POSTSCRIPT PRINTING & EXPORTING

When you're ready to print your image, you should use a PostScript printing device for most accurate results. Adobe owns and licenses the PostScript language, making PostScript printers somewhat more expensive than non-PostScript printers. You can proof your images to many non-PostScript printers. Although Illustrator images often print just fine to these printers, sometimes you can run into problems. In general, the newer the PostScript device, the faster and less problematic your printing. PostScript Level 2 and Level 3 printers provide better printing clarity and even some special effects, such as Illustrator's integration of PostScript Level 3's "smooth shading" technology (which should greatly enhance gradients and reduce banding problems). Finally, the more memory you install in your printer, the quicker your text and images will print. For crucial jobs, develop good relations with your service bureau, and get into the habit of

Out of Gamut Warning caution

If you plan to print in CMYK and see an Out of Gamut Warning in the Color palette, take this as a caution that the current color is out of the range of printable colors. Either switch your color mode to CMYK from the Color pop-up menu, or click on the Closest Approximation box next to the gamut warning for an RGB or HSB color approximation. Switching to CMYK mode will allow you to see the actual values of the plates.

New levels of PostScript

Adobe's PostScript 3 language is full of new features that improve printing time, deliver truer colors, and provide Web-ready printing. For details on PS3, refer to Adobe's "white paper" on PS3 on the Web at www.adobe.com.

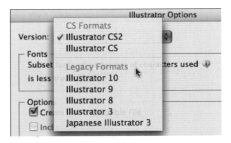

To access legacy formats, you must first choose the standard Illustrator format (.ai) from the Save or Save As dialog box; in the resulting Illustrator Options dialog, then choose the desired legacy format from the Version pop-up

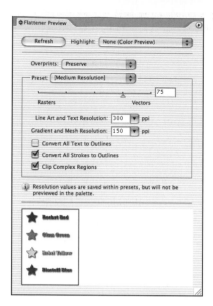

Illustrator's Flattener Preview palette

running test prints to identify possible problems. (Also see the Warning Tip "AICS2 images & files cropped!" at the beginning of this chapter.)

Correcting and avoiding printing problems

If you have trouble printing, first make sure your placed images are linked properly and the fonts needed to print the document are loaded. Second, check for any complex objects in the document (e.g., objects with many points, compound masks or shapes, or gradient meshes). (See the *Blends, Gradients & Mesh* chapter for issues regarding printing gradient mesh objects.) Use Save a Copy (to retain the original file), remove the complex object(s), and try to print. If that doesn't work, make sure File > Document Setup and the File > Print dialog box contain the correct settings for your output device.

Keep in mind that Illustrator's comprehensive Print dialog box takes on many of the functions that belonged to the Page Setup and Separation Setup dialog boxes in versions of Illustrator prior to CS. But the current Print dialog box gives you much more control over every part of the printing process.

If you're using transparency, or effects that contain transparency, you might want to preview how your art will print using the Flattener Preview palette (Window > Flattener Preview). For information on the Flattener Preview palette, and other ways to control flattening settings, see the *Transparency* chapter. Printing results will vary depending on these settings.

For detailed Illustrator printing advice, see the "Prepress and Printing" PDF excerpt from Mordy Golding's *Real World Adobe IllustratorCS2* on the *Wow! CD*.

More about controlling the size of your files

The major factors that can increase your file size are the inclusion of image objects, path pattern, brushes and ink pen objects, complex patterns, a large number of blends and gradients (especially gradient mesh objects and gradient-to-gradient blends), linked bitmapped images, and transparency. Although linked bitmaps can be large, the same image embedded as an image object is significantly larger. If your Illustrator file contains linked images, and you need to save the entire file in EPS (for placement and printing in other programs), you have the option Include Linked Files. Most service bureaus highly recommend this option, as it will embed placed images in your Illustrator file and make printing from page layout programs and film recorders much more predictable. However, since including placed images will further increase the file size, wait until you've completed an image and are ready to place it into another program before you save a copy with placed images embedded. Whether or not you choose to embed linked images, you must collect all the files that have been linked into your Illustrator documents and transport them along with your Illustrator file. Illustrator makes your task easier if you choose File > Document Info > Linked Images, which generates a text file of all images in your document; save this text file to keep for future reference or give to your service bureau as a record of the images included in your files.

ACTIONS

Actions are a set of commands or a series of events that you can record and save as a set in the Actions palette. Once a set is recorded, you can play back the actions to automate complex or repetitive tasks (such as a placing registration marks or deleting all unused styles).

Select the action in the Actions palette and activate it by clicking the Play icon at the bottom of the palette, by choosing Play from the pop-up menu, or by assigning the action to a keyboard "F key" (function key) so you can play the action with a keystroke. You can select an action set, a single action, or a command within an action to play. To exclude a command from playing within an action, disable the checkbox to the left of the command.

In order to play some types of actions, you may have to first select an object or text. Load action sets using the pop-up menu.

Minimizing file size

Before attempting to minimize the size of your file, make certain that you're working on a copy. Then start by removing all your unused colors, patterns, and brushes. You can do this easily using one handy set of Actions, included by default, in the Illustrator Actions palette. Open the palette (Window > Actions) and choose Delete Unused Palette Items, and click the Play button to automatically select and delete all unused graphic styles, brushes, swatches, and symbols. To delete only the items found in a specific palette (such as only Brushes or only Symbols), you can expand the Delete Unused Palette Items view to choose the Actions you want. Once you've removed all the unnecessary items, save the smaller version of the file.

Clean Up stray paths & points

Select Object > Path > Clean Up and check the items you want to delete from your document. Choose Stray Points, Unpainted Objects, and/or Empty Text Paths. Click OK to remove those items.

Selecting objects in an action

When recording an action, use the Attributes palette (Show Note) to name an object, and Select Object (Action pop-up) to type in the object's name (note) to select it.

If you're saving a batch of documents, and want them all to have the same resolution settings, Illustrator's new Templates feature makes it easy. Just set up a new document with the settings you want, and then save it as a template (.ait) file (File > Save as Template). Then you can base as many new documents on your template as you like—and they'll have your preferred resolution settings.

The view from the Bridge: Adobe Bridge lets you browse and manage your files with maximum convenience and control, all from a single centralized window

Adobe Stock Photos

In addition to helping you browse and manage the files already on your computer, Adobe Bridge is also your link to Adobe Stock Photos, a new feature that allows you to search for royalty-free images from a number of A-list stock photo agencies. You can find and purchase images using a shopping cart system, all from within Bridge.

Since you must record actions and save within an action set, begin a new action by clicking the Create New Set icon or by choosing New Set from the pop-up menu. Name the action set and click OK. With the new set selected, click the Create New Action icon, name the action, and click Record. Illustrator records your commands and steps until you click Stop. To resume recording, click on the last step, choose Begin, and continue adding to the action. When you've finished recording, you'll need to save the action file by selecting the action set and choosing Save Actions from the pop-up menu.

When you are recording, keep in mind that not all commands or tools are recordable. For example, the Pen tool itself is not recordable, but you can add the paths the Pen tool creates to an action by selecting a path and choosing Insert Selected Paths from the pop-up menu. Recording actions takes some practice, so don't get discouraged, and always save a backup file.

ADOBE BRIDGE AND ADOBE STOCK PHOTO

Adobe's Creative Suite 2 includes a new file browser application called Adobe Bridge. Actually, even though it's based on the file browser that was introduced in Photoshop 7, the words "file browser" really don't do it justice—Adobe refers to it as a "navigational control center" that gives you centralized access to your project files, applications, and settings. It's a bridge both in the sense of a command center *and* a link between different places. You can view, search, sort, manage, process, and share files form within Bridge, interfacing between the various Creative Suite applications.

Bridge is included with the stand-alone version of Illustrator CS2 as well as with the full CS2 suite. It can be launched independently as well as from within Illustrator, Photoshop, InDesign, and GoLive CS2. See Adobe's Web site for more information on Adobe Bridge and Adobe Stock Photos.

The Zen of Illustrator

2

The Zen of Illustrator

Zen: *"Seeking enlightenment through introspection and intuition rather than scripture."* *

You're comfortable with the basic operations of your computer. You've gone through the Tutorials in the *User Guide* or *Illustrator Help*. You've logged enough hours using Illustrator to be familiar with how each tool (theoretically) functions. You might even understand how to make Bézier curves. Now what? How do you take all this knowledge and turn it into a mastery of the medium?

As with learning any new artistic medium (such as engraving, watercolor, or airbrush), learning to manipulate the tools is just the beginning. Thinking and seeing in that medium is what really makes those tools part of your creative arsenal. Before you can determine the best way to construct an image, you have to be able to envision at least some of the possibilities. The first key to mastering Illustrator is to understand that Illustrator's greatest strength comes not from its many tools and functions but from its extreme flexibility in terms of how you construct images. The first part of this chapter, therefore, introduces you to a variety of approaches and techniques for creating and transforming objects.

Once you've got yourself "thinking in Illustrator," you can begin to *visualize* how to achieve the final results. What is the simplest and most elegant way to construct an image? Which tools will you use? Then, once you've begun, allow yourself the flexibility to change course and try something else. Be willing to say to yourself: How else can I get the results that I want?

The second key to mastering Illustrator (or any new medium) is perfecting your hand/eye coordination. In Illustrator, this translates into being proficient enough with the "power-keys" to gain instant access to tools and functions by using the keyboard. With both eyes on the monitor, one hand on the mouse, and the other hand on the keyboard, an experienced Illustrator user can create and manipulate objects in a fraction of the time required otherwise. The second part of this chapter helps you to learn the "finger dance" necessary to become a truly adept power-user.

The ability to harness the full power of Illustrator's basic tools and functions will ultimately make you a true master of Adobe Illustrator. Treat this chapter like meditation. Take it in small doses if necessary. Be mindful that the purpose of these exercises is to open up your mind to possibilities, not to force memorization. When you can conceptualize a number of different ways to create an image, then the hundreds of hints, tips, tricks, and techniques found elsewhere in this book can serve as a jumping-off point for further exploration. If you take the time to explore and absorb this chapter, you should begin to experience what I call the "Zen of Illustrator." This magical program, at first cryptic and counterintuitive, can help you achieve creative results not possible in any other medium.

*Adapted from *Webster's New World Dictionary of the English Language*

Building Houses

Sequential Object Construction Exercises

Overview: *Explore different approaches to constructing the same object with Illustrator's basic construction tools.*

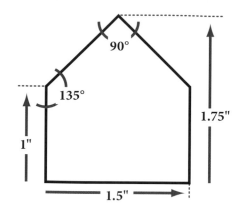

1  **zenhouse.ai**

2
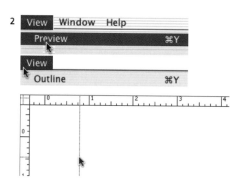

Pulling out a guide from the Ruler

3
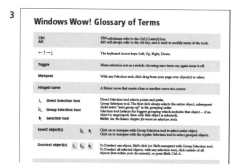

4

Hold down the Shift key to constrain movement to horizontal/vertical direction. For more modifier key help, see the end of this chapter for the "Finger Dance" lesson.

This sequence of exercises explores different ways to construct the same simple object—a house. The purpose of these exercises is to introduce you to the flexibility of Illustrator's object construction, so don't worry if some exercises seem less efficient than others.

So you can more easily follow along, set Units > General to Inches (from Preferences > Units & Display Performance). Also, please read through all of the recommendations below.

1 Use the zenhouse.ai file as a guide. Start with the file zenhouse.ai (copy it to your hard drive from the *Wow! CD*, in the Chapter 2 folder) as a guide when needed.

2 Work in Outline mode, and Show Rulers (View menu). Outline mode eliminates distractions like fills and strokes while it displays centers of geometric objects (marked by "×"). Rulers allow you to "pull out" guides.

3 Read through the *Wow! Glossary*. Please make sure to read *How to use this book* and the *Glossary* pull-out card.

4 Use "modifier" keys. These exercises use Shift and Option (Opt) or Alt keys, which you must hold down until *after* you release your mouse button. If you make a mistake, choose Undo and try again. Some functions are also accessible from the Context-sensitive menu. Try keyboard shortcuts for frequently-used menu commands.

Exercise #1:

Use Add Anchor Point tool

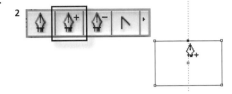

1 Open zenhouse.ai and create a rectangle and a vertical guide. Open zenhouse.ai. On the left corner where the side meets the peak, click to create a rectangle 1.5" x 1". Drag out a vertical guide and snap it to the center.

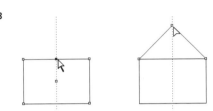

2 Add an anchor point on the top. With the Add Anchor Point tool, click on the top segment over the center guide.

3 Drag the new point up. Use the Direct Selection tool to grab the new point and drag it up into position using the zenhouse as a guide.

Exercise #2:

Make an extra point

1 Create a rectangle, delete the top path and place a center point. Create a wide rectangle (1.5" x 1"). With the Direct Selection tool, select the top path segment and delete it. With the Pen tool, place a point on top of the rectangle center point.

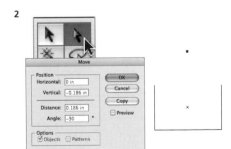

2 Move the point up. Double-click on a selection tool in the Toolbox to open the Move dialog box and enter a 1.25" vertical distance to move the point up.

3 Select and join the point to each side. Use the Direct Selection tool to select the left two points and Join (Object > Path > Join, or ⌘-J/Ctrl-J) them to the top point. Repeat with the right two points.

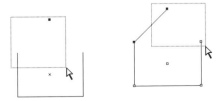

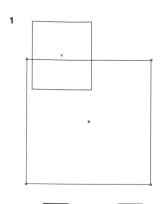

1

2

3

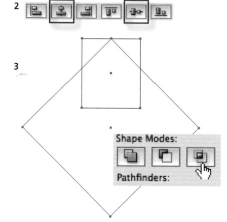

Shape Modes:

Pathfinders:

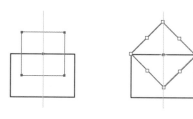

1

2

3

Shape Modes:

Path inders:

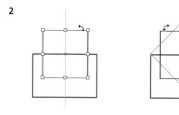

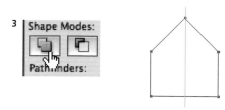

Exercise #3:

Make two rectangles,
Rotate one, Align,
apply Intersect

3

1 Make two rectangles and rotate the second. Click with the Rectangle tool to create a rectangle 1.5" x 1.75". Then click anywhere with the Rectangle tool to create a second rectangle, 3.1795" x 3.1795", and while it's selected, double-click the Rotate tool and specify 45º.

2 Align the rectangles. Select the two rectangles and, in the Control palette, click the vertical center and top Align icons. Then set the fill to white and stroke to black.

3 Apply the Intersect Pathfinder. In the Pathfinder palette (Window menu), click the Intersect shape mode. Switch to Preview mode (View menu) to see the results.

Exercise #4:

Using custom
guides, Rotate
and Add

4

1 Make two rectangles. Create a rectangle (1.5" x 1"), then drag out a vertical guide, snapping it to the center. Hold Option/Alt and, where the center guide intersects the top segment, click with the Rectangle tool. Enter 1.05" x 1.05".

2 Rotate the square. With the Selection tool, move your cursor along the square until you see a Rotate icon. Hold the Shift key and drag until the square pops into position.

3 Select and Add. Choose Select > Select All (⌘-A/Ctrl-A), then Window > Pathfinder and click the Add icon. Switch to Preview mode to see the single shape!

Exercise #5:

Use Add Anchor Points in a three-sided polygon

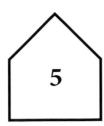

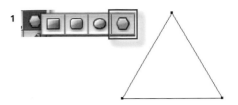

1 Create a three-sided polygon. With the Polygon tool selected, click once, then enter 3 sides and a 1.299" Radius.

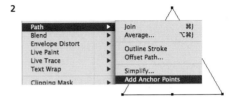

2 Use the Add Anchor Points command. With the polygon object still selected, choose Object > Path > Add Anchor Points.

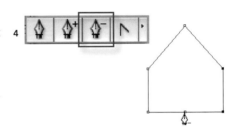

3 Average the two left points, then Average the two right points. Direct-Select the two left points and Average them along the vertical axis (Context-sensitive: Average, or Object > Path > Average), then repeat for the two right points.

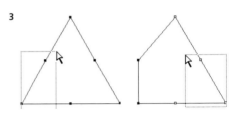

4 Delete the bottom point. With the Delete Anchor Point tool, click on the bottom point to delete it.

5 Move the top point down. Use the Direct Selection tool to select the top point, then double-click on the Direct Selection tool (in the Toolbox) to open the Move dialog box and enter –.186" vertical distance, 90° for angle.

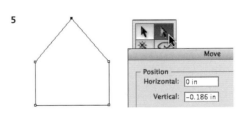

6 Slide in the sides towards the center. Use the Direct Selection tool to click on the right side of the house and drag it towards the center until the roofline looks smooth (hold down your Shift key to constrain the drag horizontally). Repeat for the left side of the house. Alternatively, select the right side and use the ← key on your keyboard to nudge the right side towards the center until the roofline looks smooth. Then, click on the left side to select it, and use the → key to nudge it towards the center. (If necessary, change your Keyboard Increment setting in the Preferences > General dialog.)

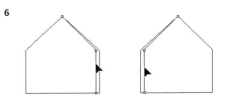

1

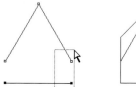

2

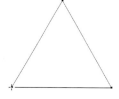

1

2

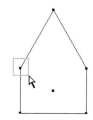

3

Exercise #6:
Cut a path and Paste in Front

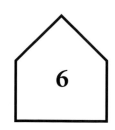

1 With zenhouse.ai, cut, paste, then move the bottom of a triangle. In the zenhouse.ai file, click with the Polygon tool and enter 3 Sides and a .866" Radius. With the Direct Selection tool, select and Cut the bottom path to the Clipboard, choose Edit > Paste in Front (⌘-F/Ctrl-F), then grab the bottom path and drag it into position.

2 Create the sides and move middle points into place. Direct-Select the two right points and join them, then repeat for the two left points. Finally, select the two middle points, and grab one to drag *both* up into position.

Exercise #7:
Join two objects

1 Make two objects. Click once with the Polygon tool, enter 3 Sides and a .866" Radius. Zoom in on the lower left corner and, with the Rectangle tool, click exactly on the lower left anchor point. Set the rectangle to 1.5" x 1".

2 Delete the middle lines and join the corners. Direct-Select marquee the middle bisecting lines and delete. Select the upper-left corner points and Average-Join by either Averaging, and then Joining the points (both from the Object > Path menu) or by pressing ⌘-Shift-Option-J/ Ctrl-Shift-Alt-J to average and join simultaneously. Select and Average-Join the upper right points.

3 Drag the top point down. Grab the top point, hold the Shift key and drag it into position.

Exercise #8:
Use Add Anchor Points, then Average-Join

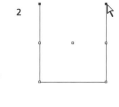

1 Using zenhouse.ai, make a rectangle, delete the top path, add anchor points, remove the bottom point. Create a tall rectangle (1.5" x 1.75") and delete the top path. Choose Add Anchor Points (Object > Path) and use the Delete Anchor Point tool to remove the bottom point.

2 Select and Average-Join the top points and move middles into position. Direct-Select the top two points and Average-Join (see Exercise #7, step 2). Then Direct-Select the middle points, grab one and, with the Shift key, drag them both into position on the zenhouse.

Exercise #9:
Reflect a Pen profile

1 Create a house profile. Drag out a vertical guide, then reset the ruler origin on the guide. To draw the profile, use the Pen tool to click on the guide at the ruler zero point, hold down Shift (to constrain your lines to 45° angles) and click to place the corner (.75" down and .75" to the left) and the bottom (1" down).

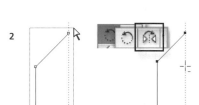

2 Reflect a copy of the profile. Select all three points of the house profile. With the Reflect tool, Option/Alt-click on the guide line. Enter an angle of 90° and click Copy.

3 Join the two profiles. Direct-Select and Join the bottom two points. Then Direct-Select the top two points and Average-Join (by pressing ⌘-Shift-Option-J/Ctrl-Shift-Alt-J, or Average then Join from the Object > Path menu).

1

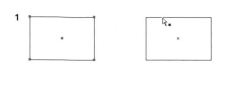

2

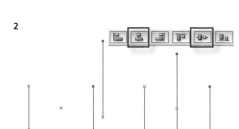

3

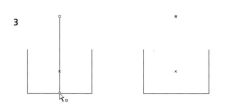

Exercise #10:
Use the Line tool and Align

1 Create a Rectangle. With the Rectangle tool, click anywhere on your Artboard and specify 1.5" x 1". With the Direct Selection tool, click on the Artboard to deselect all, then click the top edge of the rectangle and Delete.

2 Create and join the peak point. With the Line tool, click anywhere and specify a 1.75" Length and 90° Angle. Select both objects and, in the Control palette, click the vertical center and bottom Align icons.

3 Delete one of the line points. Deselect, then use the Direct Selection tool to click the bottom point of the line and Delete. To form the peak, follow Step 3 of Exercise #2.

1

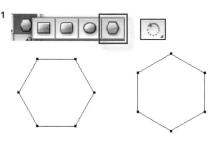

2

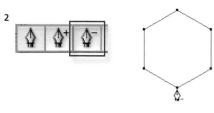

3

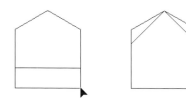

Exercise #11
Make a six-sided polygon

1 Create a six-sided polygon using zenhouse.ai. Open zenhouse.ai. Click with the Polygon tool and enter 6 Sides and a .866" Radius. Then double-click the Rotate tool and enter 30°. Align the peak of this object with the zenhouse.

2 Delete the bottom point. With the Delete Anchor Point tool, click on the bottom point to delete it.

3 Move pairs of points. Use the Direct Selection tool to select the bottom two points. Grab one of the points and Shift-drag in a vertical line into position. Direct-Select, grab and Shift-drag the middle two points into position.

Exercise #12:

With Smart Guides,
Rotate and make a
Live Paint object

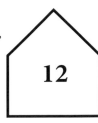

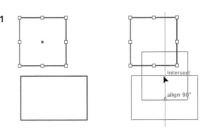

1 Make two rectangles. Enable View > Smart Guides. Create one rectangle 1.5" x 1", and one 1.05" x 1.05". Grab the center point of the square and drag it towards the center of the wide rectangle until you see "center" then move it up along this axis to the top edge until you see the words "intersect" and "align."

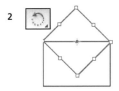

2 Rotate the square. With the square selected, double-click the Rotate tool and specify 45°.

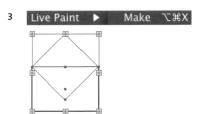

3 Make a Live Paint object. Select both objects and choose Object > Live Paint > Make.

4 Use the Live Paint Bucket to "paint out" the interior lines. Switch to Preview mode (View menu) and set the fill to white, stroke to None. Double-click the Live Paint Bucket and, in Options, disable the Paint Fills and enable Paint Strokes, and click OK. Choose None for stroke, then "paint" the interior triangular lines with None!

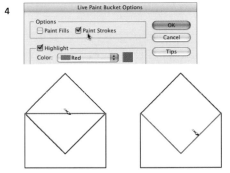

5 If you want to be able to easily paint the interior of the house as one object, delete the interior lines. Return to Outline mode (View menu). Notice that when you make a Live Paint object, it still maintains the separate shapes that made the original objects—even if you color the strokes separately. However, you *can* blend objects of the same style, like the white-filled house objects, into one object by eliminating the dividing lines.

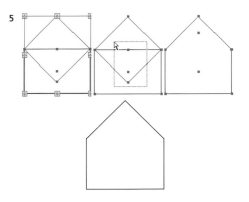

So that the entire interior of the house operates as if it is one fill, you need to delete the triangular lines that divide the interior. Using the Direct Selection tool, marquee the interior lines and Delete. Switch back to Preview mode to see that the house is still intact.

Of Grids & Lines

Three Ways to Create a Grid of Squares

Overview: *Finding different ways to construct the same simple grid.*

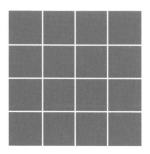

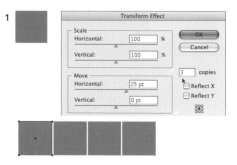

1

Make one square, apply Effect >Distort & Transform >Transform and specify a Move of 25 pt for Horizontal and 3 copies, then Effect >Transform to specify a Move of 25 pt for Vertical and 3 copies; for editable squares, choose Object > Expand Appearance

There is rarely one right way to create anything. Give three different Illustrator experts a problem to solve, and they'll come up with three different solutions. This clean logo designed by Jack Tom for Craik Consulting, Inc. (a human resource and talent company) provides a great opportunity to explore different ways to create a simple grid of blue squares separated by white lines.

Everybody's mind works differently, and the most obvious solutions to you might seem innovative to someone else. Follow your instincts as to how to construct each image. If design changes require you to rethink your approach (for instance, if the client wants the white areas of a logo to be holes that allow a background photo to show through), try a different approach.

1 Making separate small squares. With the Rectangle tool, click on your page and specify a 24 pt by 24 pt square. While it's still selected, choose a blue color from the Swatches palette. To create the horizontal row choose Effects >Distort & Transform >Transform. Specify a Move of 25 pt for Horizontal, and 3 for Copies and click OK. To fill out the grid vertically, again choose the Transform near the top of the Effects menu and click "Apply New Effect" when you see the warning. This time specify a Move of -25 pt for Vertical and 3 for Copies. If later you want to edit the rectangles separately, you can expand this live effect by choosing Object >Expand Appearance.

2 Making one large rectangle with white lines on top.
This method is a bit longer than the others, but it also allows for more design flexibility. In constructing his actual logo, Jack Tom included white lines over one large blue square, so he could control exactly how and where each line interacted with the logo "figure." He deleted part of a line below the large, white oval, and he nudged other lines slightly, horizontally or vertically.

To make a large square, choose a blue fill, click with the Rectangle tool and specify 99 pt for Width and click the word Height to automatically fill in the same number as Width (99 pt). Hold the Shift key and draw a vertical line that starts above and extends below your rectangle, and set a Fill of None and white for Stroke. To make a second line, double-click a Selection tool in the toolbox and, in the Move dialog box, enter 25 pt Horizontal, 0 for Vertical, and click Copy. Make the third line by pressing ⌘-D/Ctrl-D (which is Transform Again). For the cross lines, select your three lines, Group (⌘-G/Ctrl-G), double-click the Rotate tool, enter 90° and click Copy. To align the lines to the square, Select All (⌘-A/Ctrl-A), click the square (to designate the square as the object others align to) and, in the Control palette, click both the horizontal and vertical center Align icons.

To later "subtract" the white lines from the square (so that a background shows through), select them and choose Object > Path > Outline Stroke (your lines become thin rectangles). Next, in the Pathfinder palette (Window menu) click the Subtract from Shape icon. The stripes are "live," and can be moved, edited or deleted, leaving the square intact. To *permanently* subtract the lines from the square, select the lines and click Pathfinder Expand.

3 Splitting the square using a grid. Perhaps the simplest way to create this particular grid is to choose a blue fill and click with the Rectangle tool and specify 99-pt Width and Height. Now choose Object >Path >Split Into Grid and specify 4 rows, 4 columns; ignore the height and width but enter 1 pt for each Gutter. *Voilà!*

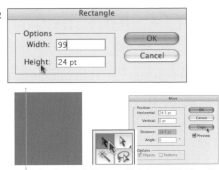

2

In a dialog box, clicking on Height or Width will copy the other value; after making a vertical line and using the Move dialog to make a copy of it

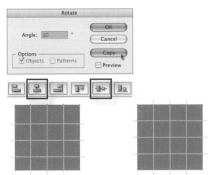

After creating the three vertical lines, using Rotate to make the horizontal copies, and aligning lines with the rectangle

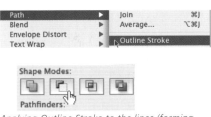

Applying Outline Stroke to the lines (forming thin rectangles), then Pathfinder Subtract (to cut the "lines" from the blue square)

3

Choosing Split Into Grid and specifying the parameters in the dialog box

Zen Scaling

Note: *Use the Shift key to constrain proportions.* ***Zen Scaling*** *practice is also on the* ***Wow! CD***.

1 Scaling proportionally towards the top Click at the top, grab lower-right (LR), drag up

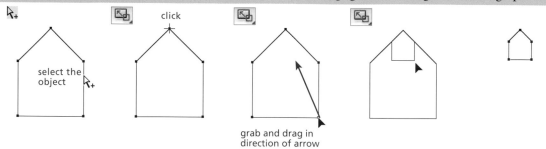

click

select the object

grab and drag in direction of arrow

2 Scaling horizontally towards the center Click at the top, grab LR, drag inwards

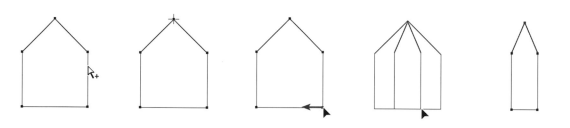

3 Scaling vertically towards the top Click at the top, grab LR, drag straight up

4 Scaling vertically and flipping the object Click at the top, grab LR, drag straight up

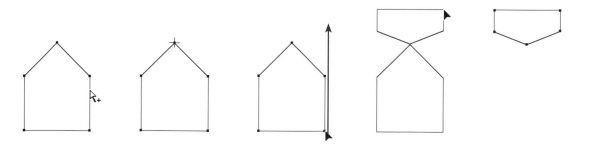

Zen Scaling (continued)

Note: *Use the Shift key to constrain proportions.* ***Zen Scaling*** *practice is also on the* ***Wow! CD***.

5 Scaling proportionally towards lower-left (LL) Click LL, grab upper-right, drag to LL

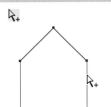 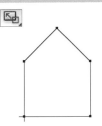  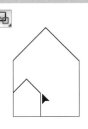

6 Scaling horizontally to the left side Click LL, grab lower-right (LR), drag to left

7 Scaling vertically towards the bottom Click center bottom, grab top, drag down

  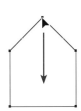 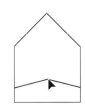

8 Scaling proportionally towards the center Click the center, grab corner, drag to center

 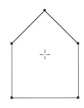  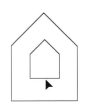

Or, to scale about the center, use the Scale tool to click-drag outside the object towards the center

Zen Rotation ↺

Note: *Use the Shift key to constrain movement.* ***Zen Rotation*** *practice is also on the* ***Wow! CD***.

1 Rotating around the center Click in the center, then grab lower-right (LR) and drag

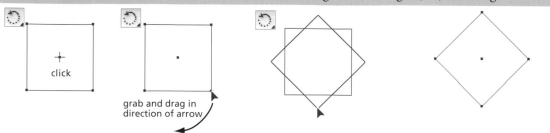

Or, to rotate about the center, use the Rotate tool to click-drag outside the object towards the center

2 Rotating from a corner Click in the upper left corner, then grab LR and drag

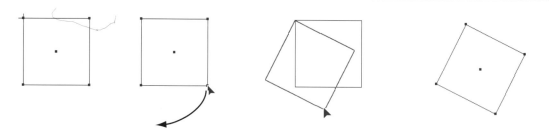

3 Rotating from outside Click above the left corner, then grab LR and drag

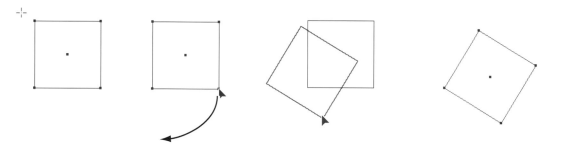

4 Rotating part of a path Marquee points with the Direct Selection tool, then use Rotate tool

Marquee the forearm with Direct Selection tool   *With the Rotate tool, click on the elbow, grab the hand and drag it around*

Creating a Simple Object Using the Basic Tools

Key: *Click where you see a RED cross, grab with the* GRAY *arrow and drag towards BLACK arrow.*

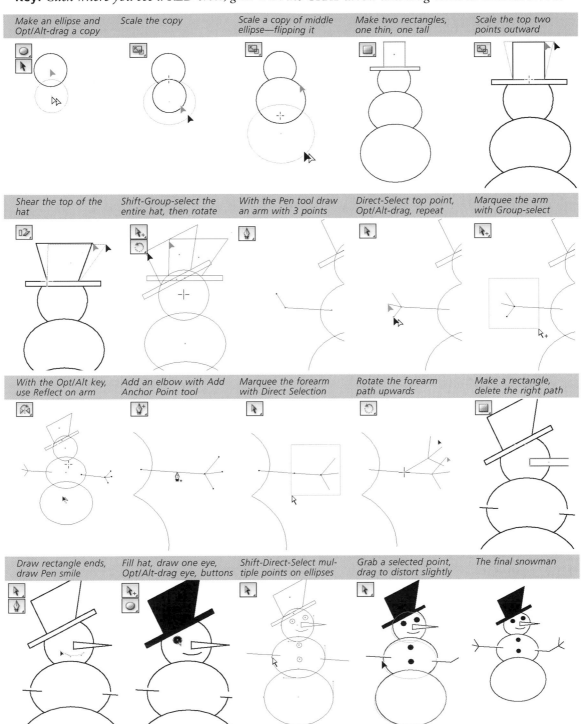

Make an ellipse and Opt/Alt-drag a copy

Scale the copy

Scale a copy of middle ellipse—flipping it

Make two rectangles, one thin, one tall

Scale the top two points outward

Shear the top of the hat

Shift-Group-select the entire hat, then rotate

With the Pen tool draw an arm with 3 points

Direct-Select top point, Opt/Alt-drag, repeat

Marquee the arm with Group-select

With the Opt/Alt key, use Reflect on arm

Add an elbow with Add Anchor Point tool

Marquee the forearm with Direct Selection

Rotate the forearm path upwards

Make a rectangle, delete the right path

Draw rectangle ends, draw Pen smile

Fill hat, draw one eye, Opt/Alt-drag eye, buttons

Shift-Direct-Select multiple points on ellipses

Grab a selected point, drag to distort slightly

The final snowman

A Finger Dance
Turbo-charge with Illustrator's Power-keys

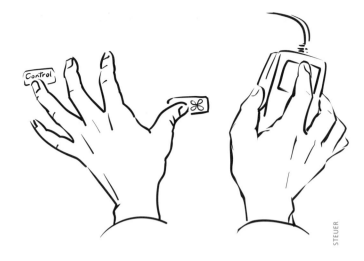

STEUER

Overview: *Save hours of production time by mastering the finger dance of Illustrator's power-keys.*

Find a summary of Finger Dance power-keys on the pull-out quick reference card

1

If you are using the mouse to choose your selection tools from the Toolbox, then you need this lesson. With some time and patience, you'll be able to free up your mouse so that practically the only thing you do with it is draw. Your other hand will learn to dance around the keyboard accessing all of your selection tools, modifying your creation and transformation tools, using your Zoom and Hand tools, and last but not least, providing instant Undo and Redo.

This "Finger Dance" is probably the most difficult aspect of Illustrator to master. Go through these lessons in order, but don't expect to get through them in one or even two sittings. When you make a mistake, use Undo (⌘-Z/Ctrl-Z). Try a couple of exercises, then go back to your own work, incorporating what you've just learned. When you begin to get frustrated, take a break. Later—hours, days, or weeks later—try another lesson. And don't forget to breathe.

Rule #1: Always keep one finger on the ⌘/Ctrl key.
Even when you're using a new tablet with keyboard characters, in most cases, the hand you are not drawing with should be resting on the actual keyboard, with one finger (or thumb) on the ⌘ key. This position will make that all-important Undo (⌘-Z/Ctrl-Z) instantly accessible.

Rule #2: Undo if you make a mistake. This is so crucial an aspect of working in the computer environment that I am willing to be redundant. If there is only one key combination that you memorize, make it Undo (⌘-Z/Ctrl-Z).

Rule #3: The ⌘/Ctrl key turns your cursor into the last used selection tool. In Illustrator, the ⌘/Ctrl key does a lot more than merely provide you with easy access to Undo. The ⌘/Ctrl key will convert any tool into the selection arrow that you last used. In the exercises that follow, you'll soon discover that the most flexible selection arrow is the Direct Selection tool.

Rule #4: Watch your cursor. If you learn to watch your cursor, you'll be able to prevent most errors before they happen. And if you don't (for instance, if you drag a copy of an object by mistake), then use Undo and try again.

Rule #5: Pay careful attention to when you hold down each key. Most of the modifier keys operate differently depending on *when* you hold each key down. If you obey Rule #4 and watch your cursor, then you'll notice what the key you are holding does.

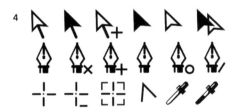

Rule #6: Hold down the key(s) until after you let go of your mouse button. In order for your modifier key to actually modify your action, you *must* keep your key down until *after* you let go of your mouse button.

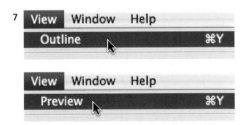

Rule #7: Work in Outline mode. When you are constructing or manipulating objects, get into the habit of working in Outline mode. Of course, if you are designing the colors in your image, you'll need to work in Preview, but while you're learning how to use the power-keys, you'll generally find it much quicker and easier if you are in Outline mode. Use the View menu, or ⌘-Y/Ctrl-Y to toggle between Preview (the default) and Outline modes.

Before you begin this sequence of exercises, choose the Direct Selection tool, then select the Rectangle tool and drag to create a rectangle.

1 Finger Dance Grabbing a selected object and moving it

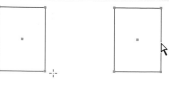

⌘
Ctrl

⌘
Ctrl

⌘
Ctrl

2 Finger Dance Deselecting an object, selecting a path and moving it

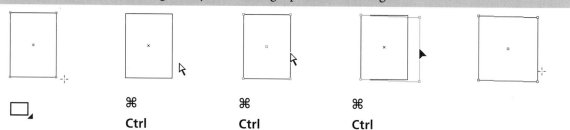

⌘
Ctrl

⌘
Ctrl

⌘
Ctrl

3 Finger Dance Moving a selected object horizontally

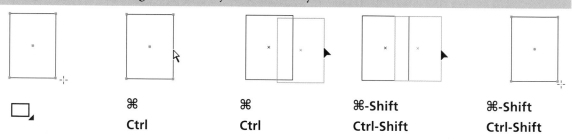

⌘
Ctrl

⌘
Ctrl

⌘-Shift
Ctrl-Shift

⌘-Shift
Ctrl-Shift

4 Finger Dance Deselecting an object, selecting a path, and moving it horizontally

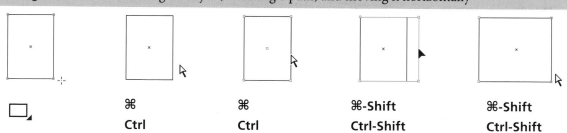

⌘
Ctrl

⌘
Ctrl

⌘-Shift
Ctrl-Shift

⌘-Shift
Ctrl-Shift

T H E   F I N G E R   D A N C E S

Before you begin this sequence of exercises, choose the Direct Selection tool,
then select the Rectangle tool and drag to create a rectangle.

5 Finger Dance Moving a copy of a selected object

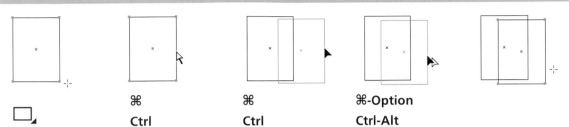

	⌘	⌘	⌘-Option	
	Ctrl	Ctrl	Ctrl-Alt	

6 Finger Dance Deselecting an object, moving a copy of a path

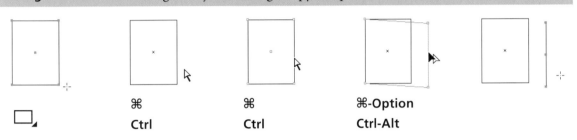

	⌘	⌘	⌘-Option	
	Ctrl	Ctrl	Ctrl-Alt	

7 Finger Dance Moving a copy of a selected object horizontally

	⌘	⌘-Shift-Option	⌘-Shift-Option	⌘-Shift-Option
	Ctrl	Ctrl-Shift-Alt	Ctrl-Shift-Alt	Ctrl-Shift-Alt

8 Finger Dance Deselecting, moving a copy of a path horizontally

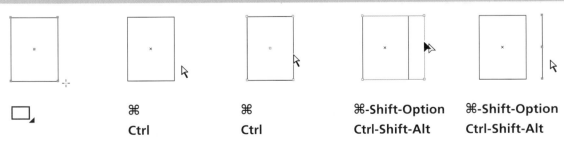

	⌘	⌘	⌘-Shift-Option	⌘-Shift-Option
	Ctrl	Ctrl	Ctrl-Shift-Alt	Ctrl-Shift-Alt

T H E   F I N G E R   D A N C E S

Before you begin this sequence of exercises, choose the Direct Selection tool,
then select the Rectangle tool and drag to create a rectangle.

9 Finger Dance Deselecting, Group-selecting, moving a copy

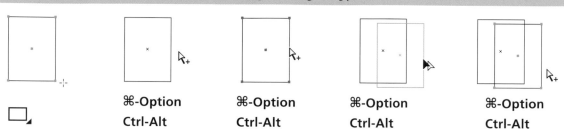

⌘-Option
Ctrl-Alt

⌘-Option
Ctrl-Alt

⌘-Option
Ctrl-Alt

⌘-Option
Ctrl-Alt

10 Finger Dance Group-selecting, moving an object horizontally

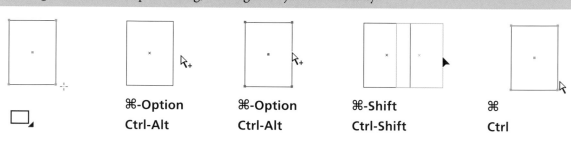

⌘-Option
Ctrl-Alt

⌘-Option
Ctrl-Alt

⌘-Shift
Ctrl-Shift

⌘
Ctrl

11 Finger Dance Moving copies horizontally, adding selections

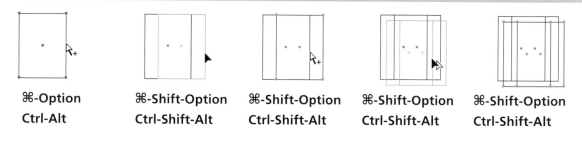

⌘-Option
Ctrl-Alt

⌘-Shift-Option
Ctrl-Shift-Alt

⌘-Shift-Option
Ctrl-Shift-Alt

⌘-Shift-Option
Ctrl-Shift-Alt

⌘-Shift-Option
Ctrl-Shift-Alt

12 Finger Dance Moving a copy, adding a selection, moving

⌘-Option
Ctrl-Alt

⌘-Option
Ctrl-Alt

⌘-Shift-Option
Ctrl-Shift-Alt

⌘
Ctrl

Drawing & Coloring

3

Drawing & Coloring

An open path shown stroked (left), filled and stroked (center), and filled only (right); note that the fill is applied as if a straight line connected the two end points

Drawing and coloring are the heart and soul of creating with Illustrator. This chapter continues the discussion of basic techniques that began in the first two chapters, rounding out the essential knowledge you'll need to work with Illustrator's drawing and coloring tools. After reading this chapter, you'll be ready to move on to the more advanced techniques in the chapters that follow.

Fill

Fill is what goes inside of a path (hence the name). The fill you choose might be a color, a gradient, or a pattern. You can even choose a fill of None, in which case there will be no fill. When you fill an open path (where the endpoints aren't connected), the fill is applied as though the two endpoints were connected by a straight line.

Stroke

The *stroke* refers to the basic "outline" of your path. While the fill gives you control over the space enclosed by a path, you can think of the stroke as the way you "dress up" the path itself to make it look the way you want. You do this by assigning various attributes to the stroke, including weight (how thick or thin it looks), line style (whether the line is solid or dashed, dash sequence (if the line is dashed), and the styles of line joins and line caps. You can also assign your path a stroke of None, in which case it won't have a visible stroke at all. (Dashed lines, joins, and caps are covered later in this chapter intro.)

Illustrator CS2 adds the ability to set how a stroke will be attached to a closed path. To do this, select a closed path and click the appropriate button to set the alignment of the stroke to the Center, Inside, or Outside of the path.

The many ways to fill or stroke an object

To set the fill or stroke for an object, first select the object and then click on the Fill or Stroke icon near the bottom

Swapping fill and stroke

When you press the X key by itself, it toggles the Stroke or Fill box to *active* (in front of the other) on the Tools and Color palettes. If you press Shift-X it swaps the actual *attributes* or contents of the Stroke and Fill boxes. For example, if you start with a white fill and a black stroke, you will have a black fill and a white stroke after you press Shift-X. **Note:** *Because gradients are not allowed on strokes, Shift-X will not work when the current fill is a gradient.*

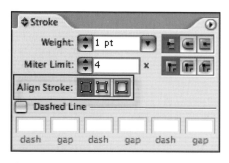

The Stroke palette, including the new Align Stroke buttons

of the Toolbox. (You can toggle between fill and stroke by pressing the X key.) If you want to set the object's stroke or fill to None, use the "/" key, or click the None button on the Toolbox or the Color palette (the little white box with a red slash through it).

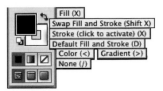

You can set the fill or stroke color you want using any of the following methods: 1) adjusting the sliders or sampling a color from the color bar in the Color palette; 2) clicking on a swatch in the Swatches palette; 3) using the Eyedropper tool to sample color from other objects in your file; or 4) sampling colors from the Color Picker. (To open the Adobe Color Picker, double-click the Fill or Stroke icon in the Toolbox or the Color palette.) In addition, you can drag color swatches from palettes to objects (selected or not), or to the Fill/Stroke icon in the Toolbox.

Color palette

The Color palette is a collection of tools that allows you to mix and choose the colors for your artwork. In addition to the sliders and edit fields for locating precise colors, this palette includes a None button so you can set your Fill or Stroke to no color at all. The Color palette also sometimes displays a Last Color proxy; this allows you to easily return to the last color you used before choosing a pattern, a gradient, or setting None. The Color palette's menu options include Invert and Complement. Invert converts a color to its negative color (as in photographic negative). Complement locates the color that Adobe calculates is the complement of a selected color).

When you're creating artwork for print, if you choose or mix a color out of the CMYK gamut, an exclamation point appears on the Color palette. Illustrator will suggest to you an "In Gamut Color" that it thinks is a close match; click on the mini swatch to accept the suggestion.

If you're creating artwork for the Web, you can choose Web safe RGB from the Palette menu, which displays the hexadecimal values for colors in the Color palette. If you choose or mix a non-Web-safe color, an "Out of Web Gamut" warning displays (it looks like a 3D cube).

Reset the Default Fill/Stroke

To change the Default Fill and Stroke colors for a document, apply a desired Fill/Stroke to an object, then Option-drag (Mac)/ Alt-drag (Win) that object to the Default style in the Graphic Styles palette. To change the Default Fill and Stroke in all new documents, do this in a start-up document.
—*Jean-Claude Tremblay*

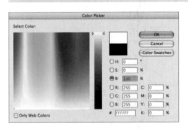
The Adobe Color Picker

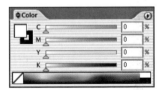

The Color palette. The sliders show the settings of the Fill or Stroke color—whichever is in front. Shown on the right is the Last Color proxy (outlined in red); when it appears, you can click it to return to the last color used before choosing a pattern or gradient, or setting a style of None

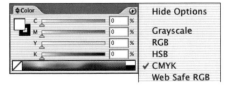

Color palette and pop-up menu

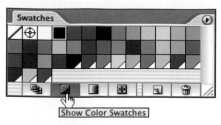

Swatches palette showing only the color swatches

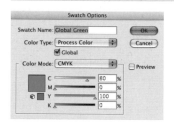

Swatch Options for a default global process color

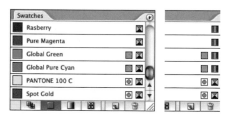

The Swatches palette, shown in list view for color swatches only; the top two swatches are process colors; the middle two are global colors; and the last two are spot colors (at left with the document in CMYK mode, at right with the same colors with the document in RGB mode)

The same swatches as in the previous caption, this time shown in thumbnail view; the left two are process; the middle two are global (includes a white triangle); the right two are spot (includes a white triangle with a "spot")

SWATCHES PALETTE

To save a color you've mixed in the Color palette, drag it to the Swatches palette from the Color palette, or just click the New Swatch button at the bottom of the Swatches palette. If you want to name the Swatch and set other options as you save it, either hold Option/Alt as you click the New Swatch button, choose New Swatch from the Swatches palette menu, or choose Create New Swatch from the Colors pop-up menu.

Whenever you copy and paste objects that contain custom swatches or styles from one document to another, Illustrator will automatically paste those elements into the new document's palettes.

The Swatch Options dialog box (which you can open by double-clicking any swatch) lets you change the individual attributes of a swatch—including its name, color mode, color definition, and whether it's a process, global process, or spot color (see below). For pattern and gradient swatches, the only attribute in the Swatch Options dialog box is the name.

Process, global, and spot colors

You can create three kinds of solid fills in Illustrator: process colors, global process colors, and spot colors. These three kinds of colors each appear differently in the Swatches palette, so they're easy to distinguish visually.

- **Process colors** are colors that are printed using a mixture of the four CMYK color values: Cyan, Magenta, Yellow, and Black. (Or, if you're doing non-print work in RGB, your process colors will be a mixture of the three RGB colors: Red, Green, and Blue.)

- **Global process colors** are process colors that have an added convenience: If you update the swatch for a global process color, Illustrator will update that color for all objects that use it in the document. You can identify a global process color in the Swatches palette by the small triangle in the lower right corner of the swatch (when the palette is in Thumbnail view) or by the Global Color icon (when the palette is in List view). You can create a global process color by enabling the Global option in either the New Swatch dialog or the Swatch Options dialog. (The Global check box is disabled by default.)

- **Spot colors** are custom colors used in print jobs that require a premixed ink rather than a percentage of the four process colors. Specifying a spot color allows you to use colors that are outside of the CMYK gamut, or to achieve a more consistent color than CMYK allows. You can specify a color as a spot color in the New Swatch dialog box (by choosing Spot Color from the Color Type menu), or you can choose a spot color from a Swatch library, such as the various Pantone libraries. All spot colors are global, so they update automatically; and, when the Swatches palette is in Thumbnail view, they have a small triangle in the lower right corner, as well as a small dot or "spot." In List view, they're marked by the Spot Color icon.

Saving custom swatch libraries

Once you've set up your Swatches palette to your satisfaction, you can save it as a custom swatch library for use with other documents. This can help you avoid having to duplicate your efforts later on. Saving a swatch library is easy thanks to the Save Swatch Library command in the palette menu. Use this command to name and save your swatch library to the Adobe Illustrator CS2 > Presets > Swatches folder. The next time you launch Illustrator, the name you gave your file will appear in the Window > Swatch Libraries menu.

This is the most efficient method in most cases, but there are other ways to make your custom Swatches palette accessible to other documents. If you want, you can choose to save the custom Swatches palette as part of your own custom Template (.ait) file, in which case it will be available when you base new files on the Template (see the *Illustrator Basics* chapter for more on Illustrator's

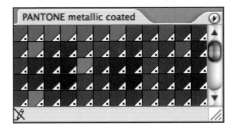

The swatches in this Pantone library all have white triangles with dots to show that they're both global and spot colors

CS2 hits the spot

Illustrator CS2 gives you the ability to use spot colors in all sorts of new places. You can now apply spot colors to raster effects like drop shadows, feathers, glows, blurs—and even 3D effects! However, you must make certain that you haven't disabled the option "Preserve spot colors if possible" in Effect > Document Raster Effects Settings (it is on by default). You can also colorize grayscale images with a spot or process color, just by dragging a color onto the image, or clicking a swatch on the Swatches palette. You can even preserve spot-color rasters or spot-colorized grayscale images when you save to EPS, PDF, or legacy Illustrator formats.

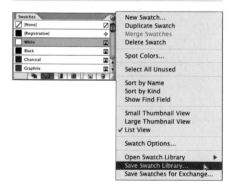

The Save Swatch Library command in the Swatches palette menu makes it easy to save custom swatch libraries

Save Swatch Library command

Keep in mind that using the Save Swatch Library command will save *only* the contents of the Swatch palette in the library it creates (as opposed to saving the whole file).

Templates feature). Or, you can simply save your file wherever you'd like, and use the Other Library menu command (available either through the palette menu's Open Swatch Library command, or via Window > Swatch Libraries) to open your custom Swatches palette. Of course, you can always open the original document when you need to access its Swatches palette—but saving it as a custom swatch library will make the swatches easily accessible.

Saving swatches for exchange

The CS2 version of Adobe's Creative Suite allows you to easily share swatches between the different CS2 applications. So, you can save your Illustrator swatches for use in InDesign, or save your Photoshop swatches for use in Illustrator, and so on. As long as your color settings are synchronized, your color swatches will remain constant as you move them between CS2 applications.

To save swatches for exchange between applications, start out in the application with the swatches you want to share. Set up your Swatches palette with the swatches you want to exchange and remove any extraneous ones. Then choose Save Swatches for Exchange from the Swatches palette menu, and save the swatch library to a convenient location. Now you can load the swatch library you've saved into any other CS2 application.

THE NEW TWO-IN-ONE EYEDROPPER

The Eyedropper tool allows you to copy appearance attributes from one object to another, including stroke, fill, color, and text attributes. In earlier versions of Illustrator, the Eyedropper functioned in tandem with the old Paint Bucket tool; the Eyedropper picked up attributes and the Paint Bucket deposited attributes.

But Adobe has retired that old Paint Bucket tool to make way for Illustrator CS2's new Live Paint Bucket tool, which is used *only* for the new Live Paint feature. (We will discuss the Live Paint Bucket's capabilities in the "Live Paint" section in the *Beyond Basic Drawing & Coloring* chapter.) That means that in CS2, the Eyedropper tool has taken over the job duties of the old Paint Bucket—so the Eyedropper now picks up *and* applies text formatting. CS2's Eyedropper has two modes: the *sampling* Eyedropper and the *applying* Eyedropper.

To copy attributes from one object to another using the Eyedropper, first select the Eyedropper from the Toolbox, and position it over an unselected object. You'll see that the Eyedropper is in sampling mode (it angles downward to the left). Click the object to pick up its attributes. Now position the Eyedropper over the unselected object to which you want to apply the attributes you just sampled, and hold down the Option (Mac)/Alt (Win) key. The Eyedropper will switch to applying mode: It angles downward to the right, and looks full. Click the object to apply the attributes sampled from the first object.

Alternatively, you can use the single-step method: First select the object with the appearance attributes you want to change, and then move the Eyedropper over the unselected object from which you want to copy attributes. Click to sample the unselected object's attributes and apply them to the previously selected object all at once. (With this method, you won't see the Eyedropper change from sampling to applying, since the whole process happens in one step.)

In addition to sampling color from objects, the Eyedropper can sample colors from raster and mesh images if you hold down the Shift key as you click.

The Shift key can also modify the Eyedropper in other ways. By default, a regular click with the Eyedropper picks up all fill and stroke attributes (it picks up the complete appearance of an object, including Live Effects). Using the single-step method described above, adding the Shift key will also allows you to sample the *color only* (as opposed to sampling the other appearance attributes as well); this will apply the color you sample to the stroke or the fill, whichever is active in the Toolbox at the time you click.

Lastly, if you hold Shift and then Option/Alt when you

From left to right: the Eyedropper tool, the cursor in normal sampling mode, in applying mode (Option/Alt), with Shift then Option/Alt key to add (not replace) appearances, and from type

Sampling from the desktop

Use the Eyedropper to sample attributes from any object on your computer's desktop, but keep in mind that the Eyedropper will only pick up RGB color when sampling from outside the current Illustrator document. To sample attributes from the desktop, first select the object whose attributes you want to change. Then select the Eyedropper tool, click anywhere on your document and continue to hold the mouse button down while you move your cursor over the desktop object you want to sample. Once your cursor is over the object, just release the mouse button and you'll see the sampled attributes applied to the selected object.

When deleting swatches

When you click the Trash icon in the Swatches palette to delete selected swatches, Illustrator does *not* warn you that you might be deleting colors used in the document. Instead Illustrator will convert global colors and spot colors used to fill objects to non-global process colors. To be safe, choose Select All Unused and then click the Trash.

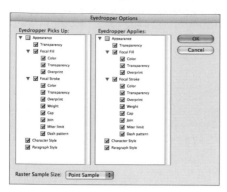

Using the Eyedropper options, you have complete control over what to pick up and/or deposit. In addition to stroke, fill, color, and text formatting, you can use the Eyedropper to copy styles and type attributes (which are discussed later in the book).

Tint hint: Use global colors

One benefit of using global colors in your Swatch palette is that you can easily specify tint percentages for any color. Just select a colored object and adjust the Tint slider in the Color palette, or type a number in the percentage field.

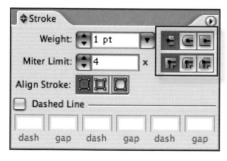

The Stroke palette with the cap/join section

At left, three lines shown top to bottom in Outline, Preview with Butt cap, Round cap and Projecting cap; at right, a 5-pt dashed line with a 2-pt dash and 6-pt gap shown top to bottom in Outline, then Preview with a Butt cap, Round cap, and Projecting cap

click, you'll *add* the appearance attributes of an object to the selected object's appearance—instead of just replacing it. (For more about appearances see the *Beyond Basic Drawing & Coloring* chapter.)

You can control which attributes the Eyedropper picks up and applies by using the Eyedropper Options dialog box (accessed by double-clicking the Eyedropper in the toolbox). You can also control the size of an area the Eyedropper samples from raster images by using the Raster Sample Size menu at the bottom of the dialog box. Choosing Single Point will sample from a single pixel; 3 x 3 will pick up a sample averaged from a 3 pixel grid surrounding the point you click on; and 5 x 5 will do so for a 5 pixel grid. (This will help you get a more accurate color sample in many cases, since it can be difficult to get the colors that the eye "blends" from many pixels by clicking on a single point.)

END OF LINES

You may discover that although stroked lines seem to match up perfectly when viewed in Outline mode, they visibly overlap when previewed. You can solve this problem by changing the end caps in the Stroke palette. Just select one of the three end cap styles described below to determine how the endpoints of your selected paths will look when previewed.

The first (and default) choice is called a Butt cap; it causes your path to stop at the end anchor point. Butt caps are essential for creating exact placement of one path against another. The middle choice is the Round cap, which rounds the endpoint in a more natural manner. Round caps are especially good for softening the effect of single lines or curves, making them appear slightly less harsh. The final style is the Projecting cap, which extends lines and dashes at half the stroke weight beyond the end anchor point.

In addition to determining the appearance of path endpoints, cap styles affect the shape of dashed lines (see illustration at left).

Corner Shapes

The Join style in the Stroke palette determines the shape of a stroke line at its corner points. Each of the three styles determines the shape of the outside of the corner; the inside of the corner is always angled.

The default Miter join creates a pointy corner. The length of the point is determined by the width of the stroke, the angle of the corner (narrow angles create longer points; see illustration at right) and the Miter limit setting on the Stroke palette. Miter limits can range from 1x (which is always blunt) to 500x. Generally, the default Miter join with a miter limit of 4x looks just fine.

The Round join creates a rounded outside corner for which the radius is half the stroke width. The Bevel join creates a squared-off outside corner, equivalent to a Miter join with the miter limit set to 1x.

FREE TRANSFORM/LIQUIFY TOOLS, DISTORT FILTERS

You can use Illustrator's Free Transform tool to distort the size and shape of an object by dragging the corner points of the object's bounding box. The shape of the object distorts progressively as you drag the handles.

One of the more recent additions to Illustrator is the suite of "Liquify" Distortion tools that arrived with Illustrator 10. They allow you to distort objects manually, by dragging the mouse over them. The Warp, Twirl, Pucker, Bloat, Scallop, Crystallize, and Wrinkle tools work not only on vector objects, but on embedded raster images as well. Use the Option/Alt key to resize the Liquify brush as you drag. These tools are a step beyond the Distort filters Illustrator had prior to version 10—they're more interactive, more intuitive, and more fun to use.

But the Distort filters in versions prior to Illustrator 10 aren't gone—they can still be found under both the Filter menu (choose the topmost of the two Distort submenus in the Filter menu) and the Effect menu (choose Effect > Distort & Transform). They do have their uses. For instance, the ability to reapply the same effect with exact precision by choosing it again from the top of the

To outline dashed strokes...

Object > Path > Outline Stroke won't expand dashes into of dashed objects. To do this, select your dashed line and choose Object > Flatten Transparency. Enable the option "Convert All Strokes to Outlines" and set the Raster/Vector slider at 100, and click OK. (If the dashes interact or overlap other objects, you must first group it with those objects—and flatten that entire group.).

—*Jean-Claude Tremblay*

A path shown first in Outline, then in Preview with a Miter join, Round join, and Bevel join

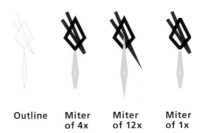

| Outline | Miter of 4x | Miter of 12x | Miter of 1x |

Objects with 6-pt strokes and various Miter limits, demonstrating that the angles of lines affects Miter limits

The Free Transform tool

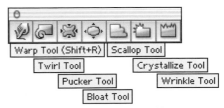

The Liquify Distortion tools' tear off palette can be accessed from the Warp tool: see "Tear off palettes" in the Illustrator Basics chapter

filter menu (if you use the versions in the Effect menu, they are live, and can be saved as Graphic Styles; see the *Live Effects & Graphic Styles* chapter for more about these live effects). They can also be used to create in-betweens for animations in cases where blends might not give the desired results, or might be too cumbersome.

The Distort filters include Free Distort, Pucker & Bloat, Roughen, Tweak, Twist, and Zig Zag. All of these filters distort paths based on the paths' anchor points. They move (and possibly add) anchor points to create distortions. Enable Preview in the dialog box to see and modify the results as you experiment with the settings.

Many of the Free Distort functions can also be performed with the Free Transform tool (to learn about the Free Transform tool, see the "Distort Dynamics" lesson later in this chapter).

PATH SIMPLIFY COMMAND

More is not better when it comes to the number of anchor points you use to define a path. The more anchor points, the more complicated the path—which makes the file size larger and harder to process when printing. The Simplify command (Object > Path > Simplify) removes excess anchor points from one or more selected paths without making major changes to the path's original shape.

Two sliders control the amount and type of simplification. Enable Show Original as well as the Preview option to preview the effect of the sliders as you adjust them. The Preview option also displays the original number of points in the curve and the number that will be left if the current settings are applied.

Adjust the Curve Precision slider to determine how accurately the new path should match the original path. The higher the percentage, the more anchor points will remain, and the closer the new path will be to the original. The endpoints of an open path are never altered. The Angle Threshold determines when corner points should become smooth. The higher the threshold, the more likely a corner point will remain sharp.

Tiffany Larsen

Tiffany Larsen used custom patterns to dress
the Big Bad Wolf in realistic fabric textures.
The gingham dress pattern was created by
drawing a checkerboard of squares with the
Rectangle tool. Within the checkerboard,
Larsen drew smaller squares of various sizes
to simulate a mottled appearance. She then
masked the grouped checkerboard into the
size she wanted and dragged it to the Swatches
palette to create a pattern. To make the lace
(shown above on a black background), Larsen
drew several circles (white Fill, no Stroke)

within a square (white Fill, no Stroke). With the
Direct Selection tool, she selected the square
and circles and made the selection into a compound path (Object > Compound Path > Make)
to create transparent holes (see the *Advanced
Techniques* chapter for more on masks). Larsen
made the selection into a pattern by choosing
Edit > Define Pattern. Using the Stroke palette,
Larsen made the stitching a 1-pt dashed line
with a 2-pt gap.

Simple Realism

Realism from Geometry and Observation

Overview: *Draw a mechanical object using the Rectangle, Rounded Rectangle, and Ellipse tools; use tints to fill all of the paths; add selected highlights and offset shadows to simulate depth.*

1

The default Fill and Stroke in the Tools palette; setting the default stroke weight for objects

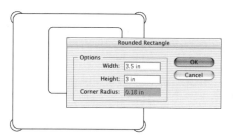

Creating rounded rectangles and ellipses to construct the basic forms

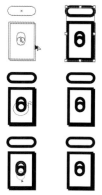

Option-Shift/Alt-Shift-dragging a selection to duplicate and constrain it to align with the original; using the Lasso tool to select specific points; Shift-dragging to constrain and move the selected points

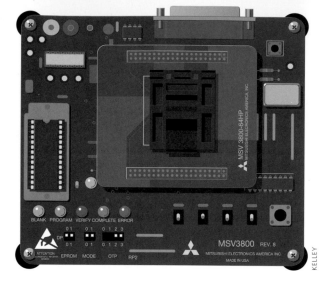

Many people believe the only way to achieve realism in Illustrator is with elaborate gradients and blends, but this illustration by Andrea Kelley proves that artistic observation is the real secret. Using observation and only the simplest Illustrator techniques, Kelley drew technical product illustrations of computer chip boards for a handbook for her client, Mitsubishi.

1 Recreating a mechanical object with repeating geometric shapes by altering copies of objects. Most artists find that close observation, not complex perspective, is the most crucial aspect to rendering illustrations. To sharpen your skills in observing the forms and details of objects, select a simple mechanical device to render in grayscale. First, create a new Illustrator document. Then experiment with the Ellipse, Rectangle, and Rounded Rectangle tools to draw the basic elements of the device. After you've made your first object—with the object still selected—click on the Default Fill and Stroke icon in the Tool palette, open the Stroke palette (Window>Stroke), and choose a stroke weight of 0.75 pt using the Weight pop-up menu. All objects you make from that point on will have the same fill and stroke as your first object.

Because mechanical and computer devices often have similar components, you can save time by copying an object you've drawn and then modifying the shape of the copy. You can easily align your copy with the original by holding the Opt-Shift/Alt-Shift keys while dragging out the copy from the selected object to the desired location. Smart Guides (View menu) can also help with alignment.

To illustrate a series of switches, Kelley dragged a selected switch (while holding Option-Shift/Alt-Shift to copy and constrain its movement), stretched the switch copy by selecting one end of the switch knob with the Lasso and dragged it down (holding the Shift key to constrain it vertically). She repeated this process to create a line of switches with the same switch plate width, but different switch knob lengths.

2 Using tints to fill the objects. At this point, all the objects are filled with white and have a stroke of black. Select a single object and set the Stroke to None and the Fill to black using the Color palette (Window > Color). Open the Swatches palette (Window > Swatches) and Option-click/Alt-click on the New Swatch icon to name it "Black-global," and enable the Global option. Click OK to save your new color. Then create a tint using the Tint slider in the Color palette. Continue to fill individual objects (be sure to set their Stroke to None) using Black Spot as the fill color, and adjust the tints for individual objects using the Tint slider until you are happy with their shades. Kelley used percentages from 10 to 90%, with most of the objects being 55 to 75% black.

3 Creating a few carefully placed highlights. Look closely at the subject of your drawing and decide where to place highlights. For lines that follow the contour of your object, select part or all of your object's path with the Direct Selection tool, copy (Edit > Copy) and Paste in Front (Edit > Paste in Front) that path or path section. Using the Color palette, change the Fill of your path to None and use the tint slider to change the Stroke to a light value of gray. While the highlight's path is still selected, you can reduce or increase the width of your

2

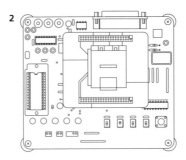

The drawn object prior to filling selected paths with gray

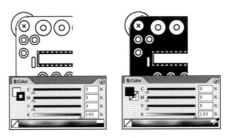

Left, the selected path set to the default stroke and fill colors; right, the selected object set to a fill of Black and a stroke of None

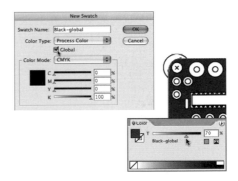

Creating a new custom global color that will then appear in the Swatches palette; setting the selected path to a fill of 70% Black using the Tint slider in the Color palette

Individual paths filled with tints of Black Spot in a range from 10% to 90%

3

Using Paste in Front on a selected, copied path to duplicate it directly on top; changing the Stroke and Fill of the duplicate path to create a highlighted outline

Using the Stroke palette Weight field to increase or decrease the width of the highlight path

Placing small circles with a Fill of 0% black (white) and a darker inset curved path to simulate depth; Option-Shift/Alt-Shift-dragging a selected path to duplicate the path and constrain its movement

4

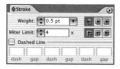

Copying a dial and choosing Paste in Back; using Arrow keys to offset the copy; setting the Fill "T" tint to 87% black to create a shadow from the copy

stroke using the Weight field of the Stroke palette. If you need to trim the length of a highlight, cut its path with the Scissors tool and then select the unwanted segments with the Direct Selection tool and delete them.

For some of the knobs and dials on her chip, Kelley used circular highlights with a value of 0% black (white) and an inset curved path with a darker value to simulate depth. Once you are satisfied with the highlights on a particular knob, select the paths (both the highlights and the knob) and hold down the Option/Alt key while dragging the objects in order to duplicate them (hold down Option-Shift/Alt-Shift to copy and constrain the paths as you drag them).

For her highlights, Kelley used lines that varied in weight from .2 to .57 pt and colors that varied in tint from 10 to 50%. She also used carefully placed white circles for some of the highlights. Try experimenting with different Cap and Join styles in the Stroke palette; see "End of Lines" section and figures in the introduction to this chapter for more on Caps and Joins.

4 Creating shadows. Follow the same procedure as above, but this time use darker tints on duplicated paths pasted behind in order to create shadows. Select a path to make into a shadow, copy it, and use Edit > Paste in Back to place a copy of the path directly behind the original path. Use your Arrow keys to offset the copy, and change the Fill to a darker tint using the Color palette.

Consider using Effects to create shadows and highlights. See the *Live Effects & Graphic Styles* chapter for information on building multi-stroke appearances and saving them as styles that you can use on other artwork.

Symbols for faster updating and smaller files

Define artwork as a symbol if you want to easily update all instances of that artwork at once (symbols also result in smaller files when you export the illustration as a Flash file). See the *Brushes & Symbols* chapter to learn more about Symbols.

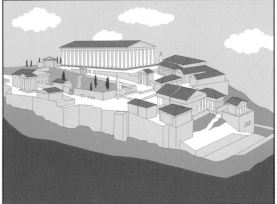

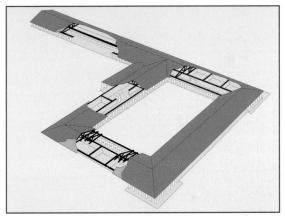

FERSTER

Gary Ferster

Using only simple filled and stroked objects, Gary Ferster created this series of illustrations on Roman Life for a children's educational

CD-ROM titled "Ancient 2000." For help making perspective guidelines, see "Varied Perspective" in the *Layers & Appearances* chapter.

Objective Colors

Custom Labels for Making Quick Changes

Overview: *Define custom spot or global colors, naming colors by the type of object; repeat the procedure for each type of object; use Select commands to select types of objects by spot or global color name to edit colors or objects.*

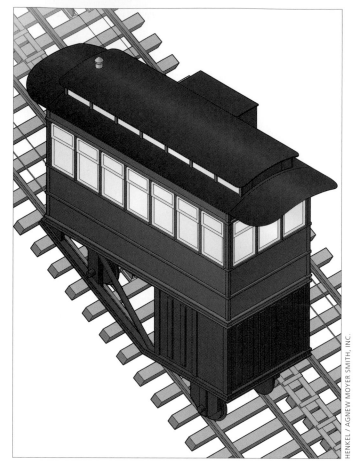

HENKEL / AGNEW MOYER SMITH, INC.

1

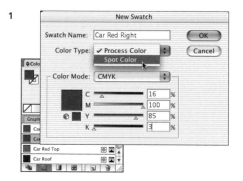

Option-clicking on the New Swatch icon to directly access Swatch Options; naming the color, then setting the color to be a Spot Color or choosing the Global option, which allows global changes and tinting

A spot color swatch with its custom label

When you need to frequently adjust the colors of an illustration, it's essential to find a way of organizing your colors. This illustration by Rick Henkel demonstrates how his firm, Agnew Moyer Smith (AMS), uses custom colors to label different categories of objects, making it simple to isolate and update colors. This method also makes it easy to find all objects in a category in order to apply any other global changes, such as changing the stroke weight or scaling, or adding transparency or effects.

1 Creating custom global or spot colors. If you define custom global or spot colors you'll be able to easily revise your colors, find objects by its colors, and make tints of your colors. In the Swatches palette, Option-click/Alt-click on the New Swatch icon. If you have premixed a color in the Color palette, this color will be loaded in the color mixer. You can then edit it using the color sliders. Now give your color a name that conveys the kind of object you plan to fill with the color and either choose Spot Color from the Color Type pop-up, or choose Process, and enable the Global option. Rick Henkel used labels such as "CamRight" and "DriveLeft" to label the colors he would use in his illustration of the Duquesne Incline. To help his selection of reliably reproducible colors, Henkel used the Agfa PostScript Process Color Guide to look up the color he actually wanted and then entered the CMYK percentages.

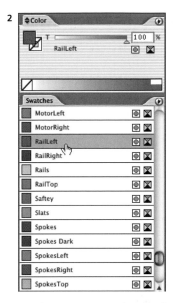

2 Repeating the procedure for all colors and labels, and changing color definitions as necessary. Create colors for each type of object to be styled differently, naming each color for the objects it will fill (to speed creation of swatches, see the Tip below right). Henkel created spot colors, properly labeled, for each type of object included in this incline railroad illustration.

The spot and global color systems makes it easy to change definitions of colors. From the Swatches palette, double-click on the color you want to change in order to open Swatch Options, where you can change the color recipe. Click OK to apply the changes to all objects containing that color.

Creating custom spot color swatches for each category of object to be styled differently

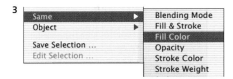

With a color swatch label selected, choosing Select > Same > Fill Color to find the objects filled with that color

After selecting the next color swatch, using the Select > Reselect command to select all objects colored with that swatch

3 Using the labels to find all like objects. To select all like objects—for example, those colored with "CamRight"—click on that color name in your Swatches palette list and choose Select > Same > Fill Color. Once selected, you can edit other attributes besides color (like stroke width, layer position and alignment).

Spot colors for four-color-process jobs

For images containing spot colors, you can print four-color-process separations from the Print dialog box by enabling the "Convert All Spot Colors to Process" Output option (though there might be color shifts).

From one swatch to another

When defining swatches with custom parameters in Swatch Options, such as Spot colors or Global process colors, instead of having to continually set similar parameters, simply select a swatch that is close to the color you want, then Option-click/Alt-click the New Swatch icon to redefine and name the Swatch.

Isometric Systems
Arrow Keys, Constrain Angles & Formulas

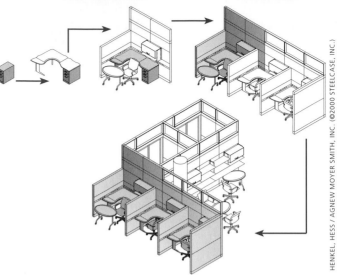

Overview: *Create detailed views of an object from front, top and side; use an isometric formula to transform the objects; set "Constrain Angle" and "Keyboard Increment;" use Lasso and Arrow keys with Snap to Point to adjust and assemble objects.*

Stubborn snapping-to-point

Sometimes if you try to move an object just slightly, it will annoyingly "snap" to the wrong place. If this happens, move it away from the area and release. Then grab the object again at the point you'd like to align and move it so that it snaps into the correct position. Smart Guides can help (View menu). If you still have trouble, zoom in. As a last resort, disable "Snap to Point" (View menu).

1

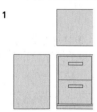

Top, front and side faces with more than one component are grouped

2

Scaling, shearing and rotating

Technical illustrations and diagrams are often depicted in isometrics, and Adobe Illustrator can be the ideal program both for creating your initial illustrations, and for transforming them into this projection. The artists at Agnew Moyer Smith (AMS) created and transformed the diagrams on these pages using their three-step iso projection. For both the initial creation and manipulation of the isometric objects in space, AMS custom-set "Keyboard Increment" and "Constrain Angle" (in Illustrator > Preferences > General) and made sure that View > Snap to Point was enabled.

1 Creating detailed renderings of the front, side and top views of your object to scale. Before you begin a technical illustration, you should choose a drawing scale, then coordinate the settings Preferences > General to match. For instance, to create a file drawer in the scale of 1 mm = 2", set the Units to millimeters and "Keyboard Increment" to .5 mm, and make sure that the "Snap to Point" option is enabled. With these features enabled and matching your drawing scale, it's easy to create detailed views of your object. To easily keep track of your object sizing as you work, choose Window > Info. If a portion of the real object is inset 1" to the left, you can use the ← key to move the path one increment (.5 mm) farther left. Finally, Snap to Point and Smart Guides (View menu) will help you align and assemble your various components. Select and group the components of the front view. Separately group the top and side so you'll be able to easily isolate each of the views for transformation and assembly. AMS renders every internal detail so they can create "cut-aways," or adjust individual groups of elements—for instance, when a drawer is opened.

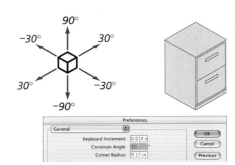

An arrow key movement chart based on a Constrain Angle of 30°; AMS groups fully transformed and assembled objects for easy selection; setting Constrain Angle in Preferences > General

2 Using an isometric formula to transform your objects, then assembling the elements. The artists at AMS created and transformed the diagrams on these pages using their three-step process, which is fully demonstrated on the *Wow! CD*. To transform your objects, double-click on the various tools to specify the correct percentages numerically. First, select all three views and scale them 100% horizontally and 86.6% vertically. Next, select the top and side, shear them at a –30° angle, and then shear the front 30°. Rotate the top and front 30° and the side –30°. The movement chart shows angles and directions.

   To assemble the top, front and side, use the Selection tool to grab a specific anchor-point from the side view that will contact the front view, and drag it until it snaps into the correct position (the arrow turns hollow). Next, select and drag to snap the top into position. Finally, select and group the entire object for easy reselection.

3 Using selection, Constrain Angle and Arrow keys to adjust objects and assemble multiple components. Try using the Lasso tool to select a portion of an object (Shift-Lasso adds points to a selection; Option-Lasso/Alt-Lasso deletes points from a selection), setting Constrain Angle to 30°; then slide your selection along the isometric axes using alternating Arrow keys. Select entire objects and snap them into position against other objects. Also, look at the movement chart (top of the page) to determine the direction in which to move, then double-click a Selection tool in the toolbox to specify a numeric movement for selections or objects.

3

You can use the Lasso to select the points you want to move

To lengthen the cart, select the points indicated and move in the direction of the arrow (–30°)

 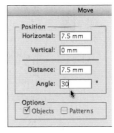

To widen the cart, select the points indicated, and either double-click on the Selection tool in the Toolbox to specify a Move numerically, or use your Arrow keys

Transforming one object into the next by Direct-Selecting the appropriate anchor points and using the Move command, or by setting and using a custom Constrain Angle and Arrow keys

Automated Isometric Actions!
Rick Henkel of AMS created *WOW Actions* that automate formulas for isometrics (on the *Wow! CD*).

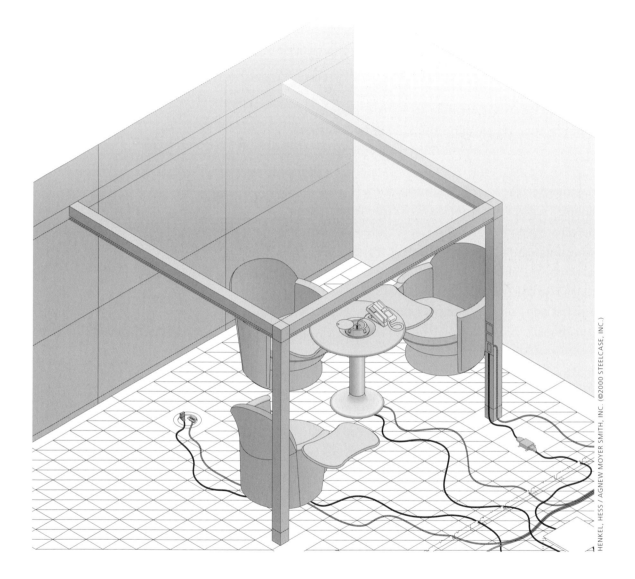

Rick Henkel, Kurt Hess /
Agnew Moyer Smith, Inc.

Agnew Moyer Smith's artists use Illustrator not only to create discrete elements, but also because it provides so much flexibility in composing an environment with those elements. Objects can be saved in separate files by category and used as "libraries" when constructing different scenes.

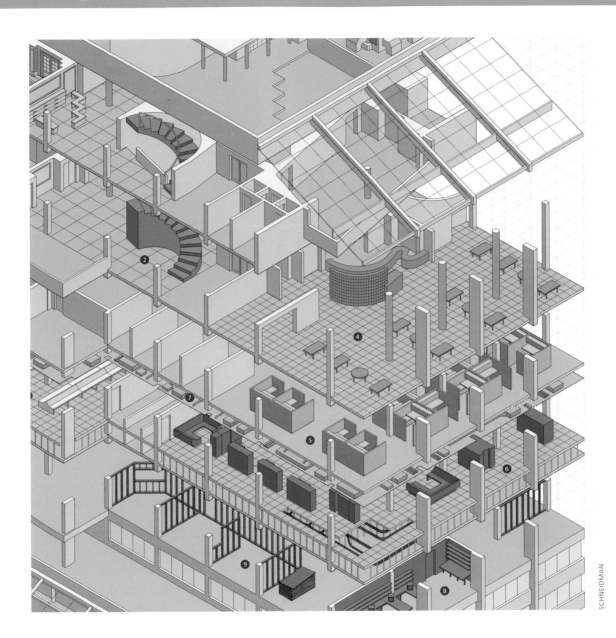

SCHNEIDMAN

Jared Schneidman

Jared Schneidman illustrated this building for a capabilities brochure for Structure Tone, an interior construction company. Schneidman manually traced a scan of an architectural drawing of the building, rendered originally in an isometric view. While drawing, Schneidman set the Constrain Angle (Preferences > General) to 30°, so he could edit objects by dragging selected points or lines along the same angles as the isometric view (he held down the Shift key while dragging to constrain movement to the set angles).

Distort Dynamics

Adding Character Dynamics with Transform

KANZLER

Overview: *Create characters and group them; use the Free Transform tool to drag one corner to exaggerate the character; draw a sun and use the Free Transform tool to add dynamics to circles.*

1

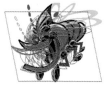

The original bug (top); then with the Free Transform tool the jaw is enlarged, the back is squashed and the entire character is skewed forward

After John Kanzler creates the cast of characters in his scenes, he often uses the Free Transform tool on each of the characters one at a time in order to add energy, movement, dynamics and action.

1 **Creating and grouping a character, then applying the Free Transform tool.** After building his bug one object at a time, Kanzler thought it needed a more menacing look, and wanted the bug to appear as if it were charging forward. By grabbing and moving various handles, he was able to enlarge the jaws while squashing the body. Then he skewed the bug to the left to give a sense of forward motion and more energy than the original. Select your objects and choose the Free Transform tool (E key). Now, this is essential throughout this lesson: grab a handle and *then* hold down ⌘ (Mac)/Ctrl (Win) to pull only that selected handle to distort the image. Look

carefully at what results from movement of each of the Free Transform handles. For his hovering wasp, Kanzler used the Free Transform tool to give the wasp a little more "personality" by pulling a corner out to one side. Notice that as you pull a *corner* sideways to expand in one direction, the opposite side distorts and compresses—if you pull a *center* handle, you will merely skew the objects, elongating them toward the pulled side.

The effect of Free Transform on the hovering wasp

2 **Applying the Free Transform tool to regularly shaped objects to add perspective and dynamics.** In creating an "action line" for his illustration, Kanzler used the Free Transform tool to make an arc of dots skew out of uniformity, while constraining the arc of the skewed path to that of the original, unskewed path. First, he applied a custom dotted Pattern Brush to a curved path (see the *Brushes & Symbols* chapter for help). Then he chose Object > Expand Appearance to turn the brushed path into a group of oval objects. By carefully tucking and pulling with the Free Transform tool, Kanzler was able to add flair to the arc while keeping the same general size.

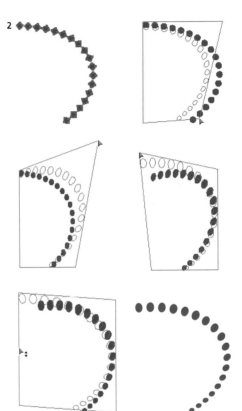

Using the Free Transform tool, pull different handles to create action and perspective effects

3 **Making a sun, then creating extreme perspective using the Free Transform tool.** To make the sun object, draw a circle (hold Shift as you draw with the Ellipse tool). In Outline mode (View menu), place your cursor over the circle centerpoint, hold Option/Alt *and* the Shift key while drawing a second, larger concentric circle and make it into a Guide (View > Guides > Make Guides). With the Pen tool, draw a wedge-shaped "ray" that touches the outer-circle guide. Select the wedge, and with the Rotate tool, Option/Alt-click on the circle's center point. Decide how many rays you want, divide 360 (the degrees in a circle) by the number of rays to find the angle to enter in the dialog box and click Copy. To create the remaining rays, keep repeating Transform Again, ⌘-D (Mac)/Ctrl-D (Win). Select all sun objects and choose Object > Group. Then, with the Free Transform tool, grab one single corner handle to skew the sun's perspective.

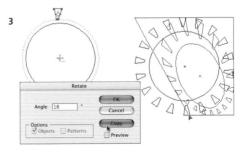

The sun object shown in Outline mode, before the process of Transform Again; and while pulling a Free Transform handle

Distort Filter Flora

Applying Distort Filters to Create Flowers

Overview: *Create rough circles; resize and rotate copies of the circles to construct a rose; fill with a radial gradient; apply the Roughen filter; apply other Distort filters to copies.*

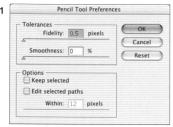

1

Setting the Pencil Tool Preferences; drawing two rough circular paths

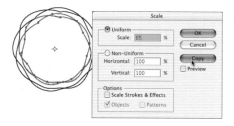

Using the Scale tool dialog window to create a reduced-size pair of circles nested within the first pair of circles

(Left) Using the Rotate tool to rotate the last-created pair of circles; (right) the complete construction of the flower before coloring—the flower center consists of a few small circles

GRACE

Artist Laurie Grace used two roughly drawn circular paths and a series of Distort filters to construct the delicate flowers in her illustration, which she colored with various radial gradients. (See the *Live Effects & Graphic Styles* chapter for examples of artwork created using "live" versions of filters, called "effects.")

1 Drawing circular paths; resizing and rotating path copies. Grace drew two rough circular paths, then resized and duplicated the two paths as the first steps in creating each rose. In a new Illustrator document, double-click on the Pencil tool to bring up the Pencil Tool Preferences window. In the Tolerances section, set Fidelity to 0.5 pixels and Smoothness to 0. In the Options section, disable "Keep selected" and "Edit selected paths." Using the Color palette, set a Fill of None and a Stroke of Black. Draw a roughly circular path, holding the Option (Mac)/ Alt (Win) key as you near the end of the circle to automatically close the path. Then draw another rough circle just within the first circle. Overlapping is okay.

Use the Selection tool or Lasso tool to select the two paths. To create a duplicate pair of circles that is smaller

than and nested within the first pair, double-click on the
Scale tool again (you should note that the previously used
reduction setting is saved) and click the Copy button.
With the last pair still selected, choose the Rotate tool and
click-drag on the image in the direction of the rotation
you want. Continue to resize/copy and rotate selected
pairs of circles until the flower form you are building is
almost filled with circles.

   To vary the petal placement in the final rose, you can
continue to rotate some of the pairs after you've created
them. Then, for the center of the rose, click on the Pencil
tool and draw a few small, nested circles. Use the Lasso
tool or the Selection tool to select all the paths that make
up the rose construction, and choose Object > Group,
then deselect all paths by choosing Select > Deselect.

2 Coloring the flower using a radial gradient. To give
the final rose illustration a color effect that mimicked
the petals of real flowers, Grace created a radial gradient
color swatch and applied it to her rose construction. Open
the Swatches palette (Window > Swatches), and click on
the "Show Gradient Swatches" button. Next, click on
the "Black, White Radial" swatch. To change the colors
of the gradient, open the Color and Gradient palettes
(Window > Color and Window > Gradient), click once on
the leftmost gradient slider (the beginning point of the
gradient) in the Gradient palette, and adjust the color
sliders in the Color palette. Grace chose 100% M for the
beginning slider. Next, click on the rightmost gradient
slider (the ending point of the gradient) and adjust the
color sliders; Grace chose 34% M and moved the K slider
to 0%. To increase the amount of 100% magenta in your
filled objects, drag the left slider to the right and release it
where you like (Grace used a Location setting of 45.51%).
Finally, create your new Gradient swatch by Option-
clicking (Mac)/Alt-clicking (Win) on the "New Swatch"
button in the Swatches palette. Name your swatch (Grace
chose "Pink Flower Gradient") and click OK. Select the
rose illustration and then set the Fill to "Pink Flower

2

Choosing a radial gradient swatch to adjust

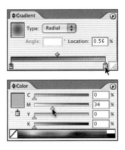

*Adjusting the color settings of the beginning
point gradient slider*

*Adjusting the color settings of the ending point
gradient slider*

Repositioning the beginning gradient slider

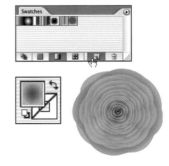

*(Top) Creating a new Gradient swatch; (bottom,
left and right) setting Fill to the "Pink Flower
Gradient" swatch and Stroke to None*

3

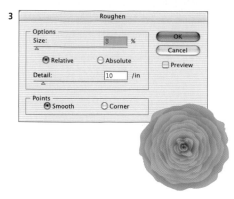

Settings for the Roughen filter; the final rose

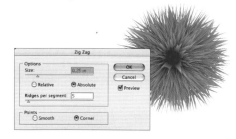

Applying additional distortion filters to copies of
the final rose illustration.

Gradient" and the Stroke to None. For more on Gradients, see the *Blends, Gradients & Mesh* chapter.

3 Applying the Roughen filter. To give her rose a realistic rough-edged petal effect, Grace applied the Roughen filter to the illustration. Use the Selection tool to select the rose, then choose Filter > Distort > Roughen. In the Roughen dialog box, enable the Preview checkbox to see the effect of the filter before you apply it. In the Roughen Options, set Size to 3%, Detail to 5/in, and Points to Smooth. Click OK to apply your chosen settings.

Grace used her final rose to create some of the other flowers in her illustration by applying more Distort filters to copies of the rose (be sure to enable the Preview checkbox for each as you work). Select the entire rose and duplicate it by holding down the Option (Mac)/Alt (Win) key as you drag the rose to a new location. With the duplicate still selected, choose Filter > Distort > Pucker & Bloat, enable Preview, and set the Bloat to 33%. Click OK to apply. On another copy of the rose, apply a Pucker & Bloat setting of –40 Pucker. With a third copy of the rose selected, choose Filter > Distort > Zig Zag and set Size to .25 in, choose Absolute, set Ridges to 5 and choose Corner in the Points section. With a fourth copy of the rose, apply an additional roughening by choosing Filter > Distort > Roughen. Set Size to .21 in, choose Absolute, set Detail to 23/in, and select Smooth in the Points section.

You can easily change the colors of the radial gradient for each of your flowers using the three-palette combination of Color, Swatches, and Gradient. Select the flower you want to change and modify the color and positioning of the sliders in the Gradient palette. When you change any attributes of your flower's Fill, it will disassociate from your "Pink Flower Gradient" swatch in the Swatches palette. In order to save any new gradient you create (that you may want to apply later to other flowers), Option-click (Mac) or Alt-click (Win) on the New Swatch button in the Swatches palette while you have your new gradient-filled object selected, name the swatch, and click OK.

Laurie Grace

Continuing with the flower theme she created in the previous lesson, Laurie Grace made some adjustments to color and size used for some of the flowers. She created variations on the other flowers by using Filter > Distort > Roughen. She created more flowers using the Pen tool to draw individual petals. She Option-clicked on the Rotate tool (Alt-click for Windows), entered 30° and clicked Copy. She used ⌘-D (Alt-D for Win) to continue the rotation around 360°. To add to the decorative design for the greenery, she used the Pen and Pencil tools to draw the stems and leaves. She then used Filter > Distort > Zig Zag and Twist on some of the pen lines and leaves. She added color by creating some gradient mesh objects (see the *Blends, Gradients & Mesh* chapter).

Intricate Patterns

Designing Complex Repeating Patterns

Advanced Technique

Overview: *Design a rough composition; define a confining pattern boundary and place behind all layers; use the box to generate crop marks; copy and position elements using crop marks for alignment; define and use the pattern.*

WEIMER

1

Top, arranging pattern elements into a basic design; bottom, adding the pattern tile rectangle behind the pattern elements

Creating crop marks based on selection of the pattern tile rectangle

Included with Illustrator are many wonderful patterns for you to use and customize, and *Illustrator Help* does a good job of explaining pattern-making basics. But what if you want to create a more complex pattern?

A simple trick with crop marks can help to simplify a tedious process of trial and error. With some help from author and consultant Sandee Cohen, Alan James Weimer used the following technique to design an intricate tile that prints seamlessly as a repeating pattern.

1 **Designing your basic pattern, drawing a confining rectangle, then creating crop marks for registration.** Create a design that will allow for some rearrangement of artwork elements. *Hint: Pattern tiles cannot contain* linked *images—to include a linked image in a pattern, select it and click Embed Image in the Control palette.*

Use the Rectangle tool to draw a box around the part of the image you would like to repeat. This rectangle defines the boundary of the pattern tile. Send the rectangle to the bottom of the Layers palette or to the bottom of your drawing layer (Object > Arrange > Send to Back). This boundary rectangle, which controls how your pattern repeats, must be an unstroked, unfilled, nonrotated, nonsheared object. Make certain this rectangle is selected, and select Filter > Create > Crop Marks. Last, Ungroup these marks (in the next step, you'll use the crop marks to align elements that extend past the pattern tile).

2 **Developing the repeating elements.** If your pattern has an element that extends beyond the edge of the pattern tile, you must copy that element and place it on the opposite side of the tile. For example, if a flower blossom extends below the tile, you must place a copy of the remainder of the blossom at the top of the tile, ensuring that the whole flower is visible when the pattern repeats. To do this, select an element that overlaps above or below the tile and then Shift-select the nearest horizontal crop mark (position the cursor on an endpoint of the crop mark). While pressing the Shift-Option or Shift-Alt keys (the Option/Alt key copies the selections and the Shift key constrains dragging to vertical and horizontal directions), drag the element and crop mark upward until the cursor snaps to the endpoint of the upper horizontal crop mark. (For any element that overlaps the left or right side of the tile, select the element and the vertical crop mark and hold down Shift-Option/Shift-Alt as you drag them into position.)

3 **Testing and optimizing your pattern.** To test your pattern, select your pattern elements (including the bounding rectangle), and either choose Edit > Define Pattern to name your pattern, or drag your selection to the Swatches palette (then double-click the swatch to customize its name). Create a new rectangle and select the pattern as your fill from the Swatches palette. Illustrator will fill the rectangle with your repeating pattern. If you redesign the pattern tile and then wish to update the pattern swatch, select your pattern elements again, but this time Option-drag/Alt-drag the elements onto the pattern swatch you made before.

Optimize your pattern for printing by deleting excess anchor points. Select pattern elements and use the Simplify command (Object > Path > Simplify).

2

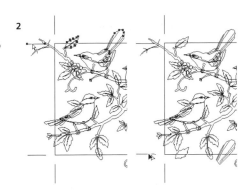

Left, selecting the flower blossom and horizontal crop mark; right, after dragging a copy of the flower blossom and crop mark into position at the top of the pattern tile artwork

Finished artwork for the pattern tile, before turning into a pattern swatch in the Swatches palette

3

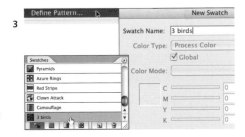

Making a new swatch using Edit > Define Pattern

Speeding redraw with patterns
After filling an object with a pattern, speed up screen redraw by setting View to Outline mode, or by rasterizing a copy of the object (keep the original object unfilled in case you need to use it later).

Brushes & Symbols

4

Brushes & Symbols

"B" Paintbrush tool; a brush in the Control palette

Brushes and Symbols blur the boundaries between Strokes, Fills, and Patterns. Using these tools and effects, you can create strokes made of fills or patterns, and fills made from strokes and other artwork.

Using Brushes and Symbols, you can create the equivalents of many traditional illustration tools, such as pens and brushes that drip and splatter, colored pencils and charcoals, calligraphy pens and brushes, and spray cans that can spray anything—from single color spots to complex artwork. You can use these tools with a pen and tablet, or with a mouse or trackball.

In addition to the Brushes examples in this chapter, you'll find numerous step-by-step lessons and Galleries involving Brushes throughout the book.

BRUSHES

There are four basic types of Brushes: Calligraphic, Art, Scatter, and Pattern. You can use Brushes for everything from mimicking traditional art tools to painting with complex patterns and textures. You can either create brush strokes with the Brush tool, or you can apply a brush stroke to a previously drawn path.

Use Calligraphic Brushes to create strokes that look like they're from a real-world calligraphy pen or brush, or to mimic felt pens. You can define a degree of variation for the size, roundness, and angle of each "nib." You can also set each of the above characteristics to be Fixed, Pressure, or Random.

Art Brushes consist of one or more pieces of artwork that get stretched evenly along the path you create with them. You can use Art Brushes to imitate drippy, splattery ink pens, charcoal, spatter brushes, dry brushes, watercolors, and more.

The artwork you use to create an Art Brush can represent virtually anything: the leaves of a tree, stars, blades of grass, and so on. Use Scatter Brushes to scatter copies of artwork along the path you create with them: flowers in a field, bees in the air, stars in the sky. The size, spacing, scatter, rotation, and colorization of the artwork can all vary along the path.

Pattern Brushes are related to the Patterns feature in Illustrator. You can use Pattern Brushes to paint patterns along a path. To use a Pattern Brush, you first define the tiles that will make up your pattern. For example, you can create railroad symbols on a map, multicolored dashed lines, chain links, or grass. These patterns are defined by up to five types of tiles—side, outer corner, inner corner, start, and end—that you create, and one of three methods of fitting them together (Stretch to Fit, Add Space to Fit, and Approximate Path).

Artwork for Creating Brushes

You can make Art, Scatter, and Pattern Brushes from simple lines and fills, and groups of objects created from them, as well as blends and some live effects. Some complex artwork cannot be used, including gradients, mesh objects, raster art, and advanced live effects such as 3D.

Working with Brushes

Double-click the Paintbrush tool to set application-level preferences for all brushes. When using Fidelity and Smoothness, lower numbers are more accurate, and higher numbers are smoother. Check the "Fill new brush strokes" option if you want the brush path to take on the fill color in addition to the stroke color. When Keep Selected and Edit Selected Paths are both enabled, the last drawn path stays selected; drawing a new path close to the selected path will redraw that path. Disabling either of these options will allow you to draw multiple brush strokes near each other, instead of redrawing the last drawn path. Disabling Keep Selected deselects paths as they are drawn, while disabling Edit Selected Paths turns off the adjusting behavior of the Brush tool even when it is near selected paths. If left enabled, the Edit Selected Paths slider determines how close you have to be in order

Closing a brush path

To close a path using the Brush tool, hold down the Option (Mac)/ Alt (Win) key *after* you begin creating the path, then let go of the mouse button just before you're ready to close the path.

Reversing brush strokes

To change the direction of a brush stroke on an open path, first select the path and then click on an endpoint with the Pen tool to establish the new direction toward that point. —*David Nelson*

Auto-replacing brush objects

To replace all applications of a brush, hold Option/Alt and drag one brush over another in the Brushes palette (you may wish to duplicate the brush being replaced first.) —*David Nelson*

Scaling brushes

To scale artwork that contains paths with applied brushes, enable Scale Strokes & Effects in Preferences > General, or in the individual transformation dialog boxes (Scale, Rotate, etc.).

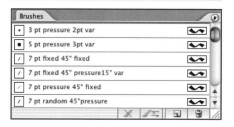

Including brush characteristics in brush name; using List View to make brushes easier to find

Brushes to layers

Scatter Brush artwork can be easily separated onto individual layers for use in animation. For details about distributing artwork to layers, see the "Release to Layers" section in the *Web & Animation* chapter introduction.

But it says I have pressure…

In previous versions of Illustrator, if you didn't have a pressure-sensitive tablet connected to your computer, you wouldn't see possible pressure settings in Calligraphic and Scatter Brush Options. Now you can actually see (and might be able to select) these pop-up options even if you're not connected to a tablet. However, unless you're connected to a tablet supporting the various pressure and tilt options, these settings will not affect your brush marks.

More about brushes

- Pasting a path that contains a brush will add the brush to the Brushes palette.
- Convert an applied brush into editable artwork by selecting the path and choosing Object > Expand Appearance.
- Drag a brush out of the Brushes palette to edit the brush art.
- To create a brush from an applied brush path, blend, gradient, or gradient mesh, expand it first (Object > Expand).

to redraw the selected path, as opposed to drawing a new path. The lower the number, the closer you must be to the selected path to redraw it.

To edit a brush, double-click it in the Brushes palette to change Brush options; or, drag it out of the Brushes palette to edit the brush and then drag the new art into the Brushes palette. To replace a brush, press Option (Mac)/Alt (Win) and drag the new brush over the original brush slot in the Brushes palette. Then in the dialog box, you can either replace all instances of the applied brush already used in the document with the newly created brush, or create a new brush in the palette.

Keep in mind that if you change the options for a brush, and in the dialog box choose to "Leave strokes," then the strokes created previously by that brush are no longer connected to that brush. In order to make changes to brush selected strokes no longer connected to a brush in the palette, you must access "Stroke Options" either by clicking the "Options of Selected Object" button, choosing it from the Brushes palette menu, or double-clicking the Stroke in the Appearance palette.

There are four colorization methods (None, Tints, Tints and Shades, and Hue Shift) you can use with Brushes. "None" uses the colors of the brush as they were defined and how they appear in the Brushes palette. The Tints method causes the brush to use the current stroke color, allowing you to create any color brush you like, regardless of the color of the brush depicted in the Brushes palette. Click on the Tips button in the Art Brush Options dialog box for detailed explanations and examples of how all four color modes work.

When drawing with a pressure-sensitive stylus (pen) and tablet, using the Calligraphic Brush tool and a pressure setting in the options dialog, you'll be able to draw with varying stroke thickness and brush shape, according to the pressure you apply to the tablet. If your tablet supports Tilt, in the Calligraphic Brush Options dialog, choose Tilt from one of the parameter pop-ups and increase the variation. For particularly dramatic results, set the Angle for tilt with a flattened shape brush with a large variation. Then the angle at which you hold your pen will affect the brush stroke, producing a dramatic variation brush-mark thickness (and or shape) as you draw. For Scatter brush pressure settings, you can vary the size, spacing, and scatter of the brush art. If you don't have a tablet, try choosing Random settings in Calligraphic and Scatter Brush Options.

SYMBOLS

Symbols consist of artwork that you create and store in the Symbols palette. From this palette, you then apply one or more copies of the symbols (called *instances*) into your artwork.

Artwork for creating Symbols

Symbols can be made from almost any art you create in Illustrator. The only exceptions are a few kinds of complex groups (such as groups of graphs) and placed art, which must be embedded (not linked).

Working with Symbols

There are eight Symbolism tools. Use the Symbol Sprayer tool to spray selected symbols onto your document. A group of symbols sprayed onto your document is called a *symbol instance set* and is surrounded by a bounding box (you cannot select individual instances inside a set with any of the selection tools). Then use the Symbol Shifter, Scruncher, Sizer, Spinner, Stainer, Screener, or Styler tools to modify symbols in the symbol instance set.

To add symbols to an existing instance set, select the instance set. Then, from the Symbols palette, select the symbol to be added—which can be the same as or different from the symbols already present in the instance set—and spray. If you are using the default Average mode, your new symbol instances can inherit attributes (size, rotation, transparency, style) from nearby symbols in the same instance set. See *Illustrator Help* for details about the Average versus User Defined modes.

Symbols to layers

Symbol artwork can be easily separated onto individual layers for use in animations. Select and target the Symbol artwork layer, then choose Release to Layers (Sequence) from the Layers palette menu. For more, see "Release to Layers" in the *Web & Animation* chapter introduction.

Symbols sprayed, sized, and stained

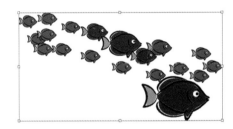

Symbols added using User Defined mode; new symbols are all same color and size

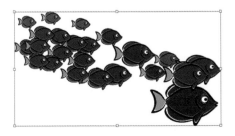

Symbols added using Average mode; new symbols inherit average color and size from symbols nearby (as defined by the brush radius)

Changing tool diameter

Instead of accessing the Symbol-ism Tools Options dialog box to change a tool's diameter, you can use the square brackets on your keyboard to interactively resize the diameter of the symbolism tool in use. Use [(left bracket) to decrease and] (right bracket) to increase. —*Vicki Loader*

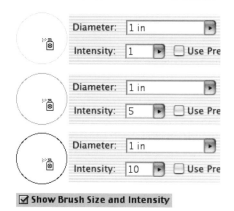

☑ **Show Brush Size and Intensity**

When Show Brush Size and Intensity is enabled, the intensity of the Symbolism tool is indicated by the shade of gray of the brush size circle

Symbol intensity vs. density

The Symbolism Intensity option controls how fast symbol instances get sprayed onto the page. The Density option controls how closely they are spaced. You can also change the Density later. Simply select the Symbol instance set, then adjust the Density slider.

Changing symbol intensity

Press Shift-[to decrease (or press Shift-] to increase) a Symbolism tool's intensity.

When you add or modify symbol instances, make sure you have both the symbol instance set and the corresponding symbol(s) in the Symbols palette selected. If you don't, the Symbolism tools can easily appear to not be working. To remove symbols from an existing instance set, hold down the Option (Mac)/Alt (Win) key and click on the symbols with the Symbol Sprayer tool. Specific details on how to create and modify symbols are covered in depth in the "Symbol Basics" lesson later in this chapter.

SYMBOLS VS. SCATTER BRUSHES

Symbols are more flexible than Scatter Brushes in terms of the types of changes you can make to them after they are applied; they can represent a greater variety of artwork (such as raster images or gradient-filled objects). However, there is one advantage to using Scatter Brushes: They allow you more control while drawing with a pressure-sensitive tablet.

Using the Symbolism tools, you can change many attributes (such as size, rotation, and spacing) to individual symbols in an instance set. Using Scatter Brushes, attributes will be applied to the whole set—you can't change attributes for single objects in a set. With Symbols, you can redefine the original artwork stored in the Symbols palette and have all the instances on the Artboard reflect those changes. Scatter Brushes also allow you to update the original artwork after you make changes (see the Tip "Auto-replacing brush objects," earlier in this chapter). Using Symbols, you can remove individual instances from a symbolism instance set. You can't delete Scatter Brush objects without first expanding the artwork.

Unlike other types of vector artwork, the art objects inside Symbols are not affected by the Scale Strokes & Effects preference. Scatter Brush artwork responds in its own unique way. For details, see the file "Scaling & Scatter Brushes.ai" on the *Wow! CD*.

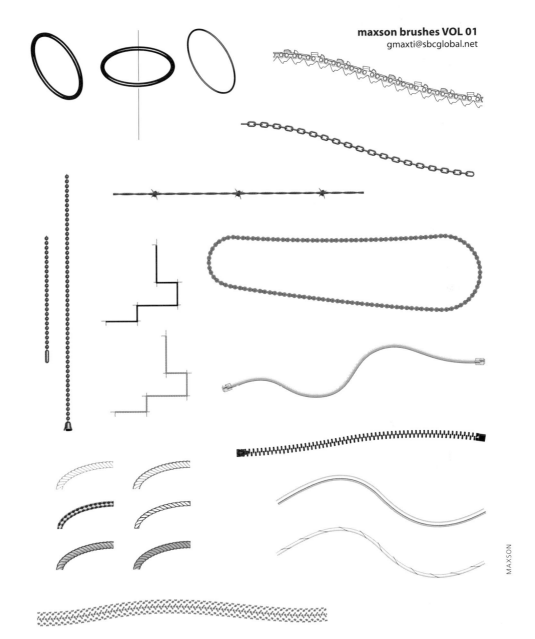

maxson brushes VOL 01
gmaxti@sbcglobal.net

MAXSON

Greg Maxson

Artist Greg Maxson creates many wonderful pattern brushes. Find this Volume 01 collection on the *Wow! CD*, and open up the file; copy one or all of the pattern paths and paste them into your file. Illustrator will automatically load those pattern brushes into your Brushes palette. Draw a line or curve, and click on the brush in the palette to transform the path into a chain, rope, wire, or zipper.

Brushes & Washes

Drawing with Naturalistic Pen, Ink & Wash

Overview: *Adjust the Paintbrush tool settings; customize a Calligraphic brush; start from an existing image; experiment by using other brushes to stroke the paths and add washes.*

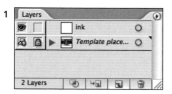

The default Layer 1 renamed Ink, and the original fountain photo placed as an Illustrator template layer below the drawing

The original photo (left), brush strokes drawn over the dimmed template photo (center), and the template hidden (right)

Maintaining your pressure

Only brush strokes *initially* drawn with pressure-sensitive settings can take advantage of pressure-sensitivity. Also be aware that you may alter the stroke shape if you reapply a brush after you experiment with another.

It's easy to create spontaneous painterly and calligraphic marks in Illustrator—and perhaps with more flexibility than in any other digital medium. Sharon Steuer drew this sketch of Place des Vosges in Paris, France using a pressure-sensitive Wacom tablet and two different Illustrator brushes. She customized a brush for the thin, dark strokes, and used a built-in brush for the underlying gray washes. When you use a pressure-sensitive, pen-like stylus and tablet to create highly variable, responsive strokes, you can edit those strokes as *paths*, You can also experiment by applying different brushes to the existing paths.

1 If you're using existing artwork as a reference, import it as a template layer. You can start drawing on a blank Illustrator artboard, but if you want to use a sketch, scanned photo, or digital camera photo as a reference, set it up as a non-printing template layer. For her template image, Steuer used a scanned TIFF photo of Place des Vosges. To place an image as a template layer, choose File > Place, locate your file, enable the Link and Template check boxes, and click the Place button. If the image imports at too large a size, unlock the template layer, enter a more reasonable Width value in the Transform palette, and press ⌘-Return (Mac)/Ctrl-Enter (Win) to resize it proportionally.

Toggle between hiding and showing the template layer using ⌘-Shift-W (Mac)/Ctrl-Shift-W (Win), or by clicking in the visibility column in the Layers palette (the icon for a template layer is a tiny triangle/circle/square, instead of the Eye icon). Illustrator automatically dims the image to make your drawing easier to see.

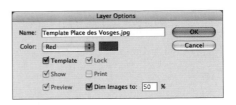

Customizing the template layer options

You can customize the template layer by double-clicking its layer and changing options in the Layer Options dialog box. When you import an image as a template, Illustrator automatically enables the Template, Lock, and Dim check boxes for you. You can't disable the Lock checkbox if the Template checkbox is enabled, but you can still unlock it in the Layers palette.

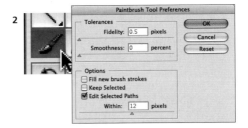

Customizing the Paintbrush Tool Preferences

2 Setting your Paintbrush Tool Preferences and customizing a Calligraphic brush. In order to sketch freely and with accurate detail, you'll need to adjust the default Paintbrush tool settings. Double-click the Paintbrush tool in the Tools palette to open Paintbrush Tool Preferences. Drag the Fidelity and Smoothness sliders all the way to the left so that Illustrator records your strokes precisely. Make sure "Fill new brush strokes" is disabled; you don't need to change the other settings.

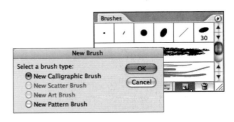

Creating a new Calligraphic brush

To create a custom brush, click the New Brush icon at the bottom of the palette and click OK for a New Calligraphic Brush. Experiment with various settings, name your brush, and click OK. For this piece, Steuer chose the following settings: Angle=90°/Fixed; Roundness=10%/Fixed; Diameter=4 pt/Pressure/Variation=4 pt. If you don't have a pressure-sensitive tablet, try Random as a setting for any of the three Brush Options, since Pressure won't have any effect. The Paintbrush uses your current stroke color (if there isn't a stroke color, it will use the previous stroke color or the fill color). Now draw. If you don't like a mark: 1) choose Undo to delete it, or 2) use the Direct Selection tool to edit the path, or 3) select the path and try redrawing it using the Paintbrush (to hide or show selection outlines, choose View>Hide/Show Edges). To edit a brush, deselect everything (Edit>Select

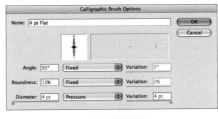

Angle, Roundness, and Diameter can be set to respond to pressure, to vary randomly, or to remain fixed; the new brush in the Brushes palette viewed with tool tips and in List View

3

Strokes made with Steuer's customized 4-pt flat brush (left); applying Adobe's default 3-pt Round brush (center), then the 1-pt Oval brush

4

The original drawing before adding a wash

A new layer (wash) created for wider wash strokes to appear under existing darker strokes on the Template placeholder layer

The gray wash strokes underneath the wider dark strokes, and the brush used to draw them

All), double-click the brush in the Brushes palette, and make changes. Illustrator will ask you if you want to apply the new settings to strokes you've already drawn with this brush; click Apply to Strokes if you want to do this or click Leave Strokes to apply the new settings only to new strokes that you'll create from this point forward, divorcing the original strokes from the edited brush. It's safer to edit a copy of a brush; to do this, drag it to the New Brush icon to duplicate it, and then edit the copy.

3 Experimenting with your artwork. Save any versions of your artwork that you like. Now try applying different brushes to specific strokes and to the entire piece. To try more Adobe-made brushes, choose Window > Brush Libraries. In this step, two Adobe brushes are applied to the same strokes as the custom brush.

4 Adding a wash. For this piece, Steuer added depth by introducing gray washes underneath the dark brush strokes. To easily edit the wash strokes without affecting the dark ink strokes, Create a new layer, and draw your wash strokes into this layer between the ink and template layers. To avoid altering other layers while you brush in the washes, you may want to lock all layers except the one on which you're drawing. To do this, Option-click (Mac) or Alt-click (Win) the wash layer's Lock icon.

Select or create a brush suitable for washes, and select a light wash color. Steuer used the Dry Ink 2 brush from the Artistic_Ink brush library included with Illustrator. In the Layers palette, click the wash layer to make it the current drawing layer, and paint away.

Drawing transparent brush strokes

By default, brush strokes are opaque. You can also draw with semi-transparent brush strokes, which you can use to simulate some types of inks or watercolors; where marks overlap, they become richer or darker. See the lesson "Transparent Color" in the *Transparency* chapter.

STEUER

Sharon Steuer

This sketch is an extended version of the pen and ink drawing in the previous lesson. In this version, Steuer wanted to add young Noah riding a bicycle past the fountain. A photo of Noah on a carousel motorcycle was a perfect reference for the sketch, but the photo wasn't facing the right direction. To flip the photo, Steuer selected the image, chose Object > Transform > Reflect, and selected the Vertical Axis option. However, the fountain drawing's existing strokes occupied the area where she wanted to add Noah. Steuer solved this using a technique that isn't available with conventional ink: She used the Pencil tool to draw a path over the existing drawing, and filled the path with white to bring back the color of the paper. This restored an empty area where she could

add the drawing of Noah, so it looked like it was there from the beginning. Steuer drew Noah on a separate layer, allowing easy editing independent of the rest of the drawing.

Lisa Jackmore

Inspired by a crumpled page from an antique garden notebook, Lisa Jackmore created a faded, textured appearance in this illustration as though pencil marks were still visible after they had been erased. Jackmore first made a palette of custom Art Brushes consisting of original and altered default Art Brushes. She created textures for the background by drawing scribble marks with the Pencil tool (using different stroke widths). For each scribble, she selected it and then dragged it into the Brushes palette to create a new Art Brush, and chose the Hue Shift colorization method so that she could vary the brush color as she drew with the art brush. Jackmore drew the vine and bird bath with a pressure-sensitive drawing tablet using varying widths of the Chalk Scribble and Thick Pencil Art Brushes. Jackmore double-clicked on the brush copy icon and in the Art Brush Options dialog box, changing the percentage to vary the width. Before drawing with these brushes, she disabled "Fill New Brush Strokes" and "Keep Selected" in the paintbrush Tool Preferences. This allowed her to draw multiple paths close to each other so she didn't accidently redraw the previous line. Jackmore then deleted any extra points within the brush strokes by tracing over a selected brush stroke with the Smooth tool.

JACKMORE

Lisa Jackmore

To create the brush details in this image, Lisa Jackmore modified custom Art Brushes that she named scribble brushes (used in the drawing opposite). She selected some of the scribble brushes and reduced the opacity by clicking Opacity in the Control palette. Jackmore made an Art Brush to build the frame by drawing a path with the Pen tool. She altered the path with a combination of the Reflect and Shear tools. Jackmore Direct- selected points along the path and reapplied the Reflect and Shear tools to achieve an ink pen look. Then she

selected the path and dragged it to the Brushes palette to make an Art Brush. Jackmore created the texture in the brown oval using a brush made of multiple strokes with the Thick Pencil Art Brush. She grouped the strokes and dragged the group to the brushes palette to make the Art Brush. She made a clipping mask to contain the large brush stroke within the oval (middle detail). To reduce the size of the brush, she double-clicked on the brush in the Brushes palette and decreased its width.

Pattern Brushes

Creating Details with the Pattern Brush

Overview: *Create interlocking chain links by drawing and cutting duplicate curve sections; select the link artwork and create a new Pattern brush; draw a path and paint it with the new brush.*

At the left, the ring drawn with the Ellipse tool and given a thick stroke; in the middle, the ellipse cut into four curve sections shown in Outline view (sections are separated to show them better); on the right, the four curve sections shown in Outline view, after using the Object > Path > Outline Stroke command

On the left, the two left curve sections copied and pasted, and colors changed to light brown in the middle; on the right, the two sections are slid to the right to form the right half link

*On the left, the half-link selected and reflected using the Reflect tool (the **X** in the middle of the guide ellipse served as the axis); on the right, both half-links in position*

One look at a Bert Monroy image and you will immediately recognize the intricacy and rich realism of his style of illustration. When crafting an image like the Rendezvous Cafe (see the Gallery image that follows for the complete image), Monroy travels between Illustrator and Photoshop, stopping long enough in Illustrator to construct the intricate shapes and details that turn his scenes into slices of life in Photoshop. The easel chain is one such detail that Monroy created in Illustrator using a custom-made Pattern brush.

1 Drawing, cutting, copying, and reflecting curves.
To build a chain-link Pattern brush, Monroy first created one link that was interconnected with half-links on either side (the half-links would connect with other half-links to form the chain once the Pattern brush was applied to a path). To create the pattern unit with the Ellipse tool, begin the center link by drawing an ellipse with a thick stroke. Copy the ellipse, Paste in Back; then turn the ellipse into a guide (View > Guides > Make Guides). You'll use this guide later when making the half-links. Now select the original ellipse and use the Scissors tool to cut the ellipse near each of the four control points (choose

View > Outline to better see the points). Shift-select the four curved paths with the Direct Selection tool and select Object > Path > Outline Stroke. Illustrator automatically constructs four closed-curve objects.

To make the right half-link, select the left two curve objects and duplicate them to make the right half-link by dragging the two objects to the right while holding down the Opt/Alt key; then change the color of the copies. For the left half-link, select the two curves you just dragged and colored, choose the Reflect tool, hold down the Opt/Alt key and click in the center of the ellipse guide (the center point is an **X**). In the Reflect dialog box, click the Vertical Axis button and click Copy to create a mirror-image of the right half-link for the left half-link.
Note: *The center link must be aligned exactly in-between the two half-links, so that the half-links join when applied to a path as a Pattern brush.*

2 **Finishing the link.** The two adjoining half-links should look like they're entwined with the link. Monroy selected the top objects of both the left and right half-links and moved them behind the center link (Object > Arrange > Send to Back). You can create a different look by selecting the top of the left half-link, and the bottom of the right half-link, and moving them to the back.

3 **Making and using a Pattern brush.** To make the brush, select the artwork and drag it into the Brushes palette. Choose New Pattern Brush in the New Brush dialog box; in the next dialog box, name the brush and click OK (leave the default settings as you find them). You can now apply the chain pattern to a path by selecting the path and clicking on the brush in the Brushes palette.

Depending on the size of your original links artwork, you may need to reduce the size of the brush artwork to fit the path better. You can do this by reducing the original artwork with the Scale tool and making a new brush, or by double-clicking the brush in the Brushes palette and editing the value in the Scale field of the dialog box.

2

Finished link artwork; at the left, the links as Monroy created them; at the right, an alternative version of the interconnected links

3
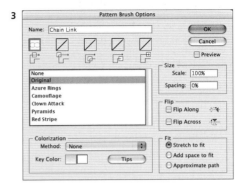

The Pattern Brush Options dialog box showing default settings

Original path on top; below, path painted with Chain Link Pattern brush

Drop Shadows

Even if your artwork is destined for Photoshop, you can make a drop shadow for it in Illustrator. Select the artwork, then choose Effect > Stylize > Drop Shadow. Copy the object (which automatically copies all of its appearances) and paste in Photoshop (Edit > Paste > Paste as Pixels). (See the *Transparency* chapter for more on appearances, and the *Illustrator & Other Programs* chapter for more on using Photoshop with Illustrator.)

MONROY

© Bert Monroy 1999

Bert Monroy

Artist Bert Monroy incorporates elements he draws in Illustrator into the detailed realism he paints in Photoshop. In this cafe scene, Monroy used Illustrator Pattern brushes for the sign post and the easel chain. For the leaves in the foreground, Monroy first drew one leaf object and made it into a Scatter brush (he used Random settings for the brush parameters). He brought resulting foliage into Photoshop where he detailed it further. (See the *Illustrator & Other Programs* chapter to learn more techniques for using Illustrator with Photoshop.)

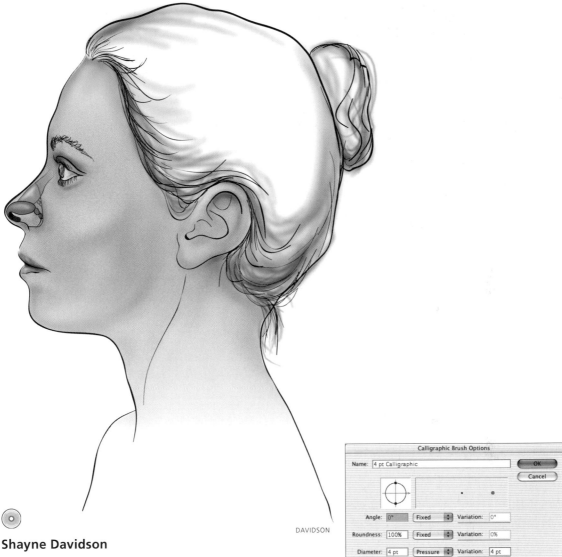

DAVIDSON

Shayne Davidson

Shayne Davidson began this medical illustration by airbrushing the soft background colors in Photoshop. After placing the image in Illustrator, she used custom-made Calligraphic brushes to draw the outlines and details. To create a brush, she opened the Brushes palette, selected New Brush from the palette's menu and picked New Calligraphic Brush from the New Brush dialog. This brought up the Calligraphic Brush Options dialog, where she left

the brush Angle at 0° (Fixed), Roundness at 100% (Fixed), and specified a Diameter (she used diameters between 0.8 and 4 points). She also set Diameter to Pressure, and Variation to the same point size as the Diameter (this establishes the maximum width of the stroke on either side of the path), and clicked OK. She repeated this process to create brushes with different diameters.

Chapter 4 *Brushes & Symbols* **105**

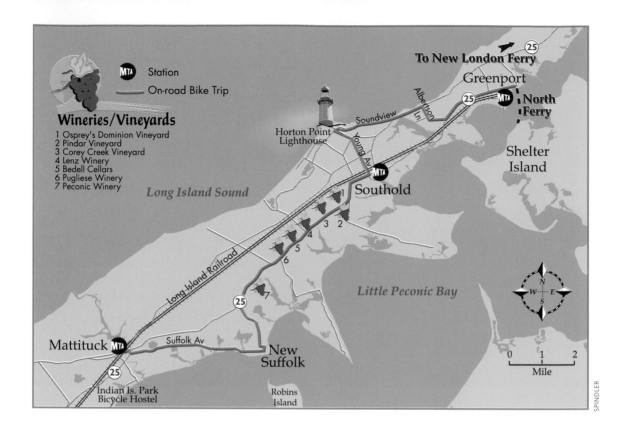

Steve Spindler / Bike Maps

When cartographer Steve Spindler begins using a new version of Illustrator, he quickly adopts its new features into his method of making maps. In this bike map of part of Long Island, New York, Spindler placed scanned photographs on a template layer to draw the vineyard grapes and lighthouse. For the grapes, he used the Tapered Stroke brush for the outlines of the leaves and the Marker brush to draw the stems (both brushes are installed with Illustrator CS2; access them from the Brushes palette menu by choosing Open Brush Library > Artistic_Ink). To create an Illustrator symbol from an object such as the grape cluster, drag artwork into the Symbols palette. To apply art as symbol instances on a map, drag a symbol from the palette onto the artboard. Spindler accesses his custom symbol libraries by choosing Open Symbol Library from the Symbols palette's menu and then selecting a file from the submenu list. Once he drags any of his symbols from the Symbol Library palette to his artwork, the symbol is added to that map's Symbols palette and is then saved with the file.

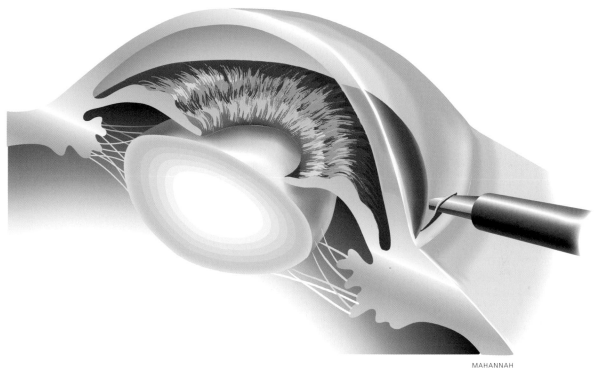

MAHANNAH

Jacqueline Mahannah

Drawing the delicate structure of the iris of the human eye to illustrate glaucoma surgery, artist Jacqueline Mahannah combined Illustrator brushes with the pressure-sensitivity of a Wacom tablet. For the iris structure, Mahannah used the Marker brush from the Ink Brushes library (accessed by choosing Open Brush Library > Artistic_Ink). She adjusted the width setting of this brush by double-clicking the brush in the palette, then editing the

Width field in the Art Brush Options dialog. Mahannah chose a light blue color for the brush and drew the innermost strokes. Then she chose a darker color and drew the next set of strokes, letting them overlap the first strokes. She continued working outward, sometimes overlapping dark brush strokes with lighter ones to suggest highlights and texture.

Building Brushes

Building Brushes for Lettering

Overview: *Draw and shape letterforms; create and vectorize brush strokes in Photoshop; bring brush paths into Illustrator and edit them; add brushes to the Brushes palette; adjust color and layering, and apply effects and transparency.*

DONALDSON

1

Hand-drawn letterform paths using Pen and Pencil tools

Donaldson hand-drew two different sets of letterforms and positioned them on two different layers; each was then painted with a different brush (see Step 4 at right)

2

Brush stroke created in Photoshop using the Paintbrush tool; below, brush stroke edited with Eraser and Airbrush tools

Timothy Donaldson's style of abstract calligraphy challenges the lettering artist to look beyond Illustrator's default brushes (like the brushes sets found under Window > Brush Libraries) to paint programs like Photoshop and Painter, where he develops brush strokes with the look of traditional art tools.

1 Drawing, smoothing and shaping letterform paths. Donaldson began the composition "abcxyz" by drawing letterform paths with the Pen and Pencil tools, going back over the paths with the Pencil to smooth them. (Use the Pencil Tool Preferences menu's Smoothness Tolerance to control how the Pencil will simplify and smooth a line you've drawn.) Once you draw the letterforms, refine them further with the Shear and Scale tools until you are satisfied with their shapes.

2 Creating brush strokes in a paint program. To build a custom brush, open any paint program that offers paintbrushes (Donaldson works in Painter and Photoshop). Start a new file in the paint program, specifying a resolution of 72 ppi and a transparent background. Set the foreground and background colors to black and white (this will make it easier when vectorizing the brush stroke in the paint program later). Next, select the Paint brush tool and edit the brush settings or preferences (opacity, blending mode, textures, pressure-sensitivity and others). (See *The Photoshop Wow! Book* by Linnea Dayton and Jack Davis, or *The Painter Wow! Book* by Cher Threinen-Pendarvis for more about painting with brushes.)

Now you're ready to paint a brush stroke. Hold down the Shift key (to constrain the cursor to straight movements) and make a stroke with the brush tool. Modify the look of the brush stroke with the Eraser or other painting tools, or with filters (but avoid filters that blur or otherwise anti-alias the brush stroke edge). If your paint program can export vector paths as an EPS or Illustrator file, then select the pixels of the brush stroke with the Magic Wand, or other selection tool, and convert the pixels to paths. Otherwise, save the image as a PSD or TIFF.

3 Opening, then editing brush strokes in Illustrator.
Bring your brush stroke into Illustrator by opening the EPS or placing the raster image. Use Live Trace (Object menu) to vectorize the raster brush stroke, or manually trace over it using the Pen and Pencil tools. You can reshape the brush artwork using the selection tools or the Pencil tool. (See the *Drawing & Coloring* chapter for more on modifying paths.) Convert your brush stroke artwork into an Illustrator brush by selecting the artwork and dragging it into the Brushes palette. Select New Art Brush from the New Brush dialog and set various brush parameters in the Art Brush Options dialog box.

4 Applying different brushes. Donaldson created multiple brushed letterforms by duplicating the layer with the paths (drag the layer to the New Layer icon in the Layers palette). For each layer with letterforms, select the paths and click on a custom brush in the Brushes palette. Alter the look of your composition by changing colors or brushes, adjusting the stacking order of layers in the Layers palette, or applying effects to modify transparency and blending (see the *Transparency* and *Live Effects & Graphic Styles* chapters for details).

3

Top, work path based on selection made in Photoshop before being saved as an Illustrator file; bottom, path in Illustrator after editing and being filled with black

4

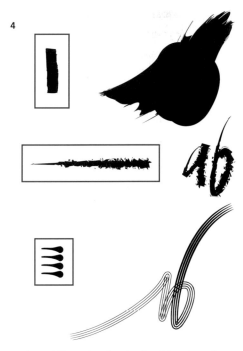

Three different brushes (outlined here in red) applied to the hand-drawn letterforms "ab"

In the background, Feather Effect applied to gray letterforms; in the middle, an 80% transparency and Multiply blending mode assigned to greenish letterforms; in foreground, red letters given a Screen blending mode with 65% transparency

Symbol Basics

Creating and Working with Symbols

Overview: *Create background elements; define symbols; use Symbolism tools to place and customize symbols.*

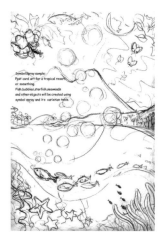

The concept sketch

The background and symbol artwork

HOLLIN

Kaoru Hollin created this Tropical Card for Adobe to use as sample art that would show the power and variety of effects possible using the new Symbolism tools. After creating a concept sketch, Hollin defined a library of symbols and then used the Symbolism tools to place and customize the symbols, almost as though they were brushes.

1 Creating the Background art. Based on her sketch, Hollin created the background art using eight simple layered objects, filled with gradients. To create the luminous colors, Hollin applied varying amounts of transparency to each of the objects. Hollin then added depth and richness to the water by applying Effect > Stylize > Inner Glow to the upper water curve, and Outer Glow to the lower water curve. Gradients, transparency, and effects are discussed in detail later in the book.

2 Creating symbols. Hollin created the artwork for each of the 20 symbols that she would use to create the piece. The simplest way to turn a piece of artwork into a symbol is to select the artwork and drag it onto the Symbols palette.

    To make your artwork on the Artboard become a symbol instance at the same time you create a symbol, hold down the ⌘ key (Mac) or Ctrl key (Win) as you drag the artwork onto the Symbols palette.

3 Applying symbols. After creating a new layer for the fish, Hollin selected the fish symbol in the Symbols palette and created the school of fish with a single stroke of the Symbol Sprayer tool. You can experiment with the Symbol Sprayer by adjusting the Density and Intensity settings (double-click on any Symbolism tool to access the Symbolism Tool Options), and the speed of your spray strokes. Don't worry about getting an exact number or precise placement for each symbol as you spray; you can fine tune those and other symbol attributes using other Symbolism tools.

4 Resizing symbols. To create a sense of depth, Hollin used the Symbol Sizer tool to make some of the fish smaller. By default, the Sizer tool increases the size of symbols within the tool's brush radius. To make a symbol smaller, hold down the Option/Alt key as you brush over it with the Symbol Sizer tool.

    To make the diameter of a Symbolism tool visible, double-click on any Symbolism tool and enable the Show Brush Size and Intensity option. As for brushes, use the] key to make the Symbolism tool diameter larger and the [key to make it smaller.

5 Modifying symbol transparency and color. To modify the appearance of symbols, use the Symbol Screener,

The artwork for the 20 symbols that were used to complete the piece

The raw fish after being sprayed on with the Symbol Sprayer tool

The Symbolism tools tear off palette, see "Tear off palettes" in the Illustrator Basics chapter

To access the other Symbolism tools, hold down Control-Option-click (Mac) or Alt-right-click (Win) and drag toward the tool you want to use until the Tool icon changes. —Mordy Golding

Hollin used the Symbol Sizer tool to make some of the fish smaller and to add depth

5

The Symbol Stainer tool set to random was used to vary the color of the fish

6

Use the Symbol Spinner tool to adjust the rotation of symbols

7

After using the Symbol Shifter tool with a smaller brush size to adjust the fish positions

8

The final fish after more fine tuning with the Symbol Sizer, Shifter, and Spinner tools

Symbols stacking order

To change the stacking order for your symbols, use the Symbol Shifter tool and:

- Shift-click the symbol instance to bring it forward.
- Option-Shift-click (Mac) or Alt-Shift-click (Win) to push the symbol instance backward.

Stainer, and Styler tools. The Screener tool adjusts the transparency of symbols. The Stainer tool shifts the color of the symbol to be more similar to the current fill color, while preserving its luminosity. The Styler tool allows you to apply (in variable amounts) styles from the Graphic Styles palette. See *Illustrator Help* for details about the coloring modes and application methods of these tools.

Hollin used the Symbol Stainer tool, set to Random, to tint the fish a variety of colors with just one stroke. Later, she also used the Stainer tool on the hibiscus and starfish, and the Screener tool on the butterflies.

6 **Rotating symbols.** To make the first rough adjustment to the orientation of the fish, Hollin used the Symbol Spinner tool set to User Defined (which sets the spin based on the direction that the mouse is moved). See "Working with Symbols" in the Introduction to this chapter and *Illustrator Help* for an explanation of the User Defined and Average modes.

7 **Moving symbols.** Hollin used the Symbol Shifter tool with a smaller brush size to adjust the position of the fish.

The Shifter tool was not designed to move symbols large distances. To maximize symbol movement, first make the brush size as large as you can—at least as large as the symbol you wish to move. Then drag across the symbol, as though you were trying to push the symbol with a broom.

8 **Deleting symbols.** At this point, Hollin felt there were too many fish in the school. To remove the unwanted fish, Hollin used the Symbol Sprayer tool with the Option/Alt key held down. She chose a narrow brush size and clicked on the fish to be removed.

Finally, in order to make the school of fish conform more to the shape of the waves in the background, Hollin used the Symbol Sizer, Shifter, and Spinner tools to make further adjustments.

POWELL

Gary Powell

Gary Powell created this illustration using his own set of custom symbols. He began with a template layer and hand-traced two pine cones and a simple branch. He combined the three into a new variation. Once he finished with the variations, he grouped and dragged them into the symbols palette. With just five symbols,

Powell used the Symbol Sprayer tool and the Symbol Spinner tool to randomly spray branches into the scene and rotate them into position. As a finishing touch, he found the cloud symbol in the Nature Symbol Library, sprayed in a few clouds, and then used the Symbol Sizer tool to give them a sense of depth.

Symbol Libraries

Making Symbols and a Symbol Preset File

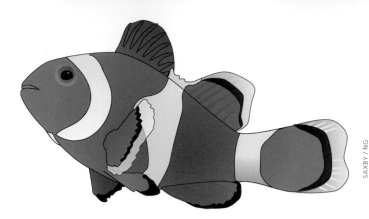

Overview: *Create artwork; add it to the Symbols palette; save the file as a preset that can be accessed from Illustrator's menus.*

The original image (photo by Richard Ng for iStock Photo, www.istockphoto.com/richard_ng)

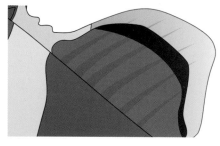

Enlargement of the dorsal fin showing the fin filled with a gradient at 75% opacity and fin rays filled with black at 12% opacity

Live Trace blues

Object > Live Trace may produce vector art from photographs automatically, but you'll probably need to tweak settings in the Tracing Options dialog to avoid complex artwork overloaded with extra objects, points and lines (For details on Live Trace see *Beyond Basic Drawing & Coloring*.)

To facilitate communication about environmental issues among scientists and environmentalists, the University of Maryland's Center for Environmental Science designed a library of symbols for use in reports, web sites and multimedia. These symbols, numbering over 1500, are free of copyright and royalty restrictions. A sampling of the symbols are included in the *Special Wow! CD IAN Symbol Pack Appendix* and on the *Wow! CD* (in the Software Demos&Links folder). For the latest update to the symbol library files, go to http://ian.umces.edu.

1 Importing and tracing an image and painting objects with gradient fills. Many sources exist for images that you can access and download from the Internet, providing a treasure-trove of visual inspiration for your symbols. Designer Tracey Saxby placed a clownfish photograph from iStockphoto (www.istockphoto.com/richard_ng) on a template layer and began tracing using the Pen and Pencil tools. If you plan to create a symbol library—a file that you access as an additional Symbols palette in Illustrator—consider keeping the artwork simple, using as few points, lines, and fills as necessary to create an expressive image. By keeping artwork simple, your symbols will smaller in file size, making them load faster if you incorporate them in a Flash movie or in another kind of digital file.

Saxby completed the clownfish by painting the objects with linear and radial gradient fills. You can also experiment with reducing opacity and applying feathering

(Effect > Stylize > Feather) to some objects, like fins or feathers, to lend transparency to the artwork and to fade the artwork into the background behind the symbol.

2 Creating an Illustrator symbol from the artwork and organizing the Symbols palette. Once she completed the artwork, Saxby opened the Symbols palette. She selected the clownfish artwork, dragged it into the Symbols palette, and then double-clicked the symbol's thumbnail to open the Symbol Options dialog where she entered "Clownfish" in the Name field.

You can rearrange the order of symbols in the Symbols palette to make it easier for you or others to find a needed symbol. To reposition a symbol, drag the symbol to a new location in the palette. Also consider naming your symbols and having Illustrator arrange them alphabetically. To do this, select the Symbols palette menu and then select Sort by Name. (Illustrator is sensitive to initial caps in symbol names; Zebrafish will precede angelfish in the Symbols palette when you select Sort by Name.)

3 Saving the symbol file as an Illustrator preset and accessing it from Illustrator. To quickly find your symbol library, save it as an Illustrator Preset. To do this, Saxby saved her symbol files by selecting Save Symbol Library from the Symbols palette's menu (the file is saved by default in Illustrator's Presets > Symbols folder). Saving your symbol file as a preset lets you quickly access a symbol file by selecting it from Window > Symbol Libraries or from the Symbols palette menu's Open Symbol Library.

Preset management

Edit all of your presets in one Illustrator file by adding your favorite brushes, graphic styles, swatches and symbols to their respective palettes in a new file. Quit Illustrator, find the file, and make four aliases (Macintosh) or shortcuts (Windows) of it. Place an alias or shortcut in each of Illustrator's Preset folders (Brushes, Graphic Styles, Swatches, and Symbols).

2

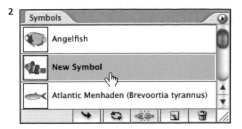

The Symbols palette after the artwork has been dragged to the palette to create a new symbol

The Symbol Options dialog after the new symbol has been double-clicked in the Symbols palette

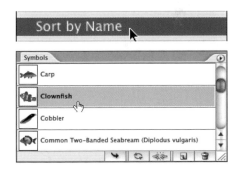

Top, the Sort by Name selection from the Symbols palette menu; bottom, the Symbols palette with the clownfish symbol among the symbols organized alphabetically using the palette menu's Sort by Name option

3

Portion of the Symbols palette menu for saving the current document in Illustrator's folder for symbol presets

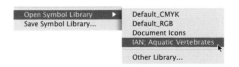

Portion of the Symbols palette menu and the submenu for selecting a symbol library preset from within an open document

Nature's Brushes

Illustrating Nature with Multiple Brushes

Overview: *Draw artwork and create an art brush; use Paintbrush tool to make objects with the art brush; create a pattern brush from brushed objects; create and use a scatter brush.*

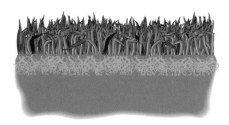

1

The three objects comprising a blade of grass

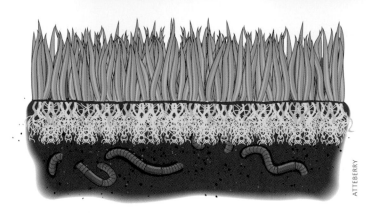

ATTEBERRY

Faced with an assignment to contrast healthy and unhealthy grass and soil for a graphic to be placed on bags of organic fertilizer, Kevan Atteberry dug deep into Illustrator's Brushes palette to build his own grass, soil, and worm brushes. With the art and scatter brushes he made, Atteberry developed an easy way to create the visually complex elements of his illustration.

The Colorization options and Tips button from the Art Brush Options dialog

The completed art brush

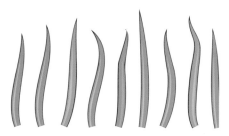

Brushed paths drawn with the Paintbrush tool

1 Drawing brush artwork, creating an art brush, and modifying copies of brushed paths. Creating a complex, natural-looking clump of grass was a challenge Atteberry solved by building art brushes. First, Atteberry drew a blade of grass using three objects that he overlapped. He selected the objects and dragged them into the Brushes palette. In the New Brush dialog, he selected New Art Brush and clicked OK. Then in the Art Brush Options dialog, Atteberry clicked on the Method menu in the dialog's Colorization section and chose Tints and Shades. (If you're unsure of how the Method options affect brushes, click the Tips button to display an informational dialog box comparing different Methods applied to colored brush strokes.)

With the brush created, Atteberry drew several paths using the Paintbrush tool, choosing a different shade of green for each blade as he drew its path. To save time when making a large number of objects, consider duplicating paths and then editing them to make them appear different. To do this, copy and paste your paths and then apply the Scale, Rotate, and Reflect tools to vary sizes and orientations of the copies. Repeat this process until you've built a complex set of brushed paths that fills up the space you've allocated in your illustration.

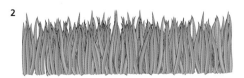

Brush paths that have been scaled, reflected, and rotated

2 Creating a pattern brush from brushed paths. You can take your artwork a step further by building a pattern brush from your artwork. This provides extra flexibility in case your illustration calls for your objects to be set along a wavy path or stretched to fill a space in your composition. To create a pattern brush, select your set of objects and drag them into the Brushes palette. From the New Brush dialog, pick New Pattern Brush; in the Pattern Brush Options dialog, keep the default setting of Side Tile and adjust the Colorization and Fit settings as needed. (Atteberry chose "Stretch to fit" that the grass would stretch automatically to fit the length of the path he would draw when continuing work on the illustration.)

Brushed paths selected to make the pattern brush

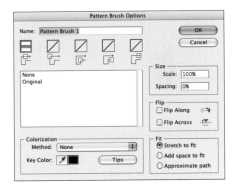

The Pattern Brush Options dialog

3 Making an art brush, drawing strokes, and covering with paths of solid and gradient fills. To show a healthy ecosystem, Atteberry drew the artwork for a worm, turned it into another art brush, and then used the Paintbrush tool to draw several paths with the worm brush. Behind the worms he drew a closed path filled with brown to make the background soil. To conceal parts of the worms, he drew brown-filled paths on a layer above the worms. For worm holes and tubes, he created dark-brown blends shaped like crescents and cylinders.

The worm artwork used to make an art brush

Path painted with the worm art brush and then partially covered by filled paths

4 Making and using a scatter brush. To add a natural complexity to the brown soil, Atteberry added random particles. He first drew small shapes that he filled with light and dark browns. Then he selected the shapes and dragged them into the Brushes palette, specifying New Scatter Brush in the New Brush dialog and adjusting the settings in the Scatter Brush Options dialog. Next, with the new brush still selected, he drew a curlicue path with the Paintbrush tool, which scattered the soil particles along the path.

Above, particle shapes used to make the scatter brush; below, the path used to paint the brush

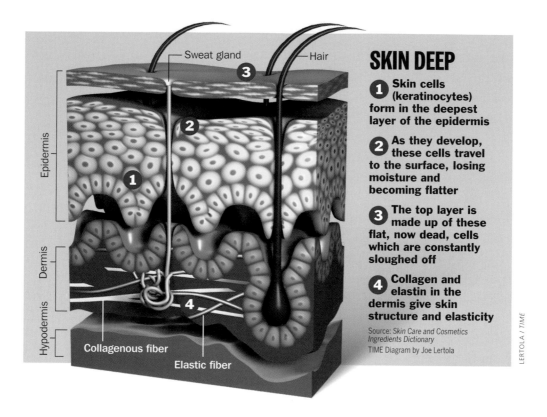

SKIN DEEP

1 Skin cells (keratinocytes) form in the deepest layer of the epidermis

2 As they develop, these cells travel to the surface, losing moisture and becoming flatter

3 The top layer is made up of these flat, now dead, cells which are constantly sloughed off

4 Collagen and elastin in the dermis give skin structure and elasticity

Source: *Skin Care and Cosmetics Ingredients Dictionary*
TIME Diagram by Joe Lertola

LERTOLA / TIME

Joe Lertola / *TIME*

For this medical infographic, artist Joe Lertola relied on the suppleness of Illustrator's Art brushes to show closely packed skin cells. To begin the top layer of cells (**1** and **2** in the illustration above), Lertola built a single cell from two blends, stacking the smaller brown blend on top of the lighter skin-colored blend. Selecting both blends, Lertola chose Object > Expand. Then he dragged the expanded artwork into the Brushes palette and selected New Art Brush from the New Brush dialog. Next, Lertola developed three more cells, varying the oval shape of each cell before turning it into an Art brush. To make the cells, Lertola drew short paths and

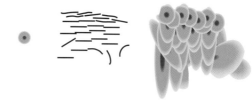

painted each with one of the four cell brushes. Lertola finished the illustration by rasterizing the skin cells in Photoshop and exporting a color and grayscale version of the cells. He imported the grayscale cells into the Lightwave 3D modeler software, where he built a model of the cells and applied the color version of the cells as a color map. (To learn more about using Illustrator artwork with other software, see the *Illustrator & Other Programs* chapter.)

Layers & Appearances

5

Layers & Appearances

Layers palette navigation

- To hide a layer, click the Eye icon. Click again to show it.
- To lock a layer, click in the column to the right of the eye (a lock displays). Click again to unlock.
- To Lock/Unlock or Show/Hide all *other* layers, Option-click/ Alt-click on a layer's Lock or Eye icon.
- To duplicate a layer, drag it to either the Create New Layer or Create New Sublayer icon.
- To select multiple contiguous layers, click one layer, then Shift-click the other. To select (or deselect) *any* multiple layers, ⌘-click/Ctrl-click a layer in any order.
- Double-click any layer to open Layer Options for that layer.

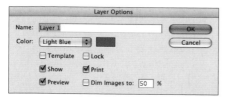

Layer Options (double-click a layer name)

Used wisely, layers can ease your workflow by dramatically improving organization of complicated artwork. Think of layers as sheets of clear acetate, stacked one on top of the other, allowing you to separate dozens of objects and groups of objects. New documents begin with one layer, but you can create as many layers and sublayers as you wish. You can also rearrange the stacking order of the layers; lock, hide, or copy layers; and move or copy objects from one layer to another. You can use the Layers palette to select objects and groups, and you can even open a layer to view and identify and select individual paths or groups contained within a layer!

A few shortcuts will help when you're adding layers to the Layers palette. Click the Create New Layer icon to add a layer in numeric sequence above the current layer. Hold Option/Alt when you click this icon to open Layer Options as you add the layer. To add a layer to the top of the Layers palette, hold ⌘/Ctrl when you click the Create New Layer icon. To make a new layer below the current layer and open the Layer Options, hold ⌘-Option/ Ctrl-Alt when you click the Create New Layer icon. Finally, you can easily duplicate a layer, sublayer, group, or path by dragging it to the Create New Layer icon at the bottom of the Layers palette. To delete selected layers, click on the Trash icon or drag the layers to the Trash. (See Tip at left.)

Sublayers can help you to stay organized. Sublayers are contained within the layer listed above them, if you delete the *container* layer holding the sublayers, all of its sublayers will be deleted as well.

Another icon in the Layers palette are targets (the circles to the right of the layer name). See the section titled "Selecting & Targeting With The Layers Palette" later in this chapter for details about the target icon, targeting objects from the Layers palette, and what all this target stuff means.

Using Layer Options

You can double-click on any group, path, compound path, clipping path, blend, mesh, guide, type, object, placed object, or raster object in the Layers palette to set Options such as the Name, Show, and/or Lock status. If you would like to know what the items are once you've re-named them, retain the name of the subcomponent. For example, you can rename a group to help organize your layer list, but keep the bracket description as part of the renaming of the layer (e.g., *floral <Group>*).

Double-click a layer name, sublayer name, or one of multiple selected layer/sublayer names to access the Layer Options discussed below:

- **Name the layer.** When creating complicated artwork, giving layers descriptive names keeps your job, and your brain, organized.

- **Change the layer's color.** A layer's color determines the selection color for paths, anchor points, bounding boxes, and Smart Guides. Adjust the layer color so selections stand out against artwork.

- **Template layer.** Illustrator's template layers are special layers that don't print or export. They're useful when-ever you want to base new artwork on existing art. For example, you can place the existing art on a non-printing template layer, and then hand-trace over it on a regular printing layer. There are three ways to create a template layer: You can select Template from the Layers pop-up menu, double-click a layer name and enable the Template option, or enable the Template option when you first place an image into Illustrator. By default, Template layers are locked. To unlock a Template in order to adjust or edit objects, click the lock icon to the left of the layer name.

There is no restriction to how many of your layers can be template layers; see Steven Gordon's map Galleries fol-lowing this chapter introduction for examples of why you might create multiple template layers.

If you can't select an object…

If you have trouble selecting an object, check/try the following:
- Is the object's layer locked?
- Is the object locked?
- Are the edges hidden?
- Is the Object Selection by Path Only box enabled (Preferences > General)?
- Locate the thumbnail in the layer list and click on the target indicator.

If you keep selecting the wrong object, try again after you:
- Switch to Outline mode.
- Zoom in.
- Try to locate the thumbnail in the layer list and click on the target indicator.
- Hide the selected object; repeat if necessary.
- Lock the selected object; repeat if necessary.
- Put the object on top in another layer and hide that layer, or se-lect Outline for the layer.
- Use the Move command: Op-tion-click/Alt-click the Selection tool in the Toolbox to move selected objects a set distance (you can move them back later).
- Check for objects with transpar-ency. Overlapping transparency inhibits selection.
- Try enabling the Type Object Selection by Path Only checkbox (Preferences > Type and Auto Tracing).

To change the stacking order of several objects:

- Reorder the layers they are on.
- Cut the bottom objects, select the topmost object, and Paste in Front with Paste Remembers Layers *off*.
- Drag selection indicators (large square) from one layer to another.
- Shift to select multiple layers and choose Reverse Order from the Layers palette pop-up.
- Move objects within a layer using Object > Arrange: Bring to Front/Bring Forward/Send to Back/Send Backward
- Select the objects you want to move; make a new layer (click New Layer icon) or highlight a layer into which you want to move these objects, and choose Object > Arrange > Send to Current Layer.
- If the selection is a blend, choose Object > Blend > Reverse Front to Back.

Italic layer names?

When a layer name is in *italic*, it's set to *not* print from within Illustrator. If the name is italic *and* you see the Template icon, it is reliably a non-printing layer (see the "Template layer" section, on previous page).

Note: *Template layers shouldn't be confused with Illustrator CS's new Templates feature. Templates are a special file format ending in .ait; whereas* template layers *are simply a special kind of layer. For more about* Templates, *see the* Illustrator Basics *chapter.*

- **Show/Hide layer.** This option functions the same way as the Show/Hide toggle, which you access by clicking the Eye icon (see the Tip "Layers palette navigation" in the beginning of this chapter introduction). By default, hiding a layer sets that layer *not* to print.

- **Preview/Outline mode.** If you have objects that are easier to edit in Outline mode, or objects that are slow to redraw (such as complicated patterns, live blends, or gradients), you may want to set only those layers (or objects) to Outline mode. Toggle this option on and off directly by ⌘-clicking/Ctrl-clicking the Eye icon in the view column. Alternatively, double-click selected layers, and in Layer Options, disable Preview to set those layers to Outline.

- **Lock/Unlock layer.** This option functions the same way as the Lock/Unlock toggle, which you access by clicking the lock column of the layer (see the Tip "Layers palette navigation" at the beginning of this chapter).

- **Print.** When you print from Illustrator you can use this feature to override the default, which sets visible layers to print. If you need a quick visual clue to ensure that a layer will not print, make it into a Template layer (see Steven Gordon's Galleries following this intro for examples).

- **Dim Images.** You can only dim raster images (not vector Illustrator objects) from 1% to 99% opacity.

The Layers pop-up menu

This section will look at functions unique to the Layers pop-up menu, not discussed in previous sections of this introduction.

With the ability to nest sublayers within other layers and create group objects comes the potential for confusion about how to find objects when they become buried in the layer list. Use Locate Object, or Locate Layer when Show Layers Only is checked in Palette Options, to find selected objects. When you've selected two or more layers, Merge Selected is available and will place *visible* objects in the topmost layer. You can consolidate all visible items in your artwork into a single layer using the Flatten Artwork command (though be aware that you might lose effects and masks applied to the layers involved). To make a flat version in another file, unlock all layers and objects, Select >All, Copy, make a new document, and Paste (with Paste Remembers Layers disabled).

Paste Remembers Layers is a great feature: When it's enabled, pasted objects retain their layer order; when unchecked, pasted objects go into the selected layer. If the layers don't exist, Paste Remembers Layers will make them for you! This feature can be turned on and off even after the objects have been copied—so if you paste, and wish that the toggle were reversed, you can Undo, toggle the Paste Remembers Layers option, then paste again. **IMPORTANT:** *Be aware that if you target a top-level layer and apply strokes, fills, effects, or transparency and then copy/paste that layer into a new document, all appearance attributes that were applied to that layer will be lost in the new document, even when Paste Remembers Layers is enabled.*

Try this workaround by Jean-Claude Tremblay (it also works to maintain masks and effects applied to the layer): Since the attributes of a top-level layer are not retained and you get no warning when pasting into the new document, you need to nest the top-layer into another layer, making it a sublayer. Then copy/paste this layer into the new document to retain the appearance attributes.

Collect in New Layer moves all of the selected layers into a new layer. Release to Layers (Build), or Release to Layers (Sequence), allows you to make individual object layers from a group of objects, such as a blend, a layer, or

New Layer...
New Sublayer...
Duplicate "Layer 2"
Delete "Layer 2"

Options for "Layer 2"...

Release Clipping Mask

Locate Object

Merge Selected
Flatten Artwork
Collect in New Layer

Release to Layers (Sequence)
Release to Layers (Build)
Reverse Order

Template
Hide Others
Outline Others
Lock Others

✔ Paste Remembers Layers

Palette Options...

Layers palette pop-up menu

If layers are too slow to open

When opening a file created by an older version of Illustrator, it can take a long time for the Layers palette to draw all the thumbnails for each path. Before you attempt to open layers to view their contents, you'll save a lot of time if you choose Palette Options from the Layers palette pop-up menu and disable the Objects option in the Thumbnails grouping. Once you've reorganized your paths in the Layers palette, be sure to re-enable the Objects checkbox in the Palette Options to view the thumbnails for your paths.

art created by using a brush. (See the *Web & Animation* chapter for applications of these options for animation.)

Reverse Order reverses the stacking order of selected layers within a container layer. Hide All Layers/Others, Outline All Layers/Others, and Lock All Layers/Others all perform actions on unselected layers or objects. And Send to Current Layer sends selected objects to your currently highlighted layer.

Palette Options customizes the layer display. This is a great help to artists who have complicated files with many layers. Show Layers Only hides the disclosure arrow so you only see the container layer thumbnail. Adding sublayers reveals the arrow, but you still can't target groups or individual paths in this mode. Row Size defines the size of the thumbnail for a layer. You can specify a thumbnail size from Small (no thumbnail) to Large, or use Other to customize a size up to 100 pixels. Thumbnail lets you individually set thumbnail visibility for the Layers, Top Level Only (when Layers is checked), Group, and Object.

CONTROLLING THE STACKING ORDER OF OBJECTS

Layers are crucial for organizing your images, but controlling the stacking order of objects *within* a layer is just as essential. The intuitive layers and sublayers disclose their hierarchical contents when you open the disclosure arrow. Following is a summary of the functions that will help you control the stacking order of objects within layers and sublayers.

Sublayers and the hierarchical layer structure

In addition to regular layers, there are sublayers and groups, both of which act as *containers* for objects or images. When you click on the Create New Sublayer icon, a new sublayer is added, nested inside the current layer. Artwork that you add to the sublayer will be underneath the art contained on the main layer. Clicking the Create New Layer icon with a sublayer selected will add a new sublayer above the current one. Adding subsequent layers adds the contents at the top of the stacking order or puts the artwork above the current layer.

Grouping objects together automatically creates a container "layer" named *<Group>*. Double-click the <Group> layer to open its options. Group layers are much like sublayers. You can target them to apply appearances that affect all the objects within the group. In some cases, such as when Pathfinder effects are applied, objects have to be grouped and the group layer must be targeted in order to apply the effect.

Note: *If you rename your <Group>, you might get confused when it doesn't behave like a regular layer. Instead of removing <Group> from the name appended to it, leave <Group> as part of the renaming of the layer.*

Paste in Front, Paste in Back (Edit menu)

When you choose Paste in Front or Paste in Back, if nothing is selected, Illustrator will paste the cut or copied object at the extreme front or back of the current layer. Whereas if you do have an object selected, Illustrator will paste the cut or copied object *exactly* on top of or behind the selected object in the stacking order. A second, and equally important, aspect is that the two functions paste objects that are cut or copied into the exact same *x* and *y* location—in relation to the *ruler origin*. This capability transfers from one document to another, ensuring perfect registration and alignment when you use Edit > Paste in Front / Back. (See the *Wow! CD* for a lesson using paste commands: 2a Zen-Layers-Moving_Pasting.ai.)

Lock/Unlock All (Object menu)

In the days before it was possible to open layers up in Illustrator and select the individual items they contain, the Lock/Unlock All commands were essential. They're a little less indispensable now, but can still be very useful if you can't locate your path from within the layer contents.

When you're trying to select an object and you accidentally select an object on top of it, try locking the selected object (⌘-2/Ctrl-2 or Object > Lock) and clicking

When is locked really locked?

Since the "Stone Age" of Illustrator, when you chose to Lock or Hide an object, it remained locked or hidden no matter what, even if the locked or hidden object was part of a group. Since the advent of *targeting* and *appearances* (see the "Selecting & Targeting With The Layers Palette" section later in this chapter for an explanation of these terms), how you *initially* select the group determines whether you are acting on the entire group (regardless of what is locked or hidden), or you are merely acting on those elements in the group that are currently visible and unlocked:

- **To act upon only the current visible/unlocked objects in a group,** either Direct-Select-marquee the group, or select the <Group> in the Layers palette by clicking the space to the right of the target icon.
- **To act on all elements in a group, including those hidden and locked,** click with the Selection tool, or click multiple times with the Group Selection tool until the group is selected (look in the Layers palette to make sure), or target the <Group> by clicking on the target icon in the Layers palette.

again. Repeat as necessary until you reach the correct object. When you've finished the task, choose Unlock All (⌘-Option-2/Ctrl-Alt-2) to release all the locked objects.

Hide/Show All (Object menu)

Alternatively, you can hide selected objects with Object > Hide > Selection (⌘-3/Ctrl-3). To view all hidden objects, choose Object > Show All (⌘-Option-3/Ctrl-Alt-3).

Note: *Hidden objects may print if they're on visible layers. If you'll be sending your file elsewhere for printing, and if your workflow includes the Hide command, make sure to chose Object > Show All before saving your final file.*

Bring to Front/Forward, Send to Back/Backward

These commands work on objects within a layer. Bring Forward (Object > Arrange) stacks an object on top of the object directly above it; Bring to Front moves an object in front of all other objects on its layer. Similarly, Send to Back sends an object as far back as it can go in its stacking order, whereas Send Backward sends an object behind its closest neighbor.

Note: *Bring Forward/Send Backward work best with simple object groupings, and may not work as expected on complex images. If it doesn't suit your needs, expand the Layers palette and relocate your path or group.*

SELECTING & TARGETING WITH THE LAYERS PALETTE

There are several ways to make selections. Click the layer's target icon or Option-click/Alt-click the layer name to select all unlocked and visible objects on the layer, including objects on sublayers and in groups. Click a sublayer's target icon to select everything on the sublayer, including other sublayers or groups. Clicking the *group's* target icon will also select all objects within that group. Shift-click the target icons to select multiple objects on different layers, including sublayers and groups. When you intend to modify the appearance of a layer, sublayer, or group, you must click on the *target* icon to make your selection first, then make your adjustments.

If you have selected artwork on the Artboard, click on the small square to select all of the objects on the layer or in the group. A larger square means that all of the objects on that layer or group are already selected. Clicking in the small space to the right of the target indicator will also select all objects on the layer, sublayer, or group.

APPEARANCES

Within an appearance are a collection of strokes, fills, effects, and transparency settings. An appearance can be applied to any path, object (including text), group, sublayer, or layer. The specific appearance attributes of a selection are shown in the Appearance palette. Attributes within the appearance are added to the palette in the order they are applied. Changing the order of the attributes will change the appearance. An object and its enclosing groups and layers can all have their own appearances.

To apply an appearance, make a selection or click on a target indicator (Layers palette). Then add transparency, effects, multiple fills, and/or multiple strokes (see the "Adding Fills and Strokes" section). When you've targeted a group, sublayer, or layer, strokes and fills will be applied to the individual objects within the selection, but any effects or transparency settings will be applied to the *target* (see Tip "Selecting vs. targeting" opposite). Drag the target indicator (in the Layers palette) from one layer to another to move an appearance, or Option-drag/Alt-drag the indicator to copy the appearance. To re-use an appearance, save it as a style in the Graphic Styles palette (for more about graphic styles see the *Live Effects & Graphic Styles* chapter).

Appearance palette

When you've selected or targeted an item, the Appearance palette displays all the attributes associated with the current selection. If there isn't a selection, the palette will display the attributes for the next object drawn. When the current target is an object, the Appearance palette always

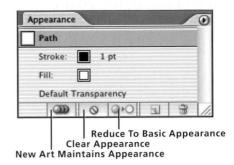

Reduce To Basic Appearance
Clear Appearance
New Art Maintains Appearance

Move or copy appearances

In the Layers palette, drag the Appearance icon circle from one object, group, or layer to another to *move* the appearance. To *copy* the appearance, hold Option/Alt as you drag the icon.

If you can't see an appearance

If you're trying to alter an appearance, but nothing seems to be changing on the screen, check for the following:
• Your objects are selected.
• You're in Preview mode.

Appearance palette indicators

The appearance indicators for Paint, Effects, and Transparency show up in the Appearance palette on layers or groups that contain elements with these attributes. (The *f* is also visible for standard strokes and fills.) See the Tip "Be a detective with files" at the end of this introduction on how to find how and where the effects in a document have been applied.

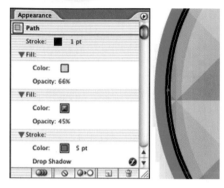

An example of multiple Strokes and Fills, including a 1-pt black stroke, a solid fill at 66% Opacity, a pattern fill at 45% Opacity, a 5-pt green stroke, and a Drop Shadow effect (see the Live Effects & Graphic Styles chapter for more about live effects)

New Art Has Basic Appearance

The Appearance palette's New Art Has Basic Appearance option is on by default. So, unless you disable this option (from the pop-up menu, or by clicking New Art Has Basic Appearance icon), Illustrator will not apply effects, brush strokes, transparency, blending modes, or multiple fills or strokes to new objects you create.

—*Brenda Sutherland*

Target all elements

When a group or layer is targeted, you can double-click the Contents line in the Appearance palette to target all the individual elements inside the group or layer.

—*Pierre Louveaux*

lists at least one fill, one stroke, and the object-level transparency. When the target is a group or layer, no Fill or Stroke is shown unless one has been applied (see "Adding Fills & Strokes" following). "Default Transparency" means 100% opacity, Normal blending mode, Isolate Blending off, and Knockout Group off or neutral.

A basic appearance isn't always a white fill and a black stroke (as suggested by the icon). An appearance is defined as a *Basic Appearance* when it includes one fill and one stroke (with either set to None); the stroke is above the fill; there are no brushes or live effects; opacity is 100%; and blending mode is Normal (the defaults).

If the current selection has more than the *basic* attributes you can choose what attributes the next object will have. The first icon at the bottom of the palette is New Art Maintains Appearance (when disabled) and New Art Has Basic Appearance (when selected). For example, if your last object had a drop shadow but you don't want the next object to inherit this attribute, click on the icon and the new object will only inherit the basic attributes.

Click on the Clear Appearance icon to reduce appearance attributes to no fill, no stroke, with 100% opacity. Click on the Reduce to Basic Appearance icon to reduce the artwork's appearance to a single stroke and fill along with the default transparency. To delete an attribute, drag it to the Trash, or click it and then click the Trash. **Note:** *Keep in mind that Reduce to Basic Appearance removes all brush strokes and live effects!*

THE FINER POINTS OF APPEARANCES
Adding fills & strokes

It's not until you start adding multiple fills and strokes to an appearance that you completely understand how useful the Appearance palette is.

Select Add New Fill or Add New Stroke from the palette pop-up menu to add these attributes to the appearance profile for a selected object, or group of objects. You can also add effects and transparency attributes to each fill or stroke by first clicking on the desired fill or stroke line in the palette, and then making the adjustments in the appropriate other palette (such as the Control palette).

The Appearance palette has a stacking order similar to that of the Layers palette. Items at the top of the palette are at the top of the stacking order. You can click on items in the palette list to select them, and you can rearrange them by dragging-and-dropping them up and down.

There are several ways to duplicate or delete a fill, stroke, or effect. You can select the attribute in the palette list and drag it to one of the icons at the bottom of the palette. You can also select the attribute and click the appropriate icon at the bottom of the palette. Finally, you can choose the appropriate item from the pop-up menu.

See the last lesson in this chapter, and the *Live Effects & Graphic Styles* chapter, for great examples of projects created using multiple strokes and/or fills.

Multiple fills & strokes

Create multiple line effects by adding multiple strokes to a path. Select a path, group, or layer and choose Add New Stroke from the Appearance palette pop-up menu. This adds a new stroke to the Appearance. In order to see the additional stroke on the path, you must give it different attributes from the initial stroke. Target one stroke (in the Appearance palette) and adjust the color, point size, shape, and/or transparency settings.

To create multiple fills, target an object, group, or layer and choose Add New Fill. As with multiple strokes, before you can see the effect of the added fill, it needs a different appearance. To vary the results of additional fills, apply an effect or different transparency settings.

If you're having trouble seeing the results of your multiple strokes, start with a wider stroke on the bottom (see the figures on the opposite page). To vary the results, try applying dashed lines and/or different end caps. For fills, try patterns or gradients with transparency. Again, see the last lesson in this chapter, and the *Live Effects & Graphic Styles* chapter, for projects that include the use of multiple fills and/or strokes.

Be a detective with files

When you need to modify artwork created by others (or open your own artwork created a while back) it's essential to have the Appearance palette and the Layers palette visible. This is because any number of applied effects or features (such as multiple strokes or fills, or transparency) may not be apparent. Click in the Layers palette on filled target indicators; in the Appearance palette you will see details about what has been applied. See the *Transparency* and *Live Effects & Graphic Styles* chapters for more on effects and appearances.

—*Vicki Loader*

Expandable text shapes

Want to make a text button? Type a word, then select the text object. Choose Add New Fill (in the Appearance palette menu) and drag this new fill below the Characters line. Click on the Fill line, apply the desired fill color, and then choose a shape from the Effect > Convert to Shape submenu. Set the Relative Extra Width and Extra Height to how far you want the button to extend around the text, and click OK. Each time you edit the text, the button will automatically resize itself.

Digitizing a Logo
Controlling Your Illustrator Template

YIP. (SAILOR JACK, BINGO & CRACKER JACK Designs are TMs of Recot, Inc., © Recot 1999.)

Overview: *Scan a clean version of your artwork; place the art on a template layer in Illustrator; hand-trace the template; modify the curve of drawn lines to better fit the template image by manipulating points and by using the Pencil tool.*

A large, clean scan of the artwork

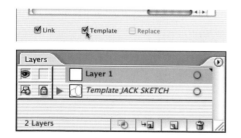

Creating the template and a drawing layer

You can easily use Illustrator's Template layer to re-create traditional line art with the computer—easily, that is, if you know the tricks. San Francisco artist Filip Yip was commissioned to modernize the classic Cracker Jack sailor boy and dog logo, and to digitize the logo for use in a variety of media. Yip scanned the original logo artwork and several sketches he drew and used the scans as sources in developing the new logo.

1 Placing a scanned image as a template and using Filters to modify the image. Select a high-contrast copy of the original artwork that is free of folds, tears, or stains. Scan the image at the highest resolution that will provide the detail you need for hand-tracing. Open a new file in Illustrator (File >New), select File >Place, click the Template option, then choose your scan, thus placing it into a new template layer. Template layers are automatically set to be non-printing and dimmed layers.

If you need to improve the quality of your scanned image to better discern details, you can edit the image with a program like Photoshop prior to placing it in Illustrator. If you've already brought the image into Illustrator, use the Filter menu to change focus or color. (If you placed the image on a Template layer, you'll need to double-click the layer name in the Layers palette and disable the Template option; this will then allow you to edit the image.) Select the image and select Filter >Sharpen to make the image more crisp. Choose the Filter >Colors menu and select options like Convert to Grayscale, Saturate, or Adjust Colors to modify image properties.

2 **Hand-tracing the template.** With the template as an on-screen tracing guide (and the original scanned artwork handy as an off-screen reference), select the Pen or Pencil tool and begin hand-tracing over the scanned image. To reduce visual clutter in small areas of the drawing, try viewing your active layer in Outline mode (while pressing ⌘-D, click on the visibility icon next to the layer's name in the Layers palette). Don't worry too much about how closely you're matching the template as you draw. Next, zoom close (with the Zoom tool, drag to marquee the area you wish to inspect) and use the Direct Selection tool to adjust corner or curve points, curve segments, or direction lines until the Bézier curves properly fit the template. (See the *Zen lessons* on the *Wow! CD* for help with Bézier curves.)

3 **Refining lines with the Pencil tool.** To modify a line, click the line to select it, then choose the Pencil tool and draw over the template with the Pencil. Illustrator automatically reshapes a selected line (instead of drawing a brand new line). You can customize the Pencil tool's settings by double-clicking the Pencil tool icon. Higher numbers in Fidelity and Smoothness result in less accurate, smoother lines, while lower numbers result in more detail and jaggier lines. You can also specify whether your newly-created line stays selected (to edit that line versus a new one) as well as the pixel distance from a selected line that indicates an edit (rather than the start of a new line).

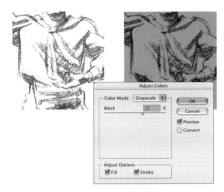

Darkening a scanned grayscale image using the Filter >Colors >Adjust Colors dialog box

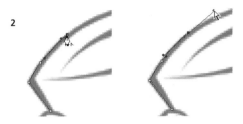

Modifying the fit of a drawn line using the Direct Selection tool to move a direction handle

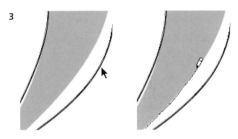

On the left, selecting a previously drawn line, and on the right, redrawing the selected line with the Pencil tool

Manually tracing an intricate object can be tedious and time-consuming; for something like the rough-edged parts of the sailor uniform with chalk on watercolor paper, try this: scan it, place it in Illustrator and apply Live Trace (Object menu)—see Chapter 7 for details on Live Trace

Organizing Layers
Managing Custom Layers and Sublayers

Overview: *Sketch and scan a composition; set up basic, named layers in Illustrator for the objects you will create; place art into sublayers; hand-trace the placed art; delete the temporary sublayers.*

Illustrator: STAHL / Art Director: JENNIFER MOORE

The initial concept sketches for the illustration

The final composition for the illustration

Beginning your illustration with well-organized layers and sublayers can be a lifesaver when you're constructing complex illustrations. Using these layers to isolate or combine specific elements will save you an immense amount of production time by making it easy to hide, lock, or select related objects within layers. Artist Nancy Stahl saved time and frustration when she was commissioned to design this illustration for an article in the Condé Nast Traveler magazine. She created multiple layers and sublayers to facilitate the manual tracing and arrangement of various components in the illustration.

1 **Collecting and assembling source materials.** Prepare your own source materials to use as drawing references and templates in Illustrator. To prepare this illustration, Stahl hand-sketched several concepts then scanned the approved composition into Adobe Photoshop where she prepared it for hand-tracing.

2 Setting up illustration layers. Before you begin to import any photos or drawings, take a few moments to set up layers and name each one to help you isolate and manage the key elements in your illustration. Before Stahl actually started drawing in Illustrator, she set up separate layers for the water, the sky, the railing, the steward, and the tray and ship. You can quickly name a layer while creating it by Option-clicking/Alt-clicking on the Create New Layer icon in the Layers palette. You can also name or rename an existing layer or sublayer by double-clicking on it in the Layers palette.

3 Placing art to use as a drawing reference. Click on the layer in which you plan to hand-trace your first object, then click on the Create New Sublayer icon in the Layers palette to create a sublayer for your drawing reference (Option-click/Alt-click on the icon to name your sublayer as you create it). Stahl created a sublayer that she named "JPEG Images." Use File >Place to select the scan or artwork to be placed into this sublayer. If you wish, you can enable the template option before placing the file. The sublayer should now be directly below the object layer in which you will be hand-tracing. Lock the sublayer and draw in the layer above using the Pencil, Pen, or other Drawing tools of your choice.

Using the Layers palette, Stahl repurposed the "JPEG Images" sublayer by freely moving it below each of the key element layers as she drew. To move a layer, drag and drop it to another position in the Layers palette.

4 Hand-tracing and drawing into your layers. Now you can begin drawing and hand-tracing elements in your compositional layers. Activate the layer or sublayer in which you want to draw by clicking on the layer's name. Make sure the layer or sublayer is unlocked and visible (there should be an Eye in the Visibility column and an empty box in the Lock column). It also helps to turn off the visibility of all non-essential layers before you begin working. From the Layers palette, you can lock, unlock,

2
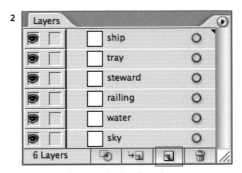
Setting up layers to isolate key elements

3
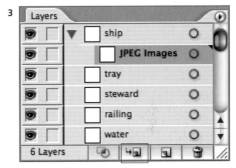
The sublayer before placing the scan

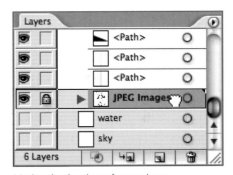
Moving the drawing reference layer

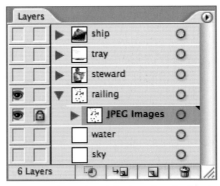
Setting up the Lock and Show options for hand-tracing an object

4

Viewing only the essential layers for each task

5

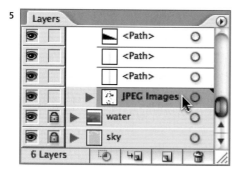

Clicking on a visible and unlocked sublayer to make it active for placing new art

6

Clicking on or dragging the sublayer to the Trash icon, or choosing Delete from the Layers palette pop-up menu

hide or show layers, as well as toggle between Preview and Outline modes, switch to your active layer, or add a new layer or sublayer (see the "Layers palette navigation Tip" on the first page of this chapter for helpful shortcuts in working with the Layers palette). By maneuvering in this way, Stahl could easily hand-trace a drawing reference or sketch in the layers above a locked layer.

5 Adding new placed art to a layer or sublayer. If you need to import art into an existing layer or sublayer, first make sure the layer is visible and unlocked, then make it the active layer by clicking on it. Use the Place command to bring the new scan or art into the selected layer. When Stahl needed additional drawing references she placed new art into the "JPEG Images" sublayer.

6 Deleting layers or sublayers when you are finished using them. Extra layers with placed art can take up extra disk space and increase the time it takes to save your document, so you'll want to delete them when you are done with them. When you finish using a drawing reference or template layer, first save the illustration. Then, in the Layers palette, click on the layer or sublayer you are ready to remove (Shift-click to select multiple layers) and either drag it to, or simply click on, the Trash icon in the Layers palette. Alternatively, you can choose the Delete option from the Layers palette pop-up menu. With these temporary layers deleted, use Save As to save this new version of the illustration with a meaningful new name and version number. Stahl eventually deleted all the sublayers she created as templates so that she could save her final cover illustration with all the illustration layers but without the excess template sublayers or placed pictures.

Easily changing placed art
Select the image you wish to replace and click on the name of the image that appears in the left side of the Control Palette; choose Relink at the top of the resulting pop-up menu.

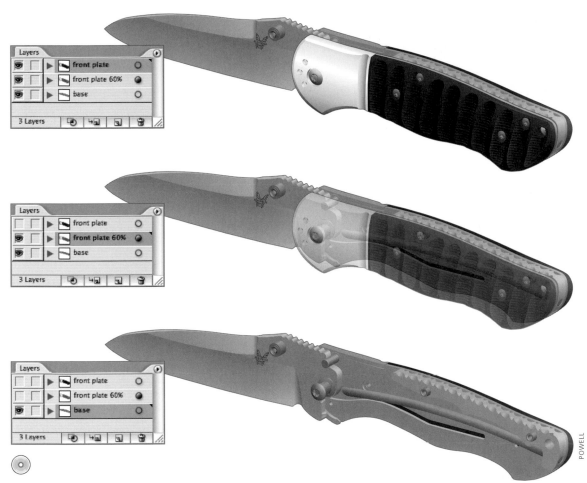

POWELL

Gary Powell

Using the same techniques as in "Organizing Layers," Gary Powell created this image for Benchmade Knife Company's training manual for product resellers. He duplicated the top layer by dragging it to the Create New Layer icon in the Links palette. He applied an Opacity value to the duplicated layer to create the transparent handle effect. When finished, he could toggle the visibility of the layers to print or export them individually.

Moving and Copying an object from one layer to another

To move a selected object to another layer, open the Layers palette, grab the colored dot to the right of the object's layer, and drag it to the desired layer (see near right). To move a copy of an object, hold down the Option/Alt key while you drag (see far right).

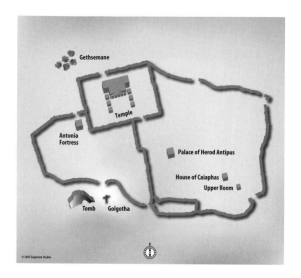

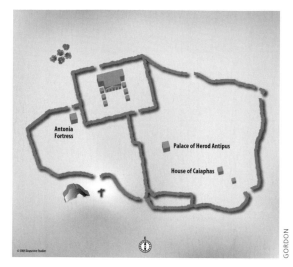

GORDON

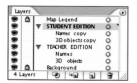

Steven Gordon / Cartagram, LLC

Steven Gordon created this map illustrating Jerusalem during New Testament times as one in a series of Bible workbook maps for Grapevine Studies. Gordon needed to design the maps for use in two versions—a detailed Teacher edition and a Student edition (in which the students would label selected map features). To simplify his work, Gordon combined both editions of each map in a single Illustrator file. He did this by first creating a layer for all of the paths and labels needed in the Teacher edition. Then, to create the Student edition, he duplicated the Teacher layer by dragging it onto the Create New Layer icon in the Layers palette. He renamed the layer and deleted the labels as required by the Student edition.

Having both editions in the same file helped in making changes and corrections. When Gordon added a building, he copied and pasted the shape on the Teacher layer and then moved the copy in the Layers palette to the Student layer. When he repositioned a building, he selected the shapes on both layers and moved them simultaneously. To output each edition, Gordon first double-clicked the Student layer and chose Template from the Layer Options dialog box. After he output the file, he repeated the process, this time turning the Teacher layer into a template layer, and returning the Student layer to its non-template condition. (Illustrator ignores non-template sublayers within a template master layer during output.)

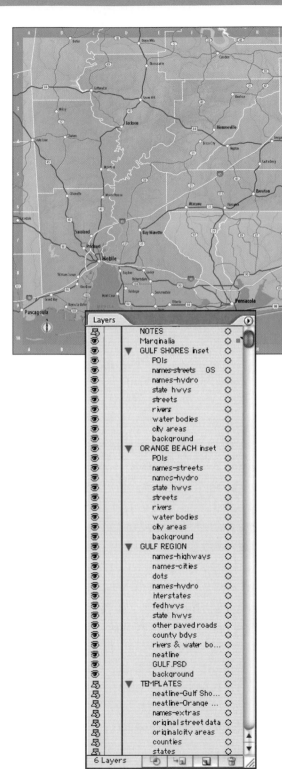

GORDON

Layers

NOTES
Marginalia
▼ GULF SHORES inset
  POIs
  names-streets   GS
  names-hydro
  state hwys
  streets
  rivers
  water bodies
  city areas
  background
▼ ORANGE BEACH inset
  POIs
  names-streets
  names-hydro
  state hwys
  streets
  rivers
  water bodies
  city areas
  background
▼ GULF REGION
  names-highways
  names-cities
  dots
  names-hydro
  interstates
  fedhwys
  state hwys
  other paved roads
  county bdys
  rivers & water bo...
  neatline
  GULF.PSD
  background
▼ TEMPLATES
  neatline-Gulf Sho...
  neatline-Orange ...
  names-extras
  original street data
  original city areas
  counties
  states

6 Layers

Steven Gordon / Cartagram, LLC

Cartographer Steven Gordon used layers to
organize this complex map. He created three
master layers, one each for the main map
and the two insets, allowing him to lock and
unlock, and hide and show, sets of layers in
the Layers palette so he could quickly find a
layer when concentrating on one of the maps.
Gordon also used template layers to store
original or extra artwork in case he needed
it later. The artwork on the template layers
was automatically excluded from the PDF files
Gordon generated to send to his client as intermediate proofs.

Nested Layers

Organizing with Layers and Sublayers

Overview: *Plan a layer structure; create layers and sublayers; refine the structure by rearranging layers and sublayers in the Layer palette's hierarchy; hide and lock layers; change the Layers palette display.*

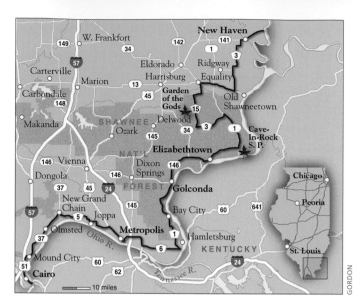

1

The completed layer structure for the map showing layers and two levels of sublayers

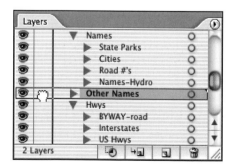

Selecting and dragging the BYWAY-road sublayer up and out of the Hwys sublayer, placing it on the same level in the hierarchy as Hwys

Layers have always been a great way of organizing artwork. Now with Illustrator, you can organize your Layers palette as a nested hierarchy, making it easier to navigate and manipulate. For this map of the Great River Scenic Byway in Illinois, Steven Gordon relied on nested layers and sublayers to organize the artwork he developed.

1 Planning, then creating and moving layers and sublayers. Gordon began by planning a layer structure for the map in which layers with similar information would be nested within several "master" layers, so he could easily navigate the Layers palette and manipulate the layers and sublayers. After planning the organization of your layered artwork, open the Layers palette and begin creating layers and sublayers. (Illustrator automatically creates a Layer 1 every time a new document is created—you can use or rename this layer.) To create a new layer, click the Create New Layer icon at the bottom of the palette. To create a new sublayer that's nested within a currently selected layer, click on the palette's Create New Sublayer icon.

As you continue working, you may need to refine your organization by changing the nesting of a current layer or sublayer. To do this, drag the layer name in the Layers palette and release it over a boundary between layers. To convert a sublayer to a layer, drag its name and release it above its master layer or below the last sublayer of the master layer (watch the sublayer's bar icon to ensure that it aligns with the left side of the names field in the Layers palette before releasing it). Don't forget that if you move a layer in the Layers palette, any sublayer, group, or path it contains will move with it, affecting the hierarchy of artwork in your illustration.

2 **Hiding and locking layers.** As you draw, you can hide or lock sublayers of artwork by simply clicking on the visibility (Eye) icon or edit (Lock) icon of their master layer. Gordon organized his map so that related artwork, such as different kinds of names, were placed on separate sublayers nested within the Names layer, and thus could be hidden or locked by hiding or locking the Names layer.

If you click on the visibility or edit icon of a master layer, Illustrator remembers the visibility and edit status of each sublayer before locking or hiding the master layer. When Gordon clicked the visibility icon of the Names layer, sublayers that had been hidden before he hid the master layer remained hidden after he made the Names layer visible again. To quickly make the contents of all layers and sublayers visible, select Show All Layers from the Layers palette's pop-up menu. To unlock the content of all layers and sublayers, choose Unlock All Layers. (If these commands are not available, it's because all layers are already showing or unlocked.)

3 **Changing the Layers palette display.** As you utilize the Layers palette, change its display to make the palette easier to navigate. Display layers and sublayers (and hide groups and paths) in the palette by choosing Palette Options from the palette menu and in the Layers palette Options dialog box, clicking Show Layers Only. To view tiny thumbnails of the artwork on each layer or sublayer, select a Row Size of Medium or Large, or select Other and set row size to 20 or more pixels in the dialog box.

2
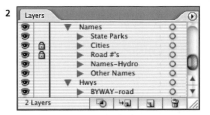
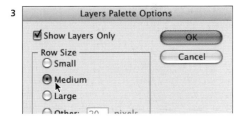

Top, a "master" layer with two sublayers locked; bottom, after the master layer is locked, the two sublayers' edit icons are not dimmed, indicating that they will remain locked when the layer is unlocked

3
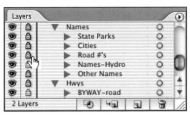

Selecting a row size in the Layers palette Options dialog box

Another way to unlock layers

A quick way to unlock all the contents of a layer: Make sure the layer itself is unlocked (the lock icon is gone) and then choose Unlock All from the Object menu.

Let Illustrator do the walking

Illustrator can automatically expand the Layers palette and scroll to a sublayer that's hidden within a collapsed layer. Just click on an object in your artwork and choose Locate Layer or Locate Object from the Layers palette's menu.

Basic Appearances
Making and Applying Appearances

Overview: *Create appearance attributes for an object; build a three-stroke appearance, save it as a style, and then draw paths and apply the style; target a layer with a drop shadow effect, create symbols in the layer, then edit layer appearance if needed.*

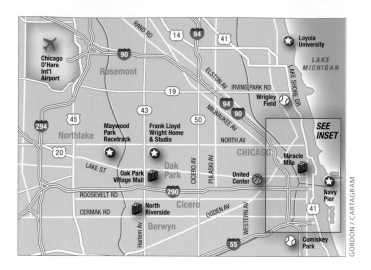

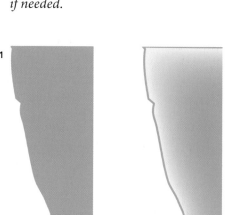

On the left, the lake with blue fill and stroke; on the right, the lake with the Inner Glow added to the appearance attribute set

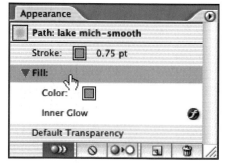

Appearance palette displaying the finished set of attributes (Gordon used the Appearance palette so that he could create a single path for the lake that contained a fill and the coastline stroke above it)

Complexity and simplicity come together when you use Illustrator's Appearance palette to design intricate effects, develop reusable styles and simplify production workflow. In this location map of Chicago, Illinois, cartographer Steven Gordon relied on the Appearance palette to easily build appearances and apply them to objects, groups and layers.

1 Building an appearance for a single object. Gordon developed a set of appearance attributes that applied a coastline, vignette and blue fill to a path symbolizing Lake Michigan. To begin building appearance attributes, open the Appearance palette and other palettes you might need (Color, Swatches, Stroke, and Transparency, for example). Gordon began by drawing the outline of the lake with the Pen tool and giving the path a 0.75-pt dark blue stroke. In the Appearance palette, he clicked on the Fill attribute and chose the same dark blue he had used for the stroke. To give the lake a light-colored vignette, he applied an inner glow to the Fill attribute (Effect > Stylize > Inner Glow). In the Inner Glow dialog box, Gordon set Mode to Normal, Opacity to 100%, Blur to 0.25 inches (for the width of the vignette edge), and enabled the Edge option. He clicked the dialog box's color swatch and chose white for the glow color.

2 Creating a style. Until Illustrator 9, you created a "patterned" line like an interstate highway symbol by overlapping copies of a path, each copy with a different stroke width. Now you can use the Appearance palette to craft a multi-stroked line that you apply to a single path. First, deselect any objects that may still be selected and reset the Appearance palette by clicking the Clear Appearance icon at the bottom of the palette (this eliminates any attributes from the last selected style or object). Next, click the Stroke attribute (it will have the None color icon) and click the Duplicate Selected Item icon twice to make two copies. Now, to make Gordon's interstate symbol, select the top Stroke attribute and give it a dark color and a 0.5-pt width. Select the middle attribute and choose a light color and a 2-pt width. For the bottom attribute, choose a dark color and a 3-pt width. Because you'll use this set of appearance attributes later, save it as a style by dragging the Object icon at the top of the palette to the Styles palette. Double-click the new style's default name in the palette and rename it in the dialog box if you want.

3 Assigning a style to a group. Draw the paths you want to paint with the new style you created above. Then choose Select All and Group. To get the three levels of strokes to merge when paths on the map cross one another, click on Group in the Appearance palette and then apply the interstate style you just saved.

4 Assigning appearance attributes to an entire layer. By targeting a layer, you can create a uniform look for all the objects you draw or place on that layer. Create a layer for the symbols and click the layer's target icon in the Layers palette. Then select Effect > Stylize > Drop Shadow. Each symbol you draw or paste on that layer will be automatically painted with the drop shadow. Later, you can modify the drop shadows by clicking the layer's targeting icon and then double-clicking the Drop Shadow attribute in the Appearance palette and changing values in the pop-up Drop Shadow dialog box.

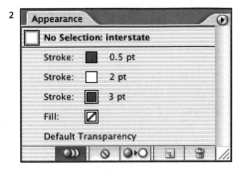

Appearance palette for Gordon's interstate highway symbol

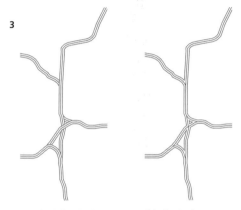

On the left, the interstates with the Style applied to the individual paths; on the right, the interstate paths were grouped before the Style was applied

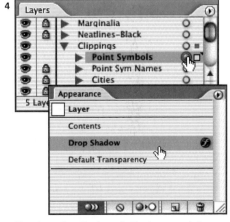

Top, targeting the layer in the Layers palette; bottom, the Appearance palette showing the Drop Shadow attribute (double-click the attribute to edit Drop Shadow values)

Varied Perspective

Analyzing Different Views of Perspective

Advanced Technique

Overview: *Draw and scan a sketch; create working layers using your sketch as a template; in each "guides" layer, draw a series of lines to establish perspective; make the perspective lines into guides; draw elements of your image using the applicable perspective guides.*

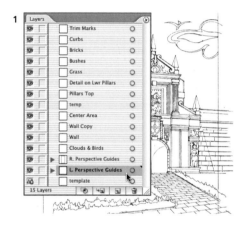

Portion of the original pencil sketch placed on a template layer with a custom layer ready for creation of guides

Locking and unlocking guides

- When guides are unlocked (uncheck View > Guides > Lock Guides), you can select any guide as an object and move or delete it.
- When a layer with guides is locked, the guides lose their "snap to" property—yet another good reason for you to keep guides on separate layers.

While any object can be made into a guide, converting lines into guides is indispensable when adding perspective to an image. To illustrate this McDonald's packaging design, Clarke Tate constructed several sets of vanishing point guides, enabling him to draw a background scene (Fort Santiago in the Philippines) that would contrast with the flat cartoon figures of Snoopy and Woodstock.

1 **Setting up the layers.** Sketch a detailed layout of the illustration on paper, shaping main elements like Tate's brick walk and wall with a perspective view. Scan your sketch and save the scan as a TIFF, then place the TIFF in Illustrator and choose Template from the Layers palette's pop-up menu. Analyze the image to determine the number of vanishing points in your illustration (points along

the scene's horizon where parallel lines seem to converge). Create new layers (click the Create New Layer icon in the Layers palette) for compositional elements; add a layer for each vanishing point in the illustration.

2 Establishing the location of vanishing points. In the Layers palette, select the first layer you'll use for developing a set of perspective guides. Referring to your template, mark the first vanishing point and use the Pen tool to draw a path along the horizon and through the vanishing point. (Some or all of your vanishing points may need to extend beyond the picture border.) With the Direct Selection tool, select the anchor point from the end of the line that is away from the vanishing point. Grab the point, then hold down Option/Alt and swing this copy of the line up so it encompasses the uppermost object that will be constructed using the vanishing point. You should now have a V that extends along your horizon line through your vanishing point, then to an upper or lower portion of your composition.

To create in-between lines through the same vanishing point, select both of the original lines, use the Blend tool to click first on the outer anchor point of one of the lines, and then on the outer anchor point of the other line. (If you need to specify more or fewer steps, you can select the blend and edit the number of steps in the Spacing > Specified Steps field of the Object > Blend > Blend Options dialog box.) For each different vanishing point, repeat the above procedure.

3 Making and using the guides. Because Illustrator cannot create guides from blended objects, you must first select each blend with the Selection tool and then expand it (Object > Blend > Expand). Next, transform the blends into guides by choosing View > Guides > Make Guides. Now pick an area of the illustration and begin drawing. You may want to lock the layers containing guides for other vanishing points so you don't accidentally snap objects to the wrong perspective.

2

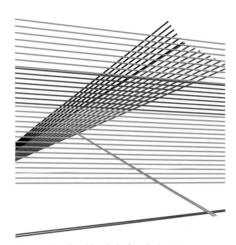

Top, dragging a perspective line to the uppermost object from the vanishing point; bottom, paths blended to create in-between perspective lines

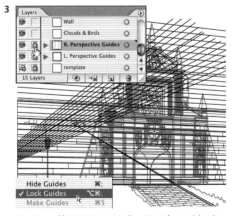

Perspective line blends before being transformed into guides

3

Turning off the "snap to" function for guides by locking the layer (left); locking guides in place by using the Lock/Unlock toggle in the View > Guides submenu

Type

6

Type

The Type tool, Area Type tool, Path Type tool, Vertical Type tool, Vertical Area Type tool, and Vertical Path Type tool. Select a Type tool and press Shift to toggle the tool between a horizontal and vertical orientation

The previous version of Illustrator, Illustrator CS, introduced major changes in terms of the way Illustrator handles type. With CS, Adobe installed a whole new text engine under Illustrator's hood—one that functions more like Photoshop and InDesign, bringing the Creative Suite applications closer together, and allowing Illustrator users to take advantage of sophisticated new type features that wouldn't have been possible in the old Illustrator. Character and paragraph styles, Unicode support, and the ability to take full advantage of the advanced capabilities of OpenType fonts are just a few of the new type features that arrived with Illustrator CS.

Of course, this step forward came with certain costs. Because Illustrator's current text engine handles type so differently, any text created in Illustrator 10 or earlier is considered *legacy text*, and must be updated before it's editable in Illustrator CS or CS2 (see Tip "Legacy text," later in this chapter). Also saving type to earlier versions of Illustrator can be challenging (see "Saving and Exporting Illustrator Type," at the end of this introduction).

Nonetheless, the advantages of Illustrator's new text engine are considerable, and allow Illustrator users to keep pace with the demands and capabilities of contemporary type design.

For Illustrator CS2, Adobe focused on improving the stability and performance of the new text engine. And CS2 adds two small but extremely useful and long-requested type formatting options: the ability to set text as underline or strikethrough.

Although you'll probably still prefer a page layout program such as QuarkXPress or InDesign for multi-page documents like catalogues and long magazine articles, and Dreamweaver or GoLive for Web page layout, this chapter will look at Illustrator's design and layout capabilities for single-page documents.

Selecting type by accident

If you keep accidentally selecting type when you're trying to select an object with the Selection tool, enable Type Object Selection by Path Only (Preferences > Type). With this option turned on, you won't select type objects unless you click directly on the baseline or path of the type. (If you have trouble finding the path, you can select the text object in the Layers palette by clicking the space to the right of the <Type> target icon, or marquee at least a full letterform with a selection tool or the Lasso tool.)

Typographic controls

Most of Illustrator's default settings for type are controlled in the Type area of Preferences. One exception is the unit of measurement for type, which is set in Preferences > Units & Display Performance.

THE SEVEN TYPE PALETTES

For creating and manipulating type, Illustrator CS2 offers no less than seven palettes, all accessible from the Window > Type submenu. Nested in with the Paragraph and Character palettes is the OpenType palette, which gives you convenient access to the options of OpenType fonts. The Glyphs palette lets you choose quickly from a wide range of special characters. The Character Styles and Paragraph Styles palettes, nested together, are where you'll manage Illustrator's automatic text formatting capabilities. And the Tabs palette (which arrived in CS to replace the old Tab Ruler) lets you manage tabs and create customized tab leaders.

The Character and Paragraph palettes may first appear in a collapsed view; cycle through display options by clicking the double arrow on the Palette tab.

THE THREE TYPES OF TYPE

There are three type options in Illustrator, accessible through the Type tool: *Point type*, *Area type*, and *Path type*. The flexible Type tool lets you click to create a Point type object, click-drag to create an Area type object, click on a path to create Path type (discussed a bit further on), or click within any existing type object to enter or edit text. Use File > Open, File > Place, and Copy and Paste commands to access type created in other applications.

Select letters, words, or an entire block of text by dragging across the letters with the Type tool; or use a selection tool to select the entire text block as an *object* by clicking on or marqueeing the text baseline (the line that the type sits on).

- **Point type:** Click with the Type tool or the Vertical Type tool anywhere on the page to create Point type. Once you click, a blinking text-insertion cursor called an "I-beam" indicates that you can now type text using your keyboard. To add another line of text, press the Return or Enter key. When you're finished typing into one text object, click on the Type tool in the Toolbox to simultaneously select

Underline

~~Strikethrough~~

A small but extremely useful enhancement: Illustrator CS2 lets you set text as underline or strikethrough

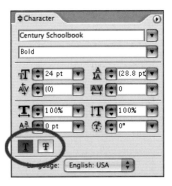

The Character palette showing the new underline and strikethrough buttons

Each type object in Illustrator has an *in port* (at the upper left) and an *out port* (at the lower right). If both ports are empty, all the text is displayed and the object isn't currently linked (or *threaded*) to any other text objects. You may also see the following port symbols:

- A red plus sign in the out port means the object contains *overflow text* (additional text that doesn't fit)
- An arrow in the in port means the object is threaded to a preceding text object, and text is flowing into the object
- An arrow in the out port means the object is threaded to a subsequent text object, and text is flowing out of the object.

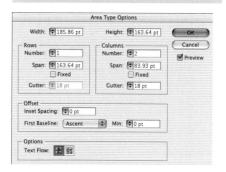

Area Type Options dialog box

Rectangle rule relaxed

When you use the Area Type Options dialog box to create rows and columns, your type container won't get automatically converted to a rectangle (as was the case in previous versions).

the current text as an object (the I-beam will disappear), and be poised to begin another text object. To edit the text click on it with the Type tool, or to select it as an object, click on it with one of the selection tools.

- **Area type:** Click and drag with the Type tool to create a rectangle, into which you can type. Once you've defined your rectangle, the I-beam awaits your typing, and the text automatically wraps to the next line when you type inside the confines of the rectangle.

Another way to create Area type or Vertical Area type is to construct a path (with any tools you wish) forming an object within which to place the type. Click and hold on the Type tool to access other tools, or press the Shift key to toggle between horizontal and vertical orientations of *like* tools (see the Tip "Type tool juggling" later in this chapter intro). Choose the Area Type or Vertical Area Type tool and click on the path itself to place text within the path. Distort the confining object by with the Direct Selection and path editing tools. The text within your Area Type object will reflow to fit the new shape of the confining object.

Illustrator's Area Type Options dialog box (Type > Area Type Options) gives you precise control over a number of important aspects of Area type. You can set numerical values for the width and height of the selected Area type object. You can set precise values for Rows and Columns (i.e., you can divide a single Area type object into multiple columns or rows that will reflow as you type), and choose whether or not those values remain fixed as you scale. You can also specify Offset options, including the amount of inset (defined as the margin between the text and the bounding path) and the alignment of the first baseline of text. And finally, you can determine how text flows between rows or columns by using a Text Flow option.

To set tabs for Area type, select the text object and choose Window > Type > Tabs. The Tabs palette will open aligned with the text box. As you pan or zoom, you'll notice the Tab ruler doesn't move with the text box. Don't sweat: If you lose your alignment, just click the little Magnet button on the Tabs palette, and the palette will snap back into alignment.

One nice feature of the Tabs palette is the ability to create your own *tab leaders*. A tab leader is a repeated pattern of characters (such as dots or dashes) between a Tab and the text that follows it. Select a tab stop on the ruler in the Tabs palette, type a pattern of up to eight characters in the palette's Leader box, then hit Return or Enter. You'll see your customized Leader pattern repeated across the width of the tab.

- **Path type:** The Path type tool (which Adobe now calls the "Type on a Path tool") allows you to click on a path to flow text along the perimeter of the path (the path will then become unstroked and unfilled).

  When you select a Path type object, you'll see three brackets appear: one at the beginning, one in the center, and one at the end of the Path type. The beginning and end brackets carry an in port and an out port, respectively, which can be used to thread text between objects (see the Tip "Ports illustrated"). The center bracket is used to control the positioning of the Path type. Hold your cursor over it until a small icon that looks like an upside down **T** appears. You can now drag the center bracket to reposition the type. Dragging the bracket across the path will flip the type to the other side of the path. (For example, type along the outside of a circle would flip to the inside.) Dragging the bracket forward or backward along the direction of the path will move the type in that direction.

  As with Area type, use the Direct Selection tool to reshape the confining path; the type on the path will automatically readjust to the new path shape.

  The Type on a Path Options dialog box (Type > Type on a Path > Type on a Path Options) lets you set a number of Path type attributes. You can choose from five different Path Type Effects (Rainbow, Skew, 3D Ribbon, Stair Step,

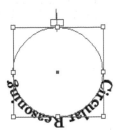

You may notice that if you try to set Path type on a circle, and the text is set to Align Center, the text will be forced to the bottom of the circle

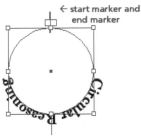

That's because each Path type object has two handles (the start marker and the end marker) that the type is centered between. When you first draw the circle and apply the Path type to it, those two handles appear together at the top of the circle, due to the fact that the circle is a closed path

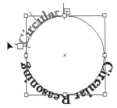

To position the text on top of the circle, all you have to do is grab the start marker handle and drag it to the 9 o'clock position, and then drag the end marker handle to the 3 o'clock position. Your text will now be centered between the two handles, on top of the circle

Moral of the story: When you're working with center-aligned Path type, be sure to keep an eye on those start and end marker handles, and make sure they're where you need them to be

To manually flip type on a path to the other side of the path, select the type and drag the center handle (the thin blue line perpendicular to the type) across the path, as indicated by the red arrow above. Note the tiny **T**-shaped icon that appears next to the cursor as you position it near the handle

The same type, after dragging across the path, but before releasing the mouse. After release, the type will be in the position indicated by the blue type above the path; you can then drag the center handle from side to side to adjust the position of the text—just don't drag across the path again or you'll flip the type back. You can also flip type across a path automatically by choosing Type > Type on a Path > Type on a Path Options, checking the Flip box (as shown on the following page), and clicking on OK

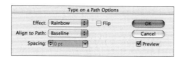

The Type on a Path Options dialog box

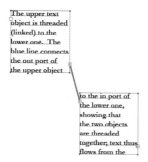

The upper text object is threaded (linked) to the lower one. The blue line connects the out port of the upper object to the in port of the lower one, showing that the two objects are threaded together; text thus flows from the first object to the second. The red plus sign in the out port of the lower object indicates that there is still more overflow text, which could flow into a third threaded object

and Gravity); a Flip checkbox that will automatically flip type to the other side of the path; a menu that lets you set the alignment of type relative to the path; and a Spacing control that lets you adjust the spacing of type as it moves around a curve. (The Path Type Effects are also available via the Type > Type on a Path submenu.)

WORKING WITH THREADED TEXT

If a text object contains more text than it has room to display, you'll see a plus sign in the small box along its lower right side. (This box is called the *out port*; see the Tip "Ports illustrated," earlier in this chapter.) To enlarge the object to allow for more text, use the Selection tool to grab the object by a bounding side, and drag to resize it (hold down the Shift key if you want to constrain proportions as you resize).

To add a new text object that can receive overflow text, use the Selection tool to select the first text object. Next, click on the red plus sign in the out port. The cursor will change to the "loaded text" cursor, which looks like a miniature text block. Then you can click on the Artboard to create a new text object the same size and shape as the original; or drag to create a text object of any size. Either way, the new text object will be *threaded* (linked) to the original, and the text that wouldn't fit in the first object will flow into the second.

Note: *Make sure Type Object Selection by Path Only is disabled in the Type area of Preferences, or the above process won't work.*

Similarly, you can link existing text objects together by clicking the plus sign on the first object, and then clicking on the path of the object that will receive the overflow text. (Keep your eye on the cursor, which will change to indicate valid "drop" locations.) You can also link objects using a menu command: Select the first object with a Selection tool, then Shift-click to select the second object as well (or marquee both objects with the Lasso or a Selection tool). Choose Type > Threaded Text > Create, and the objects are linked.

Of course, the threads between objects can be broken as easily as they're created. If you want to disconnect one object from another, first select the object. Then double-click its in port to break the thread to a preceding object, or double-click its out port to break the thread to a subsequent object. Alternatively, you can select the object and click either the in port or the out port once. Then click the other end of the thread to break it.

You can also release an object from a Text thread by selecting it, then choosing Type > Threaded Text > Release Selection. Or, if you want to remove the threading from an object while leaving text in place, select it and choose Type > Threaded Text > Remove Threading.

WRAPPING TEXT AROUND OBJECTS

These days, Illustrator handles text wrapping a little differently from the way it did in versions prior to Illustrator CS. Text wrapping is now an object attribute and is set specifically for each object that will have text wrapped around it (known as a *wrap object*). First, make sure that the object you want to wrapped with text is above the text you want to wrap around it in the Layers palette. Then select the wrap object and choose Object > Text Wrap > Make. The Text Wrap Options dialog box will appear. Here, you'll choose the amount of offset and also have the option to choose Invert Wrap (which reverses the side of the object that text wraps around). You can also wrap text around a group of objects. In order to add a new object to the text wrapped group, open the Layers palette, click the triangle to reveal the layer content, and drag the icon for your new object into the <Group>. To release an object from text wrapping, select it and choose Object > Text Wrap > Release. To change the options for an existing wrap object, select it and choose Object > Text Wrap > Text Wrap Options.

CHARACTER AND PARAGRAPH STYLES

Illustrator's Character and Paragraph palettes let you format text by changing one attribute at a time. The

---

The quick-changing Type tool

When using the regular Type tool, look at your cursor very carefully in these situations:

- If you move the regular Type tool over a closed path, the cursor changes to the Area type icon.
- If you move the Type tool over an open path, the cursor will change to the Path type icon.

Path type and closed paths

Even though the feedback you get from the Type tool cursor seems to indicate that you can only apply Path type to open paths, you actually *can* apply Path type to both open and closed paths (hold Option/Alt).

Type tool juggling

To toggle a Type tool between its vertical and horizontal mode, first make sure nothing is selected. Hold the Shift key down to toggle the tool to the opposite mode.

Hiding text threads

Users of page layout programs like InDesign or QuarkXPress will recognize the way Illustrator shows text threads graphically, by drawing a line between linked objects. If this visual gets in the way, you can toggle it on and off via View > Show/Hide Text Threads.

Illustrator's new text engine (introduced in Illustrator CS and refined in CS2) makes a lot of new type features possible. But it also means that text is handled very differently from older versions, so *legacy text* (text created in earlier versions of Illustrator) needs to be updated before it can be edited in CS2. When you open a file containing legacy text, a dialog box warns you that it contains text that needs to be updated. You can choose to update the text then and there by clicking "Update," or wait until later by clicking "OK." Text that hasn't been updated can be viewed, moved, and printed, but it can't be edited. When selected, legacy text is displayed with an X through its bounding box. When text is updated, you may see the following types of changes:

- Changes to leading, tracking, and kerning
- In Area type: words overflowing, shifting between lines or to the next linked object

You can choose to update all legacy text at any time by choosing Type > Legacy Text > Update All Legacy Text. Update specific legacy text by clicking it with the Type tool. You can also preserve legacy text on a layer below the updated text for comparison.

more powerful Character and Paragraph Styles palettes (introduced in Illustrator CS) take formatting to the next level by allowing you to apply multiple attributes to text simply by applying the appropriate style. (All four of these type-related palettes are found under the Window > Type submenu.)

New character and paragraph styles can either be created from scratch or based on existing styles. To create a new style: Using your current type styling as a default, and with a default name (all can be changed later if you like), click the Create New Style button in either the Character Styles or the Paragraph Styles palette. If you want to name your new style as you create it, choose New Character Style from the Character Styles palette menu, or New Paragraph Style from the Paragraph Styles palette menu. (You can also hold down the Option/Alt key while clicking the New Style button.) Type a name for your new style in the dialog box that appears, and click OK—your new style will appear in the Character Styles or Paragraph Styles palette.

To create a new style based on an existing one, select the existing style in the Character Styles or Paragraph Styles palette. Then choose Duplicate Character Style or Duplicate Paragraph Style from the palette menu. Your new "cloned" style will appear in the palette.

To change the attributes of a new or existing style, double-click its name in the Character Styles or Paragraph Styles palette, or select it and choose Character Style Options or Paragraph Style Options from the palette menu. The Options dialog box will let you set all your desired attributes for the style—everything from basic characteristics (such as font, size, and color), to OpenType features.

To apply a style to text, just select the text you want to format and click the name of the style in the Character Styles or Paragraph Styles palette. (This won't work if the type has *overrides*—extra formatting—applied, in which case you may need to remove the override by clicking a second time.)

TAKING ADVANTAGE OF OPENTYPE

One of the main reasons Adobe revamped the way Illustrator handles text was to allow users to take full advantage of the sophisticated features of OpenType fonts. (To underscore the point, Illustrator now ships with a bundle of free OpenType fonts, so you can put them to work immediately.) One great benefit of OpenType fonts is that they're platform-independent, so they can move easily between Mac and Windows.

When you use any OpenType font, Illustrator will automatically set standard ligatures as you type (see example at right). You can set options for other OpenType features via the OpenType palette, which is nested by default with the Character and Paragraph palettes, and is accessible via Window > Type > OpenType. The OpenType palette includes two pop-up menus that let you control the style and positioning of numerals; it also has buttons that let you choose whether or not to use standard ligatures (for letter pairs such as fi, fl, ff, ffi, and ffl), optional ligatures (for letter pairs such as ct and st), swashes (characters with exaggerated flourishes), titling characters (for use in uppercase titles), stylistic alternates (alternative versions of a common character), superscripted ordinals, and fractions.

If you'd like more information on what the various commands in the OpenType palette do, we've included a helpful guide by Sandee Cohen on the *Wow! CD* (OpenType_Guide.pdf). These pages, taken from Cohen's *InDesign CS Visual QuickStart Guide*, give you a primer on how to work with OpenType fonts.

THE GLYPHS PALETTE

Illustrator's new Glyphs palette gives you quick access to a wide variety of special characters, including any ligatures, ornaments, swashes, and fractions included in any given OpenType font. Choose Window > Type > Glyphs to display the palette. With the Type tool, click to place the insertion point where you want the special character to appear, and then double-click the character you want in

Character Styles palette

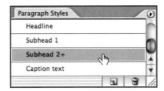

Paragraph Styles palette

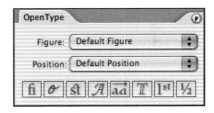

OpenType palette

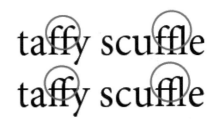

OpenType fonts automatically set standard ligatures as you type (unless you turn this feature off in the OpenType palette). In the example above, the type on the top row is set using the standard version of Adobe's Minion font. The bottom row is set using Minion Pro, one of the OpenType fonts likely installed with your Illustrator application. Minion Pro supplies the ligatures for "ff" and "ffl" (visible in the bottom row), which give the type a more sophisticated look.

Glyphs palette

Lorem ipsum dolor sit amet, consectetuer adipiscing elit. Sed at nibh. Nam ultrices erat nec pede. Vivamus est ante, aliquet vel, fermentum et, nonummy eget, ante. Morbi metus nisl, placerat ut, accumsan id, aliquet vel, nulla. Aenean scelerisque dapibus nunc. Proin augue. Vestibulum dictum. Morbi eget urna. Phasellus id augue. Nulla congue imperdiet dolor. Lorem ipsum dolor sit amet, consectetuer adipiscing elit. Sed at nibh.

Text composed using Single-line Composer

Lorem ipsum dolor sit amet, consectetuer adipiscing elit. Sed at nibh. Nam ultrices erat nec pede. Vivamus est ante, aliquet vel, fermentum et, nonummy eget, ante. Morbi metus nisl, placerat ut, accumsan id, aliquet vel, nulla. Aenean scelerisque dapibus nunc. Proin augue. Vestibulum dictum. Morbi eget urna. Phasellus id augue. Nulla congue imperdiet dolor. Lorem ipsum dolor sit amet, consectetuer adipiscing elit. Sed at nibh.

The same text composed using Every-line Composer, which automatically creates less ragged-looking text blocks with more uniform line lengths

Object rows and columns

To create rows and columns from non-type objects, select the object(s) and choose Object > Path > Split into Grid.

If you don't have the fonts...

Missing fonts? You can still open, edit, and save the file, because Illustrator remembers the fonts you were using. However, the text will not flow accurately and the file won't print correctly until you load or replace the missing fonts. Type objects that use missing fonts will be highlighted when Highlight Substituted Fonts is checked in the Type area of Document Setup.

the Glyphs palette to insert it in the text. You'll find many specialty characters (like ✳ or ✆), that once required separate fonts, sitting right there in your Glyphs palette.

THE EVERY-LINE COMPOSER

Illustrator offers two composition methods for determining where line breaks occur in blocks of text: the Single-line Composer and the Every-line Composer.

The Single-line Composer (which was the only option before CS) applies hyphenation and justification settings to one line of text at a time. But this can result in uneven, ragged-looking blocks of text, so the newer Every-line Composer thinks ahead by automatically determining the best combination of line breaks across the entire run of text. The result is even-looking text blocks with minimal hyphenation and consistent line lengths and spacing, without having to fine-tune line breaks by hand. However, if you're into micromanaging your text and you want manual control over every line break, you still have the option to choose the old Single-line Composer.

To choose between composition methods, select the text to be composed and choose Adobe Every-line Composer or Adobe Single-line Composer from the Paragraph palette menu.

MORE TYPE FUNCTIONS (TYPE & WINDOW MENUS)

- **Find Font:** If you try to open a file and don't have the correct fonts loaded, Illustrator warns you, lists the missing fonts, and asks if you still want to open the file. You do need the correct fonts to print properly; so if you don't have the missing fonts, choose Find Font to locate and replace them with ones you do have.

Find Font's dialog box displays the fonts used in the document in the top list; an asterisk indicates a missing font. The font type is represented by a symbol to the right of the font name. You can choose replacement fonts from ones on your system or those used in the document. To display only the font types you want to use as replacements, uncheck those you don't want to include in the list.

To replace a font used in the document, select it from the top list and choose a replacement font from the bottom list. You can individually replace each occurrence of the font by clicking Change and then Find. Otherwise, simply click Change All to replace all occurrences.

Note: *When you select a font in the top list, the first text object in the document using that font becomes selected.*

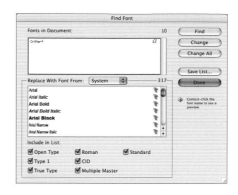

The Find Font dialog box

- **Type Orientation** lets you change orientation from horizontal to vertical, or vice versa, by choosing Type > Type Orientation > Horizontal or Vertical.

- **Change Case:** You can change the case of text selected with the Type tool via the new Type > Change Case submenu, which offers four choices: UPPERCASE, lowercase, Title Case, and Sentence case.

- **Fit Headline** is a quick way to open up the letter spacing of a headline across a specific distance. First, create the headline within an area, not along a path. Next, set the type in the size you wish to use. Select the headline by highlighting it, then choose Type > Fit Headline—the type will spread out to fill the area you've indicated. This works with both the Horizontal and Vertical Type tools.

- **Show Hidden Characters** reveals soft and hard returns, word spaces, and an oddly-shaped infinity symbol indicating the end of text flow. Toggle it on and off by choosing Type > Show Hidden Characters.

CONVERTING TYPE TO OUTLINES

You can use the Appearance palette to apply multiple strokes to editable type (see the *Layers & Appearances* chapter for details about working with multiple strokes or fills). You can also reliably mask with live, editable type! So although there are fewer and fewer reasons to convert your type to outlines, there are still some times when converting type to outlines is your best option (see "Why convert type to outlines?" following).

Choose text carefully!

Having access to dozens of fonts doesn't necessarily make you a type expert, any more than having a handful of pens makes you an artist. Experiment all you want, but if you need professional typographic results, consult a professional. Barbara Sudick designed this book.

Don't outline small type

If you're printing to a high-resolution imagesetter or using larger type sizes, you can successfully convert type objects to outlines. However, for several technical reasons, a *small* type object converted to outlines won't look as good on the computer screen, or print as clearly to printers of 600 dots per inch or less, as it would have if it had remained a font.

Illustrator supports multinational fonts, including Chinese, Japanese, and Korean. Check the Show Asian Options box in the Type area of Preferences to reveal Asian text options in the Character palette (if necessary, click on the double arrows on the Palette tab to fully expand it). To utilize multinational font capabilities you must have the proper fonts and language support activated on your system. Even then, some multinational options won't work with fonts that don't support the appropriate languages, including most fonts intended primarily for English and Western European languages.

Reflow text as in page layout

Resize a text block by its bounding box handles (select it with the Selection tool) and the text will reflow. —*Sandee Cohen*

It's Greek to me!

You can specify a size at which type will be "greeked" on screen (which means it will appear as gray bars rather than readable text). Set the greeking size by choosing Preferences > Type, and entering a size in the Greeking field. Text at or below that size will be greeked. Note that greeked text *prints* normally.

As long as you've created type with fonts you have installed on your system (and can print), and you've finished experimenting with your type elements (for example: adjusting size, leading, or kerning/tracking), you have the option to convert your live type to Illustrator objects. Your type will no longer be editable as type, but instead will be constructed of standard Illustrator Bézier curves that may include compound paths to form the "holes" in the outlined letter forms (such as the see-through centers of an **O**, **B**, or **P**).

As with all Illustrator paths, you can use the Direct Selection tool to select and edit the objects. To convert type to outlines, select all blocks of type you wish to outline (it doesn't matter if non-type objects are selected as well) and choose Type > Create Outlines. To fill the "holes" in letters with color, select the compound path and choose Object > Compound Path > Release (see the *Beyond Basic Drawing & Coloring* chapter for more about compound paths).

Note: *Outlining type is not recommended for small font sizes—see the Tip "Don't outline small type" earlier in this chapter introduction.*

Why convert type to outlines?

Here are several cases where this option may be useful:

• **So you can graphically transform or distort the individual curves and anchor points of letters or words.** Everything from the minor stretching of a word to an extreme distortion is possible. See the Galleries later in this chapter for examples. (Warp Effects and Envelopes can sometimes be used on live type for these purposes, too; see the *Live Effects & Graphic Styles* chapter.)

• **So you can maintain your letter and word spacing when exporting your type to another application.** Many programs that allow you to import Illustrator type as "live" editable text don't support the translation of your custom kerning and word spacing. Convert text to outlines before exporting Illustrator type in these instances, to maintain custom word and letter spacing.

- **So you don't have to supply the font to your client or service bureau.** Converting type can be especially useful when you need to use foreign language fonts, when your image will be printed while you're not around, or when you don't have permission to embed the fonts. If your service bureau doesn't have its own license for a font, your own license for the font may not permit you to give it to them. If this is the case, convert your fonts to outlines.

THE NEW DOUBLE-DUTY EYEDROPPER

The Eyedropper tool allows you to copy appearance attributes from one type object to another, including stroke, fill, character, and paragraph attributes. As previously discussed in the *Drawing & Coloring* chapter, because the old Paint Bucket tool has been removed to make way for Illustrator's new Live Paint Bucket tool, the Eyedropper tool has taken on new powers—it now both picks up and applies text formatting. (The Live Paint Bucket is used only for the new Live Paint feature; see *Beyond Basic Drawing & Coloring* for more on what the Live Paint Bucket does and doesn't do.)

The new double-duty Eyedropper has two modes: the *sampling* Eyedropper and the *applying* Eyedropper. To copy text formatting from one object to another using the Eyedropper, first select the Eyedropper from the Toolbox, and position it over an unselected type object. You'll see that the Eyedropper is in sampling mode (it angles downward to the left). When it's correctly positioned over the type object, a small **T** appears next to the Eyedropper. Click the type object to pick up its attributes.

Now position the Eyedropper over the unselected text object to which you want to apply the attributes you just sampled, and hold down the Option/Alt key. You'll see the Eyedropper switch to applying mode: it angles downward to the right, and looks full. As with the sampling Eyedropper, you'll see the small **T** when it's correctly posi-

Eyedropper options

To set what the Eyedropper picks up and applies, double-click the Eyedropper in the Toolbox to open the Eyedropper Options dialog box.

The sampling eyedropper, which picks up attributes, angles downward to the left. The small T next to the eyedropper appears when the eyedropper is correctly positioned—i.e., close enough to the text to sample its attributes by clicking

As you click on text with the sampling eyedropper, "ink" appears in the eyedropper to show that it has sampled the attributes of the text

The applying eyedropper, which appears when you press the Option/Alt key, functions like the old Paint Bucket used to in previous versions of Illustrator — it applies attributes to an object. Note that the applying eyedropper angles downward to the right, and is half full of ink. As with the sampling eyedropper, the small T appears when the eyedropper is correctly positioned over text. Then just Option/Alt-click the text to apply the previously sampled attributes

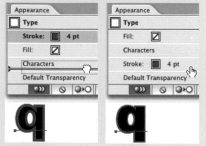
tioned over text. Click the text to apply the attributes you sampled from the first object.

Alternatively, you can first select the type object with appearance attributes you want to change, and then move the Eyedropper over the unselected type object from which you want to copy attributes. You'll see the small **T** when you're correctly positioned; click to sample the unselected object's attributes and apply them to the previously selected object.

USING THE APPEARANCE PALETTE WITH TYPE

When you work with type, you work with the letter characters or with the container that holds the characters—or both. Understanding the difference between characters and their container, (the "type object") will help you access and edit the right one when you style type. To help understand the difference, you'll need to watch the Appearance palette as you work.

Characters

When you click with the Type tool and enter text, you are working directly with the letter characters. In the Appearance palette, you'll see a blank Stroke and a black Fill listed underneath the Characters line in the palette. You can apply a color or pattern to a characters' fill and stroke. To edit a character's fill and stroke, drag across the text with the Type tool or double-click Characters in the Appearance palette.

These are some of the things you *can't* do when working with the characters (although you can with their containers): move the stroke under the fill or the fill above the stroke; apply a live effect to the fill or stroke; apply a gradient fill; add multiple fills or strokes; or change the opacity or blending mode.

The Type "object"

All text is contained in a Point, Area, or Path type object. You work with the object when you select the text with the Selection tool and move it on your page.

You can think of the type object as a group whose members are the letter characters. There are things you can do to this group that you couldn't do when working directly with the letter characters.

For example, you can add another fill (choose Add New Fill from the Appearance palette pop-up menu). Notice that the Appearance palette changes—now there is another listing of Fill and Stroke, but this time they are positioned above the Characters line in the palette. The fill and stroke you worked with at the character level still exist. You can reveal them by double-clicking Character in the palette. Doing so, however, brings you back to character editing; re-select the type object with the Selection tool to return to editing the type object rather than its characters.

When you add a new fill or stroke to the type object, its color or effects interact with the color of the characters. You can predict the visual results of changes to the type object and characters by knowing that all the fills and strokes applied to type are painted, with those listed at the top of the palette painted on top of those listed below (including the stroke and fill you see listed when you double-click Characters in the palette). So if you add a new fill and apply white to it, the type appears white (the white fill of the type object is stacked above the black fill of the characters).

To experiment with how this works, create two type objects in a large font size (72 pt, for example). Next, edit at the character level by dragging through one of the objects with the Type tool, and then changing the default black fill to red in the Appearance palette.

To edit at the type object level, select the other type object with the Selection tool. Add a new fill (choose Add New Fill from the Appearance palette menu); by default, the type object is filled with black, which will cover up the red fill you gave the character. With the type object still selected, click on the Swatches palette menu and choose Open Swatch Library > Other Library. In the dialog that opens, click on Patterns and then select Decorative >

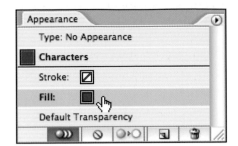

The Appearance palette showing the red fill applied to the type at the Character level

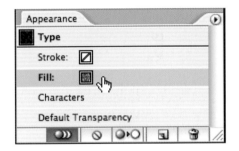

The Appearance palette showing the Chinese Spirals pattern (from the Decorative_Modern pattern library) filling the type at the type object level

BRYCE CANYON
Navajo Loop (Sunset Point)
1.3 miles (2.2 km) / 521 ft (159 m)
Moderate Hike: 1 to 2 hours
Attractions: Thors Hammer, Two Bridges, Wall Street

See Gordon's "Floating Type" lesson in the Transparency chapter to learn how to create transparent backgrounds for your area type objects

Typography

Typography

Typography

The original point type object at the top; in the middle, the same type object exported using Preserve Text Editability; at the bottom, the type object exported using Preserve Text Appearance

Decorative_Modern.ai. From the Decorative_Modern palette, click on Chinese Spirals swatch. When the type object fills with the pattern, the pattern's black objects overlay the red of the character, while its empty areas let the red show through.

Knowing the difference between a type object and its characters rewards you in this experiment. And it will help you understand later why bad things seem to happen to good type (like the black surrounding the red spirals) so that you can make good things happen to type. Reading and working through the lessons and galleries that follow will help you master the difference between characters and their type object.

SAVING AND EXPORTING ILLUSTRATOR TYPE

While the new Illustrator text engine opens the door to new levels of typographic control and flexibility, sending your typography out into the world may seem anything but controlled or flexible. Type objects in files that you save to legacy versions of Illustrator (Version 10 and before) or as EPS files will either be broken into groups of point or path type objects, or converted to outlines. Your only control is to select File > Document Setup > Type and choose Preserve Text Editability or Preserve Text Appearance from the Export menu.

As the figures at left show, choosing Preserve Text Editability breaks the word "typography" into a group of eight separate Point type objects. By contrast, choosing Preserve Text Appearance will convert all type to outlines. In either case, your type will be severely limited for others who need to use it in older versions of Illustrator.

You should test bringing Illustrator CS2 type into other applications before proceeding during a critical project or urgent deadline. While you may not need to edit the type in another program, you should ensure that it imports correctly and looks as it did in Illustrator CS2.

Lance Jackson/
San Francisco Chronicle

For the wonderful type "LONG STRANGE TRiP" in this poster for the cross-country "Green Tortoise" bus, illustrator Lance Jackson used a combination of many effects. Starting with the typeface Akzident ExtraBold, Jackson created three text blocks (one for each word) and chose a bright red fill. Combining so many effects creates unique results because of variables such as type size, kerning, and the ordering of effects, so just experiment. You can keep your type live or outline it (⌘-Shift-O/Ctrl-Shift-O). If you outline your text, you must then select it and choose Object > Compound Path > Make so it operates as one unit (see *Beyond Basic Drawing & Coloring* for more on compound paths). To emulate Jackson's effects using live effects, keep your type live and select one word at a time; then choose Effects > Distort & Transform > Zig Zag (do this to each of the words separately so you can vary the amount of Zig Zag you're applying). Next, make a green Live Effects offset version of the type so that if you change your type, the offset changes as well. Select all three words and group (⌘-G/Ctrl-G). From the Appearance palette pop-up menu, choose Add New Fill and choose a darker green color. Now

JACKSON

drag that green fill below the word "Contents" in the Appearance palette. Next, choose Effects > Distort & Transform > Transform and enter a small Move for Horizontal and Vertical (enable Preview) to offset the green version. Now select Group in the Appearance palette and start experimenting. Try applying Effects > Distort & Transform > Twist. From here, add additional live effects, or remove Twist and start again. See how this differs from Effects > Warp > Twist (see *Live Effects & Graphic Styles* for more about multiple fills and live effects). For the psychedelic border effects, Jackson used techniques similar to those in his gallery in the *Blends, Gradients & Mesh* chapter.

Curvaceous Type
Fitting Type to Curved Paths

HUERTA

Overview: *Create artwork objects; copy object paths, then cut the paths to workable length; add text to the paths and offset the text; convert type to outlines and edit character paths.*

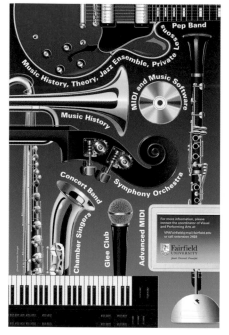

The finished poster for Fairfield University

1

The Outline view of the paths for the guitar

Using the flowing curves of musical instruments coupled with strings of text, designer Gerard Huerta captured the variety of musical studies offered by Fairfield University in this poster promoting its music program to campus and high school students. To give the type characters a more organic fit with the tight curves of some of the instruments, Huerta converted the type to outlines and then edited the shapes of the character paths.

1 Sketching and scanning the shapes, then redrawing them in Illustrator. Huerta started the poster by sketching the shapes of musical instruments by pencil. Then he scanned the drawing and placed the scan in Illustrator as a template layer. By using the Pen tool to draw the shapes, and using gradients and gradient meshes for color, Huerta built the musical instruments and then arranged them to leave space for the text he would create next.

2 Drawing paths for type and creating the type on the paths. You can draw the paths that will parallel your objects with the Pen or Pencil tool for setting type, or, like Huerta, use copies of the objects themselves. First, copy the path you want the type to parallel and paste in front (Edit > Paste in Front) so the copy directly overlays the original. Use the Scissors tool to cut the path so that it's an open-ended path instead of a closed path. Next, with the Type tool, click on the line and type the words you want on that path. Grab the type's I-beam and slide it along the path to position the text—flip it to the other side of the path if the text you typed ended up on the wrong side of the path. Make sure that the Character palette is open and your type is still selected. From the Character palette, enter a negative number in the Baseline Shift field or pick a negative number from the field's pop-up menu. Adjust the offset of the type from its path by increasing or decreasing the Baseline Shift value. Reshape the path by using the Direct Selection tool or by drawing over a section of the path with the Pencil tool.

3 **Converting type to outlines, then editing character paths.** Violins and guitars have sharply curved bodies that can make some letter characters look too angular and straight when positioned along the curve of the path. To correct this, Huerta changed the shapes of individual letter characters so that their strokes conformed more naturally to the curved shape of the path.

You can change character shapes by first converting the type to outlines. (Make copies of the type first in case you need to edit the type or its paths later.) To do this, select the Path-type object (don't select the text itself using the Type tool) and choose Type > Create Outlines. Look for characters with parallel strokes, like **m**, **n**, **h**, and **u**. Using the Direct Selection tool, move points and adjust control handles to reshape the characters. Use the Pencil tool to reshape character paths by drawing over or near a selected path. Huerta relied on the Direct Selection and Pencil tools to add curves to the straight edges of the original character shapes. He also changed the angle of some character strokes so that the characters appeared to bend with the tight curve of their paths.

Spacey characters

If you choose Auto from the Kerning field in the Character palette, Illustrator CS2 may cause letters to overlap or to be spaced too far apart on tightly curved Path-type objects. To fix this, you may need to manually kern letter pairs by clicking the Type tool between two characters and adjusting the Kerning value.

2

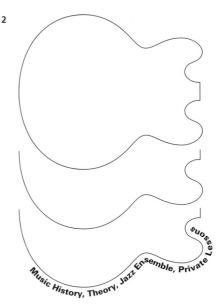

The Outline view of the original outer path for the guitar body (top); path cut from the guitar path (middle); text added to the path and then offset using a negative Baseline Shift

3

On the left, the letter **T** character from the Univers font; on the right, the **T** character after Huerta edited the character's outline paths by curving the top stroke of the letter

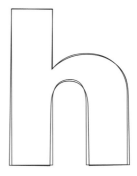

The original letter **h** character shown here as a magenta outline; superimposed on the original letter **h** is the black outline of the **h** that Huerta edited by angling the bottoms of the vertical strokes

Book Cover Design

Illustrator as a Stand-alone Layout Tool

Overview: *Set your document size; place guides and crop marks; place image files and make Area type for columns and Point type for graphic typography; visually track type to fit.*

Page layout programs such as InDesign and QuarkXPress are essential for producing multi page, complex documents. However, Rob Day and Virginia Evans often use Illustrator for single-page projects such as book jackets.

1 **Setting up your page.** Choose File > Document Setup to set up the Artboard for your design. Click on landscape or portrait page orientation and enter your Artboard size, making sure it's large enough for crop and/or registration marks (the "Size" parameter will automatically switch to "Custom"). Choose View > Show Rulers and "re-zero" your ruler origin to the upper left corner of where your page will begin (see the *Basics* chapter for more on repositioning the ruler origin), and use View > Outline/Preview to toggle between Outline and Preview modes. Although you can generate uniform grids with Preferences > Guides & Grid, for columns of varying sizes, Day and Evans numerically created two sets of rectangles: one for trims, and one for bleeds. With the Rectangle tool, click on your artboard to specify the Width and Height dimensions for the trim area. Next immediately Option-click/Alt-click on the center-point of the trim-area box to specify .25" larger in Width and Height to create a rectangle specify-

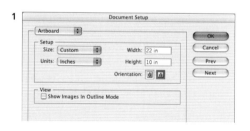

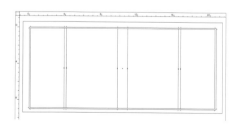

Setting up the Artboard and layout specs

ing a 125" bleed area. Day and Evans made trim and bleed boxes for the front, back, flaps, and spine. To place an overall trim mark, select the boxes that define the entire trim area and choose Filter > Create > Crop Marks.

2 Customizing your guides. Select your trim and bleed boxes (not the crop marks) and create Guides by choosing View > Guides > Make Guides.

3 Placing and refining the elements. Choose File > Place to select a raster image to import into your layout. Create rectangles or other objects which will define the area for columns of text. Click on the path of one of these objects with the Area Type tool. Once the text cursor is placed, you can type directly or paste text. Area Type is used in this layout for columns of type on the flaps. Alternatively, click on you page with the Type tool to create Point type, for titles, headlines, and other individual type elements. To track type visually, select a text object and use the ← or → key with Option/Alt. For help rotating or scaling (this applies to text objects as well), see the *Zen of Illustra-tor* chapter and the *Zen Lessons* on the *Wow! CD* (in the Ch02 The Zen of Illustrator folder in the Chapters folder) .

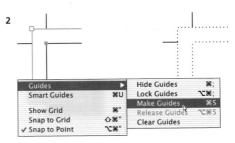

Creating "Crop Marks" versus "Crop Area"

Every time you choose Filter > Create > Crop Marks, you'll make a set of visible (selectable) Illustrator crop marks that indicate the bounding area of your cur-rent selection. Use Object > Crop Area > Make to create *one* set of *non*-selectable crop marks that are visible in Illustrator, but invisibly mark the crop area when placed into programs such as Photoshop (see "Soft-ware Relay" lesson in the *Illustrator & Other Programs* chapter). You can specify the area with a selected rect-angle or, if nothing is selected, the crop area will be sized to the Artboard. To remove a "crop area," choose Object > Crop Area > Release, or, since there can be only one Crop Area per file, make a new selection and choose Object > Crop Area > Make.

Converting trim and bleed boxes into Guides

All of the elements placed into the layout

A TIRELESS PERFORMER, CONDUCTOR, AND ambassador for opera, Plácido Domingo is one of today's greatest and most popular ten-ors His remarkably diverse and challanging repertoire includes opera, operettas, musicals, Spanish and Mexican folk songs, and popular

Close-ups of an Area Type object

PLÁCIDO DOMINGO

Close-ups of Point Type objects

CORNELIUS SCHNAUBER

CORNELIUS SCHNAUBER

CORNELIUS SCHNAUBER

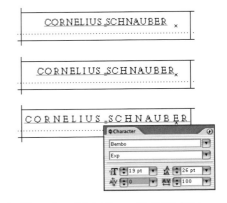

Tracking a line of Point Type with Arrow keys

Stretching Type

Fitting Type by Converting to Outline

Overview: *Enter type onto individual lines of point type objects; transform type into outlines; custom justify type by Lassoing or Direct-Selecting partial paths and stretching the horizontal strokes of the letterforms using the Arrow keys.*

1

Weinstein began by pulling out a set of vertical guides from the rulers. He then entered the body text line by line to avoid unattractive line breaks and hyphenation

Though there are more ways than ever to modify your type characters while keeping the text "live" for future editing, there are still some adjustments that require you to "outline" your type characters.

To create this beautiful *Ketubah* (traditional Hebrew wedding certificate), Ari M. Weinstein had to observe strict design guidelines, since the *Ketubah* needed to serve the dual role of legal document and work of art. The guidelines required the text to be fully justified and enclosed within a decorative border. Traditionally, in order to justify Hebrew text, calligraphers elongated the horizontal strokes of individual letterforms, instead of using paragraph justification (which would result in non-uniform word and letter spacing). To replicate this method, Weinstein needed to outline the type, so he could stretch individual horizontal strokes.

1 **Placing the text.** Having chosen a calligraphic-style Hebrew font, Weinstein entered his text line by line on unconnected Point type paths in order to avoid automatic

text wrap. This allowed him to maintain control over word placement from one line to the next. He inserted two lines below the main text for witness signatures.

2 Converting the text to outlines. Since converting type to outlines is permanent, make sure that you carefully proof and spell-check your text first. After proofing his text, Weinstein selected each single line of text and chose Type > Create Outlines (⌘-Shift-O/Ctrl-Shift-O) to convert each line of characters to outlines. Converting each line separately automatically groups the converted characters together.

3 Stretching a letter's horizontal strokes. Weinstein was now able to replicate the traditional scribal method of crafting the length of each line by stretching the horizontal strokes on the letterforms. In order to stretch a horizontal stroke, Weinstein used the Direct Selection and the Lasso tools to select the left side of a letter's outline. With these portions of the letterform selected, he then stretched them in 1-pt increments using the left Arrow key. He adjusted the spacing between entire words and individual characters by using the Group Selection tool and similarly moving them using the Arrow keys. Weinstein was able to justify the text block perfectly, using the ruler guides to the left and right of the main body text.

4 Finalizing the *Ketubah*. Weinstein was required by tradition to omit one leg of the letter *Kuf* in a word near the end of the text (the eighth word from the right on the last line of the main text). This letter segment was to be drawn by hand on the wedding day in front of the rabbi. The vertical stroke of the letter was selected and deleted. Weinstein brought his calligraphy tools along to the wedding to officially complete the *Ketubah* as part of the prenuptial proceedings. The dove at the top of the *Ketubah* encloses the bride's and groom's initials, hand drawn by Weinstein.

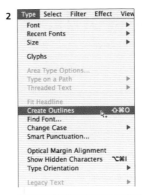

One by one, the individual lines of copy were Direct-Selected and converted to outline. Each resulting set of paths was automatically grouped for easier selection later

Direct-Selecting the path segments of the cross-strokes and stretching them with the Arrow keys

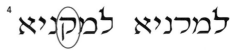

After Direct-Selecting the vertical cross-stroke of the letter Kuf, Weinstein deleted it

PAPCIAK-ROSE

Masking Words

Masking Images with Letter Forms

Overview: *Create text on top of a placed raster image; select all and make the text into a clipping mask for the placed image.*

Text using the HooskerDoo typeface (it includes the splotches), placing scanned fabric and moving it below the type using the Layers palette

After selecting the type and the image below, choosing Object > Clipping Mask > Make

With the clipping mask and type kept live, it's easy to change the typeface, the linked art, the type size, and the text

This "Africa" type treatment (using the HooskerDoo font) was created by Johannesburg South Africa-based artist Ellen Papciak-Rose. Working on shoestring budgets for non-profit organizations, Papciak-Rose often scans regional textiles and crafts to incorporate into her work.

1 Creating text and placing an image. Select a typeface with sufficient weight for an image to show through (HooskerDoo includes the splotches) and create text with the Type tool. Choose File > Place, select an image, enable Link, disable Template, and click OK. In a clipping mask, the topmost selected object becomes the mask. To use your type as a mask, in the Layers palette, expand your layer and move the <Linked File> below your type.

2 Creating the clipping mask. Select the text and the image to be masked and choose Object > Clipping Mask > Make; this will group the mask and the masked objects.

3 Making changes to image and text. Select an object or the mask to adjust its position. To select type with the Direct Selection tool, click on it (or along its baseline); select the image by clicking outside the type, where the image is. (If you have difficulty Direct-Selecting text or the image, find it in the Layers palette and click in the space to the right of its target icon.) Once you have selected the object with the Direct Selection tool or by using the cursor keys. With type selected you can change many attributes (such as size or typeface) in the Control palette, or in the Character palette (Window > /Type > Character, or ⌘-T/Ctrl-T). To change the background image, select it and click its name in the Control palette to access the Relink option, then locate the replacement file. To change the text, select it with the Type tool and retype!

Transforming Conflict, TRANSFORMiNG LIVES

The emergence of Partners in Conflict Transformation (PICOT)

SIERRA LEONE

Case study: A conflict transformation approach to peace and development work By: Richard Smith

PAPCIAK-ROSE (Photographer: Richard Smith)

Ellen Papciak-Rose

Using similar techniques as in the lesson opposite, Ellen Papciak-Rose created this cover for a 64-page book by Richard Smith (he is also the photographer). She used a cropped copy of the woman's skirt from the photo for the fabric in the words "SIERRA LEONE." Papciak-Rose chose the light blue and lime green color scheme to match the colors of the Sierra Leone flag.

Brushed Type

Applying Brushes to Letterforms

Overview: *Create centerlines for font characters; customize art brushes and apply brushes to the centerlines and outlines of the letterforms to simulate hand-rendered lettering.*

For a map title that looked artistic, Steven Gordon blended the traditional artistry of pencil and brush with the classicism of serif font characters. Because Illustrator applies brushes as strokes, not fills, Gordon drew centerlines for the font characters before painting the centerlines with natural-looking customized brushes.

1

Original characters from Garamond font, filled with gray

1 Creating letter centerlines and outlines. To re-create Gordon's painted lettering, begin by typing text in a serif font (Gordon chose Garamond Bold Condensed Italic and 112 pt from the Character palette). Select the text and give it a 20% black Fill so you can see the letterforms while drawing the centerlines later. Copy the layer with the text by dragging the layer onto the Create New Layer icon at the bottom of the palette. To create the font outline, select the text on the copied layer and convert the characters to outlines (Type > Create Outlines), then change their Fill to None and Stroke to gray. Now create a new layer (click the Create New Layer icon in the Layers palette) and drag this layer between the other two. In this new layer, draw centerlines for each font character with the Pen or Pencil tool. The paths don't have to be smooth or centered inside the letterforms because you will paint them with an irregularly shaped brush in the next step. Finally, change the gray fill of the bottom layer letters to another color or to a gradient (as Gordon did).

Letterform centerlines hand drawn with the Pencil tool in a layer above the font characters

Font characters with a radial gradient replacing the original gray fill in a layer below gray-stroked copy of font characters

2 Creating and applying custom brushes and effects. Gordon looked to Illustrator's brushes to give the letter centerlines the color and spontaneity of traditional

Top, the default Splash brush; below, the edited brush with color fills

brushwork. He opened the Artistic_Paintbrush brush palette (Window > Brush Libraries > Artistic_Paintbrush) and selected the Splash brush. To customize a brush, first drag the brush from the palette to the canvas. Select each brush object with the Direct Selection tool and replace the gray with a color. Next, drag the brush artwork into the Brushes palette and select New Art Brush from the New Brush dialog box. In the Art Brush Options dialog box, further customize the brush by changing Width to 50%, enabling the Proportional brush setting, and clicking OK. (You won't see the change in width displayed in the dialog box's preview.) Make several brush variations by copying the brush and then editing brush Direction, Width and other parameters. Now individualize your letterforms by selecting the first centerline and clicking on a brush from the Brushes palette. Try several of the brushes you created to find the best "fit." Continue applying brushes to the remaining centerlines.

To create the look of loose pencil tracings for the character outlines on the top layer, Gordon edited the Dry Ink brush from the Artistic_PaintBrush library palette, changing its Width to 10% in the Art Brush Options dialog box. He completed the look by selecting each character outline and applying the Roughen Effect (Size−1%, Distort=10%, Smooth). (See the *Layers & Appearances* and *Live Effects & Graphic Styles* chapters to learn more about using the Appearance palette and applying Effects.)

3 Finishing touches. Gordon selected all the centerlines and offset them up and left while moving the font outlines down and right from the original font characters on the bottom layer, suggesting a loose style. He also simulated the look of hand-rendering by adjusting the transparency and blending modes of the brushed letterforms: he selected the centerline objects, and in the Transparency palette, chose Multiply mode and reduced transparency to 75%. This caused the colors of brushed centerline paths to darken where they overlapped, mimicking the effect of overlapping transparent inks.

Experimenting by applying different brushes to centerlines to lend individuality to the letter

On top, the Dry Ink brush; left, the customized brush applied to the font outline; right, the Roughen Effect applied to the brushed outline

Artwork on three layers, from bottom layer (left) to top layer (right)

3

Left, the horizontal and vertical centerlines of the letter "t" with Normal blending mode and 100% opacity; right, strokes placed to form letter "t" and with Multiply blending mode and 70% opacity

Finished lettering on three layers, shown in composite view

Making a Typeface

Creating a Typeface from a Grid

Overview: *Create a grid and draw letter shapes; combine and cut shapes with pathfinders; use shapes to build other letters; use transparency to integrate the letters with other artwork.*

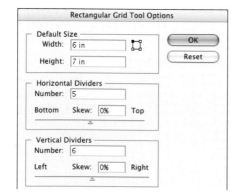

Inspired by the Cyrillic type adorning the film posters of avant garde Russian Constructivists, and drawing on her own Eastern European heritage, Caryl Gorska designed a typeface in the course of creating this self-promotion poster. After crafting the type, Gorska developed the poster artwork and added words set in her typeface.

1 Defining the working grid for creating the alphabet. Gorska began the poster by constructing the letter characters. She drew the letters directly on-screen instead of on paper because the geometric nature of the characters benefited from Illustrator's precise measuring, drawing, and editing tools (Pen, Pencil and the Pathfinders).

You'll discover another benefit of using Illustrator when you create letter characters: grids. Why grids? A grid helps save production time and improve the character of your typeface by spreading visual consistency across varied letterforms. To make a grid, decide whether the guiding shape of your letterforms will be a square or a rectangle. If it's a square, use Illustrator's Guides & Grid tab, found within the Illustrator > Preferences dialog. Simply set the size and number of subdivisions that you want in order to create an artboard-wide grid.

If the dominant letter shape is rectangular, then select the Rectangular Grid tool found within the Line Segment tool in the Tools palette. With the tool selected, click on the artboard to display the Rectangular Grid Tool Options dialog. Specify the overall grid size using the

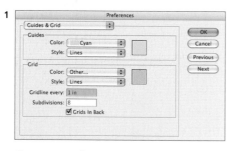

Illustrator's Preferences dialog

1

Using the Rectangular Grid Tool Options dialog to create a grid

Default Size fields and the proportions of the grid cells using the Horizontal and Vertical Dividers fields.

2 Drawing, and copying and pasting objects, to build the letterforms. Gorska made full use of Illustrator's tools in drawing and editing the letter characters: Pen and Pencil for drawing shapes, the Pathfinders for combining shapes or cutting letter counters (holes) from the shapes, and the Direct Selection tool for fine-tuning the control points of curves to vary letter proportions. Gorska started with basic characters like **o**, **e**, **b** and **r** that visually define the general look of the other letter characters. Once you complete several basic characters, arrange them in pairs or words to test how well they look together. Feel free to access the artwork of these characters when building other letters that are similar in structure. You can recycle shapes like stems, serifs, punctuation marks, and counters throughout the alphabet to speed up your work and make the typeface more visually consistent.

Adding a twist to her typeface, Gorska designed a second set of letterforms based on an oval shape using the same grid, complementing the rectangular shapes of the first set she created. This gave her the freedom to mix shapes when arranging the letters as words for a more eclectic look.

3 Drawing background art, composing words, and changing type opacity. To complete the poster, Gorska filled facial and geometric background shapes she drew with blends and gradients. Then she composed the words "red scare" from the letter characters she'd drawn earlier and positioned them over the artwork. She grouped the characters and changed their opacity in the Control palette to 20% to blend them visually with the artwork in the background. Setting her name against the gradient at the top of the poster, Gorska gave each yellow letter a stroke using the same red as the color well in the gradient behind the letters. This unified the appearance of the letters with the background colors in the poster.

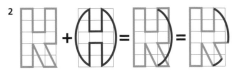

Using the parts of one letter (shown in red) in constructing another letter (shown in green)

Forming the letter counters, shown here as red shapes, by punching a hole using the Pathfinder palette's Subtract from shape area Shape Mode and then its Expand button

Letters with 20% opacity applied from the Control palette

Red-stroked letters set against a gradient

Expand your repertoire

It's easy to re-create an out-of-print typeface using non-copyrighted type found in antique books, or from a royalty-free source like Dover Publications (www.doverpublications.com). Draw the fundamental shapes and copy and paste them to construct the rest of the typeface.

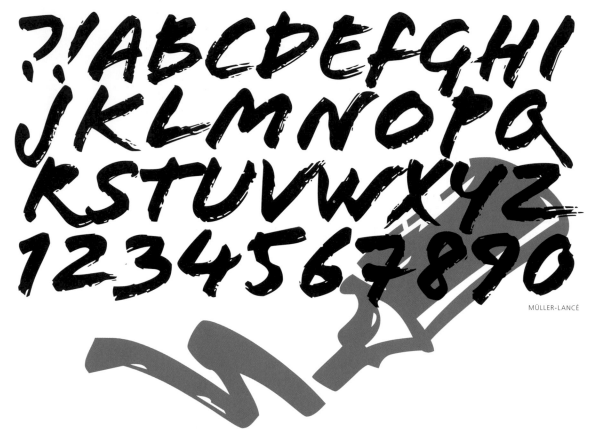

MÜLLER-LANCÉ

Joachim Müller-Lancé

The original characters of Joachim Müller-Lancé's Flood typeface were drawn with a worn felt marker during a type seminar hosted by Sumner Stone. Two years later Müller-Lancé rediscovered the drawings when Adobe asked him for new font ideas. Realizing that the original character traces were not of font quality, he redrew all of the characters using Illustrator's Pen and Pencil tools. He composed many of the characters as separate, black-filled objects, which he moved around while also adjusting width, slant, and scale until he got the look he wanted. He used the Merge command from

the Pathfinder palette to join the overlapping objects of each character into a single shape. He also drew the holes and streaks as white-filled objects below the black-filled objects and used Minus Back (also from the Pathfinder palette) to knock out the holes and streaks in the characters. Then Müller-Lancé copied the artwork for each character and pasted it directly into the appropriate character slot in Fontographer, where he completed the font.

FISHAUF

Louis Fishauf / Reactor Art + Design

Asked to create the visual identity for a pro-
posed news cafe and media tower, designer
Louis Fishauf drew the letters for the name
with the Pen tool, first assigning a thick stroke
to the paths and then outlining the strokes
(Object > Path > Outline Stroke). He moved
points in the letter tips using the Direct Selection tool, angling the tips parallel to the black
lines behind the name. To convey perspective,
Fishauf pasted copies of the letters **t** and **H**
behind the name, filled them with black, and
manually offset each of these shadows to the
left or right. For the letters **R** and **c**, Fishauf
drew the shadows with the Pen tool, keeping
the curves parallel to the white letterforms
in front.

Crunching Type

Transforming Type with Warps & Envelopes

Overview: *Create and color a title using Appearances; use a warp effect to bow type; create an outline shape to "crunch" type; give the crunched type a dynamic, curved perspective effect using an envelope warp.*

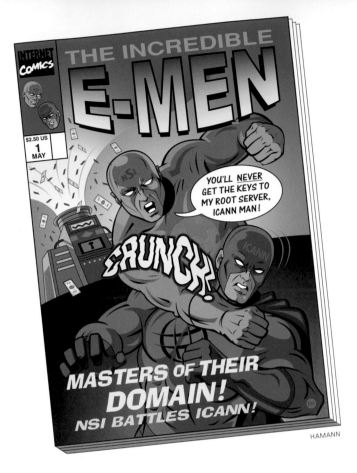

HAMANN

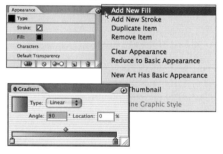

Using Add New Fill in the Appearance palette menu to add a gradient fill to the type

Warps and Envelopes are your superheroes for transforming headline type into any form you wish. No more need to convert type to outlines and laboriously move each anchor point by hand. Using Envelopes, it's literally as easy as drawing an outline and commanding the type to conform. With Warps and Envelopes, the type remains editable no matter how much you "crunch" it. Warps and Envelopes are always on hand to help rescue you from those looming deadlines!

1 Creating and coloring the E-Men title. To create the E-MEN cover title, Brad Hamann used 72-point Arial Black font, with a 2-pt black stroke. Because you can't just click on a gradient to fill type characters, he had to first select the type with a selection tool, and then choose Add New Fill from the Appearance palette menu.

2 Using a Warp effect to make the E-Men bow. There are 15 standard Warp shapes that can be turned into styles. For "E-MEN," Hamann applied Effect > Warp > Arc Lower. With Preview enabled, he used the Bend slider to bow the bottom of the letters (to 23%), then clicked OK.

Effect > Warp works in many instances, but it didn't warp his gradient fill along with the type. After applying Undo, Hamann chose Object > Envelope Distort > Envelope Options, enabled Distort Linear Gradients, and applied Object > Envelope Distort > Make with Warp, with the Arc Lower option at 23%.

3 Using a path to "crunch" type. To create the "CRUNCH!" Hamann again used the Appearance palette, this time to color "Crunch!" with a subtle gradient fill and a strong red stroke. Then, starting with a rectangle, he applied Object > Path > Add Anchor points twice, and then moved the rectangle's anchor points to form a dynamic jagged path. He then placed the path over the type, and with both the path and type selected he chose Object > Envelope Distort > Make with Top Object.

4 Using Envelope Distort > Make with Warp to create a curved perspective effect. To create a curved perspective effect, use Envelope Distort > Make with Warp to warp the "crunched" type. Because you can't nest one envelope inside another, first select your "crunched" type and choose Object > Envelope Distort > Expand. With your expanded type selected, choose Object > Envelope Distort > Make with Warp. Choose Arc in the Style pop-up menu of the Warp Options dialog box, and adjust the sliders until you find the desired curved perspective look.

5 Adjusting and adding a stroke to the type. To complete the "CRUNCH!" type, Hamann used Object > Envelope Distort > Edit Contents to adjust the type. Using the Appearance palette, he added (in order) a yellow gradient fill, a 5 point black stroke, and a 10 point red stroke to the envelope enclosing the type to get the desired final effect.

2

With Effect > Warp > Arc Lower, the gradient fill remains horizontal

Using Object > Warp > Make with Warp (with Distort Linear Gradients enabled in the Envelope Options dialog box), the gradient bends also

3

The type and path before and after applying Object > Envelope Distort > Make with Top

4

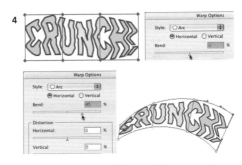

The released type; with Warp sliders set to 0 showing the starting envelope shape; the final Warp option settings; the resultant envelope

5

The final strokes and the finished type

Type Subtraction

Applying Live Subtract from Shape on Type

Advanced Technique

Overview: *Create several interleaved groups of shapes; create type objects and a shape; subtract the shape from the type using the Pathfinder palette.*

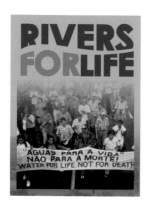

1

Left, the three groups of wave shapes made from one group (top); right, their combination in the final form used in the logo

Rotate by center

When you double-click the Rotate tool, Illustrator automatically sets the rotation centerpoint at the exact center of the selected artwork. This means your copy precisely overlays the original on the Artboard.

For a conference on protecting the world's rivers, Innosanto Nagara of Design Action designed a logo that could appear in applications as diverse as posters, report covers, and t-shirts—and stand out against a variety of backgrounds, including a solid black square and a photograph. Illustrator's Pathfinder effect subtracted Nagara's wave shapes, leaving a gap between the logo type that would remain invisible against different backgrounds.

1 Creating a wave shape, rotating and copying it, and reflecting and copying it. Nagara designed the logo as two components: the conference title, "Rivers For Life," split into two lines, and the interleaving colored waves that separated them. To re-create Nagara's design, begin by drawing a set of curved blue shapes. Instead of drawing a second set of green waves, select the blue wave shapes you just drew with the Selection tool, and then double-click the Rotate tool. In the Rotate dialog, enter 180° in the Angle field and then click the Copy button. With the copy still selected, change its fill color from blue to green.

With the set of green waves still selected, complete the interleaving of blue and green waves by creating a third set of wave shapes. Use the Reflect tool this time (you can access this tool by pressing the mouse button down on the Rotate tool icon in Illustrator's tool palette). In the Reflect dialog, set the reflection axis to Horizontal and click the Copy button. Then change the fill of the wave shapes to blue, producing a blue-to-green-to-blue series of inter-leaving wave shapes.

2 Creating two type objects, drawing a subtracting shape, then applying the Pathfinder effect. Suggesting the action of waves, Nagara decided to use a flowing wave shape to cut into the top and bottom edges of the logo's lettering. To ensure that the wave shape allows the different backgrounds to appear, you'll need to cut into the lettering with your shapes and not simply paste the shape in front of the type to visually block it.

After typing the two lines of type as separate type objects, Nagara drew a new wave shape with the Pen tool and copied it so he could use it later with the second line of type. He moved the wave shape over the type until it blocked the lettering the way he wanted.

Then he selected the type object and the wave shape and, from the Shape Modes section of the Pathfinder palette, he clicked the Subtract from shape area icon.

To maintain the separate colors in "FOR" and "LIFE," Nagara selected the first word and chose Paste in Front to overlay the wave shape in front of that second line of lettering. Selecting that word and the wave, he clicked Subtract from shape area to cut the wave shape from the object. He then repeated the sequence for the other word.

3 Selecting the subtracting and modifying the subtracting shape. When you apply one of the Pathfinder's Shape Modes to artwork, the result is a compound path in which the top object (in Nagara's case, the wave shape that subtracts from the type object below it) remains "live" and editable. You can select and modify the subtracting shape with the Direct Selection tool, or redraw with the Pencil tool if you'd like. This is especially useful when the uneven contours and counters (holes) of a line of lettering require you to tweak the subtracting shape. If you use the same object more than once, as Nagara did, you can tweak each one to make them appear a little different, giving greater spontaneity to the finished artwork.

2

Type with the wave shape that will subtract from the type

The wave placed on top of the top type object and the resulting cut in the type

Top shows the wave pasted above word "FOR" and then after then applying the Subtract from shape area from the Pathfinder palette; bottom shows these steps repeated for the word "LIFE"

The Pathfinder palette and the Subtract from shape area icon (the Subtract function remains "live" unless the Expand button is pressed)

3 RIVERS

Using the Direct Selection tool to select the subtracting shape to modify it points

Avoiding strokes

When working with a compound shape, remember that selecting the subtracting shape and applying a stroke will not change how much that shape cuts into the object below it. Adding a stroke or increasing its width will affect the bottom object—when that object is type, a stroke will change how the letter characters look.

Olde Offset Fills

Covering a Pattern with an Offset Fill

Advanced Technique

Overview: *Create a pattern using Scribble effect; apply the pattern to letter characters; add a new fill to the text object; choke the new fill by applying a negative Offset effect; use Roughen to warp type edges.*

1

Top, black rectangle; Below, with Scribble applied to fill

Scribble Options dialog box

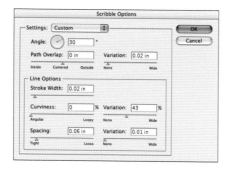

Top, Scribble effect expanded to a path; Below, Thick Pencil brush applied to scribble pattern path

ye Olde Inne

COHEN

Filling lettering with patterns is a simple way of turning familiar fonts into fresh designs. Sometimes, though, you want a pattern to fill only part of each letter character. Finding a way to block patterns from the center of letter strokes was a challenge that Sandee Cohen, AKA VectorBabe, solved in creating this logo.

1 Creating and expanding a pattern, applying a brush, saving the pattern as a swatch. Breaking the edges of type is the key to making font lettering look aged. Illustrator's Scribble effect is a perfect tool for replacing the solid fill of letter characters with an irregular pattern. Cohen started by drawing a rectangle and filling it with black. With the rectangle selected, she chose Effect > Stylize > Scribble. In the Scribble Options dialog box, Cohen customized the default values until she was satisfied with the loose drawing style the effect produced.

You can further customize the scribbled object by turning it into a path and applying a brush to it. To do this, make sure the scribble rectangle is selected and then choose Object > Expand Appearance. This converts the Scribble effect in the rectangle into a path. Cohen applied the Thick Pencil brush (from Brush Libraries > Artistic_ChalkCharcoalPencil) to the expanded scribbled path.

In order to use the scribble object with the type you'll create, convert your brushed scribble object into a pattern swatch by dragging it to the Swatches palette.

2 Creating the type and filling it with the scribble pattern. Once your pattern is made, you're ready to create your text. First, open the Appearance palette—this will help you see whether you're editing the characters or their type object as you perform the following steps. Select the Type tool from the Toolbox, click on the Artboard, and type your text (Cohen used 72-pt Caslon). Select the characters by dragging through the text with the Type tool; the text will have a black fill. Then select the Fill attribute in the Appearance palette and select your scribble pattern from the Swatches palette.

3 Adding a new fill, applying the Offset effect and using the Roughen effect. Cohen needed a way of covering up the scribble pattern in the centers of the letters. Using the Offset effect, she created a fill that covered part of the lettering underneath. To do this, first select the type object by clicking on it with the Selection tool. Now, create a new fill by choosing Add New Fill from the Appearance palette menu. The new fill, by default, will be colored black and will completely cover the pattern that filled the letters. With the new fill selected, choose Effect > Path > Offset Path and, from the pop-up Offset Path dialog box, enter a negative value in the Offset field. Be sure that the Preview box is checked so you can gauge the visual effect of the number you enter in the Offset field. (Cohen used -1 pt for Offset.)

Complete the aging of your type by applying Roughen to the type object's fill to warp its edges. Select the type object with the Selection tool and choose Effect > Distort & Transform > Roughen. Because Cohen used a font with thin character strokes and serifs, she entered a small value for Size (0.4 pt), and selected Absolute, to be sure that the edges were not overly distorted.

A pattern of change

Pattern swatches are global. If you edit or create a pattern, simply drag the artwork with the Option/Alt key depressed and drop it on the swatch in the Swatches palette. The pattern filling your type will automatically change to the new pattern.

2

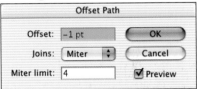

Top, the type with default black fill; right, the black fill replaced by the pattern

3

Offset Path effect applied to the new fill (shown here filled with gray instead of black), and the Offset Path dialog box

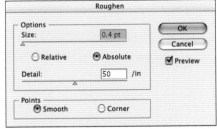

Roughen effect applied to the new fill (shown here in gray), and the Roughen dialog box

Enlargement of two letters

Antiquing Type

Applying Scribble in an Opacity Mask

Advanced Technique

Overview: *Create a type object; copy the object, then style the text with the Roughen effect; create an Opacity Mask and paste the type object; apply the Scribble effect to the Opacity Mask; return to Outline mode.*

WEINSTEIN

1

Top, the original type object with letter characters filled with black; bottom, the type object filled with a custom gradient

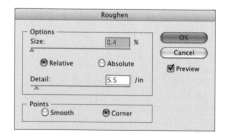

The Roughen dialog box

Every type is unique

Your settings for one type object will look different applied to another typeface. Experiment!

When you want to recreate a hand-rendered or historical look, but don't want to stray from the fonts you're already using in a project, consider using Illustrator's Effect menu and an Opacity Mask. Ari Weinstein created this poster title for the African Art exhibit at the Bundy Museum in Binghamton, N.Y. by using an Opacity Mask and the Scribble effect to chip away the edges of lettering, turning contemporary type into antiqued letters.

1 Creating text, adding a new Fill, and applying the Roughen effect. Weinstein started the poster title by typing "African Art" using the font Marigold. Before taking his type any further, Weinstein clicked on the Selection tool and then chose Edit > Copy. (You'll need a copy of the type object for the Opacity Mask that you'll make later in the second step.)

Then Weinstein was ready to start styling his type. First, he made sure the type object was still selected. He then opened the Appearance palette and chose Add New Fill from the palette menu. Weinstein clicked on the new Fill attribute in the palette and applied a gradient he had built from brown colors sampled from other artwork in the poster. (For information on creating or editing gradients, refer to the *Blends, Gradients & Mesh* chapter.)

You can simulate a hand-rendered look by applying the Roughen effect. This will change the smooth, precise edges of an object to jagged or bumpy edges. To roughen your type object, make sure the Fill attribute is not selected (deselect it by clicking in an empty area of the Appearance palette) so that Roughen will be applied to the whole object. Then choose Effect > Distort & Transform > Roughen. In the Roughen dialog, adjust the Size, Detail, and Points controls. (Weinstein chose Size=0.5, Detail=6.5, and Points=Smooth for his type.)

2 **Pasting the type object, creating an Opacity Mask, pasting the object and applying Scribble.** You can antique your type by making it look chipped or scratched. To do this, select your type object, open the Transparency palette and, from the palette menu, choose Make Opacity Mask from the palette menu. Next, click on the Opacity Mask thumbnail (the rightmost thumbnail) and make sure Clip and Invert Mask are checked. Lastly, paste the type you copied in the first step (use Paste in Front instead of Paste so this copy will overlay the original you copied).

Changes you make in the Opacity Mask will affect the transparency of the original type object—black artwork in the mask will punch holes in the original type. With the copy you just pasted still selected, choose Effect > Stylize > Scribble. In the Scribble dialog box, choose one of the ready made settings from the Settings menu, or customize the effect using the dialog box's controls. Weinstein started with the Sharp setting and then changed several of its values. With the dialog box's Preview enabled, he moved the Path Overlap slider to 0.04" to thin some of the chips in the edges. He also changed the Angle from the default, 30°, to 15°, so the chips aligned better with the angles in the type characters.

3 **Editing the type.** Once you've finished with the Scribble effect, click the artwork thumbnail (the leftmost thumbnail) in the Transparency palette. If you need to edit the type— to change the text or modify kerning, for example—you'll have to do it in *both* the original type object and in the copy in the Opacity Mask. For some edits you make to the type—like scaling or rotating—you only need to work with the type object, since the Opacity Mask will be changed simultaneously with the type object.

Choosing the Opacity Mask in the Transparency palette

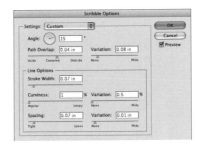

Customizing the options in the Scribble dialog

Selecting the artwork mode (instead of the Opacity mask mode) in the Transparency palette

Getting your fill

To ensure that the effects you will apply later in the Opacity Mask cut opaque holes in the artwork, make sure that the characters are filled with black. (Double-click *Characters* in the Appearance palette and check the Fill attribute.) If you then select the type object with the Selection tool and paint the object (rather than its characters) by adding a new fill in the Appearance palette, the copied type object will not adversely affect the Opacity Mask.

GORDON / CARTAGRAM, LLC

Steven Gordon / Cartagram, LLC

To create this label design, Steven Gordon simulated a sunburst using the Flare tool in an Opacity Mask. He started by drawing a rectangle and filling it with a three-color gradient. He then selected the Type tool and typed "Zion" (he left the type object black so, when used later as a mask, the artwork would remain opaque). Next, Gordon clicked on the Selection tool and copied the type object. He opened the Transparency palette and chose Make Opacity Mask from the palette menu. To select the Opacity Mask and begin working in the mask, Gordon clicked on the mask thumbnail (the right thumbnail) and then clicked on Invert Mask (he left the Clip option enabled). Next,

he chose Edit > Paste in Front to paste the type object into the mask. To make the sunburst, Gordon chose the Flare tool from the Rectangle tool pop-up menu. He positioned the cursor between the **o** and **n** letters and clicked and dragged the flare to extend it outward. To fine-tune the look of the flare, he double-clicked the Flare tool icon and, in the Flare Tool Options dialog box, he adjusted the controls for Diameter, Opacity, Direction, and other options. To return to working with the non-mask artwork, Gordon clicked on the artwork thumbnail (the left thumbnail) in the Transparency palette. He finished the label by applying a dark brown color to the selected type object.

Beyond Basic Drawing & Coloring

7

Beyond Basic Drawing & Coloring

Compound paths or shapes?

The quick answer to this question is to use compound paths on simple objects for simple combining or hole-cutting. Use compound shapes on more complex objects (such as live type or effects) and to more fully control how your objects interact. See the section "The pros and cons of compound shapes and paths" for details on when to use which.

Left to right: two ovals (the inner oval has no fill, but appears black because of the black fill of the larger oval behind it); as part of a compound path the inner oval knocks a hole into the outer one where they overlap; the same compound path with inner oval, which was Direct-Selected and moved to the right to show that the hole is only where the objects overlap

Compounds operate as a unit

Compound shapes and compound paths don't have to overlap to be useful; apply a "compound" to multiple objects whenever you want them to operate as a unit, as if they were one object.

In the preceding chapters you've learned the basics of drawing and coloring in Illustrator; this chapter will take you beyond the basics into the world of compound paths, pathfinders, and shape modes, as well as Illustrator's newest drawing and coloring features. We'll look at alternative ways to create and edit objects, and explore some of the more technical details involved in creating simple objects in Illustrator.

Illustrator CS2 introduces two exciting new drawing and coloring tools: Live Trace, which lets you transform a raster image into a detailed, accurate set of vector paths that remain live and editable; and Live Paint, which allows you to paint areas of a vector graphic more intuitively, as if you were painting by hand on paper or canvas. Illustrator CS2 also introduces a new feature called Group Isolation Mode, which can be confusing if you encounter it without knowing what it is and how it works, but which is a helpful part of working with Live Paint.

We'll discuss Live Trace toward the end of this intro, after which you'll find a special section on Live Paint and Group Isolation Mode, adapted from Mordy Golding's *Real World Adobe Illustrator CS2* book.

COMPOUND PATHS & COMPOUND SHAPES

It's often easier to create an object by combining two or more relatively simple shapes than it would be to draw the more complex result directly. Fortunately, Illustrator has tools that let you easily combine objects to get the results you want.

There are two effective ways to combine objects: 1) compound shapes, which remain "live" and editable; and 2) Pathfinder commands, which become "destructive" (permanent), and can't be returned to their original editable state except by using Undo.

Compound paths

A compound path consists of one or more simple paths that have been combined so that they behave as a single unit. One very useful aspect of compound paths is that a hole can be created where the original objects overlapped. These holes are empty areas cut out from others (think of the center of a donut, or the letter **O**), through which you can see objects.

To create a compound path, e.g., the letter **O**, draw an oval, then draw a smaller oval that will form the center hole of the **O**. Select the two paths, and then choose Object > Compound Path > Make. Select the completed letter and apply the fill color of your choice—the hole will be left empty. To adjust one of the paths within a compound path, use the Direct Selection tool. To adjust the compound path as a unit, use the Group Selection or Selection tool.

In addition to creating holes in objects, you can use compound paths to force multiple objects to behave as if they were a single unit. An advanced application of this is to make separate objects behave as one unit to mask others. For an example of this using separate "outlined" type elements, see the figure "CAREERS" by Gary Newman.

Holes and fills with compound paths

For simple holes, the Compound Path > Make command will generally give the result you need. If your compound path has multiple overlapping shapes, or you're not getting the desired holes in the spaces, take a look at "Fill Rules.pdf" on the *Wow! CD*. Or, try using compound shapes (described in the next section), which give you complete control. Certain results can be obtained only by using compound shapes.

Compound shapes

As mentioned earlier, sometimes it's easier to create an object by combining simpler objects, rather than trying to draw the complex result directly. A *compound shape* is a live combination of shapes using the Add, Subtract,

This artwork by Gary Newman is an example of separate outlined letters made into a compound path so they operate as a unit; he then used the compound path as a mask

Learn to use compound shapes

The **Minus Back** Pathfinder command is the reverse of the **Subtract** shape mode. You can create the same effect using the Subtract Shape mode by simply reversing the stacking order of the elements in your compound shape. See the *Layers & Appearances* chapter for more about object stacking order.

Expand compound shapes?

When would you want to expand a compound shape?

- If a compound shape is so complex that interacting with it is noticeably slow, then expand it.
- Anything that relies on bounding boxes will behave differently on the expanded shape if that shape has a smaller bounding box than the editable compound shape. This affects all the Align commands and certain transformations.
- Finally, you must expand a compound shape before using it as an envelope. For more about envelopes, see the *Live Effects & Graphic Styles* chapter.

—*Pierre Louveaux*

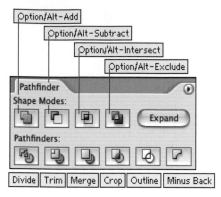

The Pathfinder Commands

Add to Shape Area (for this example as well as the ones below, the first column shows the original shapes; the second column shows the results of the operation shown in Preview mode; and the third column shows the resulting objects selected, so you can see the effects of the operation more clearly)

Subtract from Shape Area

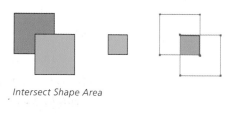

Intersect Shape Area

Exclude Shape Area

Intersect, and/or Exclude Pathfinder operations. See the figures on this page for examples of how they work.

You can make compound shapes from two or more paths, other compound shapes, text, envelopes, blends, groups, or any artwork with vector effects applied to it. To create a compound shape, choose Window > Pathfinder to display the Pathfinder palette. Then select your objects, and choose Make Compound Shape from the Pathfinder palette menu. To assign a particular Shape Mode, select one of the components of your compound shape and click on the corresponding Shape mode button on the top row of the Pathfinder palette.

Note: *Simply selecting your ungrouped objects and pressing one of the Shape Mode buttons creates a compound shape and applies the shape mode you've chosen to the objects.*

The pros and cons of compound shapes and paths

You can only make compound paths from simple objects. In order to make a compound path from more complex objects (such as live type or "envelopes"), you have to first convert them into simpler objects (see the *Type* and *Live Effects & Graphic Styles* chapters for details on how to do this); also, you'll only be able to edit them as paths. You can, however, combine complex objects using *compound shapes* and have them remain editable.

As you know by now, compound shapes allow you to combine objects in a variety of ways using Add, Subtract, Intersect, and Exclude. While keeping these Shape modes live, you can also continue to apply (or remove) Shape modes, or a wide variety of effects, to the compound shape as a unit. In later chapters, as you work with live effects such as envelopes, warps, and drop shadows, remember that you can integrate effects into your compound shapes while retaining the ability to edit your objects—even if they are editable type! Compound shapes can also help you bring objects into Photoshop (see the "Shape Shifting" lesson in the *Illustrator & Other Programs* chapter).

The power of compound shapes does come at a cost. Compound shapes require Illustrator to perform many calculations on your behalf, so as a result, too many compound shapes, or too many operations or effects applied to compound shapes, can slow down the screen redraw of your image. Although compound paths are much less powerful or flexible, they won't slow down your redraw. So if you're working with simple objects, it's best to use compound paths instead.

PATHFINDERS

The Pathfinder palette includes the top row of Live Shape commands and the lower row of permanent Pathfinder commands. You can use the Pathfinder commands Divide, Trim, Merge, Crop, Outline, and Minus Back to permanently combine or separate selected objects. You can also apply the top row of live Shape modes can also be applied as permanent Pathfinder commands. One way to do this is to hold Option/Alt when you *first* click the Shape icons to apply the Shape modes. If you've already applied the live shape, you can make that into a permanently applied pathfinder effect by selecting the objects and choosing Expand from the Pathfinder pop-up menu.

Use the Divide, Trim, Merge, Crop, and Outline Pathfinder commands are used to separate (not combine) objects—think of them as an advanced form of cookie cutters. Before you can use them, the Trim and Merge commands require that you fill objects.

Unlike objects you create using compound shapes, the results you get when you apply the Pathfinder commands alter your artwork permanently. So Pathfinder commands are preferable when you need to perform further operations on the altered paths. For example, if you apply the Divide Pathfinder as shown in the figure at right, you can then pull the resulting pieces apart, or continue to manipulate them. In contrast, you couldn't separate the two pieces resulting from the Exclude Shape Area operation (shown on the facing page), because the underlying paths aren't really altered.

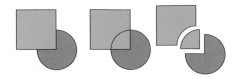

Divide Pathfinder (for this example as well as the ones below, the first column shows the original shapes; the second column shows the results of the operation shown in Preview mode; and the third column shows the resulting objects selected and/or moved apart, so you can see the effects of the operation more clearly)

Trim Pathfinder

Merge Pathfinder (note that Merge only functions correctly if both objects are the same color. Otherwise it works the same as Trim.)

Crop Pathfinder

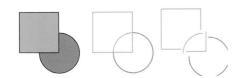

Outline Pathfinder (note that after performing the Outline operation, Illustrator applies a stroke of 0 by default. Here, we've manually applied a 2-pt stroke)

Minus Back Pathfinder

GIBLIN

You don't have to be a rocket scientist to use Live Trace in combination with Live Paint (which we discuss in a special section following this one)—the two new features were designed to work hand in hand. To create the colored rocket shown above, Ian Giblin began with the scanned drawing on the left, then used Live Trace to create the traced version in the middle. After he converted the tracing to a Live Paint group, it was easy to color the rocket using the new Live Paint Bucket

Tracing paper

Adobe has published a technical "white paper" on Live Trace entitled *Creating Vector Content: Using Live Trace.* You can find it as "creating_vector_content.pdf" on the *Wow! CD.*

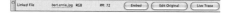

Click the Live Trace button in the Control palette to trace using the default settings

The Tracing Presets and Options button in the Control palette, from which you can open the Tracing Options dialog box or choose a tracing preset

Tracing object names

All tracing objects appear in the Layers palette with the default name "Tracing"—until you re-name them, expand them, or co-vert them to Live Paint objects.

USING LIVE TRACE

Have you ever wished that you could automatically transform a raster image—such as a photo or a scanned drawing—into a detailed, accurate set of vector paths? Illustrator's new Live Trace feature grants your wish. In a matter of minutes (and in some cases, seconds) Live Trace renders your original image into vector graphics that can then be edited, resized, and otherwise manipulated without distortion or loss of quality.

Live Trace gives you complete control over the level of detail that is traced. Live Trace options include the ability to specify a color mode and a color palette for the tracing object, fill and stroke settings, the sharpness of corner angles, blurring and resampling controls, and more. Tracing Presets allow you to store a set of tracing options for quick, convenient access the next time you want to use them.

Best of all, the tracing object you create with Live Trace remains live (that's why they call it Live Trace), so you can adjust the parameters and results of your tracing at any time. Once you're happy with your Live Trace object, you can work with it as vector paths or you can choose to convert it to a Live Paint object and take advantage of the new Live Paint Bucket's intuitive painting capabilities.

The basics of Live Trace

To trace an image using Live Trace, start by opening or placing the file that you'll be using as your source image. Once you've selected the source image, you can choose to trace the object using the default settings just by clicking Live Trace in the Control palette, or choosing Object > Live Trace > Make. If you'd like to have some control over the options for Live Trace before you trace the image, click the Tracing Presets and Options button in the Control palette (it's a small black triangle to the right of the Live Trace button) and select Tracing Options. (You can also access the Tracing Options by choosing Object > Live Trace > Tracing Options.) Search "live trace" in *Illustrator Help* for a rundown of the various options in the Tracing

Options dialog. You can enable the Preview checkbox to see what your tracing will look like before you actually execute it, but be aware that this can slow you down considerably.

Before you execute your tracing, you can choose a tracing preset in the Tracing Options dialog box (from the Preset menu), or by clicking on the Tracing Presets and Options button in the Control palette. If you make a Live Trace setting that you think you'll want to apply to other images in the future, you can save time by saving your current settings as a custom tracing preset.

To create a custom tracing preset, set your options in the Tracing Options dialog box and then click the Save Preset button. Illustrator prompts you to type a name for your new preset. Once you do that and click OK, your new preset will be available from the Preset pop-up menu in the Control palette when you have either a raster object or a Live Trace object selected. (Your preset will also be available from the Preset pop-up menu in Tracing Options.) To manage your tracing presets, choose Edit > Tracing Presets to access the Tracing Presets dialog, where you can edit or delete existing presets, create new ones, or click Export to save your presets to a file that can be shared with other users. (To load presets from an exported file, just click the Import button and locate your saved preset.)

When you've set the tracing options the way you want them, click Trace, and then sit back and watch the Live Trace feature go to work. Once Live Trace has traced your image for you, you can change the way the tracing object is displayed, or adjust the results of the tracing.

Changing the display of a Live Trace object

Because Live Trace is, by definition, live, your original source image remains untouched. So there are really two parts to a Live Trace object: the original source image, and the tracing that results from the Live Trace process. Although only the tracing result is visible by default, you can change how both parts of the Live Trace object are displayed.

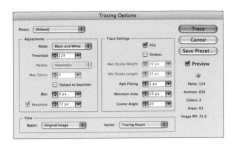

The Tracing Options dialog box is an essential stop if you want to have any control over the results of your tracing

You can manage your tracing presets from within the Tracing Presets dialog box

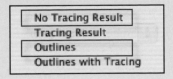

The Raster View (left) and Vector View (right) buttons in the Control palette

Seeing the source image

In Tracing Options, regardless of what display setting you choose for it, your tracing object won't be visible unless you set the tracing result's display to either No Tracing Result or Outlines from the pop-up at the bottom of the dialog box.

No Tracing Result
Tracing Result
Outlines
Outlines with Tracing

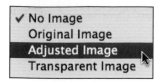

The options in the Raster View menu

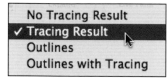

The options in the Vector View menu

Testing a trace

Save a small, representative, cropped version of your image and test your Live Trace settings with that small file. Save your settings, and then apply them to your large file!

—*Kevan Atteberry*

Quick conversion

You can make a tracing and convert it to Live Paint or a set of paths in a single step. Just choose Object > Live Trace > Make and Convert to Live Paint or Object > Live Trace > Make and Expand.

Releasing a tracing object

If you want to get rid of a tracing object—but keep the original placed image where it is—all you have to do is release the tracing object by selecting it, and then choosing Object > Live Trace > Release.

Start by selecting the Live Trace object. Once you've done that, you can change whether (and how) the original source image is displayed by choosing Object > Live Trace or clicking the Raster View button in the Control palette. Select one of the four options: No Image to completely hide the source image; Original Image to display the source image underneath the tracing result; Adjusted Image to display the image with any adjustments applied during the tracing process; or Transparent Image to see a "ghost" of the source image.

With the Live Trace object selected, you can also change how the tracing result is displayed by choosing Object > Live Trace or clicking the Vector View button in the Control palette. Select one of the four options: No Tracing Result to completely hide the result of the tracing; Tracing Result to display the full tracing result; Outlines to display only the outlines of the tracing object; or Outlines with Tracing to see the tracing result with the outlines visible.

Adjusting the results of a Live Trace

Of course, because your Live Trace object is live, you can adjust the results of the tracing whenever you want. Simply select your Live Trace object and choose a new preset from the Control palette preset pop-up menu; or, click the Tracing Options button in the Control palette; or choose Object > Live Trace > Tracing Options. If you choose Tracing Options, you'll get the same Tracing Options dialog box you saw before you traced the object, and you can continue to adjust and change any of the options at will. Then, just click Trace to reapply.

Also note that you can adjust certain basic options for your tracing result (namely Threshold and Min. Area) right in the Control palette, without even entering the Tracing Options dialog.

Using swatch libraries with Live Trace

You can create a special swatch library with only the colors you want used in your tracing, and then specify it in the

Tracing Options dialog box by choosing its name in the Palette menu. You can also specify any existing swatch library. In either case, just make sure you have the swatch library open before you open the Tracing Options dialog, or else its name won't appear in the Palette menu.

Converting to a Live Paint object or set of paths

Live Trace is designed to work hand-in-hand with the new Live Paint feature (see the special section on Live Paint following this one). Once you're happy with your tracing object, you can easily convert it to a Live Paint object so that you can color it intuitively using the Live Paint Bucket.

You can also convert the tracing object to paths if you want to work with the elements of the traced artwork as separate objects.

Whether you're converting to Live Paint or to separate paths, keep in mind that your tracing options will no longer be live and editable after you perform this step, so don't convert your tracing until you're satisfied with it.

To convert the tracing to a Live Paint object, just select the object and click the Live Paint button in the Control palette, or choose Object > Live Trace > Convert to Live Paint.

To convert the tracing to a set of paths, click the Expand button in the Control palette or choose Object > Life Trace > Expand. This will convert your object to a set of paths that are grouped together.

If you want to preserve the tracing image to be used as a guide for the paths after you've expanded them, you can choose to preserve your current display options by choosing Object > Live Trace > Expand as Viewed. So, for example, if you've chosen Outlines as the display option for your tracing result, you apply Expand as Viewed, the resulting paths will be mere outlines instead of being stroked and filled. The original image with the current display options will also be preserved and grouped together with the new paths.

The Expand and Live Paint buttons in the Control palette

Zoom before tracing

You can't change magnification or view from within Live Trace Options, so make sure to zoom in to see the area that you want to use as a reference before opening Live Trace Options.

Swatch and learn

See the "Trace Techniques" lesson, later in this chapter, for an example of working with swatches while using Live Trace.

When tracing an EPS...

Illustrator has a difficult time tracing EPS images, because it can't access the full image data. So if your source images is an EPS, it's a good idea to make sure it's embeded before you do your trace.
—*Jean-Claude Tremblay*

ATTEBERRY

See Kevan Atteberry's Galleries using Live Trace later in this chapter

Working with Live Paint
& Group Isolation Mode

A Special *Wow!* Section Adapted from:

Real World Adobe Illustrator CS2 by Mordy Golding

About Mordy Golding

Mordy Golding, an award-win-ning consultant, trainer, and former product manager for Adobe Illustrator, has been a part of our extended *Wow!* team since the second edition. This special section is adapted from Mordy's new book *Real World Adobe Illustrator CS2*, also pub-lished by Peachpit Press. You can visit Mordy's Web site at: www.designresponsibly.com

See Dave Joly's lesson demonstrating a Live Trace to Live Paint workflow later in this chapter

Controlling isolation mode

When you have a group selected, the Control palette has a button that will also allow you to enter isolation mode. You can use the same button to exit isolation mode as well.

While you can appreciate the power that vector graphics have to offer, there's an equal appreciation for how easy it is to use pixel-based paint programs like Photoshop or Painter to easily apply color to artwork. In a paint pro-gram, you can perform flood fills, where you choose a color and use a paint bucket-like tool to fill areas of the illustration with color. When working with vectors, you have to create distinct paths and shapes in order to apply a fill attribute to add color. This requirement to create dis-tinct objects can make drawing in Illustrator seem non-intuitive, or time-consuming at best.

New to Illustrator CS2, Live Paint is a feature that introduces a new concept of working with vector paths, where you can colorize vectors and edit them without hav-ing to follow the traditional vector rules that we've been detailing so far. This new feature makes it a lot easier to draw in Illustrator.

Understanding Group Isolation Mode

Before we look at the specifics of Live Paint, it's impor-tant to understand a new feature in Illustrator CS2 called Group Isolation Mode, which is especially useful when working with Live Paint (as we'll see below).

There are times when you want to draw a new object and add it to an existing group. For example, your client requests that you add the Registered Trademark symbol to a logo, which is already grouped. One way to accomplish this would be to use the Type tool to add the Registered Trademark symbol to your document. You would then select the logo, ungroup it, and then select the logo and the new trademark symbol and group the objects together.

Illustrator CS2 introduces an easier way to add objects to existing groups using Group Isolation Mode. For the logo example we used above, you would use the following method to add the trademark symbol. Using the Selection tool, double-click on any object in the logo. A gray border will appear around the perimeter of the group, indicating that the group is now isolated. When a group is isolated, any new shapes or objects that are created will become part of the group. Select the Type tool and create a text object with the trademark symbol to automatically add the symbol to the logo group. To exit isolation mode, you can either click on any object that's outside the group, or you double click on the Artboard, at which time the gray border will disappear.

A gray border around the perimeter of a group indicates that the group is now isolated.

When Live Paint Groups are selected, their different bounding box gives them away. The group on the left is a Live Paint Group; note its "fancy" bounding box as opposed to the plain bounding box of the group on the right.

Using Live Paint to color paths

First, we'll create something using Live Paint to get a feel for what the feature is all about. Then we'll discuss how the feature works and better understand how to use it in a meaningful way. Choose the Line Segment tool and draw two parallel vertical lines and two parallel horizontal lines to create a tic-tac-toe board. Don't worry if the lines or spacing aren't perfect—for this exercise you just want to make sure the lines cross each other.

Select the four lines and choose the new Live Paint Bucket tool. As you move your cursor over the four paths, the paths will become highlighted. Click once to create a Live Paint group. Now, choose a fill color (a solid color, gradient, or pattern) from the Control palette and move your cursor over the center area of the tic-tac-toe board. The enclosed area in the middle will highlight in red, which indicates an area that can be filled with color. Click once with the Live Paint Bucket tool to fill the highlighted area with color.

The resulting behavior of being able to fill areas with the Live Paint Bucket tool is very Photoshop-esque: You've filled an area that is enclosed on all sides, but you didn't fill an actual object. Choose the Direct Selection tool, select one of the paths, and move it just a bit. Notice that the color in the area updates to fill the center. If you move one of the paths far enough to the side so that it no longer

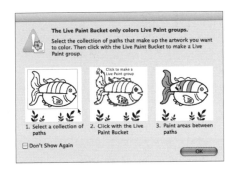

If you click with the Live Paint Bucket and you haven't selected any paths, you'll see the (very informative) dialog box shown above.

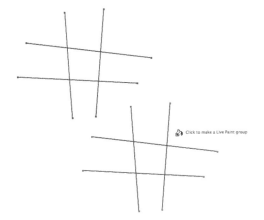

Using the Line Segment tool, you can create a simple tic-tac-toe graphic (top). If you have the Live Paint Bucket tool selected, Illustrator shows a tool tip to create a Live Paint group when your cursor passes over a valid selection (bottom).

Illustrator's Live Paint Bucket tool highlights areas that can be filled as you mouse over them, even if the Live Paint groups aren't selected

With one click of the Live Paint Bucket tool, you can fill areas that appear to be enclosed, even though there is an actual vector object there

The fill areas in a Live Paint group update automatically when you're moving the paths with the Direct Selection tool

When editing the paths in a Live Paint group, creating an opened area results in the loss of the fill attribute

Reapplying fills

Unfortunately, if you move a path so that an enclosed painted area becomes unpainted, Illustrator doesn't remember that the region was filled with a color prior to the edit. Moving the path back to its original position will not bring the fill back and you'll need to reapply the fill color.

In Group Isolation Mode, you can draw new paths into an existing Live Paint group to instantly create additional regions that can be filled with color

touches the other paths, you'll find that the fill color disappears, as there is no longer an enclosed area to fill.

Understanding Live Paint groups

Let's take a moment to understand how Live Paint works. When you select several overlapping paths or shapes and click on them with the Live Paint Bucket tool, you are creating a Live Paint group. This is a special kind of group in which object stacking order is thrown out the window. All objects in a Live Paint group are seemingly combined onto a single flat world, and any enclosed area acts as a closed shape, which can be filled with color.

While clicking on several selected paths is the easiest way to create a Live Paint group, you can also select several paths and choose Object > Live Paint > Make to create a Live Paint group. Once you've created a Live Paint group, however, you may find that you want to add additional paths or shapes to the group. To do so, draw the new paths and use the Selection tool to select the existing Live Paint group and the new paths. Then choose Object > Live Paint > Add Paths. The new paths will become part of the group and any intersecting areas will act as individual areas that you can fill with color.

Live Paint groups can also utilize the Group Isolation Mode that enables you to draw objects directly into existing groups. Using the Selection tool, double-click on an existing Live Paint group to enter Group Isolation Mode. Now, switch to any shape or path tool to add paths directly into the Live Paint group. This ability to add paths directly into a Live Paint group is extremely powerful as you can define regions for color in just a few quick steps. Illustrator no longer requires you to use Pathfinder filters to create multiple overlapping shapes for such tasks.

In the Toolbox, double-click on the Live Paint Bucket tool to change its behavior. By default, the Live Paint Bucket tool only affects the fill of a path, but you can also set the tool to apply color to strokes as well. Additionally, you can specify the color that the Live Paint tool uses to highlight closed regions.

Gap detection

Until now, all of the regions that you were filling with color were completely closed. But what happens if your paths don't exactly meet each other? That's where Illustrator's Gap Detection feature can really make a difference. Choose Object >Live Paint >Gap Options to control the settings for this feature. If you don't have any Live Paint groups selected when choosing this option, the settings you choose will become the default settings for all new Live Paint groups. You can specify different Gap Options for each selected Live Paint group in a document as well.

With Gap Detection turned on, you can specify that paint will fill areas that contain small, medium, or large gaps. Additionally, you can specify an exact amount for how big a gap can be before Live Paint considers it an open area instead of a closed one. Illustrator will preview gaps in the selected color; you can also choose to have Illustrator fill any gaps in an object with physical paths (Illustrator will always use straight paths to do so).

Releasing and expanding Live Paint groups

Live Paint groups can be expanded, at which time they will behave like ordinary vector paths. The appearance of an expanded Live Paint group will remain identical to the original, but it will be split into multiple objects for both fills and strokes. This is similar in concept to expanding live effects. To expand a selected Live Paint group, either click on the Expand button in the Control palette or choose Object >Live Paint >Expand.

From a production standpoint, there's no need to expand Live Paint groups in order to prepare a file for print. Live Paint groups print perfectly, as Illustrator performs the necessary expanding of paths at print time (similar to live effects).

Additionally, you can choose Object >Live Paint > Release to return a Live Paint group to the original paths you used to create it. Where expanding will result in Illustrator breaking up objects to preserve appearance, releasing a Live Paint group will preserve the geometry of

Coloring multiple regions

You can use the Live Paint Bucket tool to color multiple regions with a single color in one step by clicking in one region and dragging the mouse across additional contiguous regions.

You can set the Live Paint Bucket tool to apply color to stroke attributes in a Live Paint group

Mind the gap

With a Live Paint group selected, you can also open the Gap Options dialog by clicking on the icon in the Control palette.

The Gap Options dialog makes it possible to fill areas in a Live Paint group even if they aren't completely enclosed

With a Live Paint group selection, you can choose to open the Gap Options dialog from the Control palette.

Splitting Live Paint groups

With Live Paint groups that are made up of many complex paths, gap detection will impede performance. You will experience better performance by splitting very large Live Paint groups into several smaller Live Paint groups.

Using the Live Paint Selection tool, you can select visual segments of a path

In a Live Paint group, you can easily apply different stroke attributes to the segments of a path

The Live Paint Selection tool enables you to select any area of a Live Paint group

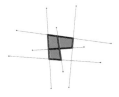

Adding a stroke to a Live Paint group at the group level makes it possible to apply stroke attributes that appear only around areas that are filled

Fixing a hole

With Live Paint objects, you can delete white areas created when you Live Trace raster images. But unlike Streamline, you can also create "holes" by simply Direct-Selecting a Live Paint object (such as the donut center), and filling it with None! —*Sandee Cohen*

the original paths, but the appearance (including colors) will be lost. (For more about appearances see the *Layers & Appearances* chapter.)

Using Live Paint to edit paths

If you think about it, Live Paint allows you to apply attributes—like fills and strokes—to paths based on their appearance as opposed to their actual makeup. It would be even nicer if you could actually edit your paths based on appearance as well, don't you think? Adobe was apparently reading your mind (a scary thought) and added another tool to the mix—the Live Paint Selection tool—which enables you to select portions of objects based on their appearance.

Let's take a look at an example: Use the Line Segment tool to draw two perpendicular lines, creating an **X**. Select both paths and press ⌘-Opt-X (Ctrl-Alt-X) or choose Object > Live Paint > Make to convert the two paths into a Live Paint group. Now, choose the Live Paint Selection tool and click on one of paths. You'll notice that you can select each segment of the line individually. What were two paths before are now four line segments. With one segment selected, press the Delete key to remove that segment from the path. Select another segment and change its stroke attribute. You can also click on one segment and then drag to select other segments in one step.

The Live Paint Selection tool can also select the fills of Live Paint areas. If you have two overlapping shapes in a Live Paint group, you can select the overlap and delete it.

At the end of the day, Live Paint adds a more flexible way to color and edit paths and also adds more value to the Pencil tool, as complete closed paths aren't required. The important thing to remember is that a Live Paint group is a group, and anything that you could do with a group in Illustrator can be done with Live Paint groups as well. For example, you can add attributes like strokes to the Live Paint group for interesting effects. Experimenting with the Live Paint feature will certainly help you when editing paths, and the good news is, it's a fun feature to use.

FOX / BLACKDOG (Art Director: Neal Zimmermann, Zimmermann Crowe Design)

© 1989 BLACKDOG

Mark Fox / BlackDog

Using techniques similar to those shown in the next lesson, Mark Fox redesigned this eagle decal for Bianchi USA—the American branch of the Italian bicycle manufacturer—under the art direction of Neal Zimmermann (Zimmermann Crowe Design).

Cutting & Joining
Basic Path Construction with Pathfinders

FOX / BLACKDOG (Art Director: Jeff Carino, Landor Associates)

Overview: *Design an illustration using overlapping objects; use the Pathfinder palette to join and intersect objects, join lines to circles, and cut objects from other objects.*

1

Fox's inked sketch drawn with a compass
NOTE: Fox created his image in reverse. As a last step, he used the Reflect tool to flip the final image (see the *Zen* chapter for help reflecting).

2

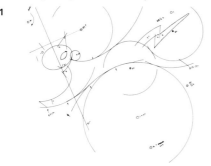

Using the Tools palette to set the Fill to None before starting to draw

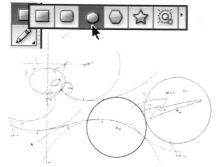

Drawing constrained circles from the center with the Ellipse tool (by holding Option-Shift/ Alt-Shift) to trace over the placed template

To redesign the classic "9 Lives" cat symbol that has appeared on Eveready batteries for over 50 years, Mark Fox began with a hand-drawn sketch. Once his sketch was approved, he inked the sketch with a Rapidograph pen and a compass, and then reconstructed the ink image in Illustrator using permanent (destructive) Pathfinder commands. The top row of Pathfinders are actually *Shape* modes that allow you to keep the objects "live" so you can make adjustments. To apply these shape modes permanently so that you can move on to the next step, select the objects and click the Expand button. Alternatively, you can apply any Shapes mode permanently in one step by holding Option/Alt when you first click the Shape icons. The bottom row of Pathfinder icons are always permanent. *Especially* when you work with permanent Pathfinders, save incremental versions of your image as you work.

1 Creating a sketch and placing it as a template

layer. Fox used a compass to create a precise drawing constructed of fluid curves. Using his inked sketch as a template, Fox then used the Ellipse tool to recreate his compass circles in Illustrator. Create your own sketch using traditional materials and then scan it, or sketch directly into a painting program (such as Painter or Photoshop). Save your sketch as PSD or TIF format, and place it into a new Illustrator document as a template. To do this, choose File > Place to locate the image you wish to use as a template, then enable the Template option and click Place (see the *Layers* chapter for more on templates).

2 Hand-tracing your template using adjoining and overlapping objects. In order to see your objects as you work, before you begin drawing make sure that you're in Preview mode (View menu), and set your Fill to None and Stroke to black. Now use the Ellipse and Rectangle tools to create the basic shapes that will make up your image. Fox used some circles to form the shapes themselves (like the rump of the cat), and others to define the areas that would later be cut from others (like the arc of the underbelly). To create perfect circles or squares hold the Shift key while you draw with the Ellipse and Rectangle tools. By default, ellipse and rectangles are drawn from a corner—in order to draw these objects from a center point, hold down the Option/Alt key as you draw. To create a circle from its center point, you'll need to hold down the modifier keys Shift-Option/Shift-Alt as you draw—don't release the modifier keys until after you release your mouse button. Because Fox measured everything in millimeters in his inking stage, he created his circles numerically. With the Ellipse tool, Fox Option-clicked/Alt-clicked on each center point marked on his template, entered the correct diameter for Width and Height, and clicked OK.

3 Constructing curves by combining parts of different circles. Once your paths are drawn and in position, use the Pathfinder palette to combine portions of different circles to create complex curves. After drawing basic circles, use the Line Segment tool to draw a line through the circles at the point where you want to join them, and choose Object > Path > Divide Objects Below. Then select the sub-sections of the divided circles that you don't want and delete. To join separate adjoining curves, click the Add to shape area Pathfinder icon. To apply Add permanently, click the Expand button.

4 Constructing objects using the Intersect Pathfinder command. If the area you wish to keep is the portion where objects overlap, use the Intersect command. Fox

3

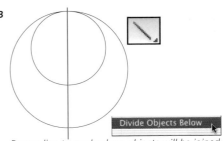
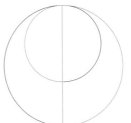

Draw a line to mark where objects will be joined and apply Object > Path > Divide Objects Below

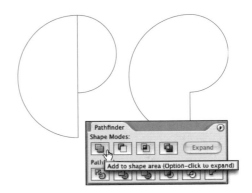

Select and delete unwanted portions of objects that won't be part of the final curve

Once only the elements you wish to be joined remain, select them and click the Add to shape area Pathfinder icon (later click the Expand button to apply Add permanently)

4

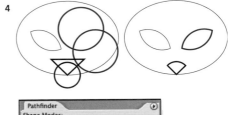

Constructing the eyes and nose using the Intersect Shape Areas Pathfinder command

5

Drawing one line from an anchor point on the circle and another angled line slightly removed

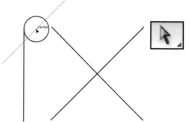

Creating a perpendicular copy of the angled line by double-clicking the Rotate tool, specifying a 90° Angle, and clicking Copy

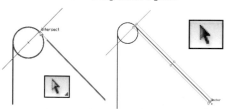

Moving the perpendicular copy to the circle's center and then making it into a guide

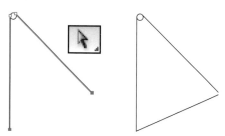

Moving the angled line tangent to the circle using the guide, then lengthening the line

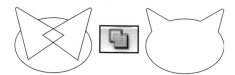

Selecting the two end anchor points of the lines and closing using Join to connect the lines

Using the Add to Shape Pathfinder command to attach the circle to the angled shape, then the completed ears to the cat-head ellipse

used Intersect to create the eyes and the nose of the cat. To make the eye shape, he drew a circle and then created a duplicate by holding Option/Alt as he moved it with the Selection tool. He then positioned the two circles so the overlap created the desired shape and selected both circles. Fox applied Intersect shape areas and Expand in one step by holding Option/Alt when he clicked the Intersect icon.

5 Attaching lines to circles. Fox connected angled lines to a tiny circle to form the cat's ear. To smoothly attach lines to circles, the lines need to lie "tangent" to the circle (touching the circle at only one anchor point). To work with precision, turn on Smart Guides (View menu).

Start with the Ellipse tool and draw a small circle. To create the first tangent line, choose the Line Segment tool, and place the cursor over the left side anchor-point of the circle. When you see the word "anchor point" click-drag downward from that anchor point to draw a vertical line.

Creating a tangent line that doesn't begin at an anchor point is trickier. Start by drawing another line slightly apart from the circle, but at the angle you desire (holding the Shift key constrain movement to horizontals, verticals, and 45° angles). To help you find the tangent point for this line, you need to create a line perpendicular to it. With your angled line selected, double-click the Rotate tool, enter 90°, and click Copy. Use either the Direct Selection or Group Selection tool to grab this perpendicular copy of your line near the middle and drag it toward the center of your circle; release the mouse when you see the word "center." With this line still selected, make it into a guide with View > Guides > Make Guides. Now select your angled line by marqueeing it with the Direct Selection tool, or click it with the Group Selection tool. Finally, with either the Direct Selection or Group Selection tool, grab the top anchor point and drag it to where the perpendicular guide meets the circle; release the mouse when you see the word "intersect."

To adjust the length of either line, switch to the Selection tool, select the line, and drag the bounding box from the middle end handle at the open anchor point.

The Add to Shape Pathfinder ignores lines, so to attach the lines to the circle, first connect the lines together to form a two-dimensional shape. Using the Direct Selection tool, marquee the two open anchor points and choose Object > Path > Join (⌘-J/Ctrl-J) to connect the points with a line.

Finally, to unite your angled shape with the circle, select them both, hold Option/Alt, and click the Add to Shape Area Pathfinder icon. Fox also used Add to Shape Area to join the ears to the head (he rotated the first ear into position, and used the Reflect tool to create a copy for the other ear—see the *Zen of Illustrator* chapter for help with rotation and reflection).

6 Cutting portions of paths with other objects. To create the rear flank of the cat, Fox used a large object to cut an area (subtract) from another circle. Use the Selection tool to select the path you'll use as the cutter and bring it to the top of the stacking order (in the exact position) either by choosing Object > Arrange > Bring to Front, or Edit > Cut and then Edit > Paste in Front (⌘-F/Ctrl-F). Select the cutter object and the objects you want to cut and click the Subtract from shape area Pathfinder icon.

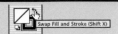

Better to see Pathfinders...

If your objects are styled with a stroke and no fill, you can swap the Fill and Stroke styling to better see the effects of a Pathfinder command. To do this, with objects selected, click on the Swap Fill and Stroke arrows in the bottom section of the Tools palette. Click again to swap it back.

6

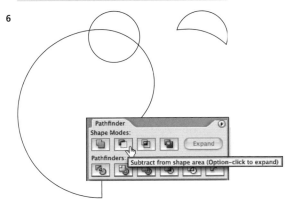

Using the Subtract from shape area to cut one object from others

Manually cut with Scissors

Although it's not as precise as using a line and "Divide Objects Below," you *can* use the Scissors tool to cut any path, including open paths. Turn on Smart Guides (View menu) and click with the Scissors tool when the word "Path" appears to place two coinciding points on the path. To separate the points, first deselect the path entirely. Then, with the Direct Selection tool, click on top of the new points to select only the top point. Then you can move or delete the selected point.

Joining open paths & closing paths smoothly

Pathfinder > Add to Shape will close open paths, joining them with a straight line. Use the following method to manually join two open paths or to close a path smoothly. Since you can only join two points at a time, start by deleting any stray points (Select > Object > Stray Points). Before you can join points with a smooth curve, you need to ensure the points are exactly on top of each other. Use the Direct Selection tool or Lasso to select one pair of end anchor points and choose Object > Path > Average (Both) and click OK, then Object > Path > Join and click OK. To Average/Join in one step, press ⌘-Shift-Option-J/Ctrl-Shift-Alt-J —there isn't a menu command for this.

Divide & Color

Applying Pathfinder Divide & Subtract

Overview: *Design an illustration using overlapping elements; create individual paths using Divide, and delete unnecessary paths; using Subtract to cut "holes" and create Compound Paths; Divide again and assign colors to divided objects.*

PIRMAN / PHOTO: JOSHUA MCHUGH

1

Creating the basic elements using the Rectangle and Ellipse tools

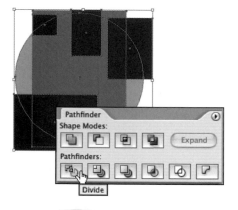

(Top) Selecting all paths and clicking on Divide in the Pathfinder palette; (bottom) selecting and deleting unnecessary paths

Illustrator's Pathfinder palette provides many ways to combine objects. To create this disco clock for a Worldstudio Foundation's "Make Time" benefit, John Pirman used the Divide and Subtract Pathfinder options to permanently alter his objects. This allowed him to adjust colors within each of the divided areas in his illustration.

1 Creating and positioning paths; dividing overlapping paths. Pirman created a circle and a number of rectangles to serve as the background (and later as the objects to Divide his figure shapes) for his clock face design. In a new Illustrator document, draw a filled circle with no Stroke using the Ellipse tool (hold the Shift key to constrain the ellipse to a circle). Then use the Rectangle tool to draw a few rectangles filled with different gray values, and a stroke of None. Use a selection tool to move the rectangles around until you are satisfied with an arrangement of rectangles in relationship to the circle. Next, choose Select > All, then open the Pathfinder palette (Window > Pathfinder) and click the Divide button (in the palette's bottom row). All overlapping paths will split into separate, editable objects. To delete the extra paths outside of this "divided circle" shape, first choose Select > Deselect, then select them, and press Delete.

2 Using Subtract to create "holes" and Divide again. Next, Pirman drew a series of silhouetted human figures with the Pen and Pencil tools and arranged them in relation to the background. For figures that included enclosed "negative space" (such as an arm partially touching another part of the body) he used Pathfinder Subtract to cut the areas as "holes," so objects behind would show through. To cut enclosed areas into permanent holes, first make sure that your enclosed paths are on top of the rest of the figure. Next, set solid fills for all the objects, with no strokes. Then select your figure and the enclosed spaces and hold Option/Alt while you click on Subtract in the Pathfinder palette (holding Option/Alt while applying a Pathfinder in the upper row of the palette makes that Pathfinder action permanent). Your figure with holes has now become a Compound Path. Use the Selection tool to reposition the complete figure, the Group Selection tool to reposition the holes, or the Direct Selection tool to edit the paths.

Pirman created a palette of blues, greens, and white to apply to his figures. He then positioned each figure over his "divided circle" background and used his background objects to divide the figures. To do this, choose different color fills for your figures and arrange them in front of your divided background (the stacking order doesn't matter). Next, select all your paths (Select > All) and click Divide in the Pathfinder palette. As before, all of the overlapping paths will now be split into individual paths. Use the Group Selection tool to select and delete paths outside of your background shape, and then to select individual sections of the figures in order to change the fill color. Pirman used colors of similar value to visually integrate the divided figures.

With his figures divided, Pirman then used his palette colors to recolor the various divided sections of the figures and continued to make adjustments to the background. To do this, color all of the paths that make up the fully divided illustration using your color palette. Using the Group Selection tool, click on the individual paths within the circle shape (hold Shift to select multiple paths) and style with any Fill color you like.

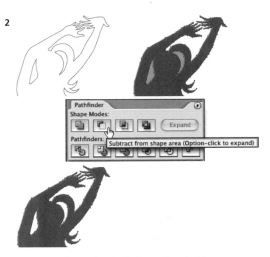

Drawing a figure that includes enclosed objects defining "negative space" (top left), selecting all the objects that create the figure and applying Pathfinder > Subtract while holding Option/Alt (top right); the figure now as a Compound Path

Filled figures; positioning the colored figure paths over the divided circle background

The process of styling individual objects with different colors.

Coloring Sketches

From Sketch to Live Trace and Live Paint

Overview: *Import a sketch into Illustrator; apply Live Trace; convert to a Live Paint Group; color with Live Paint Bucket.*

JOLY

1

The first rough draft of the robot sketch

The refined version of the sketch

Dave Joly drew this robot character as a visualization exercise for an animation project. Joly started by creating a rough sketch by hand. In Illustrator, Joly found that the new Live Trace and Live Paint features were like an express route between his sketch and a polished Illustrator drawing. Live Trace and Live Paint are well integrated for the task of filling sketches with color.

1 Drawing the initial robot concept. Joly sketched the robot using the natural media tools in Corel Painter. He then removed stray details and solidified the linework to make the image easier to trace later. When he finished, he saved the image as a Photoshop file.

Although Joly chose to start and edit his original drawing in Painter, you can also sketch an idea on paper and scan it into your computer. If necessary, you can clean up the sketch of your scan in an image editor such as Adobe Photoshop before moving it to Illustrator.

2 Tracing with Live Trace. In Illustrator, you can open a Photoshop image as a new document by choosing File > Open, or add it to an existing Illustrator document by choosing File > Place. Select the image on the Artboard and click the Live Trace button on the Control Palette.

Applying Live Trace doesn't just trace the image; it also creates a Live Trace object consisting of both the original image and the tracing. Unlike a hand-tracing, you can change the tracing options to alter the results at any time without starting over. On the Control palette, choose a tracing preset from the Presets pop-up menu, or click the Options button to open the Tracing Options dialog box where more Live Trace options are available. The default tracing preset creates high-contrast black and white line art that is well-suited for Live Paint. As a result, Joly did not need to change any Live Trace options for this project.

3 Filling areas with Live Paint. With the tracing selected, Joly clicked the Live Paint button in the Control Palette to convert it from a Live Trace object to a Live Paint Group. The object no longer contained the original image or allowed easy retracing, but it gained Live Paint attributes: Joly could fill and stroke any naturally enclosed areas in the Live Paint Group without having to draw a path to hold each fill. Joly selected the Live Paint Bucket and chose a Fill swatch from the Control Palette. Whenever Joly positioned the Live Paint Bucket over an area that could be painted using Live Paint, a red outline appeared to indicate a Live Paint region. If he wanted to paint the area outlined in red, he clicked the region or dragged across multiple regions.

Initially, gaps between the hand-drawn black lines let color spill into surrounding areas. Joly chose Edit > Undo to remove the spilled paint, and then clicked the Options button on the Control Palette to open the Gap Options dialog box. Here, you can specify the size of gap to automatically close by using the Paint Stops At pop-up menu or the Custom field. If you enable the Preview checkbox,

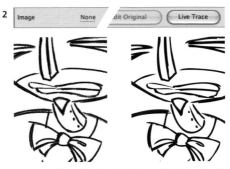

2

Image options displayed in Control Palette (top) for selected image (bottom left); the image after clicking the Live Trace button (bottom right)

Control Palette for selected Live Trace object; Options button (for Tracing Options) highlighted

3

Control Palette for selected Live Paint Group; Options button (for gap options) highlighted

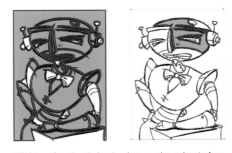

Clicking the Live Paint Bucket on the robot's face with no gap detection (left) and after applying gap detection for large gaps (right)

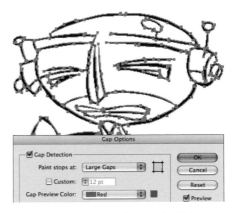

Gap Options dialog box with gaps highlighted in red on Artboard because Preview is checked

4

Additional details that Joly drew as paths in front of the Live Paint object; the Live Paint object's fills have been removed here for clarity

Very wide gap in lower left corner (top) and the blue filled path Joly drew (bottom)

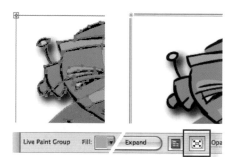

Live Paint Group border with Group Isolation Mode off (top left) and on (top right); the mode is controlled by the Group Isolation button (highlighted) on the Control Palette (bottom)

red dots on the Artboard mark the gaps detected by your Gap Options settings. For this project, Joly found that the Large Gaps setting worked well.

4 **Completing the drawing.** Joly rapidly colored the rest of the sketch using the Live Paint Bucket, changing the fill swatch as needed and clicking or dragging across Live Paint areas he wanted to fill. Joly also drew additional paths to add new details, highlights, and shading.

Some regions, like the hip at the bottom left of the illustration, had gaps that were too large for the automatic gap detection settings. Joly drew new paths for those few areas.

Joly drew his additional paths separately from the Live Paint object, filling them using the traditional method of selecting each path with the Selection tool and then clicking a swatch. However, it's possible to add paths to an existing Live Paint Group by entering Group Isolation Mode. With a Live Paint Group selected, click the Isolate Group button on the Control Palette to enter Group Isolation Mode (the border of the Live Paint Group becomes gray). When a Live Paint Group is in Group Isolation Mode, drawing a new path adds it to the selected Live Paint Group; you can then paint the new path using the Live Paint Bucket. Click the Group Isolation Mode button again to exit Group Isolation Mode.

Filling and Stroking with the Live Paint Bucket

You can control whether the Live Paint Bucket paints fills or strokes. In the toolbox, double-click the Live Paint Bucket to open the Live Paint Bucket Options dialog box, and enable or disable the Paint Fills and Paint Strokes checkboxes. If only one checkbox is enabled, pressing Shift temporarily reverses what happens when you click with the bucket. For example, by default, clicking paints fills and Shift-clicking paints strokes. With both checkboxes enabled, clicking the Live Paint Bucket automatically paints a stroke or a fill, depending on how close the bucket is to an edge.

Lance Jackson

Lance Jackson created these portraits for a San Francisco Chronicle special section on high-profile CEOs. Jackson first drew pencil sketches of the CEOs on paper. He scanned his sketches, saved them as JPEG files, and applied Live Trace to the JPEG images in Illustrator. He adjusted Live Trace settings such as Threshold to trace the precise tonal range he wanted from each sketch. Jackson expanded the Live Trace results in order to edit paths and apply additional fills as needed.

Kevan Atteberry

Illustrator Kevan Atteberry drew a sketch with a traditional paper and pencil sketch of "Lurd pieces" (top left). Atteberry creates characters in pieces so he has the flexibility to place part of a character behind another, to tweak positioning of a posture, and so forth. In the past he would just lay his scanned line drawing in layers above the colored objects (created with shaped blends), but he now applies Live Trace to his drawings first. Because each image requires slightly different settings, and because it can take a while for Live Trace to preview the changes of settings, Atteberry devised an ingenious workflow. When scanning an illustration, he also saves a small representative detail of the image. He began by placing and selecting the small Lurd detail in Illustrator, then he chose Object > Live Trace > Tracing Options. In Tracing Options, he enabled Preview, set the mode to Grayscale with the Max colors of 4, and then experimented with the blur settings so the extraneous marks for the Lurds were

minimized, while the line shape of the pencil drawing remained preserved. Saving these settings (Save Preset), he clicked Trace. Placing the main drawing, he again entered Tracing Options, chose his new settings from the Preset pop-up, and clicked Trace. Atteberry applied Object > Expand, turning the traced object into separate vector objects filled with black, white, and two grays (a detail shown above the Layers palette). To delete the whites, he clicked on one with the Direct Selection tool, chose Select > Same > Fill Color, and deleted. Because he wanted the grays to darken the colors he would be adding (not just laying gray over the colors), he used Select > Same > Fill Color to select both of the grays. In the Control palette he changed the blending mode from Normal to Multiply and reduced the Opacity to 58% (click and hold the triangle to the right of Opacity). Creating layers underneath, Atteberry used the Pen and Pencil tools with blends (see his lesson in *Blends, Gradients & Mesh*) to color the parts.

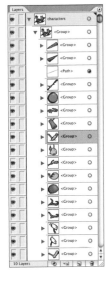

ATTEBERRY

Kevan Atteberry

Using his compositional sketch as a guide (right) and his "Lurd parts" from the Gallery opposite, Illustrator Kevan Atteberry assembled his composition. Before assembling the parts, however, Atteberry selected each "part" made up of the expanded Live Trace line work along with the inner solid shapes and shaped blends (see his lesson in the *Blends, Gradients & Mesh* chapter) and grouped (⌘-G/ Ctrl-G). This allows Atteberry to click on each part with the Selection tool to select all of it. He can then move parts easily, reorder them in the Layers palette, and form the characters. Once the characters are formed, he places them within the scene created from shaped blends.

Trace Techniques
Using Live Trace for Auto & Hand-Tracing

Advanced Technique

Overview: *Use the same image as a foundation for both a background created using Live Trace and a hand-traced foreground.*

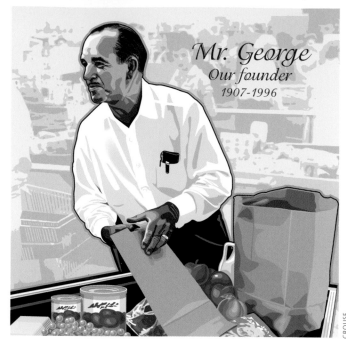

1

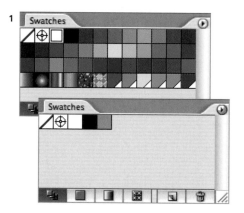

Swatches palette before and after removing unused swatches

The original photograph Crouse used as the starting point for both the Live Trace background and hand-traced foreground

Scott Crouse drew this portrait of George Jenkins, the founder of Publix Markets, as part of a series of exterior murals for the Publix grocery store chain. To communicate the warm, friendly personality of "Mr. George," Crouse applied his personal illustration style as he hand-traced the portrait from a photograph. The background image did not need to be as distinctive, so Crouse saved time by using the Live Trace feature to create it from the same photograph. For easier hand-tracing, Crouse simplifies images by limiting tonal levels and removing distracting stray bits; in many cases Live Trace can replace Photoshop for this preparatory task.

1 Preparing the document. Crouse chose Select All Unused from the Swatches palette menu, and then he clicked the trash can icon in the Swatches palette to delete the selected swatches. Removing all unused swatches from the document made it easier to see the swatches that will be created later by Live Trace.

Crouse chose File > Place to select the original photograph of Mr. George and add the photo to the page.

2 Copying the image layer. To separate the foreground and background images, you can duplicate them while keeping them aligned. Drag the original layer (not just the image) to the New Layer icon in the Layers palette, then double-click the name to rename it.

To prevent changes to layers other than the one you're editing, click the lock column to lock any layers not in use. The background is edited in the next step, so lock the foreground layer at this time.

3 Tracing the background. Crouse selected the photo and chose Object > Live Trace > Tracing Options. You can produce results similar to Crouse's by applying settings like these: For Mode, choose Grayscale; for Max Colors, enter 3 (some images need more levels); and select Output to Swatches. Leave other options at their default settings. Click Trace to commit the settings. The tracing is live, so you can change the settings at any time by choosing Object > Live Trace > Tracing Options.

4 Adjusting the background graphic's colors. To keep the viewer's focus on the subject, Crouse gave the background a light, low-contrast appearance. Selecting Output to Swatches in Step 3 added colors to the Swatches palette as global swatches applied to the Live Trace object. This is valuable because editing a global swatch updates all of its applied instances. To edit any of the new global swatches created by Live Trace, double-click them. In this case, the gray tones were changed to colors and lightened overall.

5 Simplifying the foreground copy for hand-tracing. In the Layers palette, lock the background layer and unlock the foreground. Select the foreground image and click the Tracing Options button on the Control Palette to edit the Live Trace settings for the selected image. Here, Max Colors was changed to 7, Blur to 1 px, Resample to 150 dpi, Path Fitting to 1 px, and Minimum Area to 10 px. The optimal values depend on the resolution of the image, so try different settings until you see what you want.

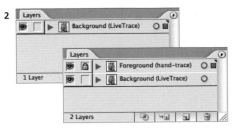

Layers palette before (top) and after (bottom) duplicating the image layer and locking the foreground layer

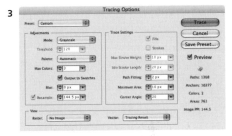

Tracing Options dialog box

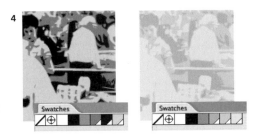

Before (left) and after (right) editing swatches output by Live Trace; white corners signify global swatches

Tracing Options button on the Control Palette, located to the right of the Preset pop-up menu

Detail of original image (left) and after adjusting for hand-tracing using Live Trace (right)

6

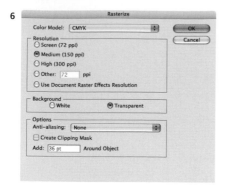

The Rasterize dialog box

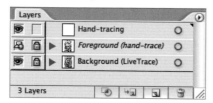

The Layers palette with the foreground tracing image layer set up as a template, and a new layer added to contain the hand-tracing

7

Completed tracing over the dimmed template (top), and with the template hidden to reveal the actual background (bottom)

6 Rasterizing the hand-tracing template. The Live Trace object contains many vector objects which could slow redraw. Converting it to a raster object simplifies the object and speeds screen redraw during hand-tracing. To rasterize the Live Trace object, select it and choose Object > Rasterize. Medium Resolution is a good compromise between a decent display speed and the ability to trace at high magnifications.

In the Layers palette, double-click the layer containing the foreground tracing image, select Template, and click OK. This locks and dims the layer, putting it in an ideal state for hand-tracing. Click the New Layer button to provide a layer to contain the paths that will be hand-traced.

7 Hand-tracing the foreground. Crouse used the Pen tool to hand-trace the template image, resulting in the foreground portrait. The goal of hand-tracing is to produce a personal interpretation of the original image, so Crouse didn't follow the template exactly; he added, edited, or removed paths as needed. Through his linework, Crouse enhanced and advanced the desired mood and feeling of the illustration and the physical and facial expressions of the subject.

When he was satisfied with his hand-tracing, Crouse used Save As to save a copy of his working file. With the original version saved, in this final copy of the file he deleted the hand-tracing template layer, leaving his hand-traced foreground over the Live Trace background.

Pre-processing a tracing image in Photoshop

Live Trace works by creating paths along significant changes in contrast. In some photos, the areas you want Live Trace to trace may not contain enough contrast. To address this, open the image in Photoshop and apply a Curves adjustment layer to increase or decrease image contrast or make other changes as needed. After you edit a placed image outside of Illustrator, use the Links palette in Illustrator to update the image link and the Live Trace object will also update.

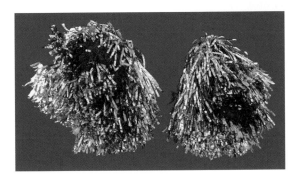

CROUSE

Scott Crouse

Using many of the same techniques as in Trace Techniques, Scott Crouse created this Illustrator CS2 rendering of a Miami Dolphins cheerleader. Crouse used Live Trace to trace a major foreground element—the pom-poms. The pom-poms are so complex that hand-tracing them would take too much time. Crouse realized that using Live Trace to trace the pom-poms would be much faster, and because of the random nature of the pom-poms, the Live Trace results would not be that different from hand-tracing them. Crouse first hand-traced the cheerleader with the Pen tool, but not the pom-poms. He then isolated the pom-poms from the rest of the original photo so that Live Trace would provide a clean outline of just the pom-poms. He did this by opening the original photo in Photoshop, tracing the outline of the pom-poms,

and then applying a single green fill color to everything but the pom-poms. For more control over the final colors, Crouse also used Photoshop to apply a Posterize adjustment layer and the Median filter. He also converted the image to Indexed Color using a 14-color Adaptive palette. He opened the edited Photoshop file in Illustrator and applied Live Trace. He used default Live Trace options with the following exceptions: He set the Mode to Color, the number of colors to 14, and checked the Output to Swatches checkbox. Crouse then edited the swatches created by Live Trace to brighten them. Finally, he deleted the green area and positioned the traced pom-poms over the rest of the drawing he hand-traced earlier.

HANSEN

Scott Hansen

For this cover of *Game Developer*, a magazine targeted at people in the video gaming industry, Scott Hansen used Live Trace to trace his sketch of a graduate (above right). Hansen wanted to portray a recent graduate considering his options in video gaming: to be a programmer, designer, or artist. Using the version he made with Live Trace as a starting point, Hansen created additional enclosed portions within the original traced objects to define areas that he intended to

be filled with different colors or tones. Hansen also "cleaned up" the traced objects that contained a lot of extra "burrs" and points. He used the Delete Anchor Point and Smooth tools to smooth the ragged sections (the final cleaned up version in Outline mode shown directly above). As with most of his projects, Hansen created the finishing details in Photoshop (see the *Illustrator & Other Programs* chapter for more on bringing Illustrator objects into Photoshop).

Scott Hansen

Before departing on a national tour, electronic music duo Dusty Brown commissioned artist Scott Hansen to create a promotional tour poster. To distress graphic pattern elements in the composition, Hansen wanted to create a vector paint stroke. He painted a real media paint stroke, scanned it, and placed it into Illustrator. Selecting the stroke, he used Live Trace to turn the paint mark into a black vector object (top black mark). So that the mark better fit the objects to which he would apply it, he used the Free Distort tool, and rotated and stretched the mark. Then, using the Direct Selection tool, he deleted some of the detailed portions of the mark, and repositioned other parts. When the stroke better matched what he had in mind, he clicked the Merge icon in the Pathfinder palette to form the final stroke (bottom mark). He brought the stroke into Photoshop as a Shape and filled it with the same cream color as the background. He duplicated the shapes on layers above the pattern elements so that they hid portions of the blue and red patterns underneath (see *Illustrator & Other Programs* for more on shapes and Photoshop).

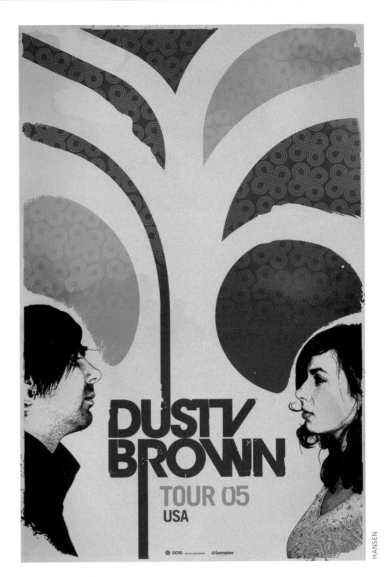

HANSEN

Blends, Gradients & Mesh

8

Blends, Gradients & Mesh

"W" Blend tool   "G" Gradient tool   "U" Mesh tool

To create volumetric fills and colors, you need to learn how to work with blends, gradients, and mesh. In the "History of Adobe Illustrator" timeline, blends came first, then gradients, then gradient mesh. Each can be both simple and very complex. So, we intermingle them in the lessons and galleries, even though we discuss these features "chronologically" in the introduction.

BLENDS

Think of blends as a way to "morph" one object's shape and/or color into another. You can create blends between multiple objects, and even gradients or compound paths such as letters. Blends are *live*, which means you can edit the key objects' shape, color, size, location, or rotation, and the resulting *in-between* objects will automatically update. You can also distribute a blend along a custom path (see details later in this chapter).

Note: *Complex blends, especially gradient-to-gradient blends, require a lot of RAM when drawing to the screen.*

The simplest way to create a blend is to select the objects you wish to blend and choose Object > Blend > Make. The number of steps you'll have in between each object is based on either the default options for the tool, or the last settings of the Blend Options (discussed in the following section). Adjust settings for a selected blend by selecting the blend, then double-clicking the Blend tool (or via Objects > Blend > Blend Options). Somewhere along the line, Adobe modified this feature, making it the most predictable method for blending—so you'll probably want to use it for most of your blends.

Another way to create blends between individual paths is to *point map* using the Blend tool. In the past, the Blend tool was used to achieve smooth transitions between blended objects. However, now that it's been modified, it's probably best to use it for special morphing or twirling effects. To use the *point map* technique, begin by clicking on an anchor point of one object, and then on an anchor point of another object. Continue clicking on anchor points of any object you want to include in the blend. You can also click anywhere on the path of an object to achieve random blending effects.

When a blend first appears, it's selected and grouped. If you Undo immediately, the blend will be deleted, but your source objects remain selected so you can blend again. To modify a key object before or after making a blend, Direct-Select the key object first, then use any editing tool (including the Pencil, Smooth, and Erase tools) to make your changes.

Blend Options

To specify Blend Options as you blend, use the Blend tool (see the *point map* directions in the previous section) and press the Option/Alt key as you click the second point. The Blend Options dialog will appear, allowing you to change any settings before making the blend. To adjust options on a completed blend, select it and double-click the Blend tool (or Object > Blend > Blend Options). Opening Blend Options without a blend selected sets the default for creating blends *in this work session*; these Options reset each time you restart the program.

- **Specified Steps** specifies the number of steps between each pair of key objects. Using fewer steps results in clearly distinguishable objects, while a larger number of steps results in an almost airbrushed effect.

- **Specified Distance** places a specified distance between the objects of the blend.

- **Smooth Color** allows Illustrator to automatically calculate the ideal number of steps between key objects in a blend, in order to achieve the smoothest color transition. If objects are the same color, or are gradients or patterns, the calculation will equally distribute the objects within the area of the blend, based on their size.

To blend or not to blend...

In addition to blending between individual paths, or groups of objects, you can blend between symbols (see the *Brushes & Symbols* chapter for more on symbols), Live Paint objects, or between Point type objects. Some of the objects that you *can't* include in a blend are meshes, raster images, and type objects that aren't Point type. When blending between objects containing brushes, effects, and other complex appearances, Illustrator blends affect options, which can help you create interesting animations (see the *Web & Animation* chapter for more on how to export animations).
—*Teri Petit*

Efficient Blending

An efficient way to make a blend is to select a manually drawn path (without a fill or stroke) and any objects you want to blend. Once you make the blend (via Object > Blend > Make), the path becomes the spine of the blended objects.
—*Jean-Claude Tremblay*

To insert objects into a blend

Direct-Select a key object and Option/Alt-drag to insert a new key object (the blend will reflow) that you can Direct-Select and edit. You can also insert new objects by dragging them into the blend in the Layers palette.

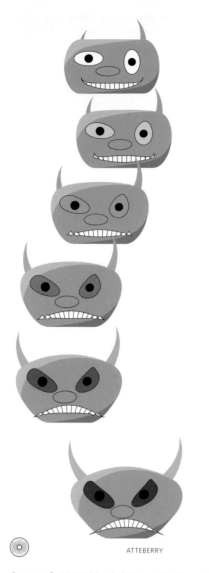

ATTEBERRY

*Groups of objects blended into each other using the Align to Path orientation, Specified Distance, and the "spines" edited into **S** curves (for more about blends see "KevanAtteberry-blends.ai" on the Wow! CD)*

Reverse Front to Back

To reverse the order of a blend with only two key objects, Direct-Select one of the key objects and choose Object > Arrange, or for any blend choose Object > Blend > Reverse Front to Back.

• **Orientation** determines whether the individual blend objects rotate as they follow the path's curves. Align to Path (the default, first icon) allows blend objects to rotate as they follow the path. Align to Page (the second icon) prevents objects from rotating as they're distributed along the path's curve (objects stay "upright" as they blend along the curve).

Blends along a path

There are two ways to make blends follow a curved path. The first way is to Direct-Select the *spine* of a blend (the path automatically created by the blend) and then use the Add/Delete Anchor Point tools, or any of the following tools, to curve or edit the path: the Direct Selection, Lasso, Convert Anchor Point, Pencil, Smooth, or even the Erase tool. As you edit the spine of the blend, Illustrator automatically redraws the blend objects to align to the edited spine.

Secondly, you can also replace the spine with a customized path: Select both the customized path and the blend, and choose Object > Blend > Replace Spine. This command moves the blend to its new spine.

You can also blend between grouped objects. Create your first set of objects and Group them (⌘-G/Ctrl-G). Now copy and paste a duplicate set (or Option/Alt and drag a copy). Select the two sets of grouped objects and blend choosing Specified Steps as the blend option. Once the objects are blended, you can rotate and scale them, and use the Direct Selection tool to edit the objects or the spine. (See "KevanAtteberry-blends.ai" on the *Wow! CD*.)

Reversing, releasing, and expanding blends

Once you've created and selected a blend, you can do any of the following:

• **Reverse** the order of objects on the spine by choosing Object > Blend > Reverse Spine.

• **Release** a blend (Object > Blend > Release) if you wish to remove the blended objects between key objects and maintain the spine of the blend (be forewarned—you may lose grouping information!).

- **Expand** a blend to turn it into a group of separate, editable objects. Choose Object > Blend > Expand.

GRADIENTS

Gradients are color transitions. To open the Gradient palette, double-click the Gradient tool icon on the Toolbox, or choose Window > Gradient. Gradients can be either radial (circular from the center) or linear.

To apply a gradient to an object, select the object and click on a gradient swatch in the Swatches palette. To view only gradient swatches, click on the gradient icon at the bottom of the Swatches palette.

To start adjusting or creating a new gradient, click on the gradient preview in the Gradient palette. Only after clicking on the preview will you see the color stops and midpoints. Make your own gradients by adding and/or adjusting the stops (pointers representing colors) along the lower edge of the gradient preview; adjust the midpoint between the color stops by sliding the diamond shapes along the top of the preview.

You can adjust the length, direction, and centerpoint location of a selected gradient. In addition, you can apply a gradient to multiple selected objects across a unified blend by clicking and dragging with the Gradient tool (see lessons in this chapter for detailed examples of how to use the gradient tool). **Hint:** *A special feature of the Gradient palette is that, even if it's docked with other palettes, you can expand its height and width to get a better view of the Gradient bar.*

To create the illusion of a gradient within a stroke, convert the stroke to a filled object (Object > Path > Outline Stroke). You can use this method to create a "trap" for gradients.

To turn a gradient into a grouped, masked blend, use Object > Expand (see the *Advanced Techniques* chapter for more on masks and masked blends).

How long can a gradient be?

Click and drag with the Gradient tool anywhere in your image window; you don't need to stay within the objects themselves.

Reset gradients to defaults

After you select an object that has an altered gradient angle (or highlight), new objects you draw will have the same settings. To "re-zero" gradient settings, Deselect All and fill with None by pressing the "/" key. For linear gradients, you can type a zero in the Angle field. Or, you can use the Gradient palette to switch between the Radial (Type) and the Linear (Type) and then back again to reset a custom angle without removing or relocating color stops.

Adding color to your gradient

- Drag a swatch from the Color or Swatches palette to the gradient slider until you see a vertical line indicating where the new color stop will be added.
- If the Fill is a solid color, you can drag color from the Fill icon at the bottom of the Toolbox.
- Hold down the Option/Alt key to drag a copy of a color stop.
- Option/Alt-drag one stop over another to *swap* their colors.
- Click the lower edge of a gradient to add a new stop.

The amazing work with mesh only starts in this chapter—don't miss the additional mesh artwork in the Advanced Techniques chapter—above is a detail of an Ann Paidrick illustration

PAIDRICK

Adding rows and columns

To add new rows and columns to your mesh, click on the mesh object with the Mesh tool (U). To add a new mesh row, click on a column mesh line. To add a new mesh column, click on a row.

Adding color to the mesh

When adding a new mesh point, the color currently selected in the Swatches palette will be applied to the new point. If you want the new mesh point to remain the color currently applied to the mesh object, hold the Shift key while adding a new point.

Moving rows and columns

When moving a mesh point, both the row and column mesh lines intersecting that point will move with it. To move a row or column mesh line independently, without moving the other, hold the Shift key while you drag a line. If you drag up or down, only the row line moves; if you drag left or right, only the column line moves.

GRADIENT MESH

This chapter begins with the basics of gradient mesh. In a later lesson, you will be taken deeper into its complexities.

If you see an amazing photorealistic image created in Illustrator, chances are it was created using gradient mesh. A *mesh object* is an object on which multiple colors can flow in different directions, with smooth transitions between specially defined *mesh points*. You can apply a gradient mesh to a solid or gradient-filled object (but you can't use compound paths to create mesh objects). Once transformed, the object will always be a mesh object, so be certain that you work with a copy of the original if it's difficult to re-create.

Transform solid filled objects into gradient mesh objects either by choosing Object > Create Gradient Mesh (so you can specify details on the mesh construction) or by clicking on the object with the Mesh tool. To transform a gradient-filled object, select Object > Expand and enable the Gradient Mesh option.

Use the Mesh tool to add mesh lines and mesh points to the mesh. Select individual points, or groups of points, within the mesh using the Direct Selection tool or the Mesh tool in order to move, color, or delete them. For details on working with gradient meshes (including the Warning Tip about printing mesh objects), see Galleries and lessons later in this chapter, as well as the *Advanced Techniques* chapter. **Hint:** *Instead of applying a mesh to a complex path, try to first create the mesh from a simpler path outline, then mask the mesh with the more complex path.*

Get back your (mesh) shape!

When you convert a path to a mesh, it's no longer a path, but a mesh object. To extract an editable path from a mesh, select the mesh object, choose Object > Path > Offset Path, enter 0, and press OK. If there are too many points in your new path, try using Object > Path > Simplify (for more on Simplify see the *Basic Drawing & Coloring* intro). —Pierre Louveaux

WEBB

Tim Webb

Tim Webb used just a few features of Illustrator to create his Victory Climb and Road lessons illustrations. The crisp woodcut appearance is a result of bold line work layered above gradient fills. Webb began by drawing the image with the Pen tool. Webb then created his color palette by importing colors from a swatch library into the Swatches palette. He then double-clicked the Gradient tool icon to open the Gradient palette and created gradients by dragging colors from the Swatches palette onto the stops of the Gradient palette. (For more detail on creating a gradient, see the gradients section of the introduction to this chapter).

After he created and saved the gradients in the Swatches palette, Webb drew closed paths and filled them with either a linear or a radial gradient, varying the direction and length of the gradient in order to give volume to the image. The woodcut appearance was created by blending between two triangular shapes on a curved path. Webb created custom art brushes to make the small rocks and the raindrops.

Simplest of Mesh

Filling a Shape with a Gradient Mesh

Overview: *Draw paths; select paths and fill with colors; select a shape and click with the Mesh tool; choose a color for the mesh highlight point; copy and paste, and scale and rotate copies to compose the illustration.*

1

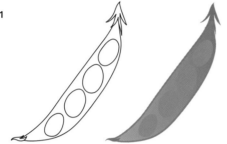

Left, the paths drawn for the soybean pod; right, the paths filled with two shades of green

2

Left, the Preview View of a gradient mesh; right, the Outline View of the selected mesh

3

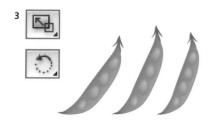

The three pods (original is on the left and the two scaled and rotated copies are on the right)

For her book for the Japanese market, "Adobe Illustrator CS," which she co-authored with Yukio Miyamoto, artist Nobuko Miyamoto found that creating a gradient mesh was easier and made a more shapely and editable gradient than creating a radial gradient with the Gradient tool.

1 Drawing and coloring the pod. Miyamoto began by drawing the vine and a soybean pod with its four beans. She filled the pod with a green gradient and then filled the bean shapes with a medium green. Use a color that contrasts with the colors around it for shapes that you'll paint later with a gradient mesh—this ensures that the mesh will not appear to fade into surrounding artwork.

2 Coloring the beans with gradient mesh. To create the gradient mesh for each bean, Miyamoto chose the Mesh tool, selected a light green for the highlight color, and then clicked on the unselected shape. When you click with the Mesh tool, Illustrator will automatically create a highlight point at the spot you clicked inside the shape. With the mesh still selected, you can change the highlight color by selecting another color from the Color or Swatches palette. If you want to move the highlight point, click on it with the Mesh tool and move it.

3 Copying, pasting, scaling and rotating. Miyamoto completed the illustration by copying and pasting the pod twice, and then scaling and rotating each copy before arranging the three soybean pods and vine.

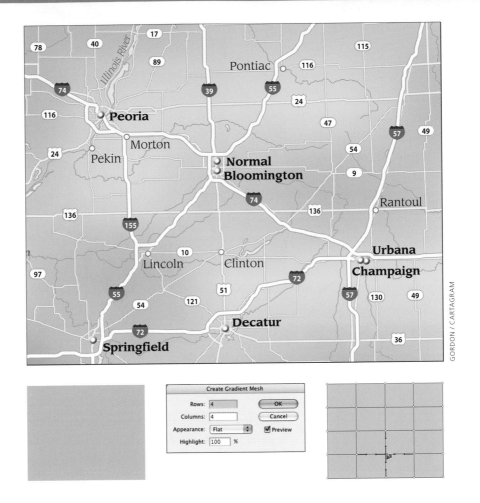

GORDON / CARTAGRAM

Steven Gordon / Cartagram, LLC

Large areas of solid color can be a necessary but boring fact of life for cartographers. With Illustrator's Mesh tool, however, they needn't stay boring for very long. In this location map, Gordon turned a solid green background into a natural-looking backdrop for his map. To create the background, Gordon first drew a rectangle and filled it with a solid green color. With the rectangle still selected, he chose Object > Create Gradient Mesh. In the Create Gradient Mesh dialog, he entered 4 in the Rows and

Columns fields, and left the Appearance menu set on the default setting of Flat. This created a mesh with editable points along the edges and inside the rectangle. Next, Gordon chose the Mesh tool and clicked on several of the points in the selected mesh. For each point inside the rectangle he clicked on, Gordon changed the original green color to a lighter yellow-green using the Color palette. For the mesh points on the edges of the rectangle Gordon clicked on, he changed the color to a darker blue-green.

Shaping Blends
Controlling Shaped-Blend Transitions

Overview: *Prepare your base objects; create modified copies of the base objects to create simple blends; further modify top objects in blends to create special blending effects; add finishing details.*

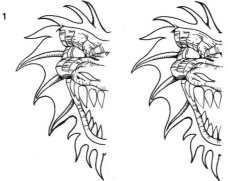

1

Atteberry's original drawing and the version he made using Live Trace

After drawing base objects, reflecting copies of the base objects that don't cross the center line

A manufacturer of theme park prizes commissioned illustrator Kevan Atteberry to create this logo to be printed on basketballs. After digitizing his initial line drawing, Atteberry colors his images with shape-to-shape blends, which he prefers over the less precise gradients, and more laborious gradient mesh. Creating shaped blends is a necessary skill to master before you can go on to the more complex techniques of masking shaped blends in the *Advanced Techniques* chapter.

1 Creating your base objects and setting options. Since his dragon is symmetrical, Atteberry drew half the face in ink on paper, scanned it in black and white at 600dpi and opened it in Illustrator. After applying Object > Live Trace, he chose Object > Expand, then selected and deleted the white objects (see the *Beyond Basic Drawing & Coloring* chapter for more on Live Trace). Then he dragged out a vertical guide from the ruler to the face's center. Using the Reflect tool he clicked on the guide, then Option-Shift/Alt-Shift-clicked on another point of the guide to reflect a copy on the other side of the guide. With the line drawing complete, he locked the layer containing the line work, and created layers underneath to create his base, solid-colored objects with the Pen and Pencil tools. For objects that didn't cross the center line, Atteberry made one version and reflected a copy to the other side. To prepare for blending, double-click the Blend tool to set Smooth Color for Blend Options.

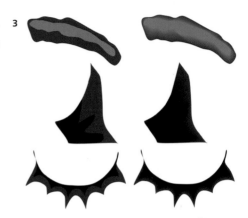

Modifying a copy of the bottom object to create smooth blend transitions

2 **Making simple, smooth blends.** For each of his blends, Atteberry begins by selecting the base object and copying. Then using Edit>Paste in Front (⌘-F/Ctrl-F), he modifies the top object and blends between the two. The modifications often include scaling the top copy of the object smaller, shifting the location of the object, or sometimes modifying the outline itself. In the example shown (the dragon's right cheek), Atteberry redrew the top object's path using the Pencil tool. Selecting both objects he chose Object>Blends>Make. Even though the top object contains many more points, the blend is still smooth.

Modifying the top object in blends to achieve special blending effects

3 **Shaping blends for special effects.** Sometimes smooth blending isn't the effect that you want. Atteberry achieves many different effects by altering the top object in the blend. Sometimes he wants to create an irregular shape (the dragon's eyebrow shown), other times he wants to create feathering or shaped effects. He uses the Direct Selection and Pencil tools, as well as the Free Transform tool and other transformation tools, to substantially modify the top shape. Although he generally just distorts the object and moves around the positioning of points, he does sometimes add new ones (using the Add Anchor Point Tool or redrawing with the Pencil). After applying the blend, because it's live, Atteberry continues to adjust the positioning and shape of the top object with all the tools at his disposal until he achieves the desired effect.

The dragon with copied and modified versions in place, and after creating all of the blends

4 **Adding finishing details.** After adding the blends to his images, Atteberry adds finishing details with solid-filled, gradient-filled, and stroked small accents. For this image, Atteberry even filled the line work with a gradient. The menacing teeth are on a layer above the line work.

The final dragon with blends and details and then with the line work (still just in black) on a layer above (the front teeth are on the top layer)

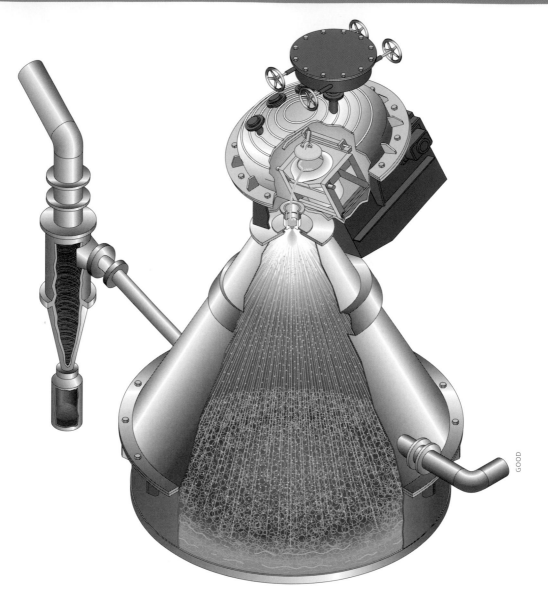

Janet Good / Industrial Illustrators

Illustrator Janet Good's image of the white-hot glow of molten metal spraying inside a chamber of liquid nitrogen is based on a drawing by Crucible Research. For the fiery glow at the top of the chamber, she first drew yellow and orange objects and then blended them. (By making the edge of the orange object jagged,

she created a blend that appears to have rays.) In a layer above the blend, Good drew several pairs of yellow and white lines, blending the pairs to form a fan of glowing light rays.

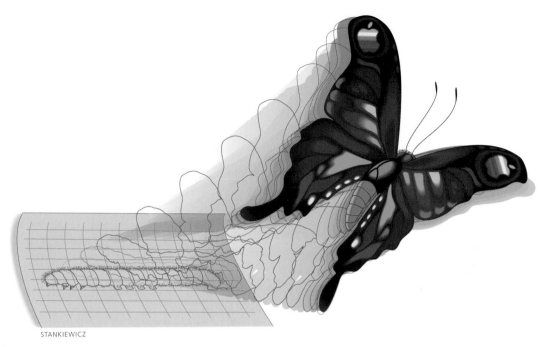

STANKIEWICZ

Steven Stankiewicz

Steven Stankiewicz uses a technique he calls "blends to blends" to smooth one colorful blend with another in his illustrations. To create a butterfly wing, he first drew the wing shape and its spots with the Pen tool and then colored each object. For the wing blend, he copied the wing object, pasted it in front, and scaled it smaller with the Scale tool. After selecting the original and the copy, he used the Blend tool to click on an anchor point on the original wing and Option-click on the corresponding point of the copied (smaller) wing. From the pop-up Blend Options dialog box, Stankiewicz chose the Smooth Color option. Then he performed the same steps to create blends for each of the wing spots. Stankiewicz decided to smooth the color transition

between each wing spot blend and the wing blend behind it. To accomplish this, he chose the Direct Selection tool and selected the outermost object in one of the wing spot blends; then he Shift-selected the innermost object of the wing blend behind it. With both objects selected, Stankiewicz clicked points on both objects that were in roughly the same position on each object. As a result, a new blend was created that smoothly bridged the blend of a wing spot with the blend of the wing behind it.

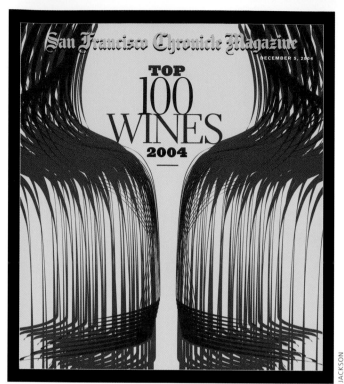

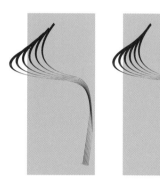

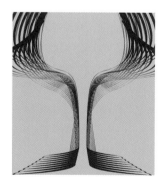

JACKSON

Lance Jackson / San Francisco Chronicle Magazine

For this *San Francisco Chronicle Magazine* cover, staff illustrator
Lance Jackson made artistic use of blended brush strokes. Jackson
customized a calligraphic brush and chose the Brush tool. Then
with a pressure-sensitive tablet, he drew a simple, elegant, gestural
silhouette evoking a wine goblet. Using a variety of tools, Jackson
modified a copy of this silhouette. Selecting the original and modified strokes, he chose Object > Blend > Make (although you can
blend live brush strokes, Jackson prefers to expand them first by
using Object > Expand). While still selecting the blend he double-
clicked the Blend tool to access Blend Options where he adjusted
the number of Specified Steps. Next Jackson expanded the blend
using Object > Blend > Expand (the expanded blend is automatically
grouped). He then adjusted the position and shape of each blend
object, and recolored the grouping. By copying these expanded
groups, Jackson created new silhouettes, modifying colors and
strokes. He created one side of the glass and used the Reflect tool to
create the other silhouette by reflecting along the Vertical axis.

GORSKA

Caryl Gorska

Gradient fills with transparencies colorize this pencil sketch based on Les Usines by Fernand Léger. Caryl Gorska placed the black and white pencil sketch on a bottom layer and selected Filter > Colors > Adjust Colors to give the sketch an overall ocher hue (shown above). On a layer above the sketch Gorska drew the geometric shapes with the Pen tool. She filled the shapes with a variety of linear and radial gradients that shared the same five colors Gorska designated in the Swatches palette. With the Gradients palette open, Gorska dragged the colors from the swatches palette to the gradient sliders and adjusted the stops. She applied the individual gradients to the shapes with the Gradient tool. Gorska adjusted the opacity ranging from 30% to 70% in the Transparency palette where she wanted the texture to show through the gradient. To further darken some areas she applied the blending mode of Multiply. The detailed image in the upper left shows the variety of gradients in the drawing without the texture of the pencil sketch underneath. For more about Transparency and Blending modes see the *Transparency* chapter.

Unified Gradients

Redirecting Fills with the Gradient Tool

Overview: *Fill objects with gradients; use the Gradient tool to adjust fill length and angle, and unify fills across multiple objects.*

picturedance.com ©joly

JOLY

The Gradient palette (left), and the Gradient tool in the Toolbox (right)

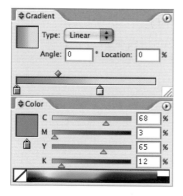

The Gradient palette customized for the flippers; when you select a gradient slider, the slider color appears in the Color palette for editing

Gradient applied to the flippers using the Gradient palette

The Gradient tool complements the Gradient palette by providing more ways to edit gradient fills, and by stretching and unifying gradients across multiple paths. For this *Sunset* magazine illustration, Dave Joly used the Gradient palette to apply initial gradients, and then used the Gradient tool to customize gradients and unify them across multiple paths, as seen in the clouds and fish scales.

1 Applying and editing gradients. The Gradient tool can edit gradients, but it can't create them. To apply an initial gradient to the flippers, Joly selected them, opened the Gradient palette, and clicked the gradient icon at the top left corner of the Gradient palette. To edit gradient colors, Joly clicked on each gradient slider and either mixed a new color in the Color palette or Option-clicked/ Alt-clicked a color swatch on the Swatches palette. He dragged the far right Gradient slider to the left to extend the ending gradient color. You can add sliders by clicking under the gradient bar, and you can drag the diamonds above the slider bar to adjust the rate of change between gradient sliders.

2 Editing a gradient using the Gradient tool. To set a new gradient length and angle, select a path and drag the Gradient tool over it. You can start and stop dragging the Gradient tool anywhere inside or outside the selected path. To constrain a linear gradient's angle to 45-degree increments, hold down the Shift key as you drag. To edit a radial gradient, you can click the Gradient tool to reposition the center, or click and drag if you want to change both the center and the radius of the radial gradient.

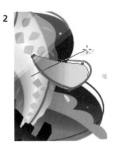

Changing a gradient's angle by dragging the Gradient tool over a selected flipper

3 Unifying gradients with the Gradient tool. Joly first selected two clouds and applied the same gradient to both. He then dragged the Gradient tool all the way from the left edge of the left cloud to the right edge of the right cloud. The length and angle of the unified gradient spanned both clouds as if they were one object.

As you drag, the Info palette displays the cursor position and the gradient distance, size, and angle. The Gradient palette displays the final gradient angle until you deselect the paths.

Dragging the Gradient tool across two clouds (top), so that the unified gradient starts in the left cloud and ends in the right cloud (bottom)

4 Editing a unified gradient. To edit the length and angle of the unified gradient across the fish scales, Joly selected all of the scales and then dragged the Gradient tool across them until he achieved the effect he wanted.

While you can also edit a unified gradient by using the Gradient palette, the Gradient tool provides additional flexibility because you can drag it to position the starting and ending points of the gradient outside the paths that make up the gradient.

÷Info		
+ X : 487 px		W : 342 px
Y : 395 px		H : −76 px
D : 350.343 px		△ : −12.529°

The Info palette provides numeric feedback as you drag the Gradient tool

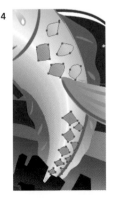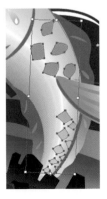

Editing the angle of the unified gradient across all selected fish scales, from a horizontal angle (left) to a vertical angle (right)

Selecting unified gradients more easily

It can be difficult to select all of the paths in a unified gradient. To simplify editing, combine the paths into a group, a compound path, or a compound shape. That way, clicking any part of the group or combined shape selects the entire unified gradient. You can also choose Select > Save Selection to save and name the selection.

Gleaming Gold

Simulating Shining Metal with Gradients

Overview: *Create the look of gold with gradients; create depth by offsetting paths and adding bevels; create custom-shaped gradients with blends*

FERSTER (Client: Intuit, Inc., Product: Quickbooks 2005)
(Creative Director: Riccardo Spina)

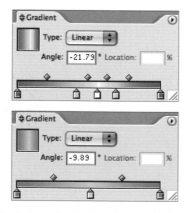

1

The coin paths pulled apart to show their fills

The Gradient palettes for the coin edge (top) and the coin center (bottom)

This logo for the popular Intuit QuickBooks line of business accounting software is used for everything from packaging to marketing materials, in print and online. It was originally designed in Illustrator and Photoshop, but the original file size was so large that Gary Ferster was asked to re-create the logo as a smaller file. Ferster's efficiently rebuilt version of the logo, created exclusively in Illustrator, takes up 93% less disk space than the original. To suggest the gleam of gold, Ferster applied gradients or blends depending on which technique was most appropriate for various parts of the illustration.

1 **Adding shiny highlights to the coin.** Ferster built the coin as a set of concentric circles, each with a different fill. The outer golden band is a large circle filled with a customized linear gradient, and the center is another circle with a similar gradient. The outermost black outline is a circle filled with black, placed just behind and made slightly larger than the outer golden circle.

By default, gradients have one starting and ending color slider. To create the metallic gleam, Ferster customized the gradients by clicking below the gradient bar to add sliders, and then applied lighter colors to the middle sliders. The outer circle uses five sliders.

2 Creating the dollar sign. Just as he did for the coin circles, Ferster created depth for the dollar sign by stacking filled paths. He started from the smaller path (the raised surface of the dollar sign). He selected the path, chose Object > Path > Offset Path, entered a positive value to create a larger duplicate (Ferster entered 5 pt), and clicked OK. The new offset path became the base of the dollar sign. With the new outer path selected, he chose the Offset Path command again, but this time entered 2 pt to create the outer border of the dollar sign.

3 Making the gleaming bevels. Ferster created bevels by cutting up copies of the inner and outer paths. He drew lines to bisect the paths at their corners, selected the lines and both dollar sign paths, and then clicked the Divide button in the Pathfinder palette. The Divide button converts all enclosed areas into separate closed paths. Ferster used the Direct Selection tool to delete line remnants but kept all closed bevel paths. He applied no stroke and linear gradients to the bevel paths. Ferster refined the gradient angles and colors with the Gradient palette because he prefers its precision compared to the Gradient tool.

Ferster also applied a radial gradient fill to the clock hub and linear gradient fills to the clock hands. He built the bar chart by applying linear gradient fills to rectangles edited for perspective by dragging points and segments with the Direct Selection tool. The sides of the bars are filled with linear gradients. For the bar tops, Ferster applied linear gradients that used three gradient sliders.

4 Adding shadows and highlight blends to the man. Ferster wanted to add airbrush-like shadows and highlights to the human figure. The shape of this shading was too organic for linear or radial gradients, so Ferster created custom-shaped blends. For each blend, he drew a base path filled with the color of the man's body, and a smaller path filled with either a highlight or shadow color. Ferster selected both paths and then chose Object > Blend > Make to blend the fills.

2

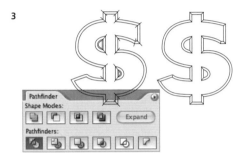

Using Offset Path to create a larger duplicate

3

Lines drawn over path intersections (left), then using the Divide button to slice along paths to create closed paths (right) for the bevels

The completed dollar sign and its gradient-filled components (left to right): The original path, the offset base path, and the filled bevels, pulled apart

4

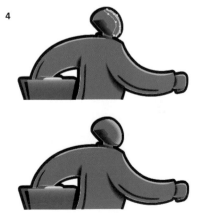

Before (top) and after (bottom) applying a blend to paths forming the highlight on his head

BEAUREGARD

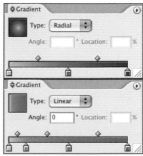

Christiane Beauregard

Christiane Beauregard created subtle color transitions throughout this illustration with linear and radial gradients. Beauregard drew each shape with the Pen tool, and as she progressed, created the gradient to fill the shape. She clicked on the gradient preview in the Gradient palette, selected the type of gradient (linear or radial), and added custom colors to the color stops and midpoints. (Two gradients Beauregard used are shown above). She adjusted the length and direction of the gradient fills within the shapes by using the Gradient tool.

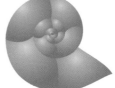

Christiane Beauregard

Using the same coloring technique as in the Fall illustration (opposite page), Christiane Beauregard created the shell (detail right) with separate shapes filled with the same radial gradient. With the shape selected, she clicked and dragged with the Gradient tool from the beginning to the end point of the area and changed the angle of the gradient to give each shape its specific highlight. She created a luminosity in the depths of the sea by varying the opacities in the gradient-filled shapes. Beauregard clicked on the word Opacity in the Control palette and reduced the Opacity of the shapes. She overlapped some of these shapes to enhance the sea's depth.

Custom Radials

Distorting Radial Fills & Recoloring Radials

PELAVIN

Overview: *Swap colors of a gradient; fill circular-oval objects with radial gradients; distort the circles to squash the gradient; scale a solid filled object up and fill it with a radial gradient; vertically scale it back down to squash the fill; select and recolor gradients.*

1

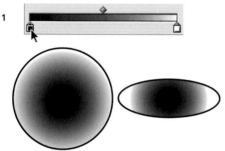

Holding Option/Alt when dragging one stop over another to swap the colors, then filling a circle and oval with a radial gradient

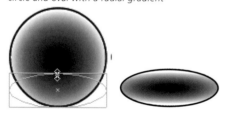

Filling a circle with a radial gradient, then squashing it using the bounding box to squash the radial fill as well

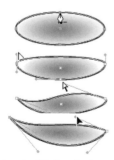

Reshaping the filled oval using path editing tools

Fill an oval with a radial gradient, and you get a circular gradient within an oval. Illustrator expert Daniel Pelavin cleverly fits a radial gradient snugly within an oval frame using a trick of scaling his object up, and down again.

For the PC Magazine awards for Technical Excellence, artist Pelavin designed the type, then created the reflective surfaces of the medal by filling the objects with a series of linear gradients. Pelavin set custom angles for the linear gradients and used the Gradient fill tool to adjust the length and position of some of the fills. In order to create the illusion of volume in the outer half of the leaf (that repeats to form the wreath), Pelavin made a circular radial fill snugly fit within the elongated oval-shaped leaf contour. To create the gold version of the award, Pelavin updated each of his gradients using his gold color scheme.

1 Squashing your circles and radials. This first method is best used with objects that don't require much editing beyond the initial shape of an oval. It's quicker to get the squashed results, but it's more editing work afterwards.

You'll first distort a circle to most closely fit your needs. Start by creating a circle using the Oval tool. Either click with the tool on your page and specify the same number for Height and Width, or drag to make an oval while holding Shift. Now open the Gradient palette and click on the black-and-white radial (circular) gradient. To reverse the gradient (or swap any gradient color with another), hold Option/Alt and drag-and-drop one stop over another. Next create a long oval; notice how the gradient doesn't fit the contour. With the Selection tool, click on the circle. Grab one of the handles of the bounding box and squash and stretch the circle. You'll see that the radial gradient distorts to match the contour.

In order to now make your oval fit a leaf shape (for instance), you now have to use the path editing tools to customize the path. As necessary, add and delete points, convert anchor points from curves to corners, and change the length and angle of the points and direction handles using the Direct Selection tool.

2 Vertically scaling your objects to squash the radial fills. Pelavin chooses to draw his objects first, and then he forces the radial gradients to fit his shapes. He drew the outer shape of his leaf with the Pen tool and gave it a solid fill (the stroke has been added so the gradients are easier to see). Then, double-clicking the Scale tool, Pelavin specified a 400% Vertical scale, 100% Horizontal. Next he chose a radial gradient from the Swatches palette and double-clicked the Scale tool again, to reverse the scaling with a 25% Vertical scaling (again 100% for Horizontal).

With his radial contour on the outer leaf, Pelavin finished the leaf cluster with a linear gradient-filled inner leaf, duplicated the leaf, and then placed a stroked outline of the combined leaves behind the filled objects.

3 Creating other color schemes. Using a copy of the silver award, Pelavin remade each of the gradients using shades of gold. He began by creating three custom global colors: light, medium and dark gold (see the *Drawing & Coloring* chapter for more on global colors). For each gradient variation, he selected one object with that fill and chose Select > Same > Fill Color. With that fill selected, in the Gradient palette he then dragged one of his new gold color swatches onto a gradient stop, or onto the gradient itself to add a new stop.

2

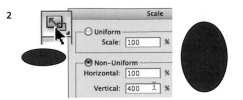

Scaling a solid-filled object up vertically by 400% by double-clicking the Scale tool

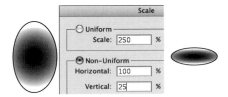

Filling the scaled oval with a radial gradient, then vertically scaling it back down by 25%

Pelavin's leaf object vertically scaled up by 400%, filled with a radial gradient, then vertically scaled down by 25%

From left to right: Pelavin's actual squashed radial fill (shown outlined), with a linear fill (shown outlined), then combined, and with finishing outline (behind the filled objects)

3

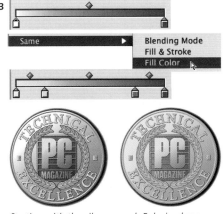

Starting with the silver award, Pelavin chose each gradient, used Select >Same >Fill Color and then customized that gradient using his new global gold colors

Rolling Mesh

Converting Gradients to Mesh and Editing

Overview: *Draw shapes and fill with linear gradients; expand gradient-filled objects into gradient meshes; use various tools to edit mesh points and colors.*

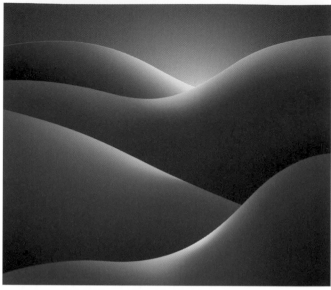

1

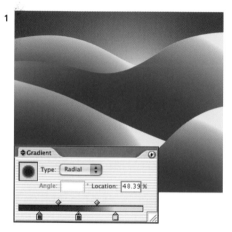

The hills shown filled with radial gradients—although there is some sense of light, it isn't possible to make the radial gradient follow the contours of the hills

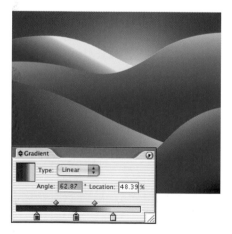

The hills shown filled with linear gradients, which are easier to edit than radial gradients when converted to gradient meshes

For many images, gradients can be useful for showing the gradual change of light to shadow (if you need to learn more about creating and applying gradient fills, first see "Unified Gradients" earlier in this chapter). For these rolling hills, artist Sharon Steuer expanded linear gradients into gradient mesh objects so she could better control the curves and contours of the color transitions.

1 Drawing shapes and then filling them with linear gradients. Begin your illustration by creating closed objects with any of the drawing tools. After completing the objects, select each object with the Selection tool and Fill it with a linear gradient fill. For each linear gradient, adjust the angle and length of the gradient transition with the Gradient tool until you can best approximate the desired lighting effect. Steuer created four hill-shaped objects with the Pen tool, filled them with the same linear gradient, then customized each with the Gradient tool. **Note:** *Although in some objects radial gradients might look better before you convert them, linear gradients create gradient mesh objects that are much easier to edit!*

2 Expanding linear gradients into gradient meshes. To create a more natural lighting of the hills, Steuer converted the linear gradients into mesh objects so the color transitions could follow the contours of the hills. To accomplish this, select all the gradient-filled objects that you wish to convert and choose Object >Expand. In the Expand dialog box, make sure Fill is checked and specify Expand Gradient to Gradient Mesh. Then click OK. Illustrator converts each linear gradient into a rectangle rotated to the angle matching the linear gradient's angle; each mesh rectangle is masked by the original object (see the *Advanced Techniques* chapter for help with masks).

3 Editing meshes. You can use several tools to edit gradient mesh objects (use the Object >Lock/Unlock All toggle to isolate objects as you work). The Mesh tool combines the functionality of the Direct Selection tool with the ability to add mesh lines. With the Mesh tool, click *exactly on* a mesh anchor point to select or move that point or its direction handles. Or, click *anywhere* within a mesh, except on an anchor point, to add a new mesh point and gridline. You can also use the Add Anchor Point tool (click and hold to choose it from the Pen tool pop-up) to add a point without a gridline. To delete a selected anchor point, press the Delete key; if that point is a mesh point, the gridlines will be deleted as well.

Select points within the mesh using either the Mesh tool or the Lasso tool, using the Direct Selection tool to move multiple selected points. Move individual anchor points and adjust direction handles with the Mesh tool in order to reshape your gradient mesh gridlines. In this way, the color and tonal transitions of the gradient will match the contour of the mesh object. Recolor selected areas of the mesh by selecting points, then choosing a new color.

If you click in the area *between* mesh points with the Eyedropper tool while holding Option/Alt you'll add the Fill color to the four nearest mesh points.

By using these tools and editing techniques, Steuer was able to create hills with color and light variations that suggest the subtlety of natural light upon organic forms.

2

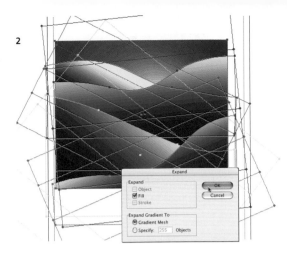

After Expanding the gradients into gradient mesh objects

3

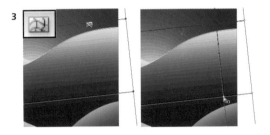

Using the Mesh tool to add a mesh line, then moving the mesh point with the Direct Selection tool

Using the Add Anchor Point tool, using the Lasso to select a point, moving selected point (or points) with the Direct Selection tool

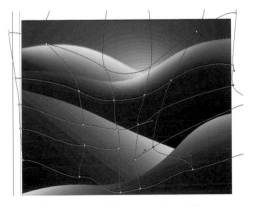

The final rearmost hill, shown after making mesh adjustments

Molding Mesh

Forming Bottles Using Gradient Mesh

Advanced Technique

Overview: *Create a basic rectangle; add mesh lines; use the Scale tool to move points in tandem; use the Direct Selection tool to edit paths; color the mesh; add finishing details.*

1

Making a basic rectangle, adding mesh points where the shape will be contoured, using the Scale tool to move groups of points inward.

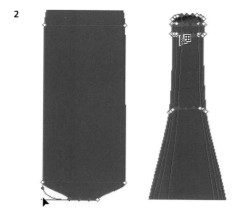

2

Using the Direct Selection tool to round curves, and adding new grid lines by clicking with the Gradient Mesh tool

Yukio Miyamoto is one of the world's experts in creating objects using the Gradient Mesh tool. This wonderful collection of bottles was created for the book and CD that he and his wife Nabuko Miyamoto write and produce; published in Japan, the *Adobe Illustrator CS* book is an amazing compendium of Illustrator techniques.

1 **Creating mesh from rectangles.** To create his complex mesh objects, Miyamoto begins with a colored rectangle. Then using the Gradient Mesh tool, he clicks on the rectangle to create basic horizontal mesh lines where he intends to modify the exterior shape of the object.

To narrow the bottle neck, Miyamoto then used the Direct Selection tool to select the anchor points at the top of the bottle. With these points selected he switched to the Scale tool. By default the Scale tool is centered on the object, so he grabbed one of the selected points and holding the Shift key, dragged towards the center of the bottle, narrowing the neck symmetrically. He also selected the bottom two points and dragged the points inward. (For details on radically modifying rectangle mesh objects see "Modeling Mesh" in the *Advanced Techniques* chapter.)

2 **Shaping mesh objects.** To continue to transform your rectangle into a rounded bottle, you'll next modify the corner points along the edge into curves. Using the Convert Anchor Point tool (hidden under the Pen tool) and the Direct Selection tool, select anchor points, smooth

anchor points and modify the corners to rounded curves. Miyamoto smoothed curves at the bottom of the bottle, holding Shift to constrain the path curves.

With the new shape contour established, Miyamoto used the Gradient Mesh tool to click within the bottle to establish vertical mesh lines, aligned with the new curve at the bottom of the bottle.

3 Modifying the mesh lines to create distortion, shadows and highlights. Light reflects and refracts on glass bottles. Once the basic inner and outer topography of the bottle is in place, Miyamoto uses the Direct Selection tool to modify the mesh lines within the bottle to mimic the affects of light. Using the Direct Selection tool, select points and groups of points to adjust their position. Click on anchor points to activate their direction handles so you can modify the length and angle of the curves.

Once your mesh lines are in place, you can select individual or groups of points, or click in areas between points and adjust colors using the Color palette sliders. You can also click on a color swatch in the Swatches palette, or pick up colors from another object by clicking in on the color you want with the Eyedropper tool. Miyamoto used a photographic reference to help him decide where to place lights and darks.

4 Creating finishing details. Although Gradient Mesh objects are an astoundingly flexible and powerful drawing tool, sometimes it's necessary to create details in layers above the mesh object. To make selections and isolated viewings of the various objects easier, create new layers for your detail objects above your mesh objects. For the blue bottle (in a layer above the mesh), Miyamoto created a few punctuations of color and light using objects drawn with the Pen tool, and filled with solid colors or custom gradients. For his beer bottle Miyamoto created type shapes, for the small milk bottle he added additional rim colors, and for the green wine bottle he added more reflections and a raised inner bottom.

3

Coloring the bottle

The finished blue bottle mesh in outline, hidden, and in Preview with details on a layer above

4

The final bottles shown with the mesh layer in Outline mode, and the finishing details (mostly gradient-filled objects) in Preview mode

Transparent Blend

Drawing Semiopaque Haze Effects

Advanced Technique

Overview: *Create blends that simulate colored water; apply a blending mode that allows objects in the water to be partially obscured.*

The Blend tool provides complete control over both color and shape transitions. Scott Crouse drew these five-step instructions for a package of denture cleaning tablets. (The large glass above is a detail of step three, and the final version includes captions.) Crouse used the Blend tool to model the complex surface of the dentures, and to show how the cleaning tablets color the water over time.

1
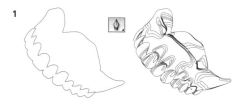

The main outlines of the dentures and tonal contours, drawn with the Pen tool (right)

1 Drawing the dentures. Crouse used the drawing tools to hand-trace the dentures from an imported photo. To set up his sophisticated shading effects, Crouse precisely drew pairs of paths marking the key contours where specific gray tones start and end. Each pair of paths would become the starting and ending paths for a blend. For each pair, he first drew a larger path with a fill matching the overall color of the gums or teeth, and then in front of that path he drew a smaller path with the shape and fill color of a highlight or shadow on that surface.

2

Two denture paths before (left) and after (center) applying a blend using the Blend command

All denture paths before applying blends (left) and after applying blends (right)

2 Creating the denture blends. Crouse applied a blend to each pair of paths he drew earlier. To blend two paths, select them and choose Object > Blend > Make. The completed blend creates a smooth transition between paths.

3 Creating the effect of light through water. Like glass, water picks up and distorts ambient light and the colors and shadows from surrounding objects. Crouse found blends to be useful here too. As with the dentures, Crouse drew pairs of paths for blends, again shaping the paths in terms of light and dark. Crouse filled each pair's larger path with 8% to 20% black and each pair's smaller path with white, then blended each pair of paths.

4 Submerging the dentures. Crouse positioned the dentures in the glass. Next, he selected the water blends and chose Object > Arrange > Bring to Front to move them in front of the dentures. While the water blends were still selected, Crouse clicked Opacity in the Control palette to change the blending mode from Normal to Multiply. Applying Multiply to the blends partially darkened the dentures so that they appeared to be submerged.

5 Showing the change in water color. Steps 2 and 3 of Crouse's illustration had to show how the cleaning solution turns green as the cleaning tablets dissolve. The packaging was not printed in full color, so the concept had to be illustrated in grayscale. To duplicate the glass and dentures, Crouse selected and then Opt/Alt-dragged them, creating a copy. To color the water, he used the Direct Selection tool to select the gray-filled paths of each water blend, and used the Color palette to darken their gray fills to 40% black. When you change the attributes of a path used in a blend, the entire blend updates.

For his steps two and three, Crouse also added a filled path to darken the water behind the dentures and blends. He also used the Ellipse tool to draw the cleaning tablet and bubbles in step two.

When blends are better than gradients

While gradients are quick and easy to set up, they are only available as simple linear and radial forms. A great advantage of blends is that they follow the shape of the paths you draw, allowing complex modeling.

3

Paths making up the glass (left) and the same paths filled (right)

Paths added to create light and water effects with blends (selected at left) and after applying a blend to each pair of paths (right)

4

Blends selected (left), and then transparent after applying Multiply blending mode (right)

5

Steps 1 to 3 of the directions (top) and the changes at each step (bottom); selected paths that were darkened (bottom left), and the larger path added to darken the background (bottom center and bottom right)

MA ZHI LIANG

Ma Zhi Liang

Ma Zhi Liang is an artist from China who painstakingly rendered this illustration from a photograph using Gradient Mesh. This portrait of his niece is a lovely example of how mesh can be used to show light, texture, and detail. The face is comprised of one mesh that makes up the "mask" of the face. Layered above the "mask" are other mesh objects that create the details of the facial features, such as the nose, eyes, and lips. Shown above are the mesh points that create the shadows and highlights in the fabric, lips, and button.

Transparency

9

Transparency

Using transparency with...

- **Fills**—apply an opacity, a blend mode, or an effect that utilizes transparency (e.g., Inner Glow).
- **Strokes**—just as with fills, apply an opacity, a blend mode, or an effect that utilizes transparency (e.g., Outer Glow).
- **Brush Strokes**—you can create scatter brushes, art brushes, and pattern brushes from transparent artwork. In addition, you can make any brush stroke (including calligraphic brush strokes) transparent by applying an opacity, blend mode, or effect that utilizes transparency.
- **Text**—apply transparency to selected text characters and/or the entire text object.
- **Charts**—apply transparency to the entire chart or the elements that make up the chart.
- **Groups**—select or target the <Group> and apply an opacity, a blend mode, or an effect that utilizes transparency (such as Feather) to that group. When you select an entire group, you will automatically be targeting the group as well.
- **Layers**—target the layer and apply an opacity, a blend mode, or an effect that utilizes transparency. —*Sandee Cohen and Pierre Louveaux*

Illustrator's sophisticated use of transparency is woven throughout the application—you use transparency whenever you apply an opacity percentage, a blending mode, an Opacity Mask from the Transparency or Control palettes, and whenever you apply certain kinds of effects (such as shadows, feathers, and glows) or styles that include those features. Although it's easy to apply transparent effects to your artwork, it's important that you understand how transparency works, because this will help you later when you print or export a document containing transparency.

If the concepts of *Appearances* or *Targeting* are new to you, it's very important that you start first with the "Appearances" section of the *Layers & Appearances* chapter. Although this is not an advanced techniques chapter, we assume that by now you have a basic knowledge of fills, strokes, and especially layers. If you're unable to keep up with this chapter, please review the *Drawing & Coloring* and *Layers & Appearances* chapters.

BASIC TRANSPARENCY

Although the Artboard may look white, Illustrator treats it as transparent. To visually distinguish the transparent areas from the non-transparent ones, choose View > Show Transparency Grid. To set the size and colors of the transparency grid, select File > Document Setup > Transparency. You can check Simulate Colored Paper if you'll be printing on a colored stock (click on the top swatch to open the color picker to select a "paper" color). Both Transparency Grid and paper color are non-printing attributes that are only visible in on-screen preview.

The term *transparency* refers to any blending modes other than Normal and any opacity settings that are less than 100%. Opacity Masks or effects, such as Feather or Drop Shadow, use these settings as well. As a result, when you apply Opacity Masks or effects, you're using Illustrator's transparency features. Be careful how you apply transparency. Correctly targeting and applying transparency is very important, especially when printing or exporting it. To make it easier, Illustrator gives you many helpful tools to increase your control over how you print and export artwork that contains transparency.

Opacity and Blending modes

To apply transparency, select an object or group by making a selection or clicking on the target indicator in the Layers palette; then, adjust the Opacity slider and/or choose a Blending Mode in the Transparency palette or Control palette. (Objects and groups are automatically targeted when you select them; if you want to apply transparency at the layer level, target the layer explicitly.) An object or group is completely opaque when its opacity is equal to 100% and is completely see-through, or invisible, when its opacity is set to 0%.

Blending modes control how the colors of objects, groups, or layers interact with one another. They are color mode–specific and yield different results in RGB and CMYK. As in Photoshop, the blending modes show no effect when they're over the *transparent* Artboard. To see the effect of blending modes, you need to add a color-filled or white-filled element behind your transparent object or group.

OPACITY MASKS

Opacity masks allow the dark and light areas in one object to be used as a mask for other objects. Black within the mask indicates areas of the masked artwork that will be completely transparent. White within the mask represents areas of the masked artwork that will be fully opaque and visible. Grays allow a range of transparency. (This works exactly like Photoshop *layer masks*).

The easiest way to create an Opacity Mask is to first create the artwork you want to mask. Next, place the object, group, or raster image you want to use as the mask above it. Select the artwork and the masking element,

Need more transparency?

Look for more lessons and Galleries involving transparency in the *Live Effects & Graphic Styles* and *Advanced Techniques* chapters.

Editing Opacity Masks

- **Disable**—Shift-click the mask thumbnail to turn it off. A red **X** will appear over the preview.
- **Enable**—Shift-click to reapply the mask.
- **Mask View**—Option-click/Alt-click the mask thumbnail to toggle between viewing and editing the masking objects on the Artboard, or the mask grayscale values.
- **Release Opacity Mask (palette menu)**—releases the masking effect.
- **Toggle between working on artwork or Opacity Mask**—click the appropriate icon to control what you are editing.
- **Link or unlink the Opacity Mask to artwork**—click between the mask and artwork to toggle the link/unlink option.

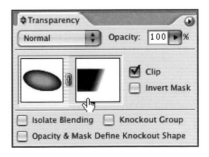

The Transparency palette with all options shown (choose Show Options from the Transparency palette menu)

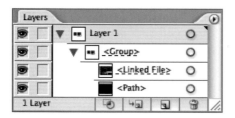

Objects being masked by an Opacity Mask are indicated by a dashed line in the Layers palette

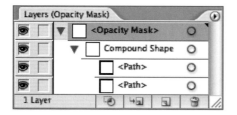

Opacity Masks are indicated with < ,> symbols in the Layers palette if you click on the Opacity Mask thumbnail in the Transparency palette

This cat by Yukio Miyamoto relies heavily on Opacity Masks (combined with mesh; see this and more in the Advanced Techniques *chapter).*

and choose Make Opacity Mask from the Transparency palette pop-up menu. Illustrator automatically makes the topmost object or group the Opacity Mask.

You may want to start with an empty mask and draw into it—in effect, painting your objects into visibility. To create an empty mask, start by targeting a single object, group, or layer. Since the default behavior of new Opacity Masks is clipping (with a black background), you'll need to turn off the "New Opacity Masks Are Clipping" option in the Transparency palette menu or your targeted artwork will completely disappear when you first create the empty mask. Next, choose Show Thumbnails from the Transparency palette menu, and double-click in the right thumbnail area. This creates an empty mask and puts you in mask editing mode; the Layers palette changes to show the Opacity Mask. Use your drawing and editing tools to create your mask. (For instance, if you create an object filled with a gradient, you'll see your artwork through the dark areas of the gradient.) While the Opacity Mask thumbnail is selected, you won't be able to edit anything else in your document. Choose to work on your artwork or your Opacity Mask by clicking on the appropriate thumbnail (the artwork thumbnail is on the left; the Opacity Mask is on the right).

A few hints can help you with Opacity Masks. First, Opacity Masks are converted to grayscale, behind the scenes, when a mask is created (even though the Opacity Mask thumbnail still appears in color). The gray values between white and black simply determine how opaque or transparent the masked object is—light areas of the mask will be more opaque and dark areas will be more transparent. In addition, if you select Invert Mask, you'll reverse the effect of dark and light values on the opacity—dark areas of the mask will be more opaque and light areas will be more transparent. To identify which elements have been masked by an Opacity Mask, look for the dashed underline in the Layers palette.

The link icon in the Transparency palette indicates that the position of the Opacity Mask stays associated with the position of the object, group, or layer it is masking. Unlinking allows you to move the artwork without moving the mask. The content of the mask can be selected and edited just like any other object. You can transform or apply a blending mode and/or an opacity percentage to each individual object within the mask.

Option-click/Alt-click on an Opacity Mask thumbnail in the Transparency palette to hide the document's contents and display only the masking element in its grayscale values. Shift-click the Opacity Mask thumbnail to disable the Opacity Mask.

See the "Opacity Masks 101" lesson in this chapter, and *Advanced Techniques,* for more on Opacity Masks.

Knockout controls

Choose Show Options from the Transparency palette pop-up menu to display the checkboxes that control how transparency is applied to groups and multiple objects. You can also click on the word Opacity in the control palette to temporarily open these settings.

With a group or layer targeted, check the Knockout Group option to keep individual objects of the group or layer from applying their transparency settings to each other where they overlap. This is particularly useful for blends containing one or more transparent objects. For this reason, Illustrator automatically turns on the Knockout Group option for all newly created blends.

Enable Isolate Blending for a selected group so the transparency settings of the objects *inside* the group only affect their interaction with each other and are not applied to objects past the bottom of the group.

The final checkbox, Opacity & Mask Define Knockout Shape, is used in very specific situations to limit the knockout of a color to the area defined by the opacity and the mask. To see any effect, you must use this option on a transparent object inside a knockout group.

This option is most useful on raster images and feathered edges. It's automatically turned on inside the appearance of Drop Shadow, Blur, Feather, and Photo-

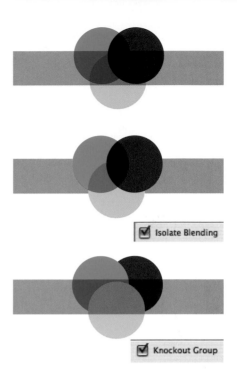

The group of circles at top show a Multiply blending mode applied to each individual circle; middle shows after enabling Isolate Blending to confine the blending mode to objects within the group; bottom shows after enabling Knockout Group to keep objects within the group from applying their blending mode to each other

Knockout Group checkbox

In addition to being 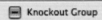 enabled or disabled, the Knockout Group checkbox has a third or neutral state that is indicated by a dash (in the Mac version) or grayed checkmark (in the Windows version). Illustrator automatically sets all newly created groups and layers to this neutral state so that simply grouping objects will not cause their transparency to change. The neutral state prevents the new group from overriding the knockout setting of the enclosing group.

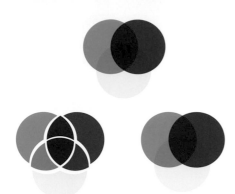

Top (live transparency): A multiply blending mode applied to each individual circle;
Bottom Left (flattened transparency, exploded view): Flattening the three circles results in seven separate regions;
Bottom (flattened transparency, non-exploded view): The final printed circles appear the same as the original

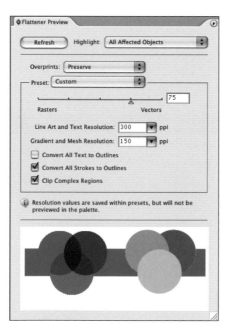

The Flattener Preview palette with all options showing (choose Show Options from the palette menu), including the Flattening Preset settings in the center of the palette. Click the Refresh button at the top of the palette, and the current document will be displayed in the preview area at the bottom of the screen. The section "Using the Flattener Preview palette," later in this chapter, explains how to use this preview to highlight areas of your art that flatttening will affect

shop effects. If it weren't, putting objects with these effects in knockout groups would produce unwanted results: The entire rectangular bounding box of Drop Shadows, Blurs, and Photoshop effects would knock out, as would the unfeathered outline of Feathered objects.

THE ART OF FLATTENING

PostScript printing devices and file formats such as EPS can only reproduce transparent artwork in "flattened" form. Illustrator's flattening process is applied temporarily if you print, and permanently if you save in a format that doesn't support transparency natively. Flattening occurs when areas of transparent overlap are converted into opaque pieces that look the same. Some of your objects may be split into many separate objects, while others may be rasterized.

As previously mentioned, Illustrator provides convenient tools that give you control over how your art is flattened. Illustrator's Flattener Preview palette (Window > Flattener Preview) lets you see how flattening will affect your art, by means of a preview built right into the palette. The Flatten Transparency dialog box (Object > Flatten Transparency) and the Advanced section of the Print dialog box also let you choose transparency and flattening settings. And the Transparency Flattener Presets dialog box (Edit > Transparency Flattener Presets) gives you quick access to your presets (discussed in the "Working with flattener presets" section following this one), allowing you to edit existing custom presets and create new ones as well.

Here are the flattening options you can adjust:

- **Name** lets you name settings to be saved as a preset.
- **Raster/Vector Balance** lets you control the degree to which your artwork is rasterized (discussed in greater detail in the "Setting Raster/Vector Balance" section a little farther on in this chapter).
- **Line Art and Text Resolution** sets the resolution for vector objects that will be rasterized when flattening.

- **Gradient and Mesh Resolution** lets you set the resolution for gradient and mesh objects that will be rasterized in the course of flattening.
- **Convert All Text to Outlines** keeps the width of text consistent during flattening by converting all type objects to outlines and discarding glyph information.
- **Convert All Strokes to Outlines** ensures that the width of text stays consistent during flattening by converting all strokes to simple filled paths.
- **Clip Complex Regions** reduces stitching artifacts by making sure that the boundaries between vector artwork and rasterized artwork fall along object paths.
- **Preserve Alpha Transparency** (Flatten Transparency dialog box only) preserves the alpha transparency of flattened objects, which can be useful if you are exporting to SWF or SVG.
- **Preserve Overprints and Spot Colors** (Flatten Transparency dialog box only) preserves spot colors and overprinting for objects that aren't involved in transparency.

To access these settings in the Flattener Preview palette, open the palette and choose Show Options from the palette menu. In the Flatten Transparency dialog box, you can select any existing preset as a starting point and then make changes in the dialog. In the Advanced section of the Print dialog box, choose any existing Preset from the Presets menu and click the Custom button to change the settings. See *Illustrator Help* for more details about Illustrator's flattening options.

Working with Flattener Presets

Once you've adjusted any of the settings above, you can save the results as a preset, so you won't have to create them from scratch the next time you want to apply the same flattening settings (or create a slight variation).

Illustrator comes with three default presets to get you started: High Resolution (for final press output and high-quality proofs such as color separations), Medium Resolution (for desktop proofs and print-demand-documents to be printed on PostScript color printers), and Low Reso-

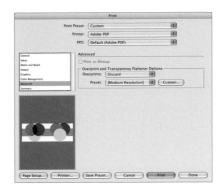

The Advanced section of the Print dialog box (choose File >Print, then select Advanced in the menu just above the preview)

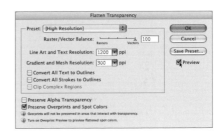

The Flatten Transparency dialog box (Object > Flatten Transparency)

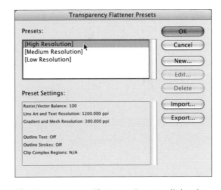

The Transparency Flattener Presets dialog box (Edit >Transparency Flattener Presets)

The Transparency Flattener Preset Options (New) dialog box that results when you click the New button in the Transparency Flattener Presets dialog box (above)

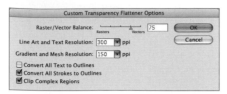

Click the Custom button in the Advanced section of the Print dialog box to display the Custom Transparency Flattener Options dialog box, where you can create a new custom preset

Overprint Preview

Previewing overprints on your screen has never been easier. Choose View > Overprint Preview to see how your overprints will look when they print. Overprint Preview also provides the best spot color simulations, although editing your file in Overprint Preview mode is slightly slower than in regular Preview mode.

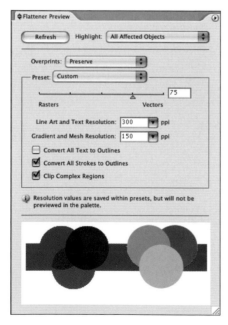

The Flattener Preview palette with artwork highlighted in red in its preview area, after choosing All Affected Objects from the Highlight menu

lution (for quick proofs to be printed on black-and-white desktop printers). You can't edit these default presets, but you can use them as a starting point, making changes and saving them as your own custom presets.

You can create and save your own custom flattening presets in any of the four following ways:

- **Using the Flattener Preview palette:** Select an existing preset from the Preset menu. Make your changes to its settings in the palette (choose Show Options from the palette pop-up menu if they aren't visible), and then choose Save Transparency Flattener Preset from the palette menu. Give your new preset a name and click OK. (If the existing preset you chose isn't one of the predefined default presets, you can also choose to apply your changes as an edit to that preset by choosing Redefine Preset.)

- **Using the Object > Flatten Transparency dialog box:** Choose an existing preset from the Presets dropdown menu, adjust the settings in the box, and click Save Preset to name and save your new settings.

- **Using the Edit > Transparency Flattener Presets dialog box:** Click the New button to create and name a new Preset; click the Edit button to make changes to an existing (non-default) preset.

- **Using the Advanced section of the Print dialog box:** Under the Overprint and Transparency Flattener Options heading, click the Custom button next to the Preset dropdown menu to create a custom preset. Click the Save Preset button at the bottom of the Print dialog box to name and save your settings into a new print preset. This option will not save a separate Transparency Flattener Preset.

To apply flattening presets when you're ready to print or export, choose an existing preset (or create a new custom preset) in the Advanced section of the Print dialog.

Using the Flattener Preview palette
The Flattener Preview palette lets you highlight areas of your artwork that will be affected when you flatten it, so you can see the effect of various settings and adjust them accordingly.

To begin, choose a preview mode from the palette menu: either Quick Preview (which gives you the fastest preview, but excludes the All Rasterized Regions option in the Highlight menu) or Detailed Preview (which enables All Rasterized Regions). Then choose an option from the Overprint menu: Preserve, to retain overprinting; Simulate, to imitate the appearance of printing to separations; or Discard, to prevent any Overprint Fill or Overprint Stroke settings that have been set in the Attributes palette from appearing on the composite.

Now you're ready to choose a flattening preset from the Preset menu (or create a new one), as described earlier in the "Working with Flattener Presets" section. When you've done that, click the Refresh button at the top of the palette, which will update the display in the palette's preview area according to the settings you've chosen. At this point, you can use the palette's Highlight menu to highlight areas that will be affected by the flattening process. You can choose from a variety of options—from All Affected Objects to specifics such as Outlined Strokes or Outlined Text. You'll see the areas in question flagged out in red in the preview. See *Illustrator Help* for more details about the various Highlight Options, and other aspects of using the Flattener Preview palette.

Setting Raster/Vector Balance

The Raster/Vector Balance setting, one of the flattening settings mentioned in "The art of Flattening" earlier in this chapter, determines how much art is rasterized and how much remains vector. In case you're unfamiliar with the terms, raster art is made up of pixels, while vectors are discrete objects. These days, most programs contain aspects of both vectors and rasters, but Photoshop is primarily raster and Illustrator primarily vector.

By default, Illustrator's Raster/Vector Balance setting is 100—which results in the greatest possible amount of art remaining in vector form. At the highest setting, the file contains the most vector objects and may produce longer print times. As you move the slider to the

More than one way to preview

Keep in mind that the Flattener Preview palette isn't intended for precise viewing of spot colors, overprints, or blending modes. Instead, use Overprint Preview mode to preview how those features will appear upon output.

The Flattener Preview palette's Highlight pop-up

Flattener Preview tools

To magnify the preview in the Flattener Preview palette, click anywhere on it with the default Zoom (magnifying glass) tool. To zoom back out, press the Option key as you click. To change the Zoom tool to the Hand tool so you can move the preview around, just hold down the spacebar and drag anywhere on the preview.

Resolution of live effects

The Flattener Preview palette can't help you fix everything that affects the output of your file. For instance, if you've applied a live effect with a specific resolution, in order to increase its resolution you'll need to reapply your effect at the resolution you desire (see the *Live Effects & Graphic Styles* chapter for more on applying live effects).

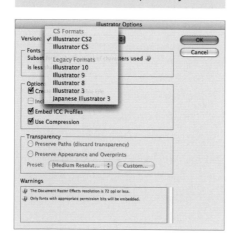

The Illustrator Options dialog box, showing the different versions to which you can save files (File > Save/Save As, then choose Adobe PDF document from the Format menu and click Save)

left, toward zero, Illustrator tries to convert vectors (like pure Illustrator files) to rasters (like Photoshop files). At a setting of zero, Illustrator converts *all* art to rasters. Usually you get the best results using the all-vector setting of 100, but if this takes too long to print, try the all-raster setting of 0. In some cases, when transparent effects are very complex, this might be the best choice. Generally, the in-between settings create awful results.

Because objects are always flattened to a white background, you might see color shifts after you flatten your artwork. To preview the way your artwork would look if flattened, you can turn on Simulate Paper (Document Setup > Transparency) or Overprint Preview (in the View menu), and you can use the Flattener Preview palette to highlight the areas that would be affected.

Using the Appearance and Layers palettes

Although Transparency can be tracked using the Flattener Preview palette, it is virtually impossible to decipher exactly what level and type of transparency has been applied to individual objects and groups without referring to the Appearance and Layers palettes. This is because you can apply transparency to individual strokes and fills, objects, sub-groups, groups, sub-layers, and layers. For example, you can apply a blending mode to an object, then group it with several other objects and apply an opacity level to the group. Later, you might even apply another blending mode to the layer containing that group.

To determine the level and type of the applied transparency, you'll first need to detect the location of the applied transparency. With the Appearance palette visible—use the Direct or Group Selection tool to click on an object within a group where you suspect that transparency has been applied. Looking at the Appearance palette will indicate whether transparency has been applied to the base object, or its fills and/or strokes; but the presence of the Transparency icons on the palette for the group and/or layer will show that cumulative transparency has been applied. Once you've determined the location of the transparency, you can use the Layers palette to locate active target icons, and look in the Appearance palette to find the type of applied transparency or effect.

THE LAST WORD ON TRANSPARENCY

When working with transparency, it is extremely important to know when your files will become flattened. When you print a file, the artwork gets flattened, but your file isn't permanently affected (because the flattening only happens to a temporary *copy* of the file during the printing process). Also, know that there are two basic kinds of EPS files you can make from Illustrator: Adobe Illustrator 9 (AI9) and newer, and Adobe Illustrator 8 (AI8) and older—and there's a big difference. (Illustrator CS2 allows you to Save As to a variety of Illustrator Legacy formats, including AI8, AI9 and AI10.) When you save as an EPS to AI9 or a newer format, two versions of your file actually get saved in the EPS—a flattened version *and* a native unflattened version. This allows you to print the file to a PostScript device (or import it into another application such as QuarkXPress). It also allows you to reopen the file in the current version of Illustrator in unflattened form so you can make edits to the file. However, saving as AI8 EPS (or earlier versions) only saves the flattened version of the file. This means that if you reopen the saved AI8 EPS file in a later version of Illustrator, you'll see that all your art is flattened. Reopening a flattened AI8 EPS file in Illustrator results in a loss of spot colors and layer information, and some of your objects may be broken apart or rasterized. In addition, this will convert all text and strokes to outlines (they become separate objects and will no longer be editable in the same way). Furthermore, if you save as AI9 or AI10, you'll lose any Illustrator CS2-specific features (they'll be expanded and lose their editability). So, it's *very* important to save in Illustrator CS2 EPS format if you need EPS. If you have to save to an earlier Illustrator EPS format, be sure to also save a copy of your file in native Illustrator CS2 format.

Stacking order is important

Stacking order plays an important role in transparency. When working with overlapping objects, changing the stacking order can change the appearance of overlapping areas. When you apply transparency to overlapping objects, make sure the stacking order is producing your intended results. Generally, it's a good practice to apply transparency to objects that are in front of other objects so they blend with the objects behind. When it comes to flattening transparency, make sure the objects you don't want to be affected by the flattening process are the topmost objects in the stacking order (such as type). You can adjust the stacking order of an object by moving it forward and backward (choose Object > Arrange). —*Gabriel Powell*

A known printing issue

Stitching is a visible transition between rasterized and vector artwork. Stitching usually happens when parts of vector objects get rasterized in the flattening process. To fix this, check the Clip Complex Regions checkbox in the flattening settings when you adjust them.

Note: *This option is only available when the Raster/Vector Balance slider is set to less than 100.*

Transparent Color
Customizing Transparent Brushes & Layers

Overview: *Create customized Calligraphic brushes; set Paintbrush Tool preferences; assign basic Transparency to individual strokes and layers; use selections to easily choose brush styles; use layers to organize different types of strokes.*

STEUER

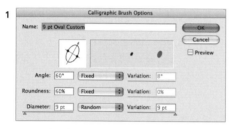

Customize the settings for each new Calligraphic brush using the Brush Options window

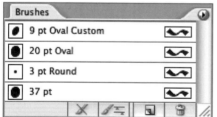

Four custom Calligraphic brushes in List view (from the Brushes palette pop-up menu)

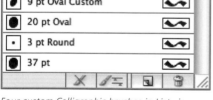

Adjusting the Opacity slider to preset the default opacity for the next brush; for quick and convenient access to the Opacity setting, use the Opacity slider in the Control palette

Illustrator provides a very forgiving way to create transparent "watercolor-like" marks. Unlike traditional media, or even digital tools such as Adobe Photoshop or Corel Painter, individual marks can be easily altered after the fact. In painting "Cyclamen in winter," artist Sharon Steuer used a few custom Calligraphic brushes, Transparency settings to adjust the appearance of overlapping marks, and Layers to control whether marks would be made above or below previous ones.

1 Creating custom Calligraphic brushes and setting the Opacity. You'll first customize a few brushes so you can better control the size of the marks you make. If you have a pressure-sensitive tablet, you can customize brushes so they respond to your touch. To make the first brush, start a new file, then open the Brushes palette and click the New Brush icon at the bottom of the palette. Select New Calligraphic Brush, and click OK. In the resulting Calligraphic Brush Options window, experiment with various settings, then click OK and make a stroke to test the brush. For her first custom brush, Steuer chose a Pressure setting for Diameter (9 pt with a 9-pt Random Variation), set the Angle to 60° and the Roundness to 60% with both Fixed, and clicked OK. For greater stroke variation, try choosing Pressure or Random options (pressure settings are unavailable and don't work unless you have a pressure-sensitive graphics tablet installed). To create additional brush variations, drag a custom brush over the New Brush icon in the Brushes palette and double-click the desired brush to adjust the settings.

To set the defaults for your next brush stroke and to paint in transparent color, first choose a Calligraphic brush and stroke color, then set the Opacity setting in the Control palette. To set opacity, click and hold the triangle to the right of the Opacity field to reveal the Opacity slider, which you can adjust. Alternatively, you can click on the word "Opacity" in the Control palette, which temporarily reveals the Transparency palette, or you can adjust the opacity and other transparency settings in the floating Transparency palette.

2 Setting Paintbrush Tool Preferences. In addition to creating your initial custom brushes, you'll need to set the Paintbrush Tool Preferences so you can freely make overlapping brush strokes. Double-click on the Paintbrush tool, then disable the Options "Fill new brush strokes" (so your brush strokes will be stroked and not filled) and "Keep Selected" (so new strokes won't redraw the last drawn stroke). With the "Keep Selected" option disabled, you can still repaint a stroke by selecting it first with a selection tool, then drawing a corrected mark within the distance specified in the Within field of the Paintbrush Tool Preferences dialog box. To create accurate marks, Steuer set the Fidelity to .5 pixels and the Smoothness to 0%. If you want Illustrator to smooth your marks, experiment with higher settings.

3 Painting and using the last selected object to determine the next brush style. For this step to work, you must turn off the New Art Has Basic Appearance feature (it's on by default); toggle it on/off in the Appearance palette. One of the wonderful aspects of working with Illustrator is that your last selected object determines the appearance for the next object you paint. To see how

2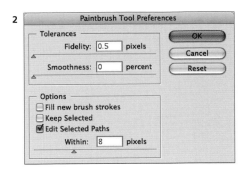

Setting the Paintbrush Tool Preferences to prevent new brush strokes from filling and to prevent redraw of marks already made

3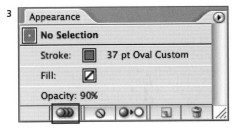

To make sure that any settings are maintained after each completed stroke, turn off the New Art Has Basic Appearance feature

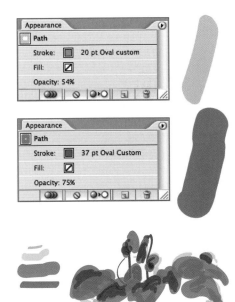

Steuer continually selects a previously painted stroke so the appearance settings from that selection are remembered for the next stroke. Working this way allows her to quickly change brushes and colors as she paints

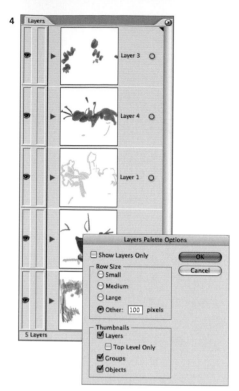

By changing the size of the thumbnails in the Layers palette (from the Layers palette pop-up), it's easier for Steuer to identify each kind of stroke and what layer it's on

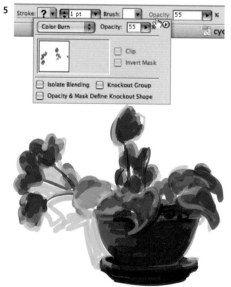

Steuer selected the layer containing a batch of flowers and experimented with different Blending Modes and Opacity settings until she was satisfied with their appearance

this works, select one of your brushes and start to paint. Notice that the brush, stroke color, and opacity you choose will continue to apply after you complete each stroke. By selecting a specific stroke that's similar to the one you want to create next, you can minimize the time it takes to customize your next brush stroke.

4 Using layers to organize different types of strokes.

To organize your artwork, keep sets of similar brush strokes in their own layers. When you are ready to make more strokes, create a new layer for them (click the New Layer icon). If you want the new set of strokes to be underneath a previous set, drag that layer below the layer containing the previous strokes. By keeping your layers organized in this way, you can use layer thumbnails to easily identify different strokes and manage the placement of new strokes. You can use layers to hide, lock, delete, and select groups of similar strokes efficiently.

Since Illustrator remembers the layer of the last selected object, your brush strokes will remain conveniently organized into separate layers. For instance, say you select a petal, then deselect it by clicking outside of the object itself (or ⌘-Shift-A/Ctrl-Shift-A): The next stroke you make will be placed at the top of the same layer. If you want the new stroke to be placed on a different layer, first select the desired layer, then begin painting.

5 Assigning Opacity and Blending Modes to selected layers.

Once you have organized different types of brush strokes into separate layers, you have the opportunity to globally adjust the Opacity and Blending Mode on entire layers. For example, after creating a batch of flowers on one layer, Steuer wanted them to appear brighter, so she changed the Blending Mode and Opacity for the entire layer by first clicking that layer's targeting circle (this selects and targets all objects within a layer, allowing any transparency settings to be applied to the entire layer). After changing the Blending Mode from Normal to Color Burn, she reduced the opacity to 55%.

STEUER

Sharon Steuer (Film by Frank Jacoby)

Artist Sharon Steuer created an opening sequence test for filmmaker Frank Jacoby's short film "Le Kiosk" by combining calligraphic brushwork with the opening still of the film. Working in RGB, she placed a TIF still (captured from Apple's Final Cut video editing program) into Illustrator as a Template. After copying brush marks containing custom "pressure sensitive" calligraphic brushes from another file, she pasted these marks into a layer above her template, automatically placing the brushes into the Brushes palette. Steuer mixed a sienna brown color, saved it as a swatch, and named it "Kiosk." Using the Control palette, she set the Blending mode to Multiply, reduced the Opacity to 80% and drew the outline of the kiosk. In new layers below the kiosk outline, she drew the background and foreground elements. Steuer selected all the marks in one of the

layers (by clicking the space to the right of the layer target icon) and then created new colors for the brush marks on that layer by Option/Alt clicking the New Swatch icon. In the resulting Swatch Options dialog she enabled Preview to see the results as she mixed a new color. By enabling Global, she could easily change the color to automatically update the color (and the marks with that color). To create the transition from drawing to opening video, Steuer duplicated the template layer (by dragging it over the New Layer icon), double-clicked it to disable the Template option, and moved it above the drawing layers. After experimenting, she set this layer to Hard Light at 40%, then duplicated the layer and saved the file. Using File > Export, Steuer saved each of five stages (building from line drawing to full image) as a TIF, and then imported them all into Final Cut.

Basic Highlights

Making Highlights with Transparent Blends

Overview: *Create your basic objects and a light-colored highlight shape; use blends to make the highlights; scale the highlights to fit.*

STEUER

1

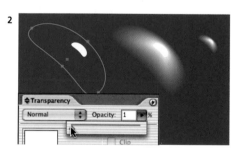

The original objects (locked in the layers palette) shown with the basic highlight shape

2

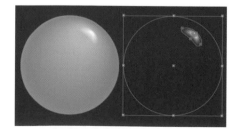

The highlight objects before blending (the outer object is set to 0% Opaque in the Transparency palette); after blending in 22 steps; the blend shown at actual size

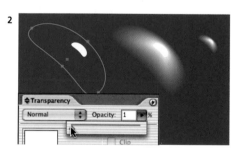

The final blend in place and shown in a "registration" circle for easy scaling on other bubbles

Using transparency, highlights are now as simple as creating a blend in the correct highlight shape. For help creating smooth contoured blends, see the *Blends, Gradients & Mesh* chapter.

1 Creating your basic objects and determining your basic highlight shape and color. Artist Sharon Steuer created this "Bubbles" image using overlaying transparent radial gradients (to see how she created the hill, see "Rolling Mesh" in the *Blends, Gradients & Mesh* chapter). She modified an oval with the Direct Selection tool to create her basic highlight shape. After creating your main objects, make a light-colored highlight object on top. Use the Layers palette to lock everything except the highlighted object (see the *Layers* chapter for help).

2 Creating the highlight. Select the highlight shape, copy it, choose Edit > Paste in Back, then Object > Lock. Now, select and shrink the front copy (for scaling help see the *Zen* chapter). Choose Object > Unlock All, then set the Opacity of this selected larger object to 0% in the Transparency palette. Select both objects, then with the Blend tool, click on one anchor point of the larger object, then Option/Alt-click on the corresponding anchor point of the smaller object and specify the number of blend steps (Steuer chose 22 steps). Steuer scaled copies of her highlight blend (with a "registration circle") for each bubble.

CASSELL

Peter Cassell / 1185 Design

As a kind of artwork not normally associated with Illustrator's hard-edged vector tools, Peter Cassell's fluffy cumulus clouds comprised one of the packaging illustrations created for an Adobe Illustrator box (see Cassell's cityscape Gallery later in this chapter). Cassell began by placing a photographic image on a template layer in Illustrator. Next, he created a gradient mesh with the maximum number of rows and columns (50). To color the clouds, he first chose View > Outline (so he could see the cloud image in a layer below the mesh). Next, he selected the Direct Selection tool, clicked on a mesh point, selected the Eyedropper tool, and then clicked in the cloud image to sample its color. He repeated this process to color the rest of the mesh to match the cloud image. To reshape parts of the grid to follow the contours of the clouds, Cassell clicked mesh points with the Mesh tool and dragged them. Where he

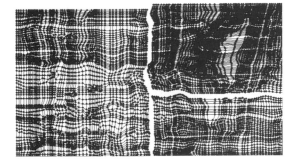

needed more detail, Cassell added rows and columns to the mesh by clicking on a mesh line or in an empty space in the mesh with the Mesh tool. As the composition became unwieldy with detail, Cassell selected overlapping sections of the mesh and copied and pasted each section into a separate file. Once he finished with a section, Cassell copied and pasted it into the final, composite file. He was careful not to adjust mesh points where sections overlapped, so he could maintain a seamless appearance where the separate sections he had worked on overlapped.

LARSEN

Tiffany Larsen

In this Illustration about Mardi Gras nightlife, artist Tiffany Larsen combined a posterized look with layers of subtle transparency to create depth and atmosphere. Larsen typically uses two colors in her illustrations. The primary color, of multiple shades, creates texture. The secondary color (red) is used as a highlight, and is limited to one or two shades and simple blocks of color. Here, Larsen also introduced a third color (turquoise) within the transparent smoke swirls. She applied varying opacities of 10%–30% using the opacity slider in the Transparency palette, all with the Blending mode set to Normal. The complex layering of transparent smoke over the solid blocks of color heightens the energy of the composition.

FISHAUF

Louis Fishauf

Louis Fishauf created the holiday glow that radiates from his mischievous Santa by using Illustrator's Gaussian Blur effect, the Transparency palette, and one of a set of custom art brushes. Fishauf created the background by drawing a large circle with a purple radial gradient and applied a 25-pixel radius Gaussian Blur. He selected the Star tool and drew a shape. He then selected Blur > Gaussian from the Effect menu, setting the Opacity to 25%. To create the illusion that the orbiting streak fades into the distance behind Santa, and to add a sense of depth to the entire image, Fishauf applied an art brush he created with short tapered ends to a 0.36-pt white stroke. He then integrated the streak into the image by giving it an opacity of 34% with the Lighten mode. As for St. Nick, Fishauf constructed the globe-like body, legs, arms, head, and hat from gradient-filled objects. He then made copies of these and pasted them behind the original set of objects, applying to each a white Fill and white Stroke ranging from 5 points to 7.26 points. A Gaussian Blur was applied to these objects, along with a uniform opacity of 68%. The gift box, computer, and Christmas tree each received individual glows. Fishauf added even more visual interest by adding a Drop Shadow to Santa's face and beard. Santa's list was created from a set of white Strokes, behind which Fishauf pasted a white-filled shape with an Opacity set to 50%, and a second copy of the shape with a gradient fill set to Lighten mode for a subtle modeled effect.

Floating Type

Type Objects with Transparency & Effects

Overview: *Create an area type object, key in text; add a new fill attribute in the Appearance palette; convert the fill to a shape; change transparency and add an Effect.*

Using the Convert to Shape effect, you can create an area type object with transparency and effects that will save you from making and manipulating two objects (a type object and a rectangle with transparency and effects below it). For a virtual guide to Bryce Canyon National Park, Steven Gordon created a transparent area type object with a hard-edged drop shadow that provided information for each of the Park's most popular hiking trails.

1

Left, the Selection tool selected; right, the Type tool selected

The type object after clicking with the Selection tool (the background photograph has been hidden in this view)

2

The Appearance palette after selecting the fill attribute and applying white to it

1 Making the area type object. Start by selecting the Type tool, dragging it to create an area type object, and then keying in your text. When you have finished typing, click on the Selection tool (the solid arrow icon) in the toolbox. This deselects the text characters while selecting the type object, preparing the object (rather than the characters) for editing in the next step.

2 Creating a new fill and converting to a shape. Open the Appearance palette and select Add New Fill from the palette menu. Drag the new Fill attribute below Characters in the palette. The Fill attribute will be automatically deselected when you move it in the palette so you'll need to click on it again to select it. Next, apply a light color to it (Gordon chose white from the Swatches palette). Now choose Effect > Convert to Shape > Rectangle. In the Shape Options dialog box, control the size of the rectangle around your type object by modifying the two Relative options (Extra Width and Extra Height). To make the shape wrap more tightly around his area type object, Gordon keyed in 0 inches for the Extra Width and Extra Height options.

3 Adjusting transparency and adding a drop shadow effect. Gordon designed each trail information box to incorporate transparency and a drop shadow, so its text would float above, but not obscure, the background photograph. To adjust the transparency of the shape you converted in the previous step, first ensure that the type object's Fill or Rectangle attribute is selected in the Appearance palette. (If either attribute is not selected, then the transparency changes that you're about to make will also affect the text characters.) Open the Transparency palette and adjust the transparency slider, or key in a value (Gordon chose 65% for transparency).

Instead of creating a soft drop shadow, Gordon opted to make a hard-edged shadow. To create this shadow, make sure the Fill attribute is still selected in the Appearance palette. Choose Effect > Stylize > Drop Shadow and in the Drop Shadow dialog box set Color to black, Blur to 0, and then adjust the X Offset and Y Offset sliders so the shadow is positioned as far down and to the right as you wish.

4 Editing the area type object. As you continue working, you may decide to resize the type object you originally created when you dragged with the Type tool. (This is different from editing the Shape Options dialog values to change the size of the transparent rectangle around the type object, as you did previously). To resize the object, click on the Direct Selection tool and then click on the edge of the type object you want to drag in or out. Because the transparent drop shadow shape was formed using the Convert to Shape effect, it is "live" and will automatically resize as you resize the type object.

Similarly, if you edit the text by adding or deleting words, the type object will resize, causing your transparent drop shadow shape to resize automatically.

The Shape Options dialog box with the Relative options edited

3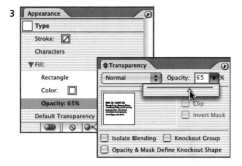

Left, the Appearance palette with the transparency attribute selected; right, the Transparency palette

The Drop Shadow dialog box

4

The Direct Selection cursor when it nears the edge of an area type object

Getting an edge

It can be hard to click the edge of a type object that has a drop shadow. To easily find the edge, choose View > Outline. Now the selectable edge will display as a black line.

Glass and Chrome

Highlights and Shadows with Transparency

Advanced Technique

Overview: *Apply transparency to white to simulate a glass highlight, and reinforce overall lighting by combining the Multiply blending mode with an underlying gradient.*

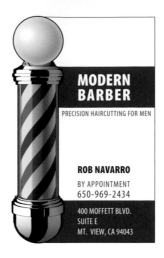

KELLEY & STOWE

The transparency and blending modes in Illustrator can greatly enhance the look of glass and chrome reflections. Andrea Kelley created this barber pole illustration for a business card designed by Jodie Stowe. To heighten the realism of the barber pole, Kelley used Illustrator's transparency features to reproduce the long, clean highlights that appear when glass and chrome reflect ambient lighting and surrounding objects. The finished business card was die-cut along the barber pole edge to set it apart from other business cards. You can use this technique by Kelley to create convincing glass and chrome highlights.

1 Placing the template image and tracing the pole.
Kelley was given a JPEG image of the original barber pole art, which was a useful reference for getting the alternating blue and red stripes just right as they wrapped around the pole. She placed the JPEG image as a template and then used the Pen tool and other drawing tools to hand-trace the objects making up the barber pole. To draw the perfectly round, white light globe on top of the pole, Kelley Shift-dragged the Ellipse tool. At this point, the chrome and glass reflections hadn't been traced yet.

2 Tracing the reflections. Next, Kelley traced the reflections—the highlight in the glass cylinder, and the dark reflections in the chrome at the bottom of the barber

1

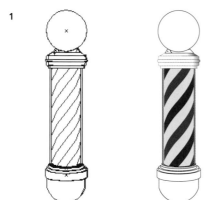

Kelley's hand-tracing without the reflected highlights and shadows, shown in Outline mode (left) and Preview mode (right)

2

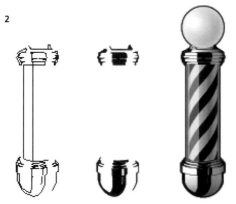

The glass highlight and chrome reflection shapes shown in Outline mode (left), Preview mode (center), and in position over the finished barber pole (right)

pole. Kelley recognized that the highlight was vertically continuous throughout the glass and chrome, so she made sure to position and align her highlight and reflection paths accordingly. She filled the glass highlight with white, and filled the dark chrome reflections with black.

To model the lighting on the frosted light globe, Kelley applied a radial gradient between white and warm gray (Kelley used 12.8% C, 12.8% Y, 16% M, 18% K), and also added a slight Inner Glow effect. To add a shine to the chrome base, Kelley applied a linear gradient between the same light gray as above, and a medium gray (16% C, 16% Y, 20% M, 16% K).

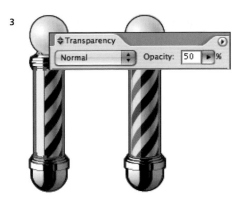

The glass highlight selected (left), and the same highlight deselected after applying 50% opacity with the Transparency palette (right)

3 Applying transparency to the highlight shape.

To reveal the objects under the glass highlight, Kelley selected the highlight and used the Transparency palette to apply an Opacity value of 50%.

4 Unifying the lighting.
Kelley reinforced the overall lighting by combining the Multiply blending mode with a gradient to create a soft, vertical shadow along the entire right side of the pole. Kelley first needed to create a separate path for the entire perimeter of the barber pole. She duplicated the pole and, with the paths still selected, she clicked the Add to Shape Area button in the Pathfinder palette to make the shapes behave as a single object. She applied a light, linear gradient to the new object.

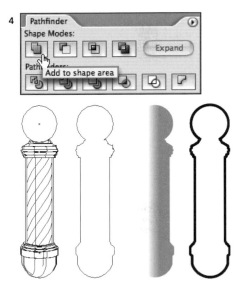

Kelley unified the lighting by uniting the pole's paths (left) with the Pathfinder palette, and filling the new path (second from left) with a linear gradient (third from left); a duplicate with a heavy stroke (right) strengthens the outline

Kelley wanted to reproduce how various pole and reflection paths would be affected to different degrees by the shadow. To control this, Kelley first positioned the gradient behind the other paths by choosing Object > Arrange > Send to Back. Kelley then applied the Multiply blending mode to pole and reflection paths so that their fills and strokes were darkened by the shadow. She created the variations she wanted by varying the Opacity values of different paths. To emphasize the overall barber pole outline, Kelley applied a 7.5-pt black stroke to a duplicate of the perimeter path, and positioned the duplicate path behind the rest of the drawing.

The Multiply blending mode was applied to the barber pole objects so that the unifying background gradient could show through

Tinting a Scan
Adding a Color to a Grayscale Image

Advanced Technique

Overview: *Prepare a grayscale image; import the image into Illustrator; colorize the image; trim the artwork to the required shape; add a vignette.*

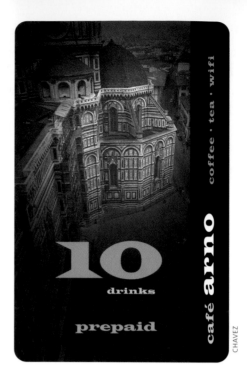

The original scanned image

The layout (left) and the image placed in the layout, initially on top of the design (right)

Conrad Chavez created this concept for a prepaid coffee card that can use different background photographs. To preserve design flexibility, Chavez imported a grayscale version of the image and added color in Illustrator so that he could change the image color at any time.

1 Scanning and preparing the image. Chavez started by scanning a photograph and saving it as a grayscale image. Save the image in a format Illustrator can place, such as a TIFF or Photoshop file. If your original image is in color, you must first convert the image to grayscale in a program like Photoshop. Color images can't be tinted in Illustrator.

2 Importing the image. Chavez chose File > Place to import the image. In the Place dialog box, he disabled the Template and Replace checkboxes. He then positioned the image on the layout.

You can also use Adobe Bridge to browse a folder of images, then import the images you want by dragging them from Bridge to the Illustrator document window.

3 Colorizing the image. Chavez selected the image, clicked the Fill box in the toolbox, and then clicked a solid color swatch in the Swatches palette to tint the image. He had already applied the dark brown swatch to other elements in the design, unifying the composition.

If applying a color doesn't change the image, make sure the Fill box is active and that the image was saved as a true grayscale image, not as an RGB or CMYK image.

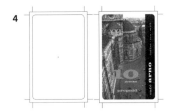

Colorizing the image (left) by selecting it and then clicking the dark brown solid color swatch on the Swatches palette (right)

4 Visualizing a trim. To preview the composition as it would appear after trimming, Chavez drew a rounded-corner rectangle at the trim size. With the rectangle in front of both the background image and the dark vertical rectangle, he selected all three objects and chose Object > Clipping Mask > Make, which created a clipping group.

Rounded-corner rectangle indicating final trim (left) and after clipping artwork to it (right)

5 Adding a vignette. Chavez created a vignette to better distinguish the foreground and background. He drew a new rectangle the size of the Artboard and used the Gradient palette to apply a radial gradient. He changed the gradient's default black slider to the same dark color swatch applied to the image. In the Control palette, he clicked Opacity and then chose Multiply from the pop-up menu to blend the gradient with the image under it.

The vignette needed to be behind all objects except the scan. In the Layers palette, Chavez not only dragged the vignette farther back in the stack but also into the clipping group, so that the vignette could be visualized within the temporary clipping group.

Applying a radial gradient to the new rectangle (left), applying the Multiply blending mode to the rectangle (right), and after dragging the vignette path into the clipping group (right)

Layers palette before (left) and after (right) dragging the vignette into the clipping group

6 Editing the vignette. Chavez decided to refine the composition by editing the vignette. He selected the vignette in the Layers palette and clicked the Gradient tool over the building to reposition the gradient center there. He dragged the Gradient palette sliders to widen both the light center and the dark edge of the gradient. Finally, to restore the bleed required for the press, Chavez selected the clipping group and chose Object > Clipping Mask > Release, and then he deleted his temporary clipping path.

Before (top left) and after (top right) gradient edits: moving the radial gradient center with the Gradient tool (bottom left) and editing the Gradient palette's slider positions (bottom right); ready for prepress with mask deleted (top right)

Opacity Masks 101

Applying Glows and Using Opacity Masks

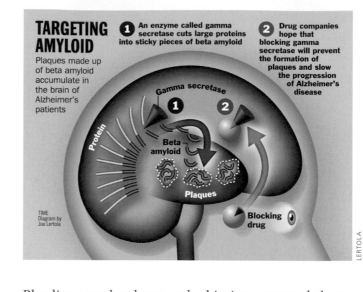

Advanced Technique

Overview: *Scan sketched artwork, place it as a template, and draw objects; apply Inner Glow; blend one object into another using an Opacity Mask.*

Pencil sketch layout of the illustration

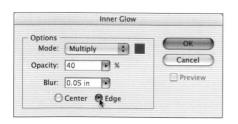

Top, head before and after applying Inner Glow; bottom, the Inner Glow dialog box

Blending complex shapes and achieving contoured glows and shadows can be daunting tasks—unless you know how to use Illustrator's Transparency palette and Effect menu. Joe Lertola makes the most of glows and Opacity Masks in this *TIME* magazine illustration, enjoying the convenience of applying raster effects in Illustrator.

1 Sketching and scanning, then drawing. Draw the objects to which you want to add a glow. Lertola placed a scan of a rough pencil layout in Illustrator as a tracing template (File > Place, and check the Template box) and drew the brain, lobes, arrows, and other elements (mostly using the Pen tool).

2 Creating Inner Glows. Heighten the visual drama of the objects you've drawn by applying glows, shadows, and other effects from the Effect menu. For example, Lertola selected the outline of the head and choose Effect > Stylize > Inner Glow. In the pop-up dialog box, he selected Multiply for Mode, entered 40% for Opacity, and set the Blur. Next, he clicked the color icon to bring up the Color Picker dialog box and chose a dark color. To start the Inner Glow color at the edge so it fades inward to the object's center, Lertola selected Edge. (To create the glow with a color chosen in the Color Picker dialog box at the center of an object—and fading outward to the edges—you would select Center.)

Similarly, you can add a drop shadow to a selected path by choosing Drop Shadow from the Effect > Stylize menu and specifying Opacity, Offset, and Blur in the Drop Shadow dialog box.

3 **Applying an Opacity Mask.** Making an object appear to blend into another object may seem difficult. Using an Opacity Mask, you can perform this trick easily. First, make sure the object that will be blended into another is in front (in Lertola's illustration, the lobe was moved in front of the brain by dragging it in the Layers palette).

To make an Opacity Mask, draw a rectangle (or other shape) in front of the object you want to fade. Fill with a black-to-white gradient, placing the black where you want to fully hide the top object and the white where you want that object fully revealed. (See the *Blends, Gradients & Mesh* chapter for more about gradients.) Next, select both the rectangle and the object to be masked (Shift-click the outlines of both objects to select them). Make sure the Transparency palette is open, and choose Make Opacity Mask from the palette's pop-up menu.

Once you've made the Opacity Mask, the object and its mask are linked together (moving the object will move the mask with it). To edit the object's path, click on the artwork thumbnail in the Transparency palette and use any of the path editing tools; to edit the mask, click on the mask thumbnail. Edit the gradient using the Gradient palette or the Gradient tool.

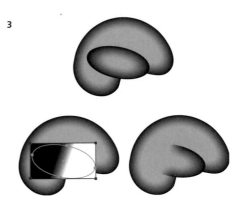

3

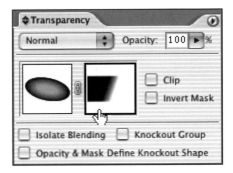

Top, brain with overlying lobe; bottom left, lobe and opacity masking object (black-to-white gradient fill) selected; bottom right, lobe following Make Opacity Mask

Entering mask-editing mode by clicking on the mask thumbnail in the Transparency palette

Transparent Kite

Revealing Hidden Details with Opacity

Advanced Technique

Overview: *Apply transparency to gradient fills as an alternative to the traditional cutaway view; adjust opacity levels for different effects.*

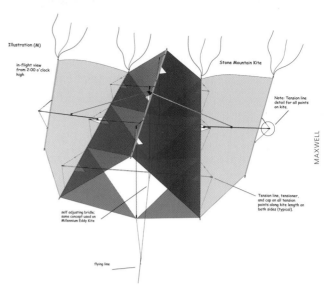

1

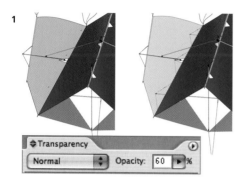

Before (left) and after (right) applying 60% opacity to left wing to reveal underlying trusses

2

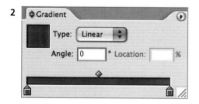

Gradient palette for the top sails

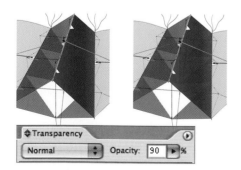

Before (left) and after (right) applying 90% opacity to top right sail

Eden Maxwell illustrated Bobby Stanfield's innovative Stone Mountain kite for a project commissioned by Encyclopedia Britannica. In 1986, this kite design set a record by staying aloft for over 25 hours. Maxwell used Illustrator's transparency features to reveal the underlying structure of the kite and to simulate the sheer, semitransparent quality of the kite fabric.

1 Applying a transparent fill to the beige wings. Maxwell applied a beige color to the wings (0% C, 25% M, 41% Y, 0% K). He wanted the truss system to be visible behind the wings, so with the left wing path selected, he set Opacity to 60%. He set the right wing Opacity to 65%.

2 Applying a transparent fill to the top sails and keels. Maxwell filled the kite's top sails with a gradient from blue (91% C, 1% M, 10% Y, 39% K), to orange (0% C, 71% M, 73% Y, 19% K). To reveal the underlying structure and simulate translucent fabrics seen at different angles, he applied 60% opacity to the top left sail and 90% opacity to the top right sail. You can specify an Opacity value in the Control palette; for more opacity options use the Transparency palette.

Finally, Maxwell applied 65% opacity to the triangular keels under the kite.

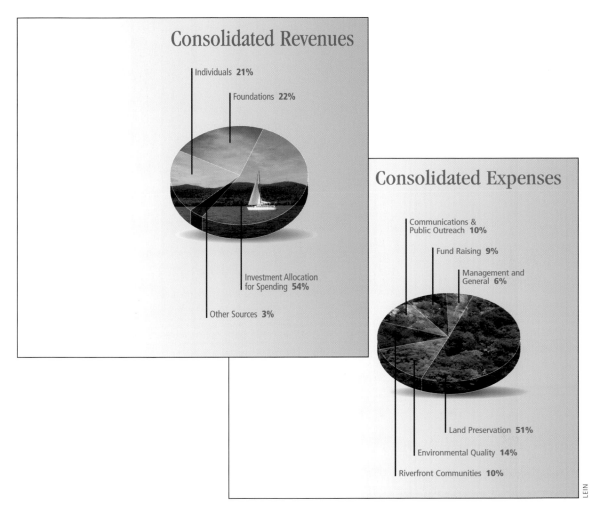

Consolidated Revenues

Individuals **21%**

Foundations **22%**

Investment Allocation for Spending **54%**

Other Sources **3%**

Consolidated Expenses

Communications & Public Outreach **10%**

Fund Raising **9%**

Management and General **6%**

Land Preservation **51%**

Environmental Quality **14%**

Riverfront Communities **10%**

LEIN

Adam Z Lein

Adam Z Lein incorporated images of New York's Hudson Valley in this pie chart for an annual report of the environmental organization, Scenic Hudson. Lein used Microsoft Excel and Excel's Chart Wizard to turn data into a chart tilted in a perspective view. Lein used the Acrobat 6 PDF maker to create a PDF of the graph. When he opened it in Illustrator, the graph retained all of the shapes as vector objects. Lein then placed a photographic image on a layer below the pie chart artwork, and used the Control palette to change the blending mode from Normal to Soft Light. Lein controlled the varying tints and shades of the underlying image by applying gradients and shades of gray to each pie piece. To fit the image inside the pie chart, Lein created a clipping mask in the shape of the pie chart. (See the *Advanced Techniques* chapter for more about clipping masks.) He then placed the charts in QuarkXPress where he added the text and data points.

CASSELL

Peter Cassell / 1185 Design

Peter Cassell's European cityscape, commissioned for an Adobe Illustrator packaging illustration, was built with mists he created using a gradient mesh as an Opacity Mask. After drawing the rough shapes of reflections in the water, Cassell drew a rectangle in a layer above the water and filled the rectangle with white. He copied the rectangle, pasted it in front, filled it with black, and then selected Object > Create Gradient Mesh to turn it into an 18 x 15 mesh. He edited the mesh by selecting mesh points with the Direct Selection tool and filling the points with gray values varying from 30%

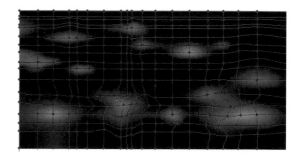

to 50% black. To shape a mist, he selected and moved mesh points. To mask the white rectangle with the gradient mesh above it, Cassell selected the mesh and the rectangle and chose Make Opacity Mask from the Transparency palette's pop-up menu.

Live Effects & Graphic Styles

10

Live Effects & Graphic Styles

These days Illustrator boasts a formidable array of live effects—from the warps and envelopes to 3D, Gaussian Blur, and Scribble effects. A few of the more robust live effects reside in their own chapters: Live Trace and Live Paint are in *Beyond Basic Drawing & Coloring*, and 3D now has its own *Live 3D Effects* chapter following this one. This chapter will focus on bringing you up to speed on working with all of Illustrator's other effects, and creating and working with Graphic Styles.

Live effects alter the look of your work but can be easily edited or removed at any time. When an effect is applied to an object, group, or layer, it will display as an attribute in the Appearance palette. The effect's position in the palette indicates which element it will modify.

The Effect menu is divided into two sections. The effects in the upper section (the 3D through Warp submenus) are mostly for use with vector images, and can be applied to either CMYK or RGB artwork. Those in the lower section (the Artistic through Video submenus) are for use with raster images, and can be applied only when your document is in RGB mode (with the exceptions of the Blur effects, Pixelate effects, and Unsharp Mask).

Although none of the effects let you save or export presets of settings that you like from within their dialog boxes, you *can* save any set of effect attributes that you like as a Graphic Style. To save your set of effects as a Graphic Style, just drag the thumbnail in the Appearance palette to the Graphic Styles palette (for more about Graphic Styles, see the final section of this chapter).

RASTER EFFECTS

Illustrator's deliberately low default resolution for the Document Raster Effects Settings (Effect > Document Raster Effects Settings) allows effects to preview faster while you're editing the artwork. But in most cases you'll need to raster your effects at a higher resolution setting. If you don't change those settings, your effects will print at that default 72 ppi (pixel per inch) setting—even if your Illustrator file is printed at a much higher resolution!

There's an important distinction between the raster effects that originated in Photoshop (and were then added in the bottom part of Illustrator's Effect menu, such as Gaussian Blur), and the raster effects developed specifically for Illustrator, such as Feather, Glow, and Drop Shadow. The Photoshop effects specify their options in pixels, whereas the native Illustrator effects specify their distances in ruler units. So if you apply a Gaussian Blur at 3 pixels, it looks much more blurry when the resolution is 72 ppi compared to 288 ppi. On the other hand, if you have a drop shadow with a 3-pt blur, it automatically adjusts to the resolution, and just covers more pixels at a higher resolution. For this reason, if you have Photoshop effects applied and you change the Document Raster Effects resolution, you may need to adjust the specific effect options, like Blur Distance, as well. (This process should be familiar to anyone who has changed the resolution of a Photoshop document containing Layer effects.)

Our output expert Jean-Claude advises that you should never send a file to be printed without setting the desired high resolution yourself and proofing it. Illustrator files created with raster effects might need adjustments, and you cannot trust that those who haven't seen your art will know how it should look, or that they know how to make adjustments to the file.

SCRIBBLE EFFECT

The Effect > Stylize > Scribble effect lets you quickly create a variety of scribble effects—from loose and *scribble* to a tight crosshatch. Scribble effects can be applied to the fill and/or stroke of an object depending on what you have targeted in the Appearance palette when you apply it.

The Scribble Options dialog box (on the next page) is divided into three sections. The Settings menu contains a fixed number of Scribble presets. Use the Angle slider to control the overall direction of the Scribble lines. A

Applying effects

Once you have applied an effect to an object, double-click the effect in the Appearance palette to change the values. If you re-select the effect from the Effect menu, you'll apply a second instance of the effect to the object, rather than change it. (In the case of 3D, avoid applying two 3D effects to a single object. Understanding what you can do in the various 3D dialog boxes will help you avoid that; see the Tip "3D—Three dialogs" in the next chapter.)

Flare—tool or effect?

The Flare tool turns up in some of the lessons and Galleries in this chapter. That's because although the Flare tool isn't technically an effect, it behaves like one—you can select and re-edit your Flare tool work using the Flare Tool Options dialog box (double-click the Flare tool to open it).

Keep spot colors with effects!

You can now use and preserve spot colors as spot colors, even with live effects such as Drop Shadow, Gaussian Blur, and Feather applied! To take advantage of this, make certain that the "Preserve spot colors when possible" option is enabled in Effect > Document Raster Effects Settings.
—*Jean-Claude Tremblay*

The Scribble effect can be applied to the stroke, the fill, or both the stroke and the fill of an object

The Scribble Options dialog box

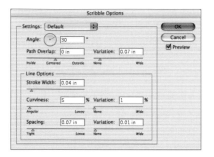

WEINSTEIN

COHEN

For more lessons with Scribble, see Ari Weinstein's "Antiquing Type" and Sandee Cohen's "Olde Offset Fills" lessons in the Type *chapter*

Crosshatching using Scribble

You don't have to duplicate a shape to create a crosshatch effect using Scribble. Instead, after applying Scribble to the object's fill (and after selecting your object), choose Add New Fill from the Appearance palette menu. Then choose Effect > Stylize > Scribble, and for the Angle setting, add 90° to the angle. —*Mike Schwabauer*

setting of 0° causes the Scribble lines to run left to right; 90° makes them run up and down. Use the Path Overlap slider to control how much the scribble stays inside or extends outside of a path boundary. In the Line Options section of the Scribble dialog, use the Stroke Width control to specify how fat or thin you want the scribble line to be. Use the Curviness slider to set how Angular or Loopy the ends of each scribble stroke should be. Use the Spacing slider to specify how tight or loose you want your strokes to be. Use the Variation sliders to further control how each attribute is applied: For a very regular machine-made look, set the slider to None, and for a more freehand and natural look move the slider toward Wide.

By combining other effects, or applying brushstrokes to your scribbles, you can create an almost infinite variety of looks. Use them as fills or masks to transform type; or save them as graphic styles to apply to other artwork.

WARPS AND ENVELOPING

Illustrator's Warp Effects and Envelope tool are robust and very powerful, offering much more than just simple transformations. Warps and envelopes may look similar at first, but there's an important difference between them. Warps are applied as live *effects*—meaning they can be applied to objects, groups, or layers. Create them by choosing from the predefined options in the Warp dialog boxes; you can save them within a graphic style. Envelopes, on the other hand, are also live, but rather than effects, they're actual *objects* that contain artwork. You can edit or customize the envelope shape, and Illstrator will conform the contents of the envelope to the contour.

Warps

Applying a warp is actually quite simple. Target an object, group, or layer and choose Effect > Warp > Arc. It doesn't matter which warp effect you choose, because you'll be presented with the Warp Options dialog box where you can choose from any of the 15 different warps. While the warp effects are "canned" in the sense that you can't make adjustments to the effects directly, you can control how a warp appears by changing the Bend value, as well as the Horizontal and Vertical Distortion values.

Once you've applied a warp, you can edit it by opening the Appearance palette and double-clicking on the warp listed there. Like any other effect, a warp can be applied to just the fill, or just the stroke—and if you edit the artwork, the warp updates as well.

Since warps are effects, you can include them in a graphic style, which can then be applied to other artwork. (For details about graphic styles see the "Graphic Styles in Illustrator" section later in this chapter introduction.)

Envelopes

While warp effects do a nice job of distorting artwork, there are times when you need more control. That's where Illustrator's envelopes come in.

There are three ways to apply envelopes. The simplest way is to create a shape you want to use as your envelope. Make sure it's at the top of the stacking order—above the art you want to place inside the envelope. Then, with the artwork and your created shape both selected, choose Object > Envelope Distort > Make with Top Object. Illustrator will create a special kind of object: an envelope. This object you created becomes an envelope container, which appears in the Layers palette as <Envelope>. You can edit the path of the envelope with any transformation or editing tools; the artwork inside will update to conform to the shape. To edit the contents of the envelope, you need to choose Object > Envelope Distort > Edit Contents. If you then look at the Layers palette, you'll notice that the <Envelope> now has a disclosure triangle that reveals the contents of the envelope—the artwork you placed. You can edit the artwork directly or even drag other paths into the <Envelope> in the Layers palette. When you're finished editing the contents, choose Object > Envelope Distort > Edit Envelope.

There are two other types of envelopes, and they're closely related. Both types use meshes to provide even

"Crunching Type" lesson in the Type *chapter*

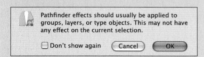
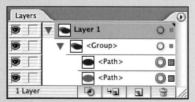
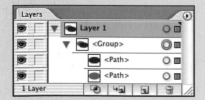
more distortion control. One of them is called Make with Warp and it's found in the Object > Envelope Distort submenu. This technique starts off by displaying the Warp dialog. When you choose a warp and press OK, Illustrator converts that warp to an envelope mesh. You can then edit individual mesh points with the Direct Selection tool to distort not only the outer edges of the envelope shape, but also the way art is distorted within the envelope itself. To provide even more control, use the Mesh tool to add more mesh points as desired.

Another way to create an envelope is to start from a rectangular mesh. Select artwork and choose Object > Envelope Distort > Make with Mesh. After you've chosen how many mesh points you want, Illustrator will create an envelope mesh. Use the Direct Selection tool to edit the points and use the Mesh tool to add mesh points.

EFFECT PATHFINDERS

The effects listed in the Effect > Pathfinder menu are effect versions of the Pathfinders described in the *Beyond Basic Drawing & Coloring* chapter. To apply a Pathfinder effect, you should either group the objects, making sure that the group is also targeted, or target the layer with the objects (which applies the effect to *all* objects on that layer). Then, select Effect > Pathfinder and choose an effect. If you don't do one of those two things, before applying the effect to a non-group, you might not see a visible result.

Pathfinder Effects vs. Compound Shapes

With live Pathfinder effects, you create a container (group or layer) and then apply one effect (Add, Subtract, Intersect, or Exclude) to the container. But in a compound shape, *each component* independently specifies whether it adds to, subtracts from, intersects with, or excludes from the components below it.

When you're using more than one or two shape modes, you'll find it simpler to work with compound shapes. One of the great benefits compound shapes have over Pathfinder effects is that compound shapes behave much more reliably when the objects being combined aren't simple.

Compound shapes can be exported live in Photoshop files, or copied in Illustrator and pasted into Photoshop as shape layers. See the *Beyond Basic Drawing & Coloring* chapter for more about Pathfinders and compound shapes.

GRAPHIC STYLES IN ILLUSTRATOR

If you think that you'll want to apply an appearance more than once, whether it's a simple stroke and fill, or a complex combination of effects, save it as a graphic style in the Graphic Styles palette. A *graphic style* is simply a combination of one or more appearance attributes that can be applied to objects (including text objects), groups, and layers. See the *Layers & Appearances* chapter to learn the basics of working with appearances.

To save a set of appearance attributes as a graphic style, in the Appearance palette (with or without an object selected), select the desired appearance attributes, and then either click the New Graphic Style icon on the bottom of the Graphic Styles palette or drag the appearance thumbnail from the Appearance palette to the Graphic Styles palette.

To apply a graphic style, simply select an object, or target a group or layer, and click on a style in the Graphic Styles palette. You can also sample a style from another object using the Eyedropper. You can also drag a style from the Graphic Styles palette directly onto an object.

To separate a graphic style from the object to which it's applied, click on the Break Link to Graphic Style icon at the bottom of the palette, or select the item from the Graphic Styles palette menu. You might want to do this when you are replacing a graphic style and don't want to change all the objects using the current graphic style to the updated or replaced version. Select two or more styles in the Graphic Styles palette, and choose Merge Graphic Styles from the palette menu to combine appearance attributes into a new style.

Envelope distort options

If your artwork contains pattern fills or linear gradients, you can employ envelopes to distort them by choosing Object > Envelope Distort > Envelope Options and checking the appropriate items in the dialog box. —*Mordy Golding*

Smart people use Smart Guides

Smart Guides can be quite helpful when you work with Warps or Envelopes, as it may become difficult to edit artwork that has an appearance applied to it. With Smart Guides turned on, Illustrator will highlight the art for you, making it easier to identify where the actual artwork is (and not the appearance). Make use of the ⌘-U/Ctrl-U keyboard shortcut to turn Smart Guides on and off. —*Mordy Golding*

Replacing graphic styles

To replace a saved appearance in the Graphic Styles palette with a new set of attributes, Option-drag/Alt-drag the thumbnail from the Appearance palette (or an object from the Artboard), to the Graphic Styles palette and drop it onto the highlighted graphic style. To replace the currently selected graphic style, make adjustments and choose Redefine Graphic Style from the Appearance palette menu. The applied styles will update.

Scratchboard Art

Combining Strokes, Fills, Effects, & Styles

Overview: *Apply multiple strokes and fills to simple objects; offset strokes; apply effects to strokes and fills; create and apply graphic styles.*

The original scratchboard art consists of simple primitive shapes

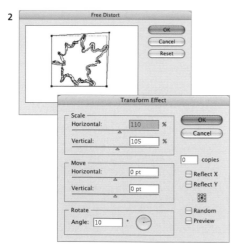

To offset a path's Stroke from its Fill, select the Stroke in the Appearance palette and apply Free Distort and Transform from the Effect >Distort & Transform menu

Sandee Cohen, author and consultant, discovered a way to simulate scratchboard art in Illustrator. Artist Gary Powell created a variation of Cohen's technique using an assortment of Art Brushes, multiple strokes and fills, and effects, which he then combined and saved as graphic styles. Once a series of effects is saved as a graphic style, you can easily apply that graphic style to multiple objects to create or quickly modify a design theme. Art directors may find this method helpful for unifying and stylizing illustrations created by a number of different artists.

1 Applying Art Brushes and Fills. To create a natural-looking stroke, Powell applied an assortment of Art Brushes to simple primitive objects. He used Waves, Weave, Dry Brush, and Fire Ash Brushes (on the *Wow! CD*), then he applied solid fills to each object. Select a simple object, then click on your choice of Art Brush in the Brushes palette or in a Brush Library. (For more on Art Brushes, see the *Brushes & Symbols* chapter.)

2 Offsetting a stroke. To develop a loose, sketchlike look, Powell offset some of the strokes from their fills. To do this, select a stroke in the Appearance palette and apply either Effect > Distort & Transform > Free Distort, or Effect > Distort & Transform > Transform to manually or numerically adjust the position of the stroke so that it separates from the fill. This gives the stroke the appearance of a different shape without permanently changing the path. (You can further reshape the stroke by double-clicking the Transform attribute in the Appearance palette and adjusting the offset of the Stroke attribute.)

3 Adding more strokes and fills to a path. To add to the sketchlike look of the square background, Powell applied additional strokes to the path. First, he chose the Stroke attribute in the Appearance palette and clicked the Duplicate Selected Item icon at the bottom of the palette. With the new Stroke copy selected, he changed the choice of Art brush. He also double-clicked the stroke's Distort & Transform effect in the Appearance palette and changed the settings to move the Stroke copy's position. Powell repeated this until he had as many strokes as he liked.

To create the scratchboard look in the leaves, Powell applied additional fills and effects to each of them. First, he chose the Fill attribute in the Appearance palette and duplicated it. With the new Fill copy selected, he changed the color and applied Effect > Stylize > Scribble. (You can apply as many fills and effects to a path as you like, then drag and drop to change their stacking order.)

4 Working with graphic styles. To automate the styling of future illustrations, Powell used the Appearance and Graphic Styles palettes to create a library of graphic styles. Whenever you create a set of strokes and fills you like, click the New Graphic Style icon in the Graphic Styles palette to create a new graphic style swatch.

Once Powell assembled a palette of graphic style swatches, he altered the look and feel of the artwork by applying a variety of graphic styles to selected paths. The use of graphic styles allows an artist or designer to create a variety of themes in a graphic style library and then apply them selectively to illustrations or design elements.

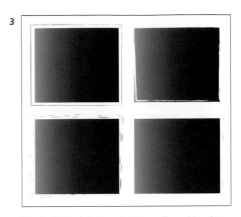

3

The individual strokes that Powell combined to create multiple strokes for the background

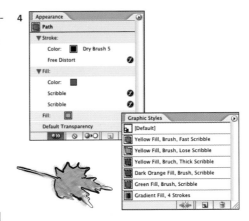

4

Multiple Strokes, Fills and Effects applied to an object shown in the Appearance palette; appearance attributes saved in the Graphic Styles palette by clicking the New Graphic Style icon

Applying different graphic styles to objects can give the same artwork several different looks and create a cohesive look throughout a project or series

Embossing Effects

Building an Embossed Graphic Style

Overview: *Apply object-level effects for highlights and shadows; build appearances, save as graphic styles and apply to layers.*

ALSPACH

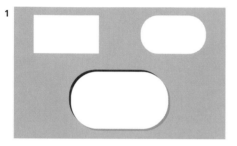

1

At the top, making the screw slots (on the left, the rectangle and on the right, the rectangle with Round Corners Effect): at the bottom, an enlarged view of the composite appearance

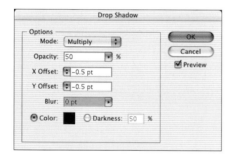

The Drop Shadow options pop-up dialog box; edit the X and Y Offset fields to adjust the position of the shadow and highlight (check the Preview box to see the effect as you work)

Resizing appearances

If you plan to resize an Illustration that contains appearances with stroke values, be sure to apply the appearances to objects, not to layers. Illustrator may fail to re-scale stroke values in layer-targeted appearances.

Ted Alspach, Group Product Manager for the Adobe Creative Suite, chose the embossed letters, numbers and lines of a license plate to demonstrate the ease and flexibility of using Illustrator's effects and appearances. In this memorial to French mathematician Pierre Bézier, inventor of the original Bézier curve, Alspach simulated the look of embossing by applying a drop shadow effect and by building a sophisticated graphic style.

1 Applying the drop shadow effect. Start the license plate by drawing the background shape, circles, curves and other linework. While technically not a raised surface, the four screw slots still require highlights and shadows to convey the impression of dimension. To create a slot, draw a rectangle with a Fill of White and a Stroke of None. Use the Round Corners Effect (Effect > Stylize > Round Corners) to give the object a more oval shape. To cast the plate's shadow on the edge of the slot, select the slot rectangle and apply the Drop Shadow Effect (Effect > Stylize > Drop Shadow). In the Drop Shadow dialog box, choose black for color, Blur 0, and Offset up and to the left (using negative numbers for "X Offset" and "Y Offset"). Then click OK. Repeat the drop shadow effect to make the highlight, except choose a light color and Offset down and to the right (using positive numbers). To further tweak the drop shadows (modifying their color or width, for example), simply double-click the attribute name "Drop Shadow" in the Appearance palette and edit the values in the dialog box.

2 Building multiple appearances. Alspach took another approach to embossing by building a sophisticated graphic style in which transparency and multiple offset fills simulate highlights and shadows.

To make the license plate lettering, type the characters in a sans serif font and convert them to outlines (Type > Create Outlines). Ungroup the characters, select a character and set its Fill to orange. To make the first embossing highlight, select the orange Fill appearance attribute in the Appearance palette and copy it by clicking the Duplicate Selected Item icon at the bottom of the palette. Now, select the lower Fill attribute in the palette, choose white from the Color palette and, in the Transparency palette, set Opacity to 25% and blending mode to Screen. Then, choose Effect > Transform > Distort & Transform to offset it up and to the left by editing the Move fields (negative Horizontal and positive Vertical). Make two more copies of this white Fill attribute by once again clicking the Duplicate Selected Item icon. Offset each copy farther up and to the left by double-clicking the Fill's Transform attribute and editing the Move values in the Transform dialog.

To start the shadows, first duplicate the lowest white Fill. Now select the bottom white Fill and set its color to black, Opacity to 50%, and blending mode to Multiply. Double-click the Fill's Transform attribute and edit the Move values to offset it down and to the right. Copy this shadow and offset it farther down and to the right. When you have finished, the Appearance palette will display six Fill attributes for the object.

3 Creating and applying a graphic style. Alspach turned the appearance set into a graphic style by dragging the Appearance palette's preview icon and dropping it in the Graphic Styles palette. He then applied the graphic style to the layer with the number characters. You can achieve the same embossing look by applying the graphic style to selected character outlines or to a group composed of the character outlines.

2

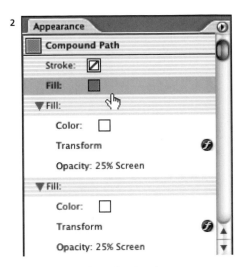

Appearance palette showing the appearance preview icon (top left), and the target of the appearance (Object)

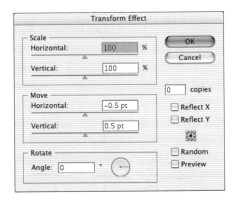

Move values in the Transform Effect dialog box to offset Fill attribute up and left

Close-up view of the embossed letter characters with the multiple highlight and shadow fills that progressively hide the background artwork

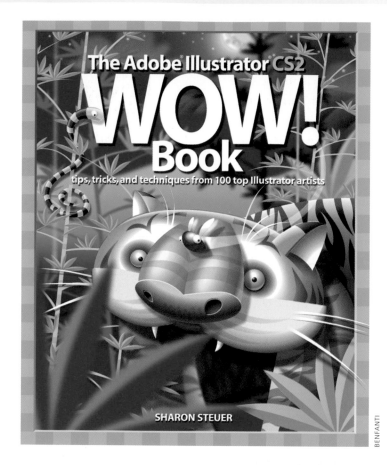

BENFANTI

Russell Benfanti

If you look closely you'll see that Russell Benfanti's lush illustrations are actually constructed of fairly simple shapes. He calls his use of color "an exercise in restraint"; consciously limiting his palettes to only a few colors per image. Using these simple shapes, rich colors, and fine attention to detail, Benfanti creates his depth of field by applying Effect > Blur > Gaussian Blur in varying degrees to objects in the foreground and background (the version at right shows the Gaussian Blurs removed). He also incorporates complex gradients shaped by masks (see Benfanti's lesson "Masking Details" in the *Advanced Techniques*

chapter). He often provides a raster version of his image to the client (using File > Export > Photoshop) to minimize the opportunity for printing error.

Ted Alspach

Ted Alspach initially experimented with Effects and the Flare tool to create an interesting desktop background, but ultimately ended up with a striking image he then made it into a large wall hanging. He created this effect with multiple fills applied to a single textured rectangle. Working in RGB mode, Alspach filled a rectangle with a multicolored gradient (center figure, left). He applied Effect > Pixelate > Color Halftone, and entered a Pixel Max. Radius of 8 (center). Alspach then applied Effect > Pixelate > Crystallize, and adjusted the cell size slider to 40 (center figure, right). He made two copies of this rectangle by selecting Duplicate Item in the Appearance palette pop-up. He made adjustments to the duplicated rectangles by selecting the Fill appearance attribute in the Appearance palette. using the Gradient tool, Alspach applied gradients of varying colors and angles. He double-clicked on the effects (Crystallize and Color Halftone) and changed the values for the Max. Radius and Screen Angles. Alspach also adjusted the Opacity (between 20% and 80%) and applied Soft Light, Multiply, and Color Burn blending modes. To make the flare, he selected the Flare tool, clicked and dragged to set the halo and click-dragged again to set the distance and direction of the rings while using the arrow keys to adjust the number of rings (bottom figure). Alspach made another copy of the rectangle and applied a blue gradient fill. He positioned this copy as the topmost fill and masked the flare to fit the image.

ALSPACH

Warps & Envelopes

Using Warping and Enveloping Effects

Overview: *Group clip art for use with Warp; apply Warp; save Warp effect as a graphic style; apply Envelope using a shaped path; add a shading effect using a mesh.*

COHEN

1

Making sure that the flag artwork is grouped.
Note: *The Appearance palette shows information for the currently targeted (not just selected or highlighted) object in the Layers palette*

The Flag Warp applied to a not-fully-grouped flag artwork. The stripes are grouped, but the stars and the union (blue field) are separate objects

2

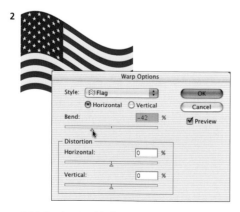

With Preview enabled, experiment with the Warp Options settings

Consultant Sandee Cohen used Illustrator's Warping and Enveloping effects to mold copies of a basic rectangular flag into a waving flag and a bow tie.

Warps are the easier of the two methods to understand and use. Simply choose one of the 15 preset shapes from the Warp menu and adjust the shape using the sliders in the Warp Options dialog box.

Envelopes let you use any path, warp preset, or mesh object to shape and mold your artwork into almost any form imaginable. You can further manipulate the shape using the envelope's anchor points. Be aware that although Warps and Envelopes leave original artwork unchanged, only Warps can be saved as graphic styles.

1 Group clip art for use with Warp effects. Cohen started with a standard United States flag from a clip art collection. First, she made sure that the flag artwork was a grouped object by selecting the flag artwork (which also targets it in the Layers palette) and checking its description in the Appearance palette. If the artwork is not a grouped object, then the effects will not be applied to the artwork as a whole, but rather to each of the paths individually (as shown in the sidebar).

2 Make a copy of the flag artwork and apply a Warp effect. Next, Cohen made a duplicate copy of the flag by selecting it and, holding down Option/Alt, dragging it to a position below the original. While the duplicate was still selected, Cohen chose Effect > Warp > Flag to bring up the Warp dialog. She enabled the Preview checkbox in the Warp dialog box so she could preview the effect her settings would have on the artwork. Cohen set the Horizontal Bend slider to –42% to create the first stage of her waving flag effect, and clicked OK to apply the Warp. She then applied a second Warp effect to the flag artwork, to complete her waving flag. With the artwork still selected, she chose Effect > Warp > Arc and, with Preview enabled, set the Horizontal Bend slider to 40%.

Note: *In the Warp dialog box, you have access to the full library of Warp shapes no matter which warp you chose from the Effect > Warp menu. Simply click and drag on the style pop-up menu in the Warp dialog box to access any of the Warp shapes. As long as Preview is enabled, you can then experiment with each Warp shape and settings to see how each will affect your artwork before you apply one.*

To remove a Warp effect, in the Layers palette target your artwork. Then, in the Appearance palette, select the Warp and click on, or drag your selection to, the Trash.

3 Save your Warp effect as a graphic style. Once you arc pleased with a particular Warp effect or effects that you have achieved, you can easily save the effects as a graphic style for application to other artwork. Begin by targeting the artwork that you applied your warp(s) and other effects to in the Layers palette. Then Option-click/ Alt-click on the New Graphic Style button at the bottom of the Graphic Styles palette to create and name your new graphic style. If the appearance you save as a graphic style has no fill or strokes, the thumbnail for the graphic style you created will be blank. When this happens, choose either the Small or the Large List View (from the Graphic Styles palette pop-up menu) to view the graphic styles by name. To apply a graphic style, simply target the object, group, or layer, and then click on the graphic style in the Graphic Styles palette.

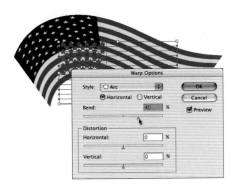

Applying a second Warp effect. Because Warps are live effects, the original flag artwork (seen here as an outline in light blue because the artwork is still selected) remains unchanged

Removing Warp effects from the artwork by highlighting the effects in the Appearance palette, and then clicking on the Trash button to delete them

3

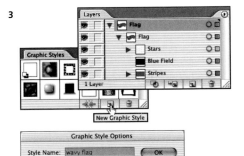

To create a new graphic style, target your artwork, then Option-click/Alt-click the New Graphic Style button, and give your new graphic style a name

Applying a Warp effect graphic style to a grouped object

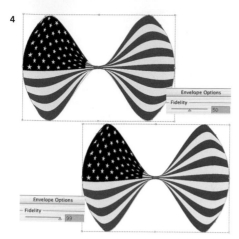

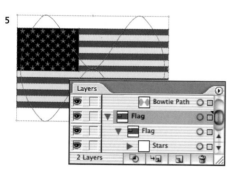

With Envelope Options fidelity set too low, red color in the lower right corner of the upper figure spills outside the bow tie shape. When the fidelity is set to 99% the artwork conforms much more closely to the envelope shape.

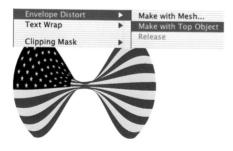

Bow tie path positioned above the flag artwork, and selected, just before making the envelope

Applying the envelope, and the resulting artwork

Using Edit > Paste in Front to create a duplicate positioned directly over the original artwork

4 Use Envelope Options to maximize Envelope fidelity. Envelopes are more versatile in the ways you can shape and manipulate them, but sometimes (especially when the shape you use to create the envelope is kinked or makes sharp changes in direction) the artwork may not conform tightly to the envelope. To minimize this problem, set the Object > Envelope Distort > Envelope Options Fidelity to 99%. Note: Setting Fidelity to 100% creates many more intermediate points along the deformed path, and is usually not necessary.

Cohen used an Envelope to give her flag the shape of a bow tie, and added some shading using a mesh.

5 Apply Envelope using a shaped Path. Cohen added points to a circle and then distorted it into a bow-tie-shaped path. To apply a shaped path of your own, place it above your flag artwork, select both the flag and your shaped path, and choose Object > Envelope Distort > Make with Top Object.

6 Add a shading effect with a mesh. Next, Cohen added a shading effect by using a mesh object on top of her bow tie flag. Begin by creating a duplicate of the bow tie flag (Edit > Copy), then paste it in front of the first one using Edit > Paste in Front to exactly align it over the original. With the duplicate still selected, choose Object > Envelope Distort > Reset with Mesh. In the Reset Envelope Mesh dialog box, make sure that Maintain Envelope Shape and Preview are both enabled. Increase the number of Rows and Columns until you are satisfied with the mesh grid in terms of how you intend to shade it. For her mesh, Cohen used 6 rows and 6 columns. Click OK, and with the mesh artwork still selected, choose Envelope > Distort > Release to free the mesh from the flag. Delete the flag artwork and keep the mesh object. When a mesh object is released from an envelope, it is filled with 20% black. Select the mesh object, then, with the Lasso or the Direct Selection tool, select points on the mesh grid and change their fill to a shadow color. Cohen selected interior grid points and gave them a value of white until she was satisfied with the mesh's shading.

Note: *Multiple contiguous points and large areas in the mesh are most easily selected using the Lasso tool.*

To see the effect of the shading on the original bow tie flag beneath the mesh, Cohen (with the mesh selected) set the Blending Mode in the Transparency palette to Multiply. This applied the Blending mode only to the selected mesh object, and not the whole layer.

Finally, using the same enveloping and mesh techniques described above, Cohen created a center for the bow tie using a copy of some of the stripes and an elongated rounded rectangle path.

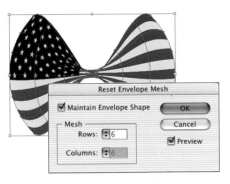

Creating a mesh object using a duplicate of the bow tie flag envelope artwork

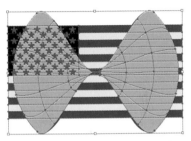

Using Envelope > Distort > Release to free the mesh from the flag artwork

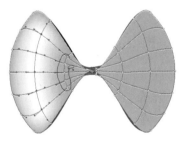

Using the Lasso to select multiple mesh points

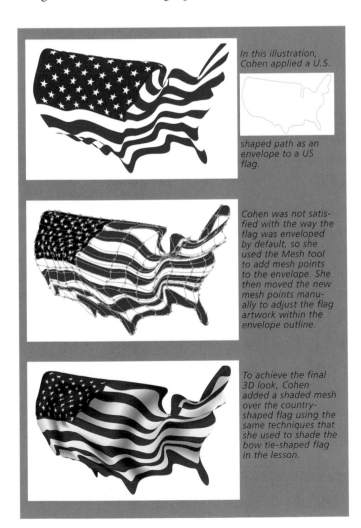

In this illustration, Cohen applied a U.S. shaped path as an envelope to a US flag.

Cohen was not satisfied with the way the flag was enveloped by default, so she used the Mesh tool to add mesh points to the envelope. She then moved the new mesh points manually to adjust the flag artwork within the envelope outline.

To achieve the final 3D look, Cohen added a shaded mesh over the country-shaped flag using the same techniques that she used to shade the bow tie-shaped flag in the lesson.

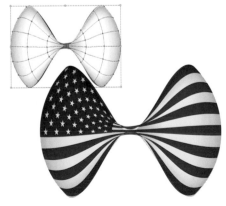

Before and after applying a blending mode of Multiply to the shaded mesh object

Scribble Basics

Applying Scribble Effects to Artwork

Overview: *Apply default Scribble effect settings; choose from preset Scribble styles; make custom adjustments to Scribble settings.*

STEAD

Hiding edges to see the effect

Applying a Scribble effect can generate a complex set of edges that make it difficult to view the artwork underneath. Get into the habit of hiding the edges of your selection before trying out an effect. Use the ⌘-H/Ctrl-H keyboard shortcut to toggle the visibility of the edges on and off.

Judy Stead's evergreen tree began simply, but with the help of Illustrator's Scribble effect, it evolved into an eye-catching Christmas card. Here, you will learn how to apply the Scribble effect to your artwork, how to make use of the preset Scribble styles, and how to make custom adjustments to the effect in order to add excitement and energy to your art.

1 Creating the base art and the variations. Stead began by using the Brush tool to create a simple, filled shape for the tree. She used a 5-pt round Calligraphic brush to create the star, and applied a red stroke and a yellow fill to the path. She drew the ornament using the same brush and stroke with a magenta fill. Stead copied and pasted this shape several times to decorate her tree. She created the base of the tree using a 12-pt oval Calligraphic brush

1

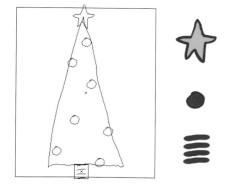

Shown here in Outline mode, Stead created her first tree by drawing with the brush tool

to draw a single horizontal stroke. She then made three copies and grouped them against a white rectangle.

Stead decided that her card would contain three variations of the first tree, so she copied and pasted them into position and gave each one a different color scheme. Beginning with the first variation, she selected the red background rectangle. She chose Effects > Stylize > Scribble, after first hiding the selection edges of her art (⌘-H) in order to observe the results more clearly. When the Scribble Options menu appeared, Stead clicked Preview. Satisfied with the Default settings, she clicked OK. These settings applied the appearance of a loose, continuous stroke to her solid red rectangle.

2 Using the Scribble presets. For her next variation, Stead first selected the light green tree and chose the Scribble style set entitled Sketch. She decided to leave the Sketch settings as they were and clicked OK. Then she selected the magenta background. After applying the Scribble style set entitled Sharp, she opened up the denseness of the effect's strokes by using the slider to change the Spacing value from 3 pt to 5 pt. The Scribble Options palette also contains sliders to control the thickness of the stroke, the general curviness of the strokes, and the degree of variation or evenness of the effect.

3 Further Scribble settings. For the final variation, Stead selected the green background and chose the Swash settings from the Options palette. Using the circular Angle slider, she changed the preset angle of the strokes from 0 to –30 degrees. Stead then selected all the tree ornaments and applied a final Scribble effect using the Dense settings from the Scribble Options palette. Stead was able to go back and readjust all her settings, as needed, by clicking the instance of the effect in each object's Appearance palette. As a final touch, Stead selected the solid red tree and sent it backward (Object > Arrange > Send Backward) so that the green Swash scribble effect would overlay the tree and provide an interesting texture.

2
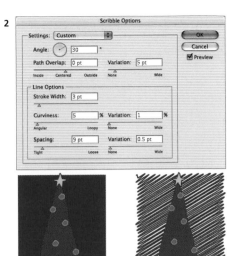

After switching the color scheme, Stead selected the red background, hid the edges, and applied a Custom Scribble (Effects menu)

For the light green Christmas tree, Stead chose the Sketch from the Scribble palette's Settings

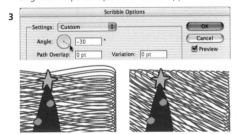
Stead applied the Scribble palette's Sharp settings to the background, changing spacing setting from 3 pt to 5 pt for a looser appearance

3

In Scribble Options, Stead applied Swash (from Settings) to the green background of the final tree art, and changed the Angle slider (which then changed the "Settings" to Custom)

MACADANGDANG

   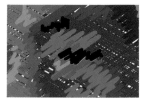

Todd Macadangdang / Adobe Systems, Inc.

Todd Macadangdang used the Scribble effect to turn this photo into an artistic crosshatch sketch. Todd started by adjusting the colors and posterizing the photograph in Photoshop, using adjustment layers. He then placed the image in Illustrator and created filled shapes based on the posterized areas. Starting with the smallest, front-most area, he clicked on the area with the Eyedropper tool to set the Fill color (with Stroke of None), then hand-traced over it using the Pencil tool. He repeated this process, working his way toward the largest, rearmost areas, using Object > Arrange > Send Backward as he went along to keep the shapes in the correct visual stacking order. Todd then applied the Scribble effect to each traced area. To give his image a greater sense of depth, he created fatter, looser Scribble strokes (using Settings such as Childlike, Loose, or Snarl) for the front-most areas and used smaller, denser strokes (with the Angle setting rotated 90°) for the larger, rearmost crosshatched areas.

Steven Gordon / Cartagram

When you mix Illustrator's brushes with live effects, you can transform the lettering of a font into art that looks hand-rendered with traditional pens and brushes. To begin this map title, Steven Gordon typed "Yakima" and then chose a calligraphic font, Zapfino, at 72 points. In the Character palette, he adjusted kerning to tighten the space between several pairs of letter characters. With the text object selected and the Appearance palette open, Gordon chose Add New Fill from the palette's Options menu and gave the new fill a dark magenta color. He duplicated the fill by clicking on the Duplicate Selected Item icon at the bottom of the palette, and then gave the duplicate a pale blue color. Lastly, he clicked on a brush in the Brushes palette and chose the

Dry Ink brush. He selected a dark blue color for the brush. Because the brush strokes were too large for the lettering effect he wanted, Gordon double-clicked the brush name in the Appearance palette, resized its width to 60% of the default size, and clicked to apply it to existing objects. To further customize the title, Gordon selected the pale blue fill in the Appearance palette, offset the fill and distorted the fill's edges using the Transform and Roughen commands from the Effect > Distort and Transform menu. He also reduced opacity by moving the Opacity slider in the Transparency palette to 35%. To finish, Gordon selected the bottom fill and applied the Roughen command from the Effect > Distort and Transform menu to tightly erode the fill's edges.

Live 3D Effects

11

Live 3D Effects

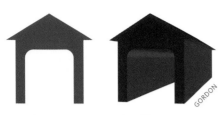

Extruding an object using the Effect >3D > Extrude & Bevel dialog box—the two-dimensional object on the left was extruded to create the three-dimensional covered bridge

2D or not 2D...?

Although Illustrator's 3D effect does a terrific job of rendering objects that look fully three-dimensional, you should bear in mind that Illustrator's 3D objects are only *truly* three-dimensional while you're working with them in a 3D effect dialog box. As soon as you're done tweaking your object and you click OK to close the dialog box, the object's three-dimensional qualities are "frozen"—almost as if Illustrator had taken a snapshot of the object—until the next time you edit it in a 3D dialog box again. On the page, it's technically an impressive 2D rendering of a 3D object that can only be worked with in two-dimensional ways. But because the effect is live, you can work with the object in 3D again any time you want, by selecting the object and then double-clicking the 3D effect listed in the Appearance palette.

3D effects are much like the other live effects, except… they're 3D. If the idea of "live effects" is new to you, you should probably take a look at the introduction to the previous chapter, *Live Effects & Graphics Styles*.

Illustrator offers you the power to transform any two-dimensional (2D) shape, including type, into a shape that looks three-dimensional (3D). As you're working in Illustrator's 3D effect dialog boxes, you can change your 3D shape's perspective, rotate it, and add lighting and surface attributes. And because you're working with a live effect, you can edit the source object at any time and observe the resultant change in the 3D shape immediately. You can also rotate a 2D shape in 3D space and change its perspective. Another exciting feature of the 3D effect is the ability to map artwork, in the form of a symbol, onto any of your 3D shape's surfaces.

To begin, think of Illustrator's horizontal ruler as the X axis and the vertical ruler as the Y axis. Now imagine a third dimension that extends back into space, perpendicular to the flat surface of your monitor. This is the Z axis. There are two ways to create a 3D shape using 3D effects. The first method is by extruding a 2D object back into space along the Z axis, and the second is by revolving a 2D object around its Y axis, up to 360°.

Once you apply a 3D effect to an object, it will show up in the Appearance palette. As with other appearance attributes, you can edit the effect, change the position of the effect in the palette's stacking order, and duplicate or delete the effect. You can also save 3D effects as reusable graphic styles so that you can apply the same effect to a batch of objects (see the *Live Effects & Graphic Styles* chapter for more about graphic styles). Of course, once the style has been applied, you can modify any of the style parameters by double-clicking the parameter in the Appearance palette (for an introduction to appearances, see the *Layers & Appearances* chapter).

EXTRUDING AN OBJECT

To extrude a 2D object, begin by creating an open or closed path. Your path can contain a stroke, a fill, or both. If your shape contains a fill, it's best to begin with a solid color. (See Tip "Solid advice on 3D colors" following.) With your path selected, choose Extrude & Bevel from the Effect >3D submenu. The top half of the 3D Extrude & Bevel Options dialog box contains rotation and perspective options that we'll examine a bit later, but for the moment we'll concentrate on the lower portion of the dialog box. Choose the depth to which you'd like your 2D object extruded by entering a point size in the Extrude Depth field or by dragging the pop-up slider. Choosing to add a cap to your object will give it a solid appearance, while choosing to turn the cap option off will result in a hollowed-out looking object (see figures at right).

You also have the option to add a beveled edge to your extruded object. Illustrator offers you ten different styles of bevels to choose from, and a dialog box in which to enter the height of the bevel. You can choose between a bevel that will be added to the original object (Bevel Extent Out), or a bevel that will be carved out from the original shape (Bevel Extent In). These options result in objects that appear radically different from each other (see the second pair of figures at right).

Note: *When you apply bevels to some objects (like stars), you might generate the error, "Bevel self-intersection may have occurred" when you click "Preview"—this may or may not actually mean that there is a problem.*

Remember that because you're working with a live effect, any changes you make to the original 2D source shape will immediately update the 3D object. The original shapes of the vector paths will be highlighted when you select the 3D shape—you can easily edit them just as you would any other path. You can always edit the settings you've entered for a particular 3D effect by double-clicking it in the Appearance palette. The appropriate dialog box will reopen where you can adjust any settings that you've previously entered.

HAMANN

Revolving an object using the Effect >3D >Revolve dialog box—the 2D shape on the left was revolved to create the 3D object on the right

Customized bevels!

All the 3D Bevels Shapes are located inside a file called "Bevels.ai" (within the folders Adobe Illustrator CS2 >Plug-ins >Bevels.ai). Each bevel path is saved as a Symbol inside this documents, so to add a custom bevel, draw a new path, drag it to the Symbols palette, name it and, resave the file.
—*Jean-Claude Tremblay*

Left to right: Turn cap on for solid, Turn cap off for hollow, Bevel Extent Out, Bevel Extent In

3D—Three dialogs

There are three different 3D effect options, and some of the features overlap. So before you apply 3D effects to an object, first decide which of the 3D effects best accomplishes your goals. If all you need to do is rotate or change the perspective of an object, use Rotate. If you want to map a symbol to the object, use either Revolve or Extrude & Bevel (you can still rotate your object from these as well). —*Brenda Sutherland*

You can rotate objects in three dimensions by using the Effect > 3D > Rotate dialog box (or the upper halves of the Revolve and the Extrude & Bevel dialog boxes). The star on the left was rotated in 3D to create the star on the right

HAMANN

Another example of rotating an object in three dimensions

3D effect—pass it on

Although in this book we generally recommend working with the New Art Has Basic Appearance setting turned off, you might want to turn it on when working with 3D effects. Otherwise, any new paths that you create subsequent to applying 3D effects to an object will also have the same appearance set, unless you first clear the appearance set from the palette, or click on the default fill and stroke icon in the Tools palette. On the other hand, if you *want* your next object to have the same 3D effects as the one you just created, leave New Art Has Basic Appearance turned off.

REVOLVING AN OBJECT

You can also create a 3D object from a 2D path (either open or closed) by revolving it around its Y (vertical) axis. Solid strokes work just as well as filled objects. Once you've selected your path, choose Effect > 3D > Revolve. In the 3D Revolve Options dialog box, you can set the number of degrees you wish to revolve the object by entering a value from 1 to 360 in the Angle text field, or by dragging the slider. An object that is revolved 360° will appear solid. An object revolved less than 360° will appear to have a wedge carved out of it. You can also choose to offset the rotation from the object's edge. This will result in a 3D shape that appears to be carved out in the center. And finally, as with extruded shapes, because the 3D options you've chosen are live effects, any changes you make to your original source object will immediately change the look of the 3D shape you've revolved.

ROTATING AN OBJECT IN 3D SPACE

The Rotate dialog box can be accessed directly by choosing Effects > 3D > Rotate. It can be used to rotate both 2D and 3D shapes. It also appears in the upper half of both the Extrude & Bevel and the Revolve Options boxes. The 3D Rotate Options dialog box contains a cube representing the planes that your shape can be rotated through. You can choose a preset angle of rotation from the Position menu, or enter values between –180 and 180 in the X, Y and Z text fields.

If you'd like to manually rotate your object around one of its three axes, simply click on the edge of one of the faces of the white cube and drag. The edges of each plane are highlighted in a corresponding color that tells you through which of the object's three planes you're rotating it. Red represents the object's X axis, a green highlight represents the object's Y axis, and blue edges represent the object's Z axis. The object's rotation is constrained within the plane of that particular axis. Remember, to constrain the rotation you must be dragging an edge of the cube. Notice the numbers changing in the corresponding text field as you drag. If you wish to rotate your object relative to all three axes at once, click directly on a surface of the cube and drag, or click in the black area behind the cube and drag. Values in all three text fields will change. And if you simply want to rotate your object, click-and-drag inside the circle, but outside the cube itself.

Changing the perspective of an object

You can change the visible perspective of your object by entering a number between 0 and 160 in the perspective text field, or by dragging the slider. A smaller value simulates the look of a telephoto camera lens, while a larger value will simulate a wide-angle camera lens, with more of an "exploded" perspective.

APPLYING SURFACE SHADING TO 3D OBJECTS

Illustrator allows you a variety of choices in the kind of shading you apply to your 3D object. These range from dull and unshaded matte surfaces to glossy and high-lighted surfaces that look like plastic. And because you can also choose how you light your object, the possible variations are limitless.

The surface shading option appears as part of both the 3D Extrude & Bevel and the 3D Revolve Option dialog boxes. Choosing Wireframe as your shading option will result in a transparent object whose contours are overlaid with a set of outlines describing the object's geometry. The next choice is No Shading, which will result in a flat-looking shape with no discernible surfaces. Choosing the Diffused Shading option results in your object having a soft light cast on its surfaces, while choosing the Plastic Shading option will make your object look as if it's molded out of shiny, reflective plastic.

If you choose either the Diffused Shading or Plastic Shading options, you can further refine the look of your object by adjusting the direction and intensity of the light source illuminating your object. By clicking the More Options button, the dialog box will enlarge and you'll be able to make changes to the Light Intensity, Ambient

Solid advice on 3D colors

You'll get best results using solid fill colors for 3D objects. Gradients and pattern fills don't produce reliable results.

For the smoothest 3D

When creating profile objects that you will extrude, revolve, or rotate into 3D, your goal should be to draw the objects with as few anchor points as possible. Since each anchor point will produce an additional surface, the more points that you have, the more irregular your form might appear. Also, extra surfaces might create potential problems you'll encounter when later mapping artwork onto the surfaces.
—Jean-Claude Tremblay

Making 3D can be slow...

Depending on processor speed and RAM, 3D effects can be slow.

Not enough steps...

If you click on the More Options button, you'll get the opportunity to adjust Surface and Shading Color options. The default setting for Blend Steps is 25—not nearly enough steps to create smooth color transitions from light to shaded areas. Since the maximum setting of 256 is smooth but slows you down, experiment to find the best resolution-to-speed setting for each image.

GOLDING

Mordy Golding used the Map Art feature to wrap the label art (above left) around the bottle (shown in detail, above right)—to create the bottle he used the 3D Revolve effect with a custom Surface Shading (for more about this art see the Mordy Golding Gallery later in this chapter)

Mapping—don't get lost!

Here are some tips to help you avoid confusion about the surface to which you're mapping symbols:

- Remember that you need to choose a surface in the dialog. Select by clicking the Arrow keys to view each surface.
- When clicking through the various surfaces, it's sometimes easier to identify the surface you want by the red highlight on the object itself, rather than by the flattened proxy in the mapping dialog box.
- Even the red highlight can fool you. If the symbol isn't mapping to a selected surface, it may be because it's being mapped to the *inside* of the surface.
- A stroke will add more surfaces to an object.
- A stroke can obscure mapped art on a side surface.

—*Brenda Sutherland*

Light level, Highlight Intensity, Highlight Size, and number of Blend Steps. The default for Blend Steps is quite low (25 out of a maximum of 256), see the Tip "Not enough steps…" on the previous page for advice about Blend Steps. Finally, you can also choose a custom Shading Color to add a color cast to the shaded surfaces.

MAPPING ART ONTO AN OBJECT

One of the most exciting aspects of the 3D effect is the ability to map artwork onto the surfaces of your 2D or 3D shape (as with the label on Mordy Golding's wine bottle at left). The key is to first define the art that you wish to map onto a surface as a symbol; select the artwork you want to map and drag it to the Symbols palette. For some images, you'll want to define a number of symbols. For instance, in Mordy's wine bottle, the label was one symbol and the printing on the cork was a separate symbol

Once you've made your artwork into symbols, you can map the symbols onto your 3D objects from the Extrude & Bevel, Revolve, or Rotate Options dialog boxes. In any of these 3D options boxes you simply click on the Map Art button, then choose one of the available symbols from the menu. You can specify which of your object's surfaces the artwork will map onto by clicking on the left and right Arrow keys. The selected surface will appear in the window; then you can either scale the art by dragging the handles on the bounding box or make the art expand to cover the entire surface by clicking the Scale to Fit button. Note that as you click through the different surfaces, the selected surface will be highlighted with a red outline in your document window. Your currently visible surfaces will appear in light gray in the Map Art dialog box, and surfaces that are currently hidden will appear dark. (See the "Quick Box Art" lesson later in this chapter for an example of mapping the 3D surfaces of a box with custom symbols.)

Note: *In order to see artwork mapped onto the side surfaces of your object, make sure that the object has a stroke of None!*

Joseph Shoulak

This tower of Tupperware (left) accompanied a San Francisco Chronicle story about the history of the Tupperware container (see his lesson later in this chapter). Shoulak created each container by using the 3D features in Illustrator. The round containers were made by drawing a 2D path of a container's profile, then applying the Effect > 3D > Revolve command to revolve the path 360° (above). He created the square containers by applying the Effect > 3D > Extrude & Bevel command to 2D paths. When a container used complex surfaces or multiple colors, Shoulak assembled it from multiple components. As he arranged the tower on the Artboard, he drew shadows and used the Control palette to adjust opacity.

Quick & Easy 3D

Simple 3D Techniques

Overview: *Draw or modify 2D artwork, prepare artwork for 3D; apply 3D Effect; expand artwork and edit objects to complete visual effects.*

1

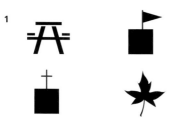

Some of the standard map symbols that Gordon modified for the map symbol set

Left, the original tent artwork objects; center, the white triangle selected; right, the tent after subtracting the white triangle from the black triangle and changing the fill color to green

---

Single-axis movements in 3D

In the 3D Extrude & Bevel Options dialog, you click on a *side* of the cube and drag to rotate artwork using the X, Y, or Z axis. If you want to move the artwork by just one axis, click instead on a white *edge* of the cube and then drag.

Steven Gordon was hired to design a set of contemporary map symbols for Digital Wisdom, Inc. that would be sold as a clip-art set of map symbol artwork and Illustrator symbols (www.map-symbol.com). To make this set stand out from other map symbol sets and fonts, Gordon explored Illustrator's new 3D Effect and found that it made it easy to turn the ordinary into the unusual.

1 Drawing artwork, visualizing 3D appearance, and using editing tools to prepare for 3D. Gordon started with some standard map symbol clip-art. For the camping symbol, he modified the tent artwork by removing the bottom horizontal object and applying a light green fill to the remaining triangle. When visualizing how the object would look in 3D, Gordon realized that the white and green triangles would both be rendered as 3D objects; instead he needed the white triangle to form a hole in the green triangle that would become the tent. He selected the white and green triangles and clicked the Subtract from Shape Area icon in the Pathfinder palette to punch a hole in the green triangle.

As you prepare artwork for the 3D Effect, refer to the *Beyond Basic Drawing & Coloring* chapter to review techniques for making compound shapes by combining or cutting objects (as Gordon did to make the tent opening), and for making compound paths (which may yield different results than applying a 3D Effect to separate artwork objects). Also, change stroke attributes for caps, joins, and miter limits to round off path intersections in the 3D rendering you'll create in the next step.

2 Apply 3D Effect, modify Position controls to extrude and rotate objects, and create a Style. When you finish creating your artwork, make sure it is selected, and then from the Effect menu, select 3D > Extrude & Bevel. In the 3D Extrude & Bevel Options dialog box, click the Preview checkbox to see what your artwork will look like using the dialog box's default settings.

Artwork in preview mode for several adjustments of the Position cube in the 3D Extrude & Bevel Options dialog box

You can change the artwork's rotation by clicking on the three-dimensional cube in the Position pane of the dialog box and dragging until the artwork moves to an orientation you like. You can also fine-tune the position by keying in values in the X, Y, and Z axes rotation fields.

To change the amount or depth of the extrusion, use the Extrude Depth slider in the Extrude & Bevel pane of the dialog box. To give the tent less depth than the default setting (50 pt), Gordon dragged the slider to extrude by 40 pt. To simulate perspective, drag the Perspective slider to adjust the amount of perspective from none/isometric (0°) to very steep (160°). Gordon used 135° for his artwork. When you are satisfied with your artwork's appearance, click OK to render the object.

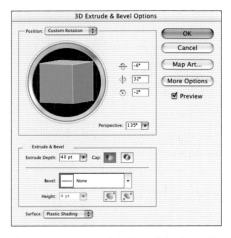

The 3D Extrude & Bevel Options dialog box with the settings Gordon used for the final version of the tent symbol

Gordon converted the 3D appearance he had created for the tent into a reusable style. Refer to the *Live Effects & Graphic Styles* chapter for instructions on creating and modifying graphic styles. You can use a style for other artwork, as way of providing a uniform 3D appearance for several objects, or as a starting point for creating a new 3D appearance for an object.

3 Editing the artwork after using the 3D Effect. After applying the 3D Effect to the tent artwork, Gordon decided to make color and shape changes to the artwork. To edit shapes or change colors of objects in the 3D artwork, you must first expand the appearance by choosing Object > Expand Appearance. (Note: this will remove the "live" editability of the artwork; it's safer to work with a copy of the artwork instead of the original.) Once expanded, ungroup the artwork (Object > Ungroup) and select and edit its paths.

Left, the tent artwork after expanding the 3D artwork (Object > Expand Appearance); right, shapes after filling with different colors

Selecting and modifying one of the shapes to create the interior floor of the tent

3D Effects

Extruding, Revolving, and Rotating Paths

Overview: *Create basic paths working with a custom template layer; extrude, revolve, and rotate paths; map artwork onto shapes.*

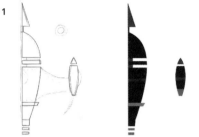

The original pencil drawing, placed as a template, and the vector shapes drawn over them

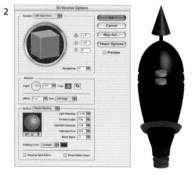

The original group of paths, selected and revolved as a group with the same settings

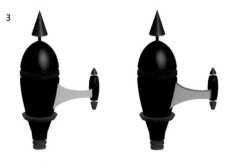

The wing shape drawn to follow the contour of the hull and then extruded and rotated slightly

HAMANN

To complete this illustration, Brad Hamann created a set of basic paths and applied a series of live 3D effects to them. He then added lighting and mapped artwork to the components.

1 Planning ahead. Because he would be rotating his shapes, Hamann needed to draw only one side of the symmetrical space cruiser. Working over a pencil drawing he had scanned in Photoshop and placed on a designated template layer, he drew one closed shape for the hull. He divided it into sections using the Pathfinder tool so he could color each part differently. He filled the paths with solid color and no stroke. When revolved, a filled path with no stroke will present the fill color as its surface color. A stroked shape that is revolved uses the stroke color as its surface color, regardless of fill color.

2 Applying the 3D Revolve effect to a group of shapes and extruding the wings. Hamann chose to revolve the group of shapes that make up the ship's hull all at the same time, because they shared the same left-side vertical rotation line. He also revolved the three shapes making up the rocket-shaped wing end as a group, using the same settings. Once the shapes were revolved, Hamann selected and moved each shape into its proper position within the group, using the Bring to Front command. He deleted the two inner green circles, because they would be invisible within the 3D model anyway.

For the wings Hamann then drew a flat shape for the right wing that followed the contour of the 3D hull and chose Effect > 3D > Extrude & Bevel. He selected an extrusion depth and rotational angle for the wing that would be visually consistent with the hull.

3 **Mapping artwork.** Hamann decided to map a star pattern, which he had previously saved as a symbol, onto the wing to liven up the look of the spaceship. He was able to return to the 3D Effects settings window by selecting the wing and clicking the Effect setting from the Appearance palette. He then clicked the Map Art button to access the Map Art window, which presented an outline of the first of the six surfaces available on the wing for mapping. Hamann chose his star pattern from the menu of available symbols. He scaled the pattern using the handles on the bounding box and then clicked OK. At this time, he also changed the wing color from green to red. Finally, Hamann selected the wing and the rocket at its end, and reflected and copied the wing to the opposite side of the spacecraft. He made a slight adjustment to the rotational angle of the new wing's Y-axis to account for its new position.

4 **Ready for takeoff.** Hamann completed his rocket ship by creating a porthole from a circular path to which he applied a 5.5-pt ochre-colored stroke. He then extruded the path and applied a rounded bevel. A blue gradient filled path, and a Gaussian Blur was applied, which completed the porthole.

3
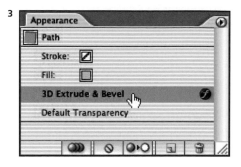

Clicking in the wing's Appearance palette to return to the 3D Effects settings window

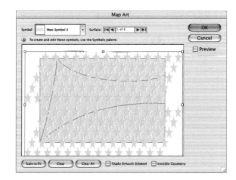

The Map Art window showing the first of the wing's surfaces available to map art onto

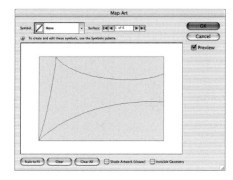

After selecting the star pattern from the Symbol menu, the pattern was scaled and positioned onto the wing outline

4

Hamann applied a rounded bevel to a circular path he had extruded to create the porthole

3D Logo Object

Revolving a Simple Path into a 3D Object

Overview: *Draw a cross-section; use the 3D Revolve feature to build a 3D object from the cross-section.*

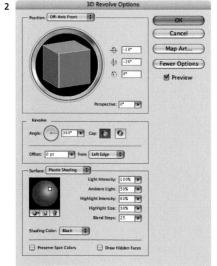

The cross-section path for the mortar, shown here with a black stroke for clarity; the actual path has a very light black fill and no stroke

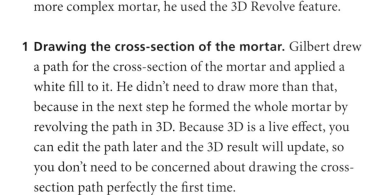

3D Revolve Options dialog box with settings for the final mortar bowl

The mortar with all rotation angles set to 0° (left), and at the default angles (right)

When Reggie Gilbert redesigned this logo for an herbal extract company, he decided to draw the mortar and pestle as 3D objects. Gilbert used the 2D basic shape tools and gradient fills to easily draw the pestle, but for the more complex mortar, he used the 3D Revolve feature.

1 Drawing the cross-section of the mortar. Gilbert drew a path for the cross-section of the mortar and applied a white fill to it. He didn't need to draw more than that, because in the next step he formed the whole mortar by revolving the path in 3D. Because 3D is a live effect, you can edit the path later and the 3D result will update, so you don't need to be concerned about drawing the cross-section path perfectly the first time.

2 Applying the 3D Revolve effect. With the cross-section selected, Gilbert chose Effect > 3D > Revolve. In the Revolve section of the 3D Revolve Options dialog box, He entered 360° for Angle, which swept the cross-section around in a full circle. The Offset option showed that by default, the center of the revolution was the path's left edge. The Surface settings shaded the mortar, using the fill color Gilbert applied to the original path (clicking the More Options button reveals Surface settings). You can rotate a 3D object by dragging the proxy cube in the 3D Revolve Options dialog box or by entering rotation angles next to the cube. Gilbert used the default values for the rotation angles and the Surface settings.

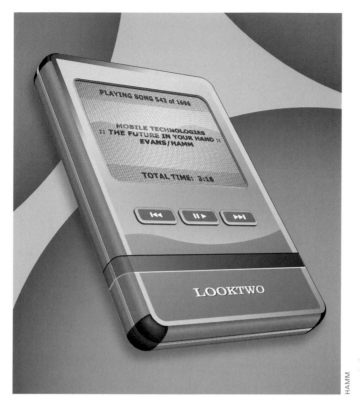

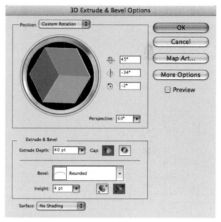

Michael Hamm

For this personal digital assistant (PDA) concept, Michael Hamm used 3D features and custom guides. He drew a rounded rectangle then chose Effect > 3D > Extrude & Bevel to specify 3D values. Hamm selected No Shading from the Surface pop-up menu in the 3D Extrude & Bevel dialog box because he wanted to shade the PDA manually. When the perspective looked good (top right), he expanded a copy of the case (Object > Expand Appearance) and applied meshes and blends to shade each side. When creating additional 3D objects like the buttons, Hamm matched them to the case perspective by copying the 3D rotation values or the Appearance from the original unexpanded 3D case, which he kept on a hidden layer. Hamm aligned objects using a layer of hand-drawn perspective guides (bottom right). He used the Rectangular Grid tool (bottom left) to draw the LCD pixel grid, and used the Free Transform tool to apply perspective (grid detail at bottom center). To combine the grid with the screen, Hamm applied 50% opacity and the Color Dodge blending mode to the grid.

Assembling in 3D

Building 3D Objects from Multiple Paths

Overview: *Draw 2D paths with rounded corners; use the 3D Extrude & Bevel effect to create 3D objects from the 2D paths; arrange the 3D objects to build a more complex 3D object.*

SHOULAK

Joseph Shoulak drew this plastic container as part of a larger illustration for a San Francisco Chronicle story about a Tupperware documentary film. Shoulak cleverly rendered complex plastic forms in Illustrator by stacking and aligning paths that were extruded and rotated using the 3D features in Illustrator.

1 **Drawing the 2D paths.** The container is like a beveled box with non-beveled lips that extend where the white base and blue lid meet. These attributes led Shoulak to draw four paths for extrusion: the white container body, the white lip, the blue lip, and the blue body. The need for four shapes will become evident when they are later extruded in 3D.

1

The Rectangle and Rounded Rectangle tools (highlighted) in the toolbox, and the Round Corners dialog box for adding round corners to rectangles that don't already have them

Seen from the top, the container consists of rectangles with round corners. To create them precisely, draw with the Rectangle tool; the rectangle for the blue top is 136 pt x 170 pt. Then choose Effect > Stylize > Round Corners and enter a Radius value of 12 pt. Alternatively, you can use the Rounded Rectangle tool, adjusting the corner radius by pressing the Up or Down arrow keys before releasing the mouse button.

The 3D effects in Illustrator pick up the fill and stroke colors applied to paths. Shoulak filled the rectangles with the blue and white colors of the container body and lid. He set the stroke color to None, because a stroke color would have colored the sides of the objects.

These four paths will eventually form the entire container

2 Extruding the 2D paths into 3D. Shoulak selected the blue container lid and chose Effect > 3D > Extrude & Bevel. He entered an Extrude Depth of 40 points. Shoulak also applied a bevel by choosing the Classic style and entering a Height of 4 points. He also adjusted the 3D rotation angles (X axis: 77, Y axis: 35, Z axis: -10). When he was satisfied, he clicked OK.

For the other three paths, Shoulak used the same rotation angles, but slightly different extrusion and bevel settings. For the thin blue lip path, he entered an Extrude Depth of 10 points with no bevel. For the thin white lip, Shoulak entered an Extrude Depth of 5 points with no bevel. For the white container base, he used an Extrude Depth of 45 pts with a 4-pt Classic bevel.

Enable the Preview checkbox to see your changes interactively, but be aware that previewing 3D effects can take time. Because a 3D effect is live, you can edit it by selecting the object using the effect, then double-clicking the effect name in the Appearance palette. If selecting 3D objects becomes a challenge, you can select objects using the Layers palette, or working in Outline view. (3D objects in Outline view appear without the 3D effects.)

3 Assembling the objects. To complete the illustration, Shoulak repositioned the four 3D objects into their final arrangement. He used the Control palette to center all four objects horizontally. Then he moved each path up or down until they fit together perfectly.

There are several ways to keep objects along a vertical axis as you move them. You can Shift-drag an object, drag an object vertically with View > Smart Guides enabled, press the up or down arrow keys to nudge the object, or enter a value into just the Y value in the Control palette or Transform palette.

While you can rotate individual 3D objects by using the 3D Extrude & Bevel dialog box, you can't position 3D objects relative to each other in 3D space. 3D objects on the Artboard behave like 2D page objects—you can position them only on the Artboard's 2D space.

3

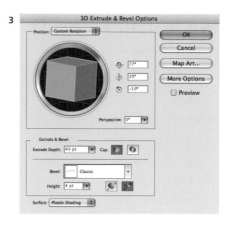

The 3D Extrude & Bevel dialog box settings for the larger blue lid piece

The four paths after applying extrusion settings

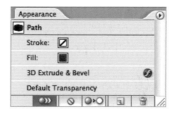

Appearance palette showing applied 3D effect

3

The Control palette with the Horizontal Align Center button highlighted; Align buttons appear when multiple objects are selected

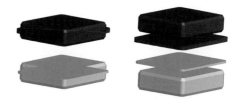

The four extruded paths after horizontal centering (left) and after repositioning them vertically (right), closing in on their final positions

Quick Box Art
Converting 2D Artwork to 3D Packages

Overview: *Start with a 2D package drawing; create symbols from package sides, use 3D Extrude and Bevel to rotate a box in perspective; map side art to each surface.*

The prepress-ready flat box drawing

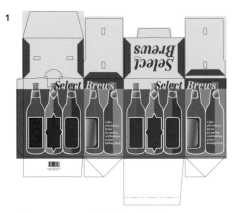

The three required sides separated from the main drawing

Gary Moss designed this easy-to-carry box for assorted beer bottles. The client requested a rendering of the finished box for a catalog. Moss used the 3D Extrude & Bevel effect to simulate the final three-dimensional box and to quickly map the box sides to their surfaces.

1 **Drawing the flat box.** Moss created a design sketch in Illustrator. Then using an Illustrator file provided by the box manufacturer, he applied precise dimensions to his sketch to meet the printing specifications, including all necessary sides, folds, bleeds, and die cuts.

2 **Separating the sides.** Moss created a copy of the flat box drawing, then used the Selection and Direct Selection tools to delete everything except the three sides that would be visible in the simulated box. For the 3D box, he wouldn't need the bleeds that extended beyond the actual edge of a side, so Moss trimmed them back, resizing the bleed paths to meet the actual box edge.

3 Creating symbols from the sides. Moss planned to use the 3D Extrude & Bevel feature to map the art to the sides of the box; this feature requires each side to be made into an Illustrator symbol first. If you're not using other symbols, you can delete them to reduce palette clutter: In the Symbols palette, choose Select All Unused, and click the Delete Symbol button. To create a symbol, select the objects making up one side and click the New Symbol icon in the Symbols palette. Repeat for each side.

In Illustrator, a symbol is normally used to creatively reuse an object many times. Mapping art in the 3D Extrude & Bevel feature is a special use of symbols.

4 Creating the 3D form. Moss drew a rectangle the size of the box front. With the rectangle selected, he chose Effect > 3D > Extrude & Bevel. He set the Extrude Depth to 120 points (the side panel width). He adjusted the rotation angles (X axis: -20, Y axis: 30, Z axis: -10), and to add slight linear perspective, he set Perspective to 19°.

5 Mapping the art. To apply art to each box surface, Moss used the Map Art feature in the 3D Extrude & Bevel dialog box. Click the Map Art button, click the arrows to select next and previous surfaces (the current surface highlights in red on the Artboard), and select the desired symbol. Click the Scale to Fit button to size the art to the surface, or use the handles to position, rotate, or size the art manually. It may be simpler to create the symbols at the proper orientation and size, as shown in step 3.

If mapped art doesn't preview, it may be mapped to the non-visible surface of a side. When viewing non-mapped surfaces in the Map Art dialog box, a light gray surface faces you, while a dark gray surface faces away.

6 Finishing the illustration. Although the 3D Extrude & Bevel dialog box provides lighting controls (click More Options to see them), Moss wanted to add more creative lighting and shading effects by hand in Photoshop. In Photoshop, choose File > Open to open an Illustrator file.

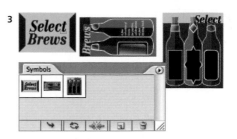

Symbols created from each side of the bottle box, after deleting all unused symbols

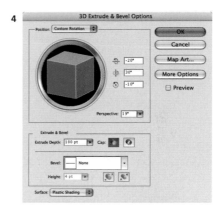

3D Extrude & Bevel dialog box (top), the 2D front side before (bottom left) and after (bottom right) applying 3D extrusion

Map Art dialog box (top) and the art on the Artboard (bottom) as each side is mapped

Mike Schwabauer / Hallmark Cards

To announce a company blood drive, artist Mike Schwabauer produced this illustration that was emailed as a low-resolution graphic and printed as a sign. For the background flag, Schwabauer started with flat, rectangular flag artwork. He selected the Free Transform tool to rotate and scale the flag. Then he chose Object > Envelope Distort > Make with Warp. In the Warp Options dialog box, he selected Flag from the Style menu. Schwabauer modified the default settings for the Flag style. When he had the look he wanted, he clicked OK. To fade the flag, he drew a rectangle large enough to cover the flag and filled it with a black-to-white gradient. After selecting the rectangle and the flag, he opened the Transparency palette and chose Make Opacity Mask from the palette menu. For the blood drop, Schwabauer drew half of the blood drop shape. Then he chose Effect > 3D > Revolve and customized the set-

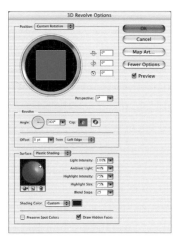

tings in the 3D Revolve Options dialog box. After clicking OK, he changed the object's transparency in the Transparency palette to 93% to make the drop look more like a liquid. To complete the blood drop, Schwabauer selected the blood drop object and chose Effect > Stylize > Drop Shadow. In the Drop Shadow dialog box, he set Mode to Multiply, Opacity to 50%, Blur to 0.12 inches, and Offset to –0.5" (X) and 0.2" (Y).

SHARIF

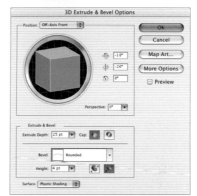

Robert Sharif

Robert Sharif used the power of Illustrator's 3D Extrude & Bevel effect to transform and combine a set of flat shapes into a stunningly realistic rendering of a classic Fender electric guitar. Robert chose Off-Axis-Front as the position for each shape he wanted to extrude, including the red guitar body, the wooden neck/headstock, and a grouped set of shapes containing the fingerboard, frets, and dot-shaped position markers. Because each extrusion shared the same position, the extruded pieces all lined up. Robert varied the value of the extrude depth for each piece, from a deeper extrusion for the body (25 pt), to a shallower extrusion for the white face plate (0.65 pt). Robert also chose to add a variety of bevels to various parts of the guitar, including rounded bevels to the body and neck, and a classic bevel to the control knobs. The three white pickups, the fret board, and other square edged parts were extruded with the Bevel set to None. To create the soft highlights on the guitar body, Robert used the Plastic Shading

rendering style. The 3D Extrude & Bevel effect was also used to create the screw heads for the tuning pegs, whose shafts were created using 3D Revolve. The tuning peg handles and other parts of the guitar were made using gradient-filled shapes.

WAI

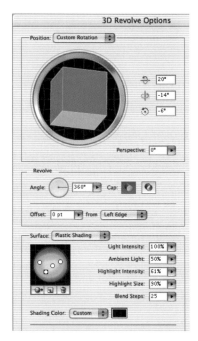

Trina Wai

Trina Wai created her playful panda by taking full advantage of Illustrator CS's 3D Revolve and 3D Extrude and Bevel effects. She started with a series of very simple flat shapes and ended with a truly organic look. Wai began by drawing an open path for one side of the panda's head. Choosing Effect > 3D > Revolve, she rotated the path 360° along its left edge. To create the soft shiny reflections of the panda's fur, Wai specified plastic shading as the surface type and added additional light sources using the New Light button. The bamboo stalk was also revolved from a simple open path, then rotated and grouped with a set of flat leaf shapes. Wai then extruded the main body parts by selecting 3D Extrude and Bevel. Each shape received its own extrusion depth ranging from 150 pt for the legs and body, 37.5 pt for the ears, 30 pt for the nose and 7 pt for the areas

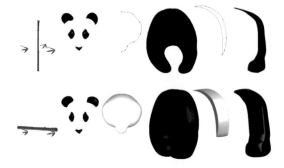

surrounding the eyes. Each shape also received a rounded bevel and plastic shading lit with a single light source. The small eyes were created using a blend between a large black circle and a smaller gray circle.

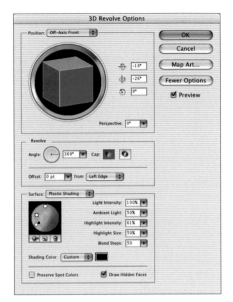

GOLDING / ADOBE SYSTEMS, INC.

Mordy Golding

To demonstrate the 3D effect of Illustrator CS for Adobe Systems, Inc., Mordy Golding created a wine label and then dragged the label to the Symbols palette (so he could use it next to create the 3D rendering). He drew a half-bottle shape and selected Effect > 3D > Revolve. In the 3D Revolve Options dialog box, Golding clicked the Preview checkbox and then clicked on the Map Art button. From the Map Art dialog box's Symbol menu, he selected the wine label symbol he had created previously. Back in the 3D Revolve Options dialog box, Golding adjusted the preview cube, changing the rotation angles until he was satisfied with the look of the bottle. He finished the effect by adding lights, using the New Light icon in the Surface panel of the dialog box; this created the cascading highlights on the bottle. After creating the cork, using the same technique as he used for the bottle, Golding selected the bottle, moved it above the cork, and changed its opacity to 94% in the Transparency palette.

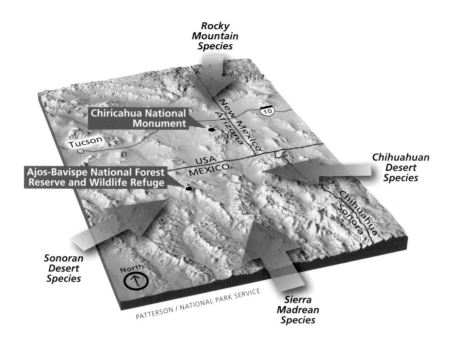

PATTERSON / NATIONAL PARK SERVICE

Rocky
Mountain
Species

Chiricahua National
Monument

Tucson

Ajos-Bavispe National Forest
Reserve and Wildlife Refuge

USA
MEXICO

Chihuahuan
Desert
Species

Sonoran
Desert
Species

North

Sierra
Madrean
Species

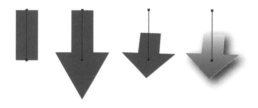

Tom Patterson / National Park Service

Cartographer Tom Patterson used Illustrator's
3D effect to show species movement across the
Sonoran Desert. Patterson drew a straight path
with the Pen tool and chose a 20-pt stroke. To
turn the path into an arrow, he chose Effect >
Stylize > Add Arrowheads. In the Add Arrowheads dialog box, he selected an arrowhead
design (11) and specified 25% for Scale. Next,
Patterson chose Effect > 3D > Rotate and in the
3D Rotate Options dialog box, he enabled the
Preview and dragged the three-dimensional
cube in the Position pane to adjust the spatial
orientation of the arrow. When the arrow
looked right, he clicked OK. To fill the arrow,
Patterson first chose Object > Group to change
the arrow from an object to a group. Then he
selected Add New Fill from the Appearance
palette menu and applied a custom gradient
to the new fill. He repeated these steps to create the other three arrows. To finish, Patterson
targeted the layer containing the arrows and
changed opacity to 80% in the Transparency
palette; he also added a drop shadow (Effect >
Stylize > Drop Shadow) to the layer.

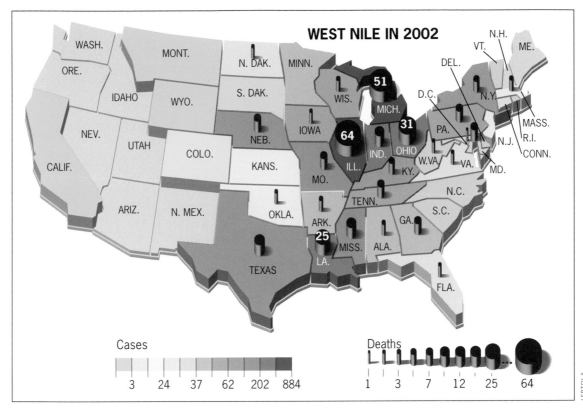

WEST NILE IN 2002

Cases

3 24 37 62 202 884

Deaths

1 3 7 12 25 64

LERTOLA

Joe Lertola / TIME

Joe Lertola of *TIME* Magazine relied on the 3D Effect (Effect > 3D > Extrude & Bevel) to turn an otherwise flat map into an eye-catching 3D thematic map. After drawing all the artwork, Lertola created groups for the gray states and the colored states. To give each group a different height, he applied the 3D Effect to each group, but specified a different Extrude Depth value in the 3D Extrude & Bevel Options dialog box for each group (6 pt for the gray states and 24 pt for the colored states). Lertola completed the effect by adding a second light (he clicked on the New Light icon in the Surface panel) to change the position of the highlight and shadow of each group.

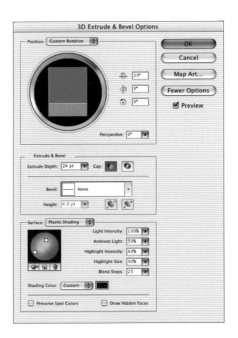

Advanced Techniques

12

Advanced Techniques

Clipping Mask	▶	Make
Compound Path	▶	Release

Choose Clipping Mask >Make from the Object menu or use the Make/Release Clipping Mask button on the Layers palette

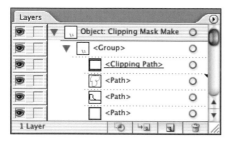

Choosing Object >Clipping Mask >Make puts all of the masked objects into a group with the clipping path at the top of the group

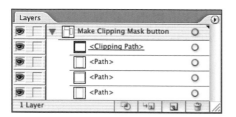

Clicking the Make/Release Clipping Mask button at the bottom of the palette turns the first item within the highlighted group or layer into a clipping path, without creating a new group

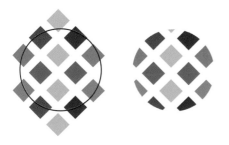

Before masking (left), the circle is positioned as the topmost object in the stacking order, so it will become the clipping path when the Clipping Mask is created (right)

This chapter combines techniques found throughout this book and expands upon them. We'll often use masks to control which portion of an object or image is visible, and which is hidden. With masking effects in particular, the techniques will be easier to follow if you're comfortable with layers and stacking order (see the *Layers & Appearances* chapter), as well as blends and gradients (the *Blends, Gradients & Mesh* chapter), and are willing to experiment with Pathfinders and Shapes (the *Beyond Basic Drawing & Coloring* chapter).

Illustrator features two kinds of masks: Clipping Masks and Opacity Masks. Although this chapter will include lessons and Galleries using both in a variety of techniques, this Introduction will only focus on Clipping Masks. Since Opacity Masks are made using the Transparency palette, the *Transparency* chapter covers the basics of creating and working with Opacity Masks.

CLIPPING MASKS

A Clipping Mask gathers *all* selected objects into a group and then converts the topmost object of that group into a *clipping path*; this clips (hides) portions of the other objects in the group that extend beyond the clipping mask boundaries. Regardless of its previous attributes, a clipping mask always becomes unfilled and unstroked. After you've created a Clipping Mask, you can edit the masking object, as well as the objects within the mask, using the Lasso, Direct Selection, or any path-editing tools.

In the Layers palette, there are two indicators of an active Clipping Mask. First, your <Clipping Path> will be underlined and will remain underlined even if you rename it. Second, with an active Clipping Mask, you'll see dotted lines, instead of the standard solid lines, between the clipped items in the Layers palette.

To make a Clipping Mask from an object, you must first create that object. Make sure it's above the objects to be clipped, then create the Clipping Mask using one of two options. Use either the Make/Release Clipping Mask button on the Layers palette, or the Object > Clipping Mask > Make command. Each has its inherent advantages and disadvantages. The Object menu command gathers all the objects into a new group as it masks, allowing you to have multiple masked objects within a layer. It also gives you the ability to freely move masked objects within a layer structure without breaking the mask. However, if you have a carefully planned layer structure, it will be lost when everything is grouped. In contrast, the Layers palette command maintains your layers' structure as it masks, but you can't have separately masked objects within a layer without building sublayers or grouping them first. This makes it difficult to move masked objects as a unit. In terms of releasing either type of mask, see the Warning Tip on the next page.

Masking technique #1: The Layers palette options

To mask unwanted areas of art within a *container* (meaning any group, sublayer, or layer), first create an object to use as your mask—make sure it's the topmost object in your container. Next, highlight that object's *container* and click the Make/Release Clipping Mask button on the Layers palette. The result: The topmost object, or container *within* the highlighted container, becomes the clipping path, and all elements within that container extending beyond the clipping path are hidden.

Once you've created a Clipping Mask, you can move objects up or down within the container (layer, sublayer, or group) to change the stacking order. However, if you move items outside of the Clipping Mask container, they will no longer be masked. Moving the clipping path itself outside of its container releases the mask completely. To release a Clipping Mask without reordering objects or layers, select it and choose Object >Clipping Mask > Release. You can also use the Make/Release Clipping Mask button in the Layers palette, but unexpected results may occur (see Warning Tip on the next page).

PAPCIAK-ROSE

See the Type chapter for masking with live type

If you have only one Clipping Mask within a layer, you can safely highlight the container for the mask and click the Make/Release Clipping Mask button to release it. However, if you have a layer, sublayer, or group that contains more than one Clipping Mask, choosing this option with the top layer highlighted may release all Clipping Masks within that layer. The safest way to release a Clipping Mask is to select it and choose Object > Clipping Mask > Release.—*Jean-Claude Tremblay*

To insert objects into a Clipping Mask, make certain that Paste Remembers Layers (in the Layers palette menu) is off, then Cut or Copy the objects you wish to insert. Next, select an object within the mask and use Paste in Front or Back to place the copied object into the mask. Alternatively, you can drag the new object into the mask using the Layers palette (see the *Layers & Appearances* chapter).

Once an object is a Clipping Path, you can move it anywhere *within* its layer or group in the Layers palette—it will still maintain its masking effect!

Masking technique #2: The Object menu command

You can also create masks for objects using the Object menu command. Use this method when you want to confine the Clipping Mask to a specific object or group of objects that need to be easily duplicated or relocated. Since this method modifies your layer structure, don't use it if you need to maintain objects on specific layers.

As before, start by creating an object or compound object that will become your Clipping Mask. Make sure that it's the topmost object, then select it and *all* the objects you want to be masked (the topmost object will become the mask). Now, choose Object > Clipping Mask > Make. When you use this method, all the objects, including the new clipping path, will move to the layer that contains your topmost object and will be collected into a new <Group>. This will restrict the masking effect to only those objects within the group; you can easily use the Selection tool to select the entire clipping group. If you expand the <Group> in the Layers palette (by clicking the expansion triangle), you'll be able to move objects into or out of the clipping group, or move objects up or down within the group to change the stacking order. This chapter includes many examples that show how to use this command to create intricate contours by masking complex groups, such as blends.

MASK PROBLEM-SOLVING STRATEGIES
Using type or compound paths as a mask

You can use editable type as a mask to give the appearance that the type is filled with any image or group of objects. Select the type and the image or objects with which you want to fill the text. Make sure the type is on top, then choose Object > Clipping Mask > Make.

To use separate type characters as a single Clipping Mask, you have to first make them into a Compound Shape or Compound Path. You can make a Compound Shape from either outlined or live (i.e., non-outlined) text. You can make a Compound Path only from outlined text (not live text). Once you've made a Compound Path or Shape of your separate type elements, you can use it as a mask. (See Tip "Compound Paths or Shapes?" in the *Beyond Basic Drawing & Coloring* chapter. And see the *Type* chapter for examples of masking with type.)

You can also use multiple objects as a mask. You'll need to first select the objects and convert them to a Compound Path (Object > Compound Path > Make), or a Compound Shape (from the Pathfinder palette). In either case, your multiple objects form one compound object that can then become a single masking object. For examples, see the first two chapters in this book.

Mask error message

If you've tried to make a Clipping Mask, but you get the message. "Selection cannot contain objects within different groups unless the entire group is selected," the objects you've chosen to mask are part of a subset of a group of objects. To create a mask with these objects, Cut or Copy your selected objects, then Paste in Front (⌘-F/Ctrl-F). Now you'll be able to apply Object > Make Clipping Mask.

Opening legacy documents that contain masks

Before Illustrator 9, if you selected objects on different layers and chose to Make Mask, you'd create a "layer-mask" that would hide all objects between the selected objects, with the topmost object becoming your mask. If you open one of these files in the current version of Illustrator, you'll see that all your layers are now contained within a new layer called a "master layer."

Now, if you want to mask across layers, you have to manually create your own "master layer" into which you'll place everything you want to mask. To do this, select all the layers you wish to mask (click on the topmost layer, then Shift-click on the bottom layer), and choose Collect in New Layer from the Layers pop-up menu—this places all of your layers within a new "master layer." Although you can now make any topmost object your mask (including a group or sublayer), it's easiest to create or move an object for this purpose into the "master layer" itself.

Figuring out if it's a mask

Here's how to spot whether a current selection contains a mask or is being masked:

- The <Clipping Path> entry in the Layers palette will remain underlined if it is a mask, even if you've renamed the entry.
- An enabled Object > Clipping Mask > Release means a mask is affecting your selection.
- An Opacity Mask is indicated with a *dotted* underline.
- Choosing Select > Object > Clipping Masks can help you find masks within a document as long as they aren't inside linked EPS or PDF files.

Memory-intensive masks

Too many masks, or complex masking paths, may demand too much RAM and prevent you from printing. To test if a specific mask is the problem, select it and its masked objects, temporarily Hide them (Object > Hide), and then try to print. Hiding the masked objects will free up memory.

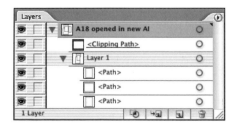

When you open a legacy file with layer-masks, the masked layers become sublayers of the masking layer, because all masking objects must be on the same container layer

Masking Details

Using Masks to Contour & Hide Elements

Advanced Technique

Overview: *Create basic elements; make basic masks; mask compound path objects with Live Effects; make compound paths to act as masks; create an overall cropping mask.*

1

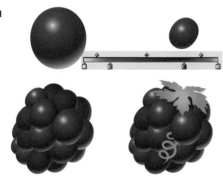

Making radial gradients for a grape shapes, drawing and combining basic objects

Masking to make two-toned leaves; making shadows by masking and setting the fills to Multiply mode; the final grapes with masking and shadows throughout

To truly be an Illustrator expert, you must master a range of masking techniques. Russell Benfanti's lush and masterful illustrations are filled with masks. This lesson looks at four applications of masking in Illustrator.

1 Contouring masks for detail and shadows. First create your basic objects using any tools, including blends and gradient mesh. Benfanti used ovals filled with radial gradients customized using the Gradient tool, so that the blue would appear as a reflection on the bottom edge.

In a layer above his grapes, Benfanti drew a two-toned leaf. He began by drawing the outline shape, filled it with a radial gradient, and copied it. Then he quickly drew teardrop shaped wedges extending beyond the leaf-shapes, filled with a darker green gradient. With the leaf shape still on the Clipboard, he used Paste In Front (⌘-F/Ctrl-F). Next, selecting *all* the leaf objects, he chose Object>Clipping Mask>Make (⌘-7/Ctrl-7).

To create the shadow for the leaf, he used Paste In Back (⌘-B/Ctrl-B) to paste another copy of the leaf underneath. He then shifted the position of this "shadow" down and to the right, and gave it a medium blue solid fill. To fit that object within the silhouette of the grapes (not extend beyond it), he needed to make a contouring object that matched the silhouette of the grapes. Selecting the grapes, he copied and used Paste In Front. In the Pathfinder palette he held Option (Alt) and clicked the first Add to Shape icon to permanently unite the grapes into one simple contouring-outline object.

Masking objects must be above the objects they mask, so move your grape-contour object above the "shadow" using the Layers palette. With the grapes contour above the blue leaf, Benfanti selected both and made a new clipping mask (⌘-7/Ctrl-7). To make the shadow more realistic, he selected only the blue leaf object and from the Control palette Opacity pop-up, he changed the blending mode from Normal to Multiply (you can change the blending mode before applying the mask). Benfanti also created shadows for individual grapes and the stem curl.

2 Masking roughened compound paths. To make the watermelon stripes, Benfanti drew arcs over the oval using the same gradient as the oval, and chose Object > Compound Path > Make, unifying the color. He then used the Gradient and Color palettes to make the colors of the arc gradient warmer and lighter. To ripple the selected arcs he chose Effect > Distort & Transform > Roughen, and used Preview to decide on Size: 2%, Relative, Detail: 5.53/in, and Corner. He used a copy of the melon oval as a mask so the arcs stay within the contour.

3 Using compound paths to mask. You can use multiple objects to act as one masking object by first making the selected objects into a compound path. For Benfanti's orange sections, he created the overall shapes and the inner textures. Next he drew section wedges, selected them all and chose Object > Compound Path > Make. Selecting the textures of the orange with this compound path, he used ⌘-7 (Ctrl-7) to section the orange. Before adding the finishing details, he selected the compound path mask object, and applied a darker orange gradient that shows through as a background.

4 Cropping the image with a layer mask. Benfanti placed all layers within one enclosing layer. Loose in that enclosing layer he created a rectangle that would define the cropping area. Finally, he clicked the master layer to highlight it, and then the Make Clipping Mask icon.

2

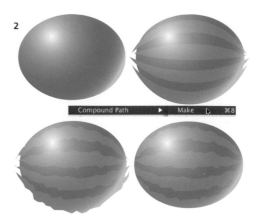

The original oval, making arcs and combining them into a compound path, applying Roughen, and masking with a copy of the original oval

3

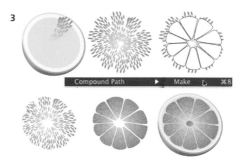

Making the basic orange elements; making wedge objects into one compound path; using the compound path as a mask; finishing details

4

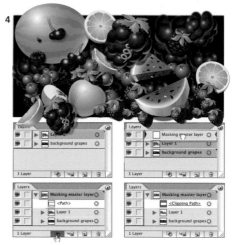

The final illustration before cropping the margins and the original Layers palette; after making a new layer, dragging the two original layers into it, clicking the Create Layer Mask icon and the final palette showing the clipping mask

Mask Upon Mask

Creating Reflections with Many Masks

JONEN

Advanced Technique

Overview: *Create an arc blend; widen the blend; fade the blend; apply a compound-path clipping mask; add a custom gradient; create final refraction and fading details.*

Linotype commissioned Frank Jonen to create a new icon suite for the Linotype Library GmbH font collections (Bad Homburg, Germany, www.linotype.com). Jonen used many masking techniques to achieve the rainbow reflections and glare for the logo (center above) representing Linotype's line of "standard" fonts (the gold logo is above left, and the platinum logo is above right).

1

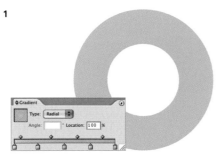

Creating a compound path and filling the duplicate with a custom radial gradient

1 Creating a disk gradient. Create a circle defining an outer disk shape by holding Shift when you drag with the Ellipse tool. Next, holding Option-Shift (Alt-Shift), from the center of your previous circle, draw a second circle to define the center hole area. Now select both circles and choose Object > Compound Path > Make to cut the first hole from the second, like a donut. With his disk created, Jonen filled the compound path with a custom, muted-color radial gradient. Keeping the compound path selected, he adjusted the colors and stops until the colors transitioned where he wanted them (see the *Blends, Gradients & Mesh* chapter for help with gradients).

2

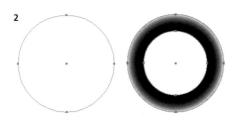

Fading the disk with a black-to-white blend on top of a white circle, making the blend into an Opacity Mask over the white circle, then placing this Opacity Mask over background disk and applying Soft Light mode at 30% opacity

2 Fading the disk. To make the disk vary in tonality, Jonen created a "fader" using an Opacity Mask. After turning on Smart Guides (View menu), with the Ellipse tool, he held Option-Shift (Alt-Shift) and dragged from the current circle's center to create a new circle slightly smaller than the outer disk, and filled it with white (no stroke). After copying this white circle, he pasted a copy on top (⌘-F/Ctrl-F) and then swapped the fill and stroke (Shift-X) so it had a white stroke and no fill. Jonen then created a smaller black-stroked circle from the same center (not as small as the CD hole). Selecting the two stroked circles (if you have trouble selecting, expand the Layers palette to view the <Path> objects and Shift-click to the right of the target icons to select both stroked <Path> objects), he then chose Object > Blend > Make. Unlocking the white-filled circle underneath, Jonen selected it along with the new blend. From the Transparency palette pop-up he chose Make Opacity Mask, then he set the blending mode to Soft Light, reduced the Opacity to 30%, and made sure to enable Clip.

3 Creating arc blends. Blends are probably the best way to create arcs of color. To re-create Jonen's blend, you'll blend between five different colored lines. On a new layer above, draw the first line from the circle center point beyond the edge of the outer disk, and give it a 1-pt bluish stroke (make sure Opacity is 100% and Blending Mode is Normal). Hide the disk layers. Make the second line by selecting the top anchor point of the line with the Direct Selection tool, grab it and swing it up about 15° and press down the Option/Alt key, holding until after you release the mouse. Color this line Cyan, the then repeat the duplication process above (varying the distance) to create the third (green), fourth (yellow), and fifth (red) lines. Before you blend these lines together, select the outer two (bluish-purple and red) and copy (you'll need these lines on the clipboard for the next step). Next, double-click the Blend tool to set Blend Options as Smooth Color. Finally, select all the lines and choose Object > Blends > Make.

4 Widening the end colors. To prepare the rainbow to fade along the edges, Jonen created wider versions of the outer colors. To do this, choose Paste in Front (⌘-F/ Ctrl-F) to paste the copied lines in perfect registration with the blend. In the Layers palette, make a new layer above the blend and move the lines into that new layer by dragging their selection indicators. Now hide the blend layer, showing just your copied lines. Starting with the bluish line, expand it with the Pen tool into a triangular wedge-shape: Start with the upper anchor point to con-

3

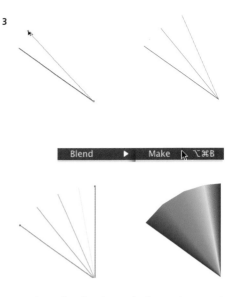

Drawing a first line then swinging copies up and recoloring, making a Smooth Color blend

4

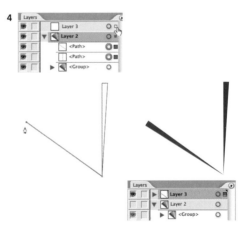

Copying and pasting in front the outer strokes, widening the copies

Showing the rainbow blend underneath, grouping the wider shapes with the blend objects

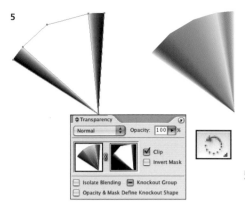

5

Creating a black-to-white larger object and applying it as an Opacity Mask for the rainbow and using the Rotate tool to make a copy

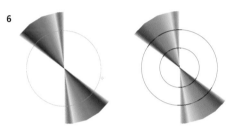

6

Drawing two circles centered on the rainbow center point with the Ellipse tool

Selecting the two circles to make a compound path

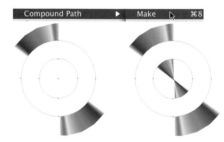

Selecting the compound path and the rainbow and choosing Object >Clipping Mask >Make

tinue the line, then click to create a perpendicular segment that extends out wider than the blend below. Then click the Swap Fill and Stroke icon in the toolbox (or press Shift-X), so that the new triangular color object is filled, not stroked with that blue color. Repeat this for the red line. Show the rainbow layers, Select All (⌘-A/Ctrl-A), and Group (⌘-G/Ctrl-G).

5 **Fading the rainbow with an Opacity Mask and duplicating it.** To fade the rainbow along the edges, Jonen used three objects to create an Opacity Mask. On a new layer above, he created a small black-to-white blend along the edge of the rainbow. Drawing a black line outside of and slightly longer than the rainbow, he held Option/Alt while moving the upper anchor point (as he did in making the lines in step 3), and changed the stroke copy to white. Selecting and blending these strokes, he then created a mirror version of this blend on the other side of the rainbow (you can recreate this blend, or use the Reflect tool to reflect a copy). Lastly, with the Pen tool, Jonen drew a white-filled triangle covering the remainder of the rainbow, overlapping into the white of the blends. After grouping the black-and-white objects, Jonen selected the rainbow and black-and-white groups, opened the Transparency palette, and chose Make Opacity Mask from the pop-up menu. To create a copy of the rainbow, with the Rotate tool hold Option/Alt and click on the rainbow-blend point, enter 180°, and click Copy.

6 **Masking the rainbows with a copy of the compound path.** Next, mask the rainbows with a copy of the background disk. One way to copy the disk is to expand the layer containing the background disk objects and locate <Compound Path>. Enable the view icon if it's still hidden, and click on the right side of the palette to select it. Now click the New Layer icon, and drag the selection indicator for the <Compound Path> to the new layer while holding Option/Alt. Since you're going to make these circles into a mask, it doesn't matter that the circles

are filled; creating the mask removes all styling. To apply this compound path as a mask, select it along with the rainbows, and choose Object>Clipping Mask>Make (if you have trouble isolating objects, use the Layers palette to lock or hide objects that are in the way).

7 Fading the rainbow with more masks. Jonen changed the blending mode for both rainbow objects to Overlay. Then, selecting each rainbow group separately, he reduced its opacity—60% for the top group, and 50% for the bottom rainbow group.

8 Creating a bright "reflection." To create a lighter "reflection," Jonen created an Opacity Mask applied to a white disk. Starting from the circle centerpoint, he drew a black line, a center white line, and an outer black line. Selecting the three lines, he chose Object>Blend>Make. After rotating a copy of this blend across the circle (hold Option/Alt, click on the circle centerpoint, enter 180°, and click Copy), and grouped these blends to form a "butterfly" <Group>. Selecting the donut-shaped compound path in the Layers palette, Jonen copied, and then selected the butterfly blends. Using ⌘-B (Ctrl-B), he pasted a copy of the compound path directly behind the butterfly objects. Giving this compound path a white fill and no stroke, he selected it and the butterfly objects and chose Make Opacity Mask (with Clip enabled).

9 Making glare. Lastly, Jonen created a crescent-shaped glare on half the disk. You can make a crescent by drawing two circles, one slightly larger than the outer disk, and one smaller than the hole. With the Pen tool, draw two arcs defining the ends of the crescent. Then select all and click the Divide Pathfinder icon. After deselecting, Direct Select and delete the excess objects. Selecting his crescent, Jonen set a white fill (no stroke), copied, and used ⌘-F (Ctrl-F). He applied a radial gradient fill (gray to black) to this upper crescent, selected both, chose Make Opacity Mask, and reduced the opacity to 50%.

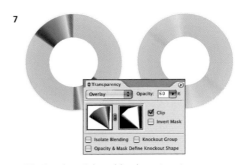

7

Moving the rainbow blends on top, Jonen changed the blending mode to Overlay and reduced the opacity (60% for the top rainbow and 50% for the bottom one)

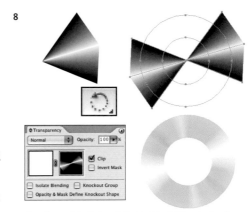

8

Creating a black-to-white-to-black blend, duplicating it to form a "butterfly" shape; then applying this as an Opacity Mask over a copy of the compound-path disk object (filled white)

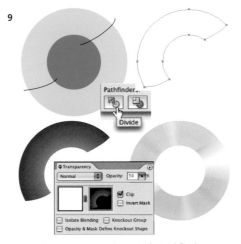

9

Creating a crescent using Divide Pathfinder on a pair of circles with paths defining the cut lines; filling one crescent with white and a copy with a radial gradient, making an Opacity Mask and reducing opacity to 50%

BRAD NEAL / THOMAS • BRADLEY ILLUSTRATION & DESIGN

Brad Neal

Brad Neal combined an attention to detail with Illustrator's wide range of drawing and rendering tools to create this photo-realistic image of a Ford Taurus stock car. Beginning with a contour shape filled with a flat color, Neal overlaid a series of custom blends to replicate the subtle modeling of the car's surface. Neal simulated the grill work at the front of the car by overlaying a series of four dashed stroked paths. The racing logos on the side of the car were drawn by hand, grouped, and positioned using the Shear tool. The Taurus, Valvoline, and Goodyear logos were fitted to the contour of the body with the help of the Envelope Distort tool. To achieve the realistic look of the front right wheel, Neal created custom blends with outer edges that blended smoothly into the flat color of the underlying shapes. Neal created a drop shadow for the car using a carefully controlled blend. This blend had an inner path that contained a solid black fill that blended to white as it approached the outer edge.

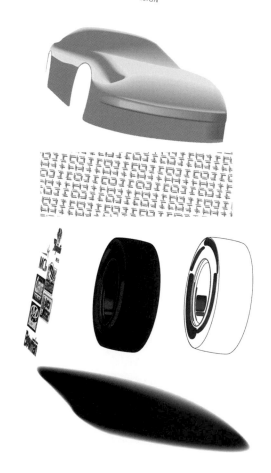

CATER(©INMOTION 2003)

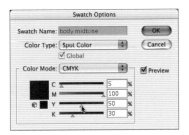

David Cater

David Cater created this Mini Cooper image for reproduction on T-shirts, posters, and note cards. Knowing that different clients would want the car in a variety of colors, he started by creating two spot color swatches for the mid and shadow tones of the car. He then used those two spot colors (global process colors would also work) to create the handful of gradients he used to fill each of the approximately 1,500 shapes he used to create the car. Because he was careful to color only the body panels using gradients created from those two colors, he was later able to easily change the color of the car by simply double-clicking on each of the two color swatches and using the CMYK sliders to redefine the colors. Although he could have used blends more extensively (he only used a few for the cowlings along the front and side of the car), Cater found it faster and easier to use simple gradient-filled shapes.

FERSTER

FERSTER

Gary Ferster

In creating a product illustration, Gary Ferster strives to combine realism with a dramatically appealing view of the product. For the Jeep and the sneaker, Ferster began by scanning photographs of the products and placing these grayscale TIFFs on template layers (see "Digitizing a Logo" in the *Layers & Appearances* chapter). On layers above the templates, he drew the objects' outlines with the Pen tool and then drew the base objects that would be used to create blends, created his blends, and then masked the blends with copies of the outlines. For each sneaker lace, Ferster created several dark-colored blends overlaying a light background. Then he masked each of the blends and background with the lace outlines.

Chris Nielsen

Drawing with the Pen tool and using Path-finder's Divide mode, Chris Nielsen created a series of shapes with increasing complexity to create photo realism. Nielsen began by placing an original photograph on a bottom layer to use as a guide for both shape and color values. Using the Pen tool he drew the larger shapes first, (such as the pipe shown above). He continued to draw shapes to define the object by first drawing all the dark red shapes, then those having a lighter value. Once the lines of the pipe were drawn for several values (such as dark red and light red), he selected all the paths, and from the Pathfinder palette selected Divide. Nielsen continued to draw more shapes to further define the area and repeated the process of using Pathfinder and Divide to break down the areas into increasingly smaller shapes. (The pipe detail shows steps 1,2,7 and the final 11th step). Nielsen then filled the shapes with colors sampled from the underlying photograph using the Eyedropper tool. If you look closely, you can see a reflection of Nielsen (taking the photograph) in the round chrome shape directly below the red pipe.

Glowing Starshine

Drawing Stars with Gradients and Strokes

Advanced Technique

Overview: *Create a star shape on top of a circle and adjust the shape using the Direct Selection tool; add a glow by applying a radial gradient to the star and circle shapes.*

1

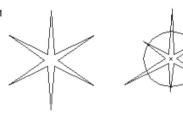

The original star, and the modified star positioned over a circle

2

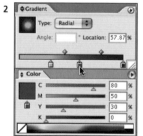

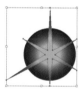

Color palette displaying color for selected slider on the Gradient palette with star shape selected

Gradient-filled shapes on the sky background

Illumination is the key to creating a realistic nighttime sky. This technique by Kenneth Batelman will help you create glowing lights of all sizes, simply and directly.

1 Drawing a big star. Batelman used the Ellipse tool to create a circle, and then the Star tool to draw a star on top of the circle. To make the star shape more interesting, he repositioned some of the star points using the Direct Selection tool.

2 Applying a radial gradient. To make the star glow, Batelman applied a radial gradient to the star. The gradient slider at the edge matches the sky color (he used 100% C, 80% M, 60% Y, and 20% K), and the slider at the center is the star glow at its brightest (he used 30% C, 5% M, 0% Y, and 0% K). Batelman added a third gradient slider between the original two, set to an intermediate color (he used 80% C, 50% Y, 30% M, 0% K). Applying the same radial gradient to the circle adds a halo effect to the star (for more on creating and storing gradients see the *Blends, Gradients & Mesh* chapter). To keep the star and glow together, he selected the star and circle and chose Object > Group (⌘-G/Ctrl-G).

Batelman created the small stars by overlapping specialized dashed strokes; see the Gallery opposite for details on this technique.

BATELMAN

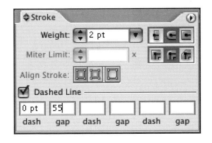

Kenneth Batelman

Batelman blanketed his sky with small stars by using dashed-line paths drawn with the Pencil tool. He created dots along the path by entering a Dash value of 0. For the Gap value, Batelman entered a value between 20 and 90 points. He chose the rounded options for both the cap and join so that the dots would be circular instead of square, and then set Weight values ranging from .85 to 2.5 points. By overlapping multiple paths with varying weights and dash gap values, Batelman's "dashes" appear to be points of light that vary in size and spacing. The Stroke palette settings shown above left are for the path of small stars selected above right.

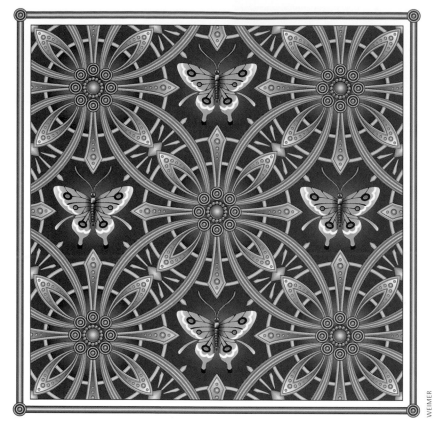

WEIMER

Alan James Weimer

Alan James Weimer constructed this pattern tile (detail right) using the steps described in the "Intricate Patterns" lesson in the *Drawing and Coloring* chapter. Once he had filled the tile elements with gradients and blends, Weimer Option-dragged (Alt-drag) the tile to the right to form the first row. To create the repeating pattern, Weimer diagonally Option-dragged (Alt-drag) copies of the first tile row onto a grid of guidelines to create a row above and a row below the first row. To crop the pattern into the square, he drew a square on the same layer as the tiled design, and at the bottom of the layers palette, he clicked the Make/Release Clipping Mask icon. On a layer above the mask, he added a border composed of blended, stroked rectangles for the sides and created the corner medallions with blended, stroked concentric circles. He then added a gradient-filled circle to the center of the medallion. For the background, Weimer used a solid fill beneath a layer of radial gradients which are positioned underneath the butterflies.

WEIMER

Alan James Weimer

To make the two medallions for a horizontal "tile" (right), Alan Weimer used the circle-and-guides technique described on the opposite page. After arranging the medallions and other elements to form the tile, he Option-dragged (Alt-drag) the tile to the right to form the first row. To create the repeating pattern, Weimer diagonally Option-dragged (Alt-drag) copies of the first tile row onto a grid of guidelines to form rows above and below the first row. To visually "crop" the design, he drew a rectangle on the same layer as the tiled design, and, at

the bottom of the Layers palette, clicked the Make/Release Clipping Mask icon. In a layer above the mask he added a border composed of blended, stroked rectangles.

LAMANTIA

Marc LaMantia

Marc LaMantia scanned one of his photographs to create this illustration of a subway exit, in which he used the techniques described on the opposite page. In this piece, LaMantia depicts the beauty of a single moment of an ordinary day in New York City. Transparency effects were used throughout the entire illustration (see the *Transparency* chapter). Many of the shadow areas (such as within the steps) are

actually made of transparent pink, red, and magenta shapes, layered above black. Rarely is a color used at full opacity. The layering of numerous transparent layers (all in Normal mode) brings enormous depth and interest to the posterized style. When viewing the image in Outline mode (above right), the level of detail becomes apparent.

GILBERT

Reggie Gilbert

To create his photorealistic fire station, illustrator Reggie Gilbert laid his bricks like a master. He began by creating five different rectangles and customizing a gradient for each using the Gradient palette. Then creating one solid-colored brick on an angle, duplicated that brick, and moved the duplicate along that angle, a distance away. Selecting the two angled bricks he double-clicked the Blend tool to set Blend Options to Specified Steps for Spacing, and entered 8. Gilbert then chose Object > Blend > Make to create the blend, then Object > Expand to break the blend into 10 separate objects. He next used the Direct Selection tool to select individual bricks to move them slightly out of alignment, giving the line of bricks a more organic look. Then he again selected each of the angled bricks and this time use the Eyedropper tool to click on one of the pre-made gradients to fill it with that gradient. With

this line of bricks complete, he grouped them (⌘-G/Ctrl-G) and starting with the blended line of bricks, he'd customize a new line. By creating each line of bricks with deliberate randomness Gilbert avoids the appearance of repeating patterns in the bricks. To create the windows (shown against blue at top), he drew the objects, grouped them, then filled them with a custom light-to-slightly-darker gradient in the hue of the objects that behind the glass. In the Layers palette he targeted the <Group>, and in the Control palette he reduced the opacity and applied Effect > Stylize > Feather (for the windows shown above he used 40% Opacity and 9 pt Feather).

CROUSE

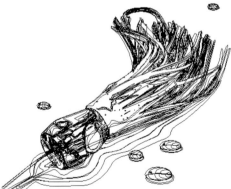

Scott Crouse

Scott Crouse required the flexibility of a vector drawing and the realism of a photograph for use in a variety of mediums (various sizes of signs and banners). He created this fishing lure with a combination of blends and solid filled paths. Crouse made the realistic head,

beads of water, and the shadows with blended shapes. He layered vibrant solid filled shapes to construct the tail. Crouse used the contrast of the filled shapes next to the blended objects to emphasize the fine detail in this vivid illustration.

CROUSE

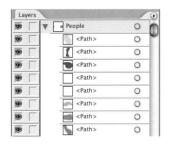

Scott Crouse

Scott Crouse created this photorealistic scene using layers of meticulously drawn and colored shapes (palette shown above). After drawing paths with the Pen tool to define an area, he colored the shapes with similar values (detail above right). In select areas such as the blue car trunk, he created a gradient. Crouse worked in a scale larger than what the final output required, so that after he reduced the image, the viewer would see smooth color transitions, not separate shapes. His technique created an illustration as lifelike as the photo from which Crouse drew inspiration (shown above the Layers palette at left).

Modeling Mesh

Shaping and Forming Mesh Objects

Advanced Technique

Overview: *Create an outline for smoke; create a simple rectangular mesh; bend the mesh using the Rotate and Direct Selection tools; align the mesh to your outline; add columns to lend a 3D effect; color your mesh; use the Screen Blend mode to make the smoke transparent.*

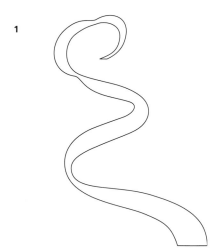

Create an outline of the desired final smoke form

Smoke outline locked in a layer, with the starting mesh above

Ivan Torres molded a mesh as though it were a piece of clay to form the smoke in his art piece "Meshsmith." One of the highlights of this lesson is Torres's use of the Rotate tool to bend *portions* of a mesh (as opposed to using it to rotate *whole* objects).

1 Setting up your artwork. Start by using the Pen or Pencil tool to create an outline of a smoke form. Lock the smoke outline in a layer, then place a rectangle at the base of the smoke. Convert the rectangle to a mesh, using the Object > Create Gradient Mesh command, with 1 column and 3 rows. Keep your starting mesh simple; it is easier to add rows as needed later.

2 Making the rough bends. Make your first big bend using the Rotate tool. Start by Direct-Selecting all but the bottom two points of the mesh. Next with the Rotate tool click on the inside of the first curve of the smoke outline to place the center for rotation, and then grab the top of your mesh rectangle and drag it around the center of rotation to form the first curve (see images at right).

At each bend or pinch in the smoke, you will need a row in order to make the next bend. If an existing row of your mesh is nearby, Direct-Select it and move it over the bend or pinch. To add a row, click with the Mesh tool on the edge of the mesh outline, at the bend or pinch. Once you have placed or added a mesh row at a bend or pinch, leave those points out of the next selection as you work your way up the smoke. Repeat this step until you reach the top of your smoke outline.

3 Aligning and straightening the mesh rows. Once you have the mesh roughly aligned, zoom in at each pinch and bend where you placed a mesh row and make it straight and perpendicular to the curve. Straightening out the mesh rows is essential for your final smoke to look correct and work smoothly.

4 Aligning the mesh curves with the smoke. With the Direct Selection tool, start at the bottom and click a section of the mesh curve. Adjust the direction handles so they align with the smoke outline. You may have to go back and forth between the next and previous sections of the curves in order to properly adjust the sides of the mesh to fit the smoke outline.

5 Adding columns to lend a 3D effect. The final 3D form of the mesh will be defined by where the highlight and shadow colors are placed on the mesh. If you were to draw evenly spaced columns around the actual smoke and photograph it, the columns in the photograph would appear to be closer together near the edges of the smoke outline and farther apart in the middle of column. To create this

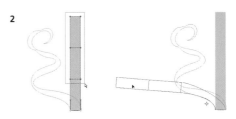

2

Selecting top portion of mesh. After clicking on inside of the first curve to set the rotation point (blue crosshair in lower right), clicking the top of the rectangle, and dragging to left and down

Working up the smoke, rotating the mesh at each major bend; placing mesh rows at pinches and using the Direct Selection tool to adjust

3

Aligning the rows with the pinches in the outline, making them straight and perpendicular to the sides of the curve

4

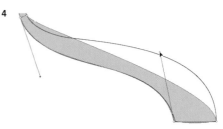

Starting from the bottom, using the Bézier handles to align the curves of the mesh to the outline of the smoke

5

Adding columns to the smoke mesh using the Gradient tool and spacing them closer at the edges to create a rounded 3D look

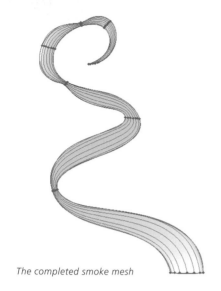

The completed smoke mesh

6

Creating a highlight at a mesh point

7

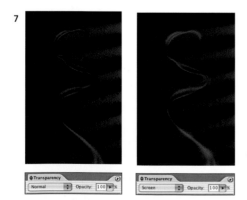

The smoke before and after setting the Blend Mode to Screen on the Transparency palette

3D effect, use the Mesh tool to add a first column by clicking on the center of the bottom edge of the smoke. Next, add two more columns close to each outside edge of the smoke. Then, place two columns between the center and the next closest columns on each side—not exactly in between, but closer to the outside edge.

Because of your careful work in steps 3 and 4 above, your new columns will be parallel to—and flow smoothly through—the pinches and bends of your smoke outline.

6 Coloring the mesh. Torres chose a dark blue color for his smoke (if you want to use a different color you will have to adjust the color choices in the steps below). To see where the mesh points are as you work, turn on Smart Guides from the View menu, or ⌘-U/Ctrl-U. In order to make the selection line color interfere less with the mesh color as you work, use a dark shade of blue for the selection line color (choose Dark Blue from the Layer Options Color menu). Also, learn to use the single-key navigation shortcuts to quickly switch between the Mesh (U), Eyedropper (I), and Direct Selection (A) tools.

Start by adding a middle blue value to the whole mesh. Next, from the Color palette pop-up menu, choose HSB, and then use the Brightness ("B") slider to create lighter highlight or darker shadow tints of your starting color. At the center of where highlight or shadow areas should be (either on a point, mesh line, or between the mesh lines), click with the Direct Selection tool and choose a color or swatch, or pick up a color using the Eyedropper tool. If you add a point with the Mesh tool it will remain selected, so you can easily adjust the fill color using the HSB sliders. For final tweaking of the highlights and shadows, use the Direct Selection tool or Lasso tool to select areas, and then make adjustments using the HSB sliders.

7 Making the smoke transparent. Select your smoke and on the Transparency palette, experiment with various combinations of the Screen Blend mode and Opacity settings until you get the desired effect.

MIYAMOTO

Yukio Miyamoto

As with most of his mesh art, Yukio Miyamoto began this illustration of a Yamaha French horn by manually tracing over a photo with the Pen tool, then filling the objects with solid fills. In layers above the basic tracing, Miyamoto drew the reflections and details of the tubular structure and filled them with linear gradients. He used the Mesh tool to define several reflections within the horn, with the most obvious on the horn's bell. He then created other areas of reflection with clusters of solid and gradient-filled objects (as on the bell and the valves). Miyamoto made the background out of a large, rectangular, gradient mesh. Within this mesh,

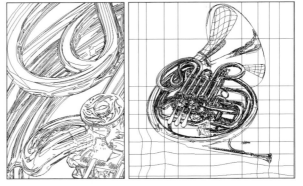

he created the horn's shadow. The magnificent level of detail is evident even when the image is viewed in Outline mode (a detail is shown directly above left; the full image in Outline is above right).

Ann Paidrick

For this Illustration, Ann Paidrick placed an original photograph on a bottom layer to use as a drawing guide. Paidrick began by blocking out all the shapes in the illustration by drawing rectangles based on the relative size and shapes of each object. She filled the shapes with a base color sampled from the underlying photograph. Paidrick selected and changed the shape into a mesh (Object > Create Gradient Mesh). In the Create Gradient Mesh dialog, she specified 2 columns and 2 rows (so they formed a cross) and a flat appearance. This produced mesh points that were more evenly distributed and required less adjustments after other mesh points were added. She Direct-Selected the mesh, added points with the Mesh tool, and adjusted the points to form the shape she desired (such as a leaf). She continued to

sample color from the photograph to color the mesh points. In some areas, Paidrick created an Opacity Mask to create a smooth color transition into darker areas (detail above). To create the mask, she created a new object, and pasted two copies in front. She filled the bottom copy with black and the top with white. With the top object selected, she double- clicked on the Scale tool in the Tools palette and decreased its size. She selected both the black and white objects and chose Object > Blend > Make. Paidrick then selected the blend objects, along with the mesh object, and chose Make Opacity Mask from the Transparency palette, blending that area into the background. She masked the spots on the lily's petals using the same technique. Lastly, Paidrick added a rectangular background filled with a linear gradient.

PAIDRICK

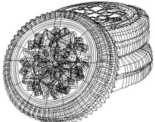

Ann Paidrick

In addition to the technique used in the drawing opposite, Ann Paidrick used symbols to enhance the realistic appearance of this glass of iced tea (palette detail at right). To make the tiny bubbles at the top of the tea, she created blended circles of various sizes and colors to make a symbol set. (See the *Brushes & Symbols* chapter for more about symbols). Paidrick created numerous complex gradient mesh shapes to complete the amazing level of detail in the objects. Some of these gradient mesh shapes are shown in the cookie detail above (shown in outline view).

MIYAMOTO

Yukio Miyamoto

The "Molding Mesh" lesson in the Blends, Gradients & Mesh chapter shows how Yukio Miyamoto created these amazing mesh bottles. To create the reflections in this version, Miyamoto used the Reflect tool to reflect a copy of the bottles along the base of the bottles. He next pulled a horizontal guide from the ruler to align with the end of the table top. For each of the reflections, he targeted the mesh and in the Transparency palette he reduced the opacity to 80%. To make the reflections fade, he used Path> Offset Path and entered 0 as the Offset. He filled this outline with a white-to-gray gradient, and then used the Gradient tool to run from white at the guideline to gray at the bottle bottom. To make certain that the reflection stopped abruptly at the table edge,

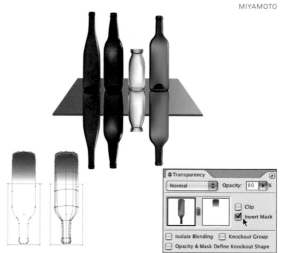

he grouped each gradient bottle with white rectangle covering the neck half of the bottle, and ending at the guidline. He then selected each pair of gray and mesh bottle objects, chose Make Opacity Mask from the Transparency palette pop-up, and then he enabled the Invert Mask option.

Web & Animation

13

Web & Animation

This chapter focuses on how you can use Illustrator to prepare artwork for on-screen display. Although everything in this chapter relies heavily on Illustrator, some of the techniques also involve working with other applications (see the *Illustrator & Other Programs* chapter).

Artists produced the animations and Web graphics in this chapter using a number of other programs, including Macromedia's Flash and Dreamweaver; Adobe's Premiere, After Effects, and GoLive; Thorsten Lemke's GraphicConverter; and Bare Bones Software's BBEdit.

Web designers will find that Illustrator supports a wealth of file formats, and a streamlined work flow for creating Web graphics. Save for Web, in the File menu, makes it easy to optimize graphics for the Web, by letting you visually compare examples of different quality settings and file compression options side by side, in a multi-view dialog box. And Pixel Preview allows you to view precise antialiasing right in Illustrator.

WORKING IN RGB IN ILLUSTRATOR

To create artwork in RGB, first start with a new RGB file (File > New and Color Mode > RGB Color in the dialog box). Choose a Web safe RGB palette of colors if you want to create colors that are never dithered when viewed on 8-bit monitors. If you plan on using an RGB document exclusively for the Web, use the new North America Web/Internet color setting (Edit > Color Settings).

A FEW THOUGHTS ON RGB AND CMYK COLOR

- **You should work in the RGB color mode (space) if you're creating graphics for on-screen display.** If you're designing for the Web, it's particularly important to keep file sizes to a minimum, and the final files must be in RGB (see "The Web Swatches library" following).
- Don't convert the same artwork repeatedly between RGB and CMYK. Converting RGB to CMYK forces one

Facts about CMYK and RGB

Since Illustrator allows you to mix colors in CMYK, RGB, or HSB color modes, be aware of which color palette is displayed when you're creating colors. If your file is in RGB color mode, switch the color palette to RGB or Web safe RGB. If you're doing print work, you would normally work in CMYK color mode, but in order to apply some Photoshop filters, you must work in RGB color mode. If you intend to use your artwork for both print and the Web, your best bet is to work first in CMYK (with its narrower color gamut) and then create the final Web output by exporting to an RGB format and adjusting colors to approximate the original CMYK colors.

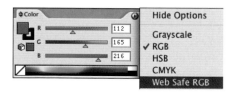

Choosing color models from the Color palette's pop-up menu. You can also cycle through color models by Shift-clicking on the Color Spectrum. Selecting a different color model to mix colors does not change the color mode of the file

If you need Photoshop...

Don't forget to look at the *Illustrator & Other Programs* chapter for details about working with Illustrator and Photoshop.

range of colors (a gamut) into a smaller range of colors. This process involves either clipping or compressing certain colors, and can make the colors in your file appear muddy or muted. If you absolutely need both CMYK and RGB versions of your artwork, maintain two versions of your art—one in RGB and one in CMYK. To experiment with clipping or compressing colors between gamuts, see *Illustrator Help* on choosing the appropriate rendering intent in the Color Settings dialog box.

- **If you're going to use your artwork for both print and on-screen viewing, create in CMYK and then export the art to RGB.** Since the CMYK color space has a smaller color gamut than RGB and is able to produce predictable color output for print, it makes sense to create your artwork in CMYK *before* exporting it to RGB for display on a monitor. RGB has a wider gamut, so it won't clip or compress the colors of your CMYK document when you convert it to RGB.

The Web Swatches library

Sticking to the Web safe color palette—which consists of the 216 colors that are most reliable for creating artwork for the Web—is no longer considered as important in Web design as it once was. Monitors have developed to the point where most users can now display thousands or millions of colors. Still, if you want to be very cautious and make sure that even those using very old equipment will see your colors exactly as you've specified them, the Web safe palette remains available for use.

Illustrator includes a non-editable Web safe swatches library. To access this library, choose Open Swatch Library > Web from the Swatches palette menu, or choose Window > Swatch Libraries > Web. To create a smaller custom library from the Web safe library, simply drag the desired color swatches to the Swatches palette for storage and save the file. (Remember to clear the Swatches palette before you build your custom library—see "Setting up your palettes" in the *How To Use This Book* section.)

Converting CMYK to RGB

If you already have artwork prepared in CMYK and you need to change the color mode for on-screen RGB viewing, make sure you first save a copy of your file, then choose File > Document Color Mode > RGB Colors. Remember, try not to convert your artwork back and forth between color spaces, because your colors can become muddy or muted (see text at left for more details).

Rasterizing art for the screen

The process of turning vector art into a pixel-based image is called *rasterizing*. Anyone creating artwork for the Web or for multimedia applications might, at some point, need to rasterize vector art, with the exception of SWF and SVG (see the "SVG" section later in this chapter). There are two options for rasterizing art in Illustrator. If you want to permanently rasterize an object, select it and choose Object > Rasterize. However, you can keep your artwork editable by using the option found in the Effect menu (Effect > Rasterize). This way, your art takes on the appearance of rasterization, but its underlying vector structure is maintained and can still be edited. Each Rasterize dialog box provides options that make it easy to control how your artwork is rasterized.

ASSIGNING URL'S AND SLICING

Illustrator's Attributes palette lets you create an image map area and assign a URL (Uniform Resource Locator) to selected objects in your artwork. Creating image maps is an essential tool for Web designers because it allows them to create links to other Web pages by defining clickable parts of the artwork. Illustrator creates a separate HTML (HyperText Markup Language) file containing the URL information, which can be imported into an HTML editor such as Adobe GoLive, Macromedia Dreamweaver, or Bare Bones Software's BBEdit.

To assign a URL to a selection, open the Attributes palette (Window > Attributes), select the type of image map from the Image Map pop-up, and type the URL into the URL text field (see the Gulf Shores Web page Gallery in this chapter for more on making image maps). If you need to verify whether your URL is valid or not, simply click the Browser button in the Attributes palette. This will launch your default Web browser and automatically open the link if it is valid. You can export the file by using Save for Web and choosing Save as Type: HTML and Images (*.html).

Illustrator also provides another way for you to assign URLs or links to objects—by using Web slices. Web slicing is a way to divide a large image into several smaller pieces that are displayed in HTML as a table. This allows you to optimize individual parts of your artwork in different formats (e.g., GIF, JPEG, SVG), and helps the files download faster to a Web browser. To apply a slice to an object, select the object and choose Object > Slice > Make. If you have guides within your document, you can use them to slice your artwork by choosing Object > Slice > Create from Guides.

To assign a URL to a Web slice, apply a slice to an object and then, with the object still selected, choose Object > Slice > Slice Options. In the URL field, enter the correct link information. You can also get to the Slice Options dialog box by double-clicking on a slice with the Slice Select tool in the Save for Web dialog box.

When you apply a slice to an object, group, layer, or document guide using the Object menu, you've actually assigned a slice as an "attribute." This means that if you update your artwork, your slice will update automatically. So, once you make a slice, you never have to re-create it.

If you want to create a slice whose position remains unchanged when you update the artwork from which the slice was originally generated, choose Object > Slice > Create from Selection, or draw the slice using Illustrator's Slice tool. (In ImageReady, this kind of slice is called a *user slice*.) Slices applied as attributes are exported as *layer-based slices* when you choose File > Export > Photoshop (*.PSD) and you select the Write Slices option. If you edit the exported layers in Photoshop or ImageReady, the corresponding slices will reshape themselves just as they would have done in Illustrator. This PSD export option only works on slices attached to elements that are not contained inside any groups or sublayers. All other slices are exported as user slices.

RELEASE TO LAYERS

Illustrator gives you the ability to take each one of your multiple objects or blended objects to distribute onto its own layer. For example, having the objects on separate layers makes it easier to develop animations (see the "Macromedia Flash (SWF) export" section following this chapter. It explains how to move Illustrator art into Macromedia Flash for animation work).

Highlight a layer, group, live blend, or symbol set in the Layers palette by clicking on it—merely selecting or targeting the artwork won't work. Next, choose Release to Layers (Sequence) from the palette menu. This creates each new layer within the current layer or group and consists of a single object. Use this option when you want each element to be separately manipulated in another program, or you want the animation to be sequential (one, then the next).

To perform an additive effect, choose Release to Layers (Build). Instead of containing a single object, each

Save for Web

Save for Web provides many options for optimizing Web graphics:

- **Tools:** A limited set of tools lets you zoom, pan, select slices, and sample colors in the artwork.
- **Views:** Multiple views are available for you to compare compression settings against the final image quality.
- **Settings:** Preset compression settings are easily accessed from the Preset pop-up menu. If you are new to Web graphics, start with one of these settings. You'll notice that as you select different presets, the options for the specific file type are updated under the Settings grouping. Save your own settings by choosing Save Settings from the pop-up menu to the right of the Settings menu.
- **Color Table:** The color table updates the number of colors in the image for GIF and PNG-8 file formats. You can lock colors or shift to a Web safe color by clicking on the icons at the bottom of the palette.
- **Image Size:** To change the dimensions of the final optimized file, but not the original artwork, click on the Image Size tab and enter a new size.
- **Browser button:** To preview the optimized image in a browser, click on the browser button at the bottom of the dialog box.

- **Color Table:** 8-bit images have a maximum of 256 colors. The Perceptual table is more sensitive to colors than the human eye can differentiate. Selective gives more emphasis to the integrity of the colors and is the default setting.
- **Colors:** You can have up to 256 colors in a color table. However, the image might not need that many. Select a smaller number of colors when you optimize by adjusting the number of colors in the color table—the fewer colors, the smaller the file.
- **Dither:** Blends colors in a limited color palette. Diffusion dither is usually best. Vary the amount of dither to reduce banding of solid-color areas by adjusting the Dither slider. Leave it off for clean-edged vector graphics.
- **Transparency:** Choose this for non-rectangular artwork that you want to put over multicolored backgrounds. To reduce edge artifacts, choose a color to blend with the transparent edges from the Matte pop-up.
- **Interlacing:** Allows viewers to see a low resolution version of the image as it downloads, which continues to build until the image is at full resolution. A non-interlaced image draws one line at a time.

new layer is generated with one more object. You end up with the same number of layers, but what appears on those layers is very different. Use this option when you want to create a "building animation" that contains the previous elements.

When releasing objects to separate layers, keep in mind that their stacking order in the Layers palette can affect the final animation. With scatter brush art, it's sometimes hard to predict the order in which the individual objects will be released to the layers; stacking order is dependent on the direction of the path. You can reverse the direction of a path by clicking on an end anchor point with the Pen tool. You can reverse blends by choosing Object > Blend > Reverse Front to Back.

EXPORT FILE FORMATS
Save for Web

An important feature for Web designers is the ability to export optimized files from the Save for Web dialog box. GIF and JPEG are the Web's two most common image formats (see the Tip "GIF or JPEG?" in this chapter). The GIF format's compression works well with vector-based images or files that have large areas of solid color. GIF files support transparency; JPEGs don't.

JPEG provides variable levels of compression and works best for continuous-tone images (such as photos or gradients). Although JPEG is a "lossy" format (when you optimize the file size you lose image detail), this trade-off still tends to result in good-quality images, making JPEG a particularly useful format for Web designers.

JPEGs can also be a useful alternative to a PDF file. For example, a JPEG file can be used to transfer a layout for client approval. JPEGs are much smaller than PDFs while sacrificing very little image detail, and smaller files transfer more easily (and sometimes more reliably) via the Internet. Other JPEG options include progressive and optimized. A progressive JPEG is similar to an interlaced GIF—it first appears blurry, then builds up with increasing clarity until the image is fully displayed.

Note: *If Progressive is checked, checking Optimized will not make the file any smaller.*

To save a version of your artwork for use on the Web, choose File > Save for Web and adjust the various optimization settings (see the Tip "Save for Web" in this chapter). If you've defined slices in your file, use the Slice Select tool to click on and select the slice you want to optimize, then select a file type from the Optimized file format pop-up.

If you want to compare the compression of two or more settings, click on one of the other views, either 2-Up or 4-Up. The final file format, size, download time, and compression specifics are listed under each preview panel.

Finally, if you want to export your artwork, click the Save button to specify how you want to save files. If you have slices, you can choose to export the images and the HTML as well. If you opened Save for Web only to define the optimization settings for your slices, you can press the Done button to get back to your file, Illustrator remembers all the settings you just applied. See *Illustrator Help* for a complete description of format options.

Note: *PNG, SWF, and SVG are available file formats in the Save for Web dialog box, but these formats may require browser plug-ins in order to be viewed on the Web.*

Macromedia Flash (SWF) export

Many multimedia artists and designers use Illustrator with Macromedia Flash to create Web pages and animations. Illustrator CS2 allows you to export Illustrator artwork as SWF files (File > Export, then choose Macromedia Flash from the Format menu) with more options and improved control over such details as how layers are mapped to animation frames and how files are compressed. Illustrator CS2 also makes it easier to preserve the appearance of stylized text.

Be aware that exporting as SWF may break your artwork into many simple objects. An alternative workflow used by many artists is to create the basic line art in Illustrator, save the file as an EPS, and then open it in Flash for

---

Selectively exporting artwork

When exporting your artwork from the Save for Web dialog box, Illustrator includes every object within the document, even if it exists outside the Artboard. If you enable the Clip to Artboard option in the Image Size tab, only the objects that exist within the Artboard will be exported. To export just a portion of your artwork, first create a rectangle around the art you wish to export and choose Object > Crop Area > Make, then open Save for Web.
—Jean-Claude Tremblay

SVG Browser Plug-in

Illustrator ships standard with (and installs by default) the SVG 3.0 browser plug-in. If you're creating SVG graphics, make sure that whoever is viewing them also downloads the free SVG 3.0 viewer that's available from the www.adobe.com/svg Web page.

Transparency and Web colors

Even if you've been working in RGB mode with Web safe colors, if you've used Illustrator's transparency in your file, you will end up with out-of-gamut shades when the artwork is rasterized or flattened. Files with extensive transparency use should be saved as JPEG, not as GIF, to avoid excessive dithering.

Illustrator now supports the Adobe Color Picker. Double-click on the color proxy in the Toolbox or on the Color palette to open the Color Picker. Enable the Only Web Colors checkbox to limit the Color Picker to Web safe colors.

Change ruler to pixel units

Control-click (Mac)/Right mouse-click (Win) on the ruler (View > Show Rulers) and select "Pixels" to display the units as pixels.

Auto-opening select libraries

Set any swatch library to open automatically when you launch Illustrator (Window> Swatch Libraries). Select Persistent from the palette's pop-up menu. Choose it again to reset the palette to close by default.

SVG or SVGZ (compressed)?

SVG compressed is gzipped or "gnu-zipped," and is the W3C-sanctioned version of "raw" SVG. The Adobe SVG Viewer automatically decompresses the file on the client browser and displays it as normal. So there is little difference between the formats, except that one is much smaller. An exception occurs when you use a database to serve information to a client. In this case, you will need a script to decompress and then re-compress the file.—*Andrew T. Watanabe*

coloring and finishing. If you have very simple artwork, you also can try copying and pasting art directly from Illustrator to Flash.

Here are some strategies for maximizing the quality and usefulness of your Illustrator files in Flash:

- **Use Illustrator symbols for repeating objects.** Illustrator lets you convert both raster and vector artwork into *symbols* that you can *place* multiple times, instead of using multiple copies of the original art (see the *Brushes & Symbols* chapter for more about symbols). Each time you place an instance of a symbol, you are creating a *link* to the symbol stored in the palette, rather than duplicating the artwork. This reduces the size of your Illustrator file, and can also reduce the size of any SWF files you export from Illustrator—as long as you haven't used the Stainer, Screener, or Styler on your symbols. Using those tools can actually increase the size of your exported SWF file, because what were instances in the AI file will become unique symbols in the SWF file.

- **Use flat colors rather than blends, gradients, or gradient mesh objects.** You'll make smaller SWF files if you use Flash to add your gradient colors. If you must use gradients or gradient mesh objects, recognize that you'll be creating bitmapped images that will result in larger file sizes.

- **If you import or create rasterized art for the Internet,** rasterize at 72 ppi, not the default, to keep file sizes small.

- **To export a file's layers or paths selectively,** hide the ones you don't want before exporting.

- **If the object you want to export to Flash contains a dashed stroke,** expand it (see the Tip "Outlining Dashed Strokes" in the *Drawing & Coloring* chapter). Or you can use your operating system's clipboard to copy the stroke from Illustrator and paste it into Flash. To preserve the dash and gap pattern of the Illustrator object, choose Preferences > File Handling & Clipboard and then select PDF for the Copy As option. If you don't do this, the dash and gap pattern will be converted to the default pattern in Flash.

- **Choosing Export AI Layers to SWF Files turns each Illustrator layer into a separate Flash file.** This is the preferred method of exporting Illustrator elements for animation.

SVG

Illustrator supports the export of Scalable Vector Graphics (SVG). SVG is an emerging standard for a Web graphic format that contains a combination of elements such as vectors, gradients, type, raster effects, and JavaScript events, all based on the popular XML standard. SVG is also a text-based format, which means it can be easily edited even after the file has been uploaded to a Web server. SVG is potentially a very exciting file format, because it combines very small file sizes with crisp artwork that, like Illustrator vector art, can be zoomed into and scaled up or down with no loss of quality. As with Flash, in order for exported SVG files to be viewed in a browser, a special viewer (plug-in) is required. The SVG plug-in is automatically installed in your browser when you install Illustrator.

The SVG format supports JavaScript interactivity and static image display. To add a JavaScript event to your artwork you must know JavaScript! Open the SVG Interactivity palette (Window > SVG Interactivity); select an object and choose an event from the pop-up menu, then type a JavaScript command into the JavaScript text field.

A final note: Illustrator CS2 supports the SVG-Tiny format, which is optimized for wireless mobile devices. You can save rich graphical content as SVG-Tiny for use in designs for mobile media.

Pixel preview

Choose View > Pixel Preview and zoom in to 200% or more to display a rasterized preview of your vector artwork.

No more SVG export?

Illustrator now lets you save as SVG directly from the Save and Save As dialog box. If you check the Preserve Illustrator Editing Capabilities option, a native version of the AI file will be included in the SVG file, allowing for complete editability in Illustrator.

Go, Go Dynamic!

You can take dynamic graphics a step further if you're using Adobe GoLive 6.0 or higher, which understands Illustrator's variable content. Simply save your file in SVG format and import it into GoLive as an Illustrator Smart Object. You can change the variables you defined in Illustrator in GoLive.

CSS layers

Illustrator allows you to export CSS (Cascading Style Sheets) layers. Newer browsers take advantage of DHTML, which allows you to overlap artwork layers. Top level layers can be converted to CSS layers on export from the Save for Web dialog box, and you can specify which layers to export from the Layers tab there.

Layering Frames

Turning Layered Artwork into Key Frames

Overview: *Draw artwork for print; design animation sequences using artwork; create layers and lay out art and text in positions for animation key frames; export layers as Shockwave Flash frames.*

1

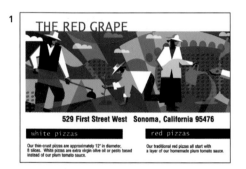

Artwork originally created for The Red Grape's printed restaurant menu

Planning an animation sequence by positioning objects and text at beginning and end of the sequence

After designing the brand identity, menu artwork, and a wall mural in Illustrator for The Red Grape, a Sonoma, California restaurant, Hugh Whyte of Lehner and Whyte faced one more task. He needed to turn his artwork into Flash animations for the restaurant's Web site (www.theredgrape.com). The key to recycling the artwork was to develop a productive workflow between Illustrator and Macromedia Flash that would allow Whyte and Mark Murphy of DigitalKick to work within the software that each designer knew best.

1 Drawing artwork and planning objects and type for key frames. While his drawings of people and food were originally designed for the printed menus, Whyte returned to the artwork and prepared it for the Web as a Flash animation.

If you are more comfortable designing in Illustrator than in Flash, stay in Illustrator and use the artwork you've already created. Think about how your artwork will move in the animation sequences you plan. Identify the starting and ending locations of each object in an animation sequence. Also note where objects will change direction as they move during the sequence.

2 Arranging artwork on layers. To facilitate their collaboration, Whyte and Murphy devised a workflow in which Whyte created in Illustrator what Murphy would use as key frames in Flash. You can do the same (even if you will be producing the final animation yourself in Flash) and enjoy the ease of using Illustrator to build the foundation of your animation.

Begin by creating a new file (File > New). In the default layer of the new file, arrange objects and text in the positions you plan for the first frame of the animation. Next, duplicate the default layer by dragging the layer name and dropping it onto the Create New Layer icon at the bottom of the Layers palette (see the *Layers & Appearances* chapter for more on managing layers and the artwork on them). In the new layer, arrange the objects and text for their next positions in the animation sequence. These positions might be the final ones in the animation, or points in the middle of the sequence where something occurs (for example, a text object stops moving). Continue creating new layers, copying and pasting artwork, and positioning the artwork, until you've created as many layers as you'll need to cover the beginning, end, and any important intermediate frames of the animation.

Keep in mind that you don't need to make every frame that will appear in the final animation. That would be unnecessary! Instead, create layers and arrange the text and graphic objects on them for the critical frames (which will be used as "key frames" in Flash). Once exported, the Flash software will generate the in-between frames (or "tweens") to fill in the frames you haven't created, saving time and producing a smaller Flash file size.

3 Exporting the Illustrator layers as Shockwave Flash frames. When Whyte finished building the file, he deleted any artwork or layers that weren't required as Flash frames.

To save the file, choose File > Save for Web and, from the Export dialog box, choose SWF from the Format pop-up (just below the word Preset), and choose Layers to SWF Frames from the pop-up below that. Set the other dialog options as you prefer and then click OK. (For more controls choose Export then Macromedia Flash (SWF).)

2

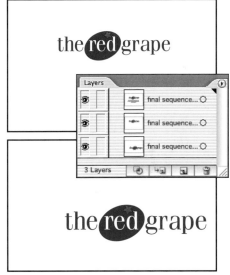

Artwork for the final animation sequence arranged on three layers; the Layers palette showing the layers in the sequential frame order of the animation

3

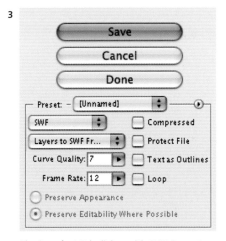

The Save for Web dialog with SWF Format Options and Layers to SWF Frames chosen

Webward Ho!

Designing a Web Page in Illustrator

Overview: *Set up a document for Web page design; use layers to structure artwork for pages and frames; save layouts as template images; slice text and artwork and save an HTML file and sliced image files.*

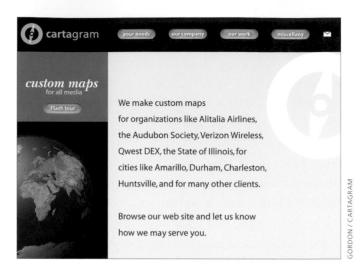

GORDON / CARTAGRAM

Gordon constructed the Cartagram Web site around a two-frame design; the black rectangle represented the top frame's Web page, used for the logo and main navigation controls; the other colored rectangles served as a design grid for dividing areas of the Web pages that would load in the bottom frame

216 colors, or millions?

The palette of 216 non-dithered, Web safe colors was designed for text and graphics displaying on 8-bit monitors. But how many people are restricted to 8-bit color anymore? Not many. Most computers are now equipped with 24- or 32-bit video boards, rendering Web safe colors unnecessary. So you can choose from millions of colors, not just 216.

If you are comfortable designing and drawing in Illustrator, why go elsewhere to design your Web pages? Steven Gordon uses Illustrator to design and preview Web pages, create comps for client approval, export a layout as a template for use in Adobe GoLive, and slice and optimize artwork before saving it for use on Web pages.

1 Choosing document settings. With Illustrator, you can draw and organize artwork to design a simple Web page or a more complex page with multiple frames. To start your page, create a new document (File > New). In the New Document dialog box, set Units to pixels, specify an Artboard size in pixels equal to that of your intended Web page size, and choose RGB Color for Color Mode. You may want to create a grid (Preferences > Guides & Grid) that will help you align and constrain artwork.

Also, if your artwork will be exported in a bitmap format like GIF or JPEG, consider turning on pixel preview (View > Pixel Preview)—this lets you see the anti-aliasing of your artwork. (See Tip, "Anti-antialiasing," for a technique that helps you reduce the amount of blurring that affects artwork when it is antialiased.)

2 Structuring pages with layers and adding artwork. Let the Layers palette help you organize the layout and content of your Web page. (See "Nested Layers" in the *Layers*

& Appearances chapter for more on making and manipulating layers.) Gordon created separate layers for the top and bottom frames of his page, and sublayers for multiple pages he designed for the bottom frame. He toggled layer visibility on to preview the layout and content of different pages in the bottom frame of his page design.

Once you've set up the layer structure of your document, you're ready to add content to your page design. As you create text and graphics, and import images, use familiar Illustrator tools and palettes to help make and arrange objects. Gordon relied on the Align palette to easily align and distribute navigation buttons in the top frame and to center or justify colored background rectangles for both frames (using the Align to Artboard option in the Align palette).

3 Saving a Web page design and importing it into GoLive. Once your page design is complete, export it as a GIF or JPEG and import the file into Adobe GoLive as a "tracing image" to help you construct a finished HTML page. If you set up the Artboard to match the dimensions of the Web pages you'll construct in GoLive, you can crop your Illustrator artwork so that it matches those dimensions when exported as a bitmapped image. To do this, either create cropmarks from the Artboard (see the *Type* chapter for instructions on making cropmarks) and then use File > Export, or skip the cropmarks and choose File > Save for Web (which automatically crops artwork to the Artboard).

When you begin working in GoLive, import the image you just exported from Illustrator and use it as a template to guide you in building the page. First, choose Window > Tracing Image; then, in the Tracing Image palette, click the Source checkbox and the Browse icon to select your Illustrator-exported image. Next, adjust the HTML page's frame widths, and create text boxes and other objects in GoLive that match the Illustrator image. Repeat these steps with other exported images when building other pages in GoLive.

2

The layer structure for the Web page design, showing the top and bottom frames, and two sublayers representing separate pages designed to load in the bottom frame

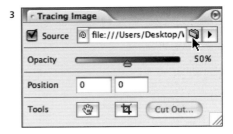

3

The Tracing Image palette in Adobe GoLive5; Gordon clicked the Browse icon to locate the layout image file he had exported previously using Illustrator's Save for Web command

Anti-antialiasing

When artwork is saved as a bitmapped image, straight lines and other objects may be anti-aliased (blurred). To minimize this, first set Keyboard Increment to 0.5 pixels in the Preferences > General dialog box. Then make sure both View > Pixel Preview and View > Snap to Pixel are turned on. Next, draw and position your objects. Finally, turn off View > Snap to Pixel, and nudge aliased objects in 0.5-pixel increments as needed, using the Arrow keys.
—*Mordy Golding*

4

The numbered slices created after using the Object >Slices >Create from Selection command

5

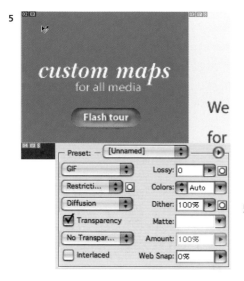

In the Save for Web dialog box, a preview of the slices is displayed; Gordon clicked in a slice with the Slice Selection tool to select it and then specified settings related to file format and other image characteristics in the Settings portion of the dialog box

Object or clipping path?

When making a slice using the Object >Slices >Create from Selection command, you'll need to decide whether the clipping path or the artwork it masks will become the slice. Clicking on a masked object will make a slice out of the object instead of the clipping path. Click carefully!

4 Slicing artwork. Instead of using your Illustrator artwork as a template in GoLive, consider using Illustrator's slices to turn text, artwork, and placed images into elements you can use when building your HTML pages. Slices also let you divide a large image or layout into smaller areas that you can save as separate, optimized images. These images will load simultaneously, and usually faster than a single large image in a Web browser.

You can use artwork selections, guides, or the Slice tool to divide your Illustrator design into slices. Gordon's design was divided by colored backgrounds and a masked image. (You can use non-contiguous objects for slicing; Illustrator will add slices to fill in any gaps between objects.) To make the slices, first choose Object >Slice > Clip to Artboard, then select an object and choose Object >Slice >Create from Selection. Repeat these steps until you've created all of the slices you need. If you need to remove a slice, select and delete it; or in the Layers palette drag its name (<Slice>) to the palette's trash icon.

5 Saving slices, and using and previewing the HTML page. When you've finished slicing your artwork, you can save the slices as text and images. Choose File >Save for Web; in the dialog box, click on the Slice Select tool and click one of the slices. Pick the settings that you want to use for saving that selected slice. Gordon selected GIF as the file format for the two blocks with solid color fills and text.

For the globe image, he chose JPEG as the file format and enabled Optimized to make the file size smaller. After clicking on Save, Gordon entered a file name for the HTML file (which automatically became the root name of each of the sliced image files), and made sure that HTML and Images were selected in the Format pop-up menu. After Illustrator saved the HTML file and the sliced image files, Gordon opened the HTML file in GoLive to add head tags (like meta tags) and then previewed the file in a Web browser.

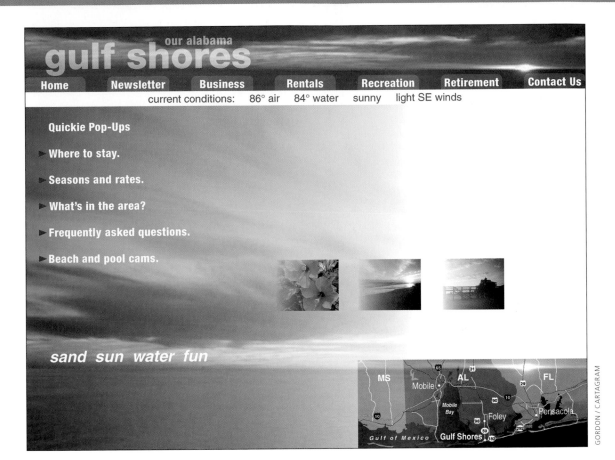

GORDON / CARTAGRAM

Steven Gordon / Cartagram

To build image-mapped buttons at the top of a travel Web page, Steven Gordon first placed a TIFF image in Illustrator to serve as a background image. Next, he drew a button shape with rounded corners and gave it a white Fill and a 25% Opacity using the Transparency palette. He copied the button six times and arranged the buttons in a row above the background image. To space the buttons evenly, Gordon positioned the left and right buttons, selected all buttons, and then clicked the Horizontal Distribute Space icon in the Align palette. To map the buttons to URLs, he selected each button shape and in the

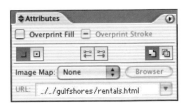

Attributes palette chose Rectangle from the Image Map pop-up menu. He then keyed in the button's URL link in the URL field. In the Save for Web dialog box, Gordon selected JPEG as the output file format, clicked Save, and then chose HTML and Images from the Format pop-up menu. He entered a file name in the Name field and clicked Save.

Off in a Flash

Making Artwork for a Flash Animation

Overview: *Sketch character artwork; create brushes and blend objects for moving parts in the animation; export the artwork as a static Macromedia SWF file and a SWF animation; preview animations in Illustrator.*

ATTEBERRY

1

Character parts sketched with a custom calligraphic brush (see the Brushes & Symbols *chapter for help with brushes)*

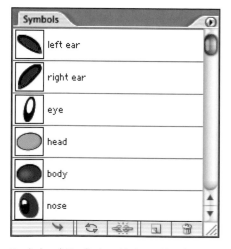

Symbols palette displayed in Large List View

Seattle artist and animator Kevan Atteberry knows how to get the most from Illustrator when preparing artwork for animation in Macromedia Flash. Besides making his Illustrator file a sketchpad filled with the eyes, ears, arms, and legs of the character he will animate later in Flash, Atteberry uses the Layers palette to preview parts of the animation. He also exports a Flash animation from Illustrator to view as a draft version as he works on the final animation in Flash.

1 Sketching characters, drawing body parts. Atteberry began with a custom calligraphic brush, sketching a series of facial expressions and figure poses, honing the visual character of a lemur until he was satisfied with the characterization and ready to construct the lemur's body parts. Once you're done drawing your character's parts, you can keep your artwork as Illustrator objects or turn the artwork into symbol instances. It takes fewer steps to convert your artwork to symbol instances in Illustrator than to bring your artwork into Flash and make symbols there. Also, if you plan to export a Flash movie from Illustrator, turning your character parts into symbol instances results in a smaller and faster-loading Flash file.

To make symbol instances, select the artwork for each part body you drew and Shift-drag it into the Symbols palette. After you release the mouse button, Illustrator adds the artwork as a symbol in the Symbols palette and replaces the selected artwork with an instance of the symbol that was just made. (See the *Brushes, & Symbols* chapter for more on symbols and instances).

2 Making brushes, creating blends for objects, expanding blends, and creating symbols. For any part you animate, you will need to create a sequence of parts—for example, a leg that moves from straight to bent. Atteberry created art brushes for the lemur's moving parts, so he could paint each part in the motion sequence with the brush. (This saved the effort of creating separate art for each part in the sequence.) First, draw a straight version of the part. When you have the look you want, drag-and-drop it on the open Brushes palette. In the New Brush dialog box, choose New Art Brush.

Next, you'll create artwork for the two extremes in the motion sequence. Draw the straight part, and a few inches away draw the bent part. Select both paths and apply the art brush to both. Now, to make other parts in the movement sequence, make sure both paths are selected and choose Object > Blend > Make; then choose Object > Blend > Blend Options and key in the number of steps in the Spacing: Specified Steps field. Consider using a small number of blend steps—Atteberry uses three or four—so that if used as frames in a Flash animation, your SWF file will have a smaller number of frames and a smaller file size. Finally, expand the blend (Object > Blend > Expand) and ungroup it so you have separate objects to use in constructing poses for the motion sequence.

3 Exporting an SWF animation. Once your artwork is complete, you can export the file as a draft or final animation that you can view in a browser or in the Flash player. To prepare your file for animation, first add as many

2

Two of the brushes Atteberry created for the moving parts

The straight and bent lemur legs representing the extremes of a motion sequence that Atteberry used to create a Blend

A blend using three steps created between the straight and bent lemur legs

AI instances to Flash symbols

If you make symbols in Illustrator and want to import them into Flash, be sure to make instances of your symbols first. When you export an SWF file from Illustrator, the Symbols palette is not exported with the SWF file. Flash will recognize Illustrator's instances in the SWF file, however, and add them as symbols to its own Library.

Exporting an SWF file

In Illustrator use Save for Web or, for more extensive options, Export for saving an SWF file to import into Macromedia Flash.

Previewing a motion sequence using Illustrator's Layers palette as a crude film projector

layers as frames needed to show the motion sequence. Treating each layer as an animation frame, assemble the artwork for a particular pose or step in the motion sequence on each layer. Move from layer to layer, creating renditions of the character on each layer until the character has performed all of the poses or movements you want to preview. When you have completed all the layers, select File > Save for Web. From the Format pop-up, select SWF (just below the word Preset) and, from the pop-up below that, choose AI Layers to SWF Frames. If your animation will use a lot of frames, or will include complex motion sequences that require many intermediate poses or steps, create the final animation in Flash instead of in Illustrator. Flash's tweening commands automatically create many of the intermediate poses you would otherwise assemble manually in Illustrator.

There is another animation technique you can use to preview motion—from within Illustrator itself. Atteberry constructed a draft version of part of the animation to preview the look of objects and of the motion sequence. To do this, you can construct a preview by first following the steps described above for positioning poses on successive layers. After you've filled all your layers with artwork, select Palette Options from the Layers palette menu. Click on the Show Layers Only checkbox to enable this option and key in 100 pixels in the Other field. To preview the animation, position the cursor over a Layers palette scrolling arrow and press the mouse button to cause the layer thumbnails to scroll like frames in a projector.

4 Exporting an SWF file to import into Macromedia Flash. To create complex animations, instead of Save for Web, choose File > Export and choose Macromedia (SWF) from the format pop-up. After naming your file and choosing the file destination, use the Format Options dialog box to choose options for creating SWF animations. One choice available only from Export is AI Layers to SWF file; this can be a very useful option for continuing to work on your artwork in Macromedia Flash.

Pasting into Flash

You can copy Illustrator artwork and paste into Flash. Be careful, though—some Illustrator artwork with complex styles and bitmap effects will not look correct when pasted in Macromedia Flash.

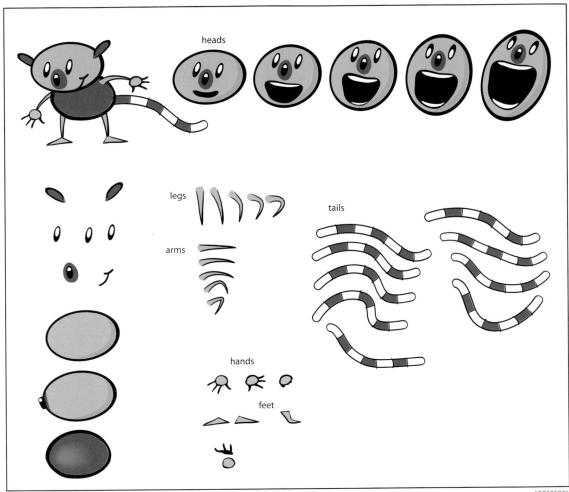

ATTEBERRY

Kevan Atteberry

To assist in constructing his animation "Millard and the Pear," which is described in the previous lesson, artist Kevan Atteberry developed a file of recyclable parts—a cartoon "morgue"—from which he copied parts and pasted them in the file in which he created the animation. To trim the file size of the animation, Atteberry converted the artwork for parts into symbol instances by Shift-dragging them to the Symbols palette. When he needed to edit a symbol,

Atteberry selected the instance and chose Object > Expand. After editing the artwork, Atteberry selected the artwork and Shift-dragged it to the Symbols palette to automatically convert it back into a symbol instance.

Animating Pieces

Preparing Files for Creating Animations

Illustrator with After Effects

Overview: *Make basic elements; cut elements using the Knife tool; order the <Path> elements and separate them into layers; export the file to create the actual animation.*

1

After drawing the **huge** *letter forms using the Pen tool, Lush created "records" and ™ with the Text tool, then converted the text to outlines so he could modify the forms with the Direct Selection tool (final objects shown above in Outline and below in Preview modes)*

2

The art shown after Lush cut the objects, in Outline mode above, and Preview mode below (the preview pieces have been moved so that you can see the cuts)

Terry Lush created the Illustrator portion of this animation for an ongoing "latest record release banner" on the hugerecords.com website.

1 Creating the basic elements. Use any tools to create your basic elements. For his animation, Lush drew the "huge" outlines with the Pen tool, based on the typeface Bauhaus. He then created the "records" and ™ text with the Type tool, and converted the text to outlines (Type > Create Outlines, or ⌘-Shift-O/Ctrl-Shift-O) so he could slightly modify the letterform paths with the Direct Selection tool. Lush saved his files in stages as he worked.

2 Cutting lines. To visualize where to cut elements, draw lines to use as guides (⌘-5/Ctrl-5 turns objects into guides). Lush used the Knife tool (under the Scissors tool) to cut the letters into pieces. To make straight cuts, he held Option (Alt) while click-dragging with the Knife (adding Shift for straight lines). Objects are shown at left first in Outline then Preview mode (the pieces shown in Preview have been moved apart so you can see the cuts).

3 Ordering the animation and distributing elements into layers. To figure out the order in which the pieces should appear in the animation, Lush expanded the layer containing the separate (cut) <Path> elements. First, while hiding all the paths, he experimented with showing paths one at a time until he determined the order in which he wanted the paths to appear. He then reordered the <Path> elements to match that viewing sequence.

Once you've rearranged the paths in the correct order within a layer, you'll need to distribute each <Path> onto its own layer. To do this, click the name of the enclosing layer and, from the Layers palette pop-up, choose Release to Layers (Build). Now select these sublayers (click the top one and Shift-click the bottom one) and drag them above the enclosing layer so they are no longer sublayers.

4 Making the animation and creating variations. Lush imported the layered Illustrator file into After Effects (download a tryout version from adobe.com/products/tryadobe). In After Effects, he selected all layers and trimmed the length of the layers to 7 frames. Choosing Animation > Keyframe Assistant > Sequence Layers, he set the parameters for the sequence so that each layer would be held for seven frames and then crossfade for two frames to the next layer. Keyframe Assistant automatically sequenced the layers (in order), and created the crossfades by generating keyframes with the correct opacity for each transition. With the file saved, Lush exported the After Effects movie in QuickTime format. Bringing this animation into his 3D program, Cinema 4D, he mapped the animation to the front surface of 3D-rendered, Times Square–like billboard. To create variations (such as the one at 30° rotation shown at right), Lush worked once more in Illustrator with a copy of the file. He selected all elements (without grouping them), double-clicked the Rotate tool, entered a 30° angle and clicked OK. He then saved this version and imported it into After Effects where he created a variation of the animation using the same procedures described above.

3

After cutting the objects, then after rearranging the pieces in the order of the desired animation

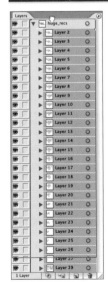

With the containing layer selected, choosing Release to Layers (Build), then moving the sublayers out of the containing layer

4

Selecting all of the objects in Illustrator to rotate the entire cut group of objects 30° for a variant of the animation

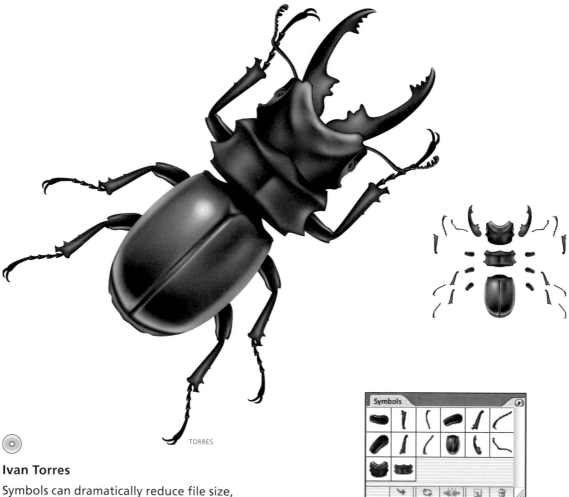

TORRES

Ivan Torres

Symbols can dramatically reduce file size, especially in art destined for the Web. Artist Ivan Torres began this beetle by first creating individual body parts, many of which were complex gradient meshes. (To learn more about creating and editing gradient meshes, see the *Blends, Gradients & Mesh* chapter.) Then he converted the parts into symbols by dragging and dropping each onto the Symbols palette. To assemble the beetle from body part symbols, Torres dragged the parts from the Symbols palette and dropped them on the Artboard, creating instances of the symbols.

To create the body parts with mirrored twins on opposite sides of the beetle body, he used the Reflect tool, chose Vertical and clicked Copy. When he had completed the illustration, Torres chose File > Save for Web and selected SWF from the format pop-up, and AI File to SWF File from the pop-up below that. After opening Flash (SWF), Torres imported the Illustrator Flash file (File > Import) and then used Flash's tools to manipulate the body part symbols to create an interactive animation.

Illustrator & Other Programs

14

Illustrator & Other Programs

f you're a FreeHand User...

Find "Moving from FreeHand to Illustrator" on the *Wow! CD*—a PDF Excerpt from Mordy Golding's *Real World Adobe Illustrator CS*.

Open sesame

If you're working in an application that doesn't allow you to save in a format that Illustrator imports (such as PSD, EPS, or PDF), but does print to PostScript, you may be able to get the vector data by printing to File and then opening the PostScript file in Illustrator.

When EPS is *not* recommended

If your application can place or open native AI, native PSD, or PDF 1.4 or later formats, it's better to use those than EPS, because they may preserve transparency, layers, and other features.

Which formats can you link?

Any BMP, EPS, GIF, JPEG, PICT, PCX, PDF, PNG, Photoshop, Pixar, Targa, or TIFF file can be placed as linked (rather than embedded).

So you think it's linked?

Flattening transparency of a linked image automatically embeds the image. In addition to increasing the file size, you can no longer update the link.

This chapter showcases some of the ways you can use Illustrator together with other programs. Although the range of work you can create using Illustrator is virtually limitless, combining other programs with Illustrator increases your creative opportunities, and in many instances can save you significant time in creating your final work.

We'll begin by discussing how you can place artwork in Illustrator, and then we'll provide a general look at how Illustrator works with other programs. Next we'll examine how Illustrator works with specific programs, including Photoshop, InDesign, Acrobat, and 3D programs. For information about working with Illustrator and Web or animation programs, see the *Web & Animation* chapter.

PLACING ARTWORK IN ILLUSTRATOR

Illustrator can place more than two dozen different file formats. The major choice you'll need to make is whether to link or embed the placed file. When you link a file, you don't actually include the artwork in the Illustrator file; instead a copy of the artwork acts as a placeholder, while the actual image remains separate from the Illustrator file. This can help reduce file size, but keep in mind that linking is supported only for certain formats (see Tip at left). On the other hand, when you embed artwork, you're actually including it in the file. The Links palette keeps track of all the raster images used in your document, regardless of whether they were created within Illustrator, opened, or introduced via the Place command.

In general, you should embed artwork only when:
- The image is small in file size.
- You're creating Web graphics.
- You want more than just a placeholder with a preview (e.g., you want editable objects and transparency).
- You want to apply live effects or filters.

And you should link (rather than embed) when:

- Your illustration uses several copies of the same image.
- The image is large in file size.
- You want to be able to edit the placed image using its original application.
- You can make changes to a linked file and resend only the linked file to your service bureau or client. As long as it has exactly the same name, it will auto-update without further editing of the Illustrator document itself.

ILLUSTRATOR & OTHER PROGRAMS

The first consideration when moving artwork between Illustrator and other programs is to decide which objects in your artwork have to remain as vectors and which you can allow to become rasterized. Next is whether you want to move the artwork between two open programs on your desktop (e.g., by using Copy and Paste or Drag and Drop) or if you will be moving your artwork via a file format. Finally, consider whether you want to move only a few objects or the whole file. Techniques for the above vary, depending on the program and are described in the corresponding program sections below.

Depending on the application, when you drag or paste objects between Illustrator and another open program, your objects will either drag or paste as vectors or as raster objects. In general, any program that supports PostScript drag and drop behavior will accept Illustrator objects via Drag and Drop (or Copy and Paste). In order for this to work, before copying and pasting, make certain that the AICB (Adobe Illustrator Clipboard) is selected in the File Handling & Clipboard panel of the Preferences dialog box. Then you can copy the objects between AI and the other application.

When you copy and paste, or drag-and-drop Illustrator art into a raster-based program (other than Photoshop), it's likely that your art will be automatically rasterized at the same physical size, or pixels-per-inch ratio, that you have specified in that raster-based program. (See the section "Illustrator & Adobe Photoshop,"

Resolution of placed images

Ensure optimal image reproduction by properly setting the pixels per inch (ppi) resolution of raster images before placing them into Illustrator. The ppi of images should be 1.5 to 2 times the size of the line screen at which the final image will print. For example, if your illustration will be printed in a 150 dpi (dots per inch) line screen, then the resolution of your raster images would typically be 300 ppi. Get print resolution specifications and recommendations from your printer *before* you begin your project!

Extract Embedded Images

To extract embedded raster images from Illustrator, save as an .ai with PDF compatibility on (it *is* on by default). In Photoshop CS2 (PSCS2) choose File > Open; in PSCS or PS6, choose File > Import > PDF Import. Next choose the .ai file, then choose Image from the Select pop-up (top left). Click the image thumbnails (press Shift or ⌘/Ctrl to click multiples) and click OK to open (extract) the images.
—*Jean-Claude Tremblay*

Illustrator File Handling and Clipboard Preferences dialog box; to copy and paste vectors set the clipboard preferences as shown above

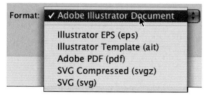

Options available from Save As

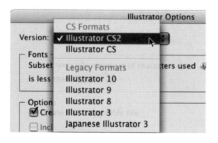

After choosing Adobe Illustrator Document, the Version pop-up choices give you access to Illustrator CS and Legacy Formats

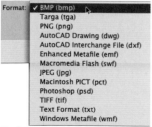

Options available from Export

following, for details about Illustrator's special working relationship with Photoshop.)

You can Save, or Export, your Illustrator artwork to many formats. From the File menu you can Save, Save for Web, Save for Microsoft Office, and Save As Template. From Save As you can choose Adobe Illustrator Document, Illustrator Template (.ait), EPS, PDF, or SVG. In order to save in legacy Illustrator .ai formats (so it can be opened in previous versions of Illustrator), you first choose Adobe Illustrator Document from the Save As > Format pop-up. From the Version pop-up in the resulting Illustrator Options dialog, you can choose Illustrator CS or Legacy Formats from Illustrator 10 and earlier.

From Export, you can access additional formats including: PSD, GIF, JPEG, PICT, PNG, SVG, SWF, and TIFF. Know which file formats your other application supports and the type of information (vector, raster, layers, paths) you want to bring from Illustrator into the other program to determine which format to choose.

ILLUSTRATOR & ADOBE PHOTOSHOP

As the lessons and Galleries in this chapter demonstrate, the creative possibilities for using Illustrator and Photoshop together are limitless.

Moving artwork between Illustrator and Photoshop via a file format is fairly straightforward, since Photoshop can open or place Illustrator files, and Illustrator can open and export Photoshop PSD files.

Fortunately, rasterizing isn't the one-way street it used to be, thanks to a marvelous new feature Photoshop CS2 introduces called *Smart Objects*, which greatly improves the process of bringing Illustrator art into Photoshop.

Smart Objects in Photoshop can be scaled, rotated, or warped without loss of data, and when you edit one instance of a Smart Object, Photoshop will automatically update all of your associated Smart Objects.

But the best news for Illustrator users is that you can create Photoshop Smart Objects from Illustrator data just by using the Clipboard (copying and pasting, dragging and dropping), or by inserting an Illustrator file using File > Place. You'll then have your choice of editing the placed Illustrator data either within Photoshop as rasters, or externally in Illustrator as vectors.

When you double-click an Illustrator Smart Object in Photoshop's Layers palette, Photoshop will automatically launch Illustrator and open a working copy of your artwork. You can then edit the artwork in Illustrator and save the file, at which point Photoshop will re-rasterize it. Presto! To edit the Illustrator file with raster tools, you must convert the smart objects to a layer using Layer > Smart Object > Convert to Layer, or via Layer > Rasterize > Smart Object. For more info about Photoshop's Smart Objects and how they work, see the Photoshop CS2's *Photoshop Help*.

The rules governing how Illustrator layers get translated into Photoshop layers (and whether or not those layers get rasterized in the process) are complex. You can find a few examples of how to move Illustrator objects (such as simple paths, text, compound paths, and compound shapes) between Illustrator and Photoshop in lessons following in this chapter.

ILLUSTRATOR & ADOBE INDESIGN

When you Copy and Paste artwork from Illustrator into InDesign, the artwork is pasted as either PDF or AICB, depending on which option you specified in the Illustrator File Handling & Clipboard panel of the Preferences dialog box. PDF preserves transparency, while AICB can break your artwork into smaller opaque native InDesign objects that mimic the transparency of your original artwork. Be aware that your artwork is imported as one object, which is not editable using InDesign, and not listed in InDesign's Links palette.

To place native Illustrator files in InDesign, you must have saved your Illustrator artwork with the Create PDF Compatible File option enabled. Doing so will also preserve your gradients, patterns, and transparency (which allows underlying artwork to show through).

Why is it a "smart object"?

When you paste or place Illustrator data into Photoshop, Photoshop rasterizes it just like it always has. The difference is, now when you place the Illustrator file, Photoshop makes it into a Smart Object (SO) by default. When you transform the SO, Photoshop will always "sample" from the original source, so there will be no degradation of resolution. If you choose to edit the SO (double-click its icon in the Layers palette), Photoshop will allow you to edit the embedded source data in Illustrator, then update the results when you save and return to the parent (Photoshop) document.

Pasting objects into InDesign

Before copying and pasting Illustrator objects into InDesign, you must first set preferences in both Illustrator and InDesign:

- In Illustrator, enable the AICB (details on the AICB in the "…Other Programs" section).
- In InDesign, disable the Clipboard Preference "Prefer PDF When Pasting" (depending on your version of InDesign, you'll find the preference either in Preferences > General, or in Preferences > File Handling).

(Adapted from InDesign Help *with the search word "Illustrator")*

— Options —
☑ Create PDF Compatible File

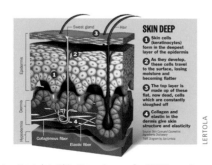

Joe Lertola's Skin Deep image for TIME *used Illustrator and Lightwave 3D. See his Gallery in the* Brushes & Symbols *chapter*

ILLUSTRATOR, PDF, & ADOBE ACROBAT

Acrobat's Portable Document Format (PDF) is platform and application independent—this means the format allows easy transfer of files between different operating systems, such as Mac OS, Windows, and even UNIX, as well as between different applications.

There are a number of ways to specify how PDFs are created in Illustrator. By default, the Adobe Illustrator Document CS2 format includes a PDF compatible file option that allows others to open your .ai file directly in Acrobat. If you're not sure if this default is active, choose Save As and, with Adobe Illustrator Document format chosen, click Save; in the resulting dialog make certain that the "Create PDF Compatible File" option is enabled, and Save your Illustrator file.

For full control over PDF options previously available only from Acrobat Distiller, from Save As choose Adobe PDF (pdf) from the pop-up and click Save. In the Adobe PDF Options dialog box, you can set many features including enabling the "Create Acrobat Layers From Top-Level Layers" option to save your layered Illustrator files as layered Acrobat 6 or 7 files. Illustrator PDF files can also preserve Illustrator editability and native transparency support; it can also conform to a widespread standard like PDF/X1a.

PDF files created by other programs can be edited in Illustrator, but you can only open and save one page at a time, and text that appears in one flow or text box in the PDF may be broken up into multiple text lines when opened in Illustrator.

ILLUSTRATOR & 3D PROGRAMS

In addition to Illustrator's 3D effects (see the *Live 3D Effects* chapter) you can also import Illustrator paths into 3D programs to use as outlines and extrusion paths. Once you import a path, you can transform it into a 3D object. Strata's 3D StudioPro, SketchUp!, and Lightwave 3D are just a few of the many 3D programs that you can use in combination with Illustrator.

MONROY

Bert Monroy
(Photoshop)

Bert Monroy capitalized on layered, resolution-independent artwork that he created in Illustrator and brought into Photoshop to create this image of a neon sign. Although he uses photos for visual reference, all of his images are completely hand-drawn with digital tools, and don't include any photo-collage. Monroy's techniques for creating photorealistic images from 2D software are illustrated in his books, *Bert Monroy: Photorealistic Techniques with Photoshop & Illustrator* and *Photoshop Studio with Bert Monroy* (both New Riders Publishing).

Software Relay

An Illustrator-Photoshop Workflow

Illustrator with Photoshop Overview: *Create paths in Illustrator; build a registration rectangle; organize layers for Photoshop masking; export as a PSD file; copy Illustrator paths and paste in Photoshop for masking.*

MAGIERA

1

Two stages in the construction of the image in Illustrator: left, the shapes as drawn; right, the shapes with fills

Why crop area?

Creating a crop area will automatically set the canvas size of a PSD file you export from Illustrator. Also, by making the crop area the same size as the Artboard, you can easily register the image after you've modified it in Photoshop. Just choose File > Place, select the image file, click OK, and then drag a corner until it snaps to a corner of the Artboard.

To illustrate mascots for Salt Lake City's 2002 Olympic Winter Games, Utah artist Rob Magiera drew shapes in Illustrator. He then exported the artwork as a Photoshop (PSD) file so he could airbrush highlights and shadows in Photoshop. While working in Photoshop, Magiera sometimes copied an Illustrator object and pasted it in Photoshop to serve as a selection or to modify a Quick Mask. (See the "Shape Shifting" lesson in this chapter to learn another way to move artwork between Illustrator and Photoshop.)

Although Magiera's illustration would be completed in Photoshop, his client needed the original Illustrator artwork for other uses.

1 Placing a sketch in Illustrator, drawing shapes, and making a registration box. Magiera began by scanning pencil sketches and saving them in TIFF format. He created a new Illustrator file with dimensions that were larger than the drawings he would make and then created

a crop area the size of the document by choosing Object >
Crop Area > Make (this will help when you place the
Photoshop image back into Illustrator). Next, he placed
the scanned image on a template layer in Illustrator (see
the *Layers* chapter for more on templates) and drew the
mascot shapes with the Pen and Pencil tools. He filled the
shapes with color, leaving the outlines unstroked.

In order to more easily modify rasterized shapes
once you get them into Photoshop, make sure you organize your major artwork elements onto separate layers
(for help see the "Organizing Layers" lesson in the *Layers* chapter). (On export to PSD, Illustrator preserves as
much of your layer structure as possible without sacrificing appearance.) For objects that overlapped other objects
(like the bear's arm or the coyote's leg), Magiera created
new layers and moved the overlapping objects onto separate layers so he could easily mask them in Photoshop
when he began airbrushing them.

Knowing that he would bring some of the paths he
had drawn into Photoshop to help with masking, Magiera
devised a way to keep paths registered to other pasted
paths and to the raster artwork he would export from
Illustrator. You can accomplish this by making a "registration" rectangle in Illustrator that will keep your artwork in the same position relative to the rectangle (and
the Photoshop canvas) each time you copy and paste. To
make this rectangle, first create a new layer in the Layers
palette, and then drag it below your artwork layers. Next,
draw a rectangle with no stroke or fill that is the same size
as the Artboard. Center the rectangle on the Artboard.
With the rectangle matching the size and position of the
Artboard, copies of the rectangle will be pasted in Photoshop automatically aligned with the canvas.

Now you're ready to export your Illustrator artwork.
Select File > Export, and from the Export dialog box
choose Photoshop (PSD) from the Format pop-up.

2 Working with Illustrator paths in Photoshop. After
opening the exported PSD file in Photoshop, Magiera

The Illustrator Layers palette organized with
separate layers for shapes (shown as selected
objects) to be masked in Photoshop

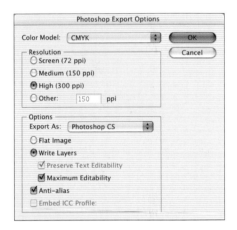

Illustrator's Export: Photoshop Options dialog

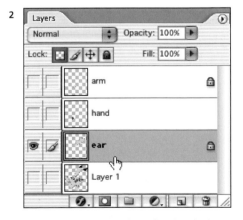

The Photoshop Layers palette showing the layer
structure of the Illustrator-exported PSD file

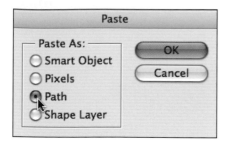

Photoshop's Paste dialog box for pasting paths

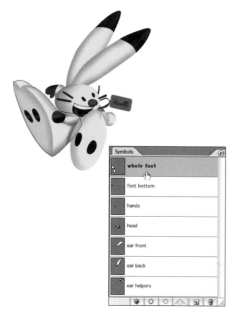

At top, the bunny figure with the "whole foot" work path selected; bottom, Photoshop's Paths palette showing the selected work path

Masking a shape with a shape

If you mask a raster shape with a pasted Illustrator path in Photoshop, be aware that the mask applies antialiasing to pixels that are already antialiased, resulting in an incorrect appearance. A better way to mask raster shapes in Photoshop is to use the Layers palette's Lock Transparency Pixels option or the Layer > Group with Previous command.

used different masking techniques as he airbrushed highlights and shadows. To mask within a shape, Magiera usually enabled Lock Transparent Pixels for the layer on which the shape was located. If you use the Quick Mask working mode, you can create new masks from objects copied in Illustrator and pasted in Photoshop. To do this, in Illustrator, select both an object *and* the registration rectangle and then choose Edit > Copy. Next, in Photoshop, choose Edit > Paste and in the Paste dialog box, choose Paste as Pixels. Notice that the artwork is in the same position on the Photoshop canvas as it was relative to the registration rectangle in Illustrator. With each pasted path, you can generate a selection and either add to or subtract from your working Quick Mask.

As Magiera worked in Photoshop, he occasionally modified a raster shape and then needed to update the Illustrator path that he originally used to generate the shape. To do this, first make a copy of the Illustrator path and the registration rectangle. Then, in Photoshop, choose Edit > Paste and, from the Paste dialog box, choose Paste as Path. Now you can modify the shape's path with Photoshop's drawing tools. When you finish, Shift-select the modified path and the registration rectangle path (click close to an edge of the canvas to select the rectangle) and choose Edit > Copy. Return to Illustrator, select the original registration rectangle, choose Edit > Paste, and drag a corner of the pasted registration rectangle until it snaps to the corresponding corner of the existing registration rectangle. Now you can delete the original path that you are replacing with the modified path.

When Magiera finished airbrushing in Photoshop, he saved the file (which was still in PSD format).

3 Bringing the Photoshop image into Illustrator. For some of the changes to raster shapes he made in Photoshop, Magiera chose to edit the original path in Illustrator. He selected File > Place and imported the image into the Illustrator file, snapping it to the registration rectangle. He edited the paths using the Pen and Pencil tools.

CHAN

Ron Chan
(Photoshop)

Illustrator Ron Chan began this illustration for the Catellus Web site by dividing and joining objects using the Pathfinder palette (see more about the Pathfinder palette in the *Beyond Basic Drawing & Coloring* chapter). After filling his objects with color, Chan brought the artwork into Photoshop, where he selected individual elements and added textures to lend a more organic look the illustration. Similar results can be achieved using Effect menu commands, with transparency and Opacity Masks (see the *Transparency* and *Live Effects & Graphic Styles* chapters for help with effects, the Transparency palette, and Opacity Masks.)

Shape Shifting

Exporting Paths to Shapes in Photoshop

Illustrator with Photoshop
Advanced Technique

Overview: *Draw paths in Illustra-tor; convert paths to compound shapes; export in PSD format; apply effects in Photoshop.*

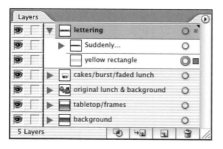

The original Illustrator artwork and the Layers palette shown before the frame, the yellow burst, and the yellow background (behind the type) were turned into compound shapes

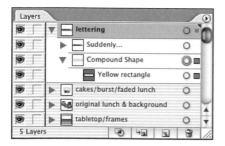

The palette showing objects in a compound shape

Artist Brad Hamann prepared this colorful illustration in Illustrator before exporting it as a PSD file and open-ing it in Photoshop, where he applied live effects that he could not have created in Illustrator. The key to bringing editable paths into Photoshop is to turn the objects you want to keep as paths into compound shapes. Then, after you export your document as a layered PSD and open it in Photoshop, you will see that your compound shapes have become editable shape layers while the rest of your artwork has been rasterized.

1 Drawing and layering artwork. Hamann used the Pen tool to draw objects and relied on the Blend, Reflect, and Rotate tools to create repeating elements (such as the slanting lines on the side of the milk box). For two of the objects he drew (the yellow burst and the yellow back-ground behind the title), Hamann decided to leave each with a simple fill color in Illustrator and use Photoshop's layer styles and lighting effects to "paint" the objects. Moreover, in order to keep the outer frame looking neat in Photoshop, he had to export it as a single vector object. To do all this, Hamann converted these objects to com-pound shapes so they would be exported as Photoshop shape layers when he created a PSD file.

Once you've identified the objects you will bring into Photoshop as paths, select each object. From the Pathfinder palette pop-up menu, choose Make Compound Shape. (Choose Release Compound Shape from the Pathfinder palette pop-up menu if you need to turn compound shapes back into regular objects.) Hamann's compound shape frame had two components: a copy of the burst object in Subtract mode, and a rectangular frame. See the *Beyond Basic Drawing & Coloring* chapter introduction for details about working with compound shapes and shape modes.

If a compound shape is to remain an editable path when exported from Illustrator, make sure that it's not inside a group or on a sublayer. If it is, use the Layers palette to drag it out from all groups and sublayers (see the *Layers & Appearances* chapter for help with layers).

2 Exporting a Photoshop (PSD) file. Export your Illustrator file by choosing File > Export, then choose Photoshop (PSD) format and click OK. In the Photoshop Options dialog box, pick a resolution setting that matches the requirements of your printing or display medium and make sure that within the Options section, that all available options are selected.

Note: *See the intro to this chapter for information on more ways to move artwork between Illustrator and Photoshop.*

3 Applying effects to shape layers in Photoshop.
When Hamann opened the exported PSD file in Photoshop, each Illustrator compound shape appeared as a shape layer in Photoshop's Layers palette. To add a layer effect to a shape layer, Hamann double-clicked the shape layer in the Layers palette. He applied Bevel and Emboss effects to his yellow rectangle and starburst shape layers, and even reshaped the shape paths using Photoshop's Direct Selection tool. Finally, he added some Photoshop effects (such as Strokes) to duplicates of some of the shape layers, and applied the Add Noise filter (Gaussian) to a duplicate of the background.

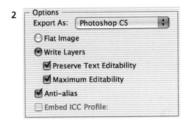

Compound shape to raster

If you turned a stroked object into a compound shape and exported a PSD file, but then found your shape rasterized in Photoshop, don't panic. Either select the. object in Illustrator and choose Round Join in the Stroke palette, or remove the object's stroke.

2

A portion of the Options section of the Illustrator File > Export > Photoshop (PSD) dialog box

3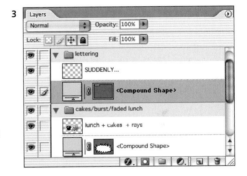

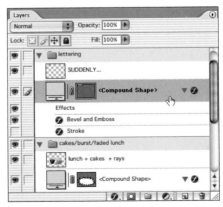

Top shows the Photoshop Layers palette as the PSD is first opened; bottom shows layer effects applied to some of the shape layers

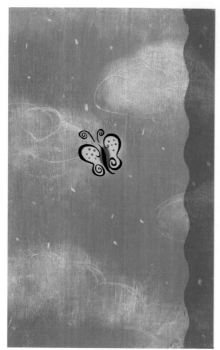

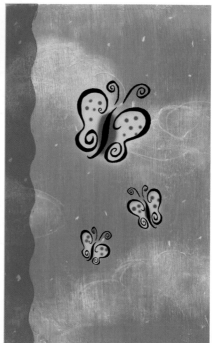

Judy Stead
(Photoshop)

Judy Stead combined Photoshop, Illustrator, and traditional painting techniques to design the cover of this Scholastic Book Fairs journal. (Shown above are the back and front covers.) Stead alternated among the three approaches throughout her entire creative process. She first painted the blue clouds on a gesso-textured board with acrylic paint, pastels, and a white pencil (see image inset at right). The image was scanned into Photoshop and the color was adjusted from aqua blue to orange (Image > Adjustments > Hue/Saturation). Stead drew the butterfly in Illustrator, using one of the default Calligraphic brushes and a Wacom drawing tablet, which allowed

her to create a line that varied in width (see the *Brushes & Symbols* chapter). She then exported the file to Photoshop as a PSD file and made several copies of the butterfly, varying rotation, orientation, and size. Stead drew the wavy book spine in Illustrator. In Photoshop, the clouds, spine, and butterflies were combined into a layered Photoshop file. Stead set the blending mode of the cloud layer to Multiply, so the cloud texture was visible through the individual elements. She then added airbrushed detail to the butterfly and continued to adjust the color of the element using Hue/Saturation until she was satisfied with the overall effect.

STEAD

Judy Stead
(Photoshop)

Judy Stead often begins her illustrations by making traditionally painted backgrounds that are manipulated in Photoshop. With one painted background, (shown above right) Stead can create several others varying in color by using the Image Menu. Stead scanned the background into Photoshop and chose Image > Adjustments > Hue/Saturation. To enhance a specific color, she chose Image > Adjustments > Selective Color. Further adjustments were made on a duplicated layer where Stead applied Blending Modes such as Multiply and Hue. The background image was saved in Tiff format. To import the background into Illus-

trator, Stead chose File > Place. She then drew with the Charcoal brush imported from the Artistic_ChalkCharcoalPencil Brush Library. In the Transparency palette, Stead applied various Blending Modes to enhance specific areas. After drawing a shape, such as a leaf, she opened the Transparency palette and selected the Blending Mode, Overlay. The colored circles underneath the word "think" have the Blending Modes of Overlay, Hue and Multiply (top to bottom). The colored circles also have either a Gaussian Blur (Effect > Blur > Gaussian Blur) or a brush applied to the stroke.

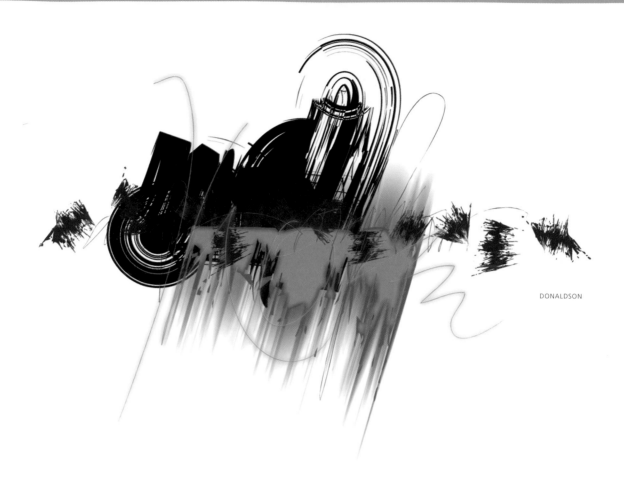

DONALDSON

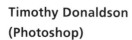

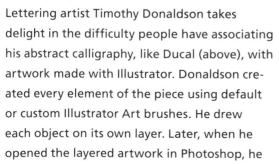

Timothy Donaldson (Photoshop)

Lettering artist Timothy Donaldson takes delight in the difficulty people have associating his abstract calligraphy, like Ducal (above), with artwork made with Illustrator. Donaldson created every element of the piece using default or custom Illustrator Art brushes. He drew each object on its own layer. Later, when he opened the layered artwork in Photoshop, he selected objects, applied blurs and drop shadows and adjusted transparency. Some of these Photoshop treatments can also be achieved using the Effect menu and the Transparency palette. (See the *Transparency* and the *Live Effects & Graphic Styles* chapters for more on the Appearance and Transparency palettes and the Effect menu.)

GREIMAN

April Greiman
(Photoshop)

April Greiman, of April Greiman Made in Space, took advantage of Illustrator's ability to produce resolution-independent vector graphics when creating this large wall mural for the Cafe & Fitness Center at Amgen. Greiman began with source photos and original images. In Photoshop, she combined the images, adjusted the hue, saturation, and opacity and made adjustments with levels and curves. A variety of filters were applied to the images, such as Gaussian Blur, Motion Blur, Ripple, and Noise. Greiman knew that when the image was enlarged, the pixelated effect would enhance the image, just as she wanted. When Greiman was satisfied with the Photoshop image, she saved it as a PSD file. The PSD file was imported into Illustrator and text was added. The text was created on several layers with varying opacities. The size of the Illustrator image was 21 inches x 5 inches, and the final mural measured 36 feet by 11.3 feet. The pixels in the Photoshop image were greatly distorted when enlarged to the final mural size. This desired pixelated effect was combined with crisp text that Illustrator can produce at any magnification. The final image was output from Illustrator and printed directly on vinyl.

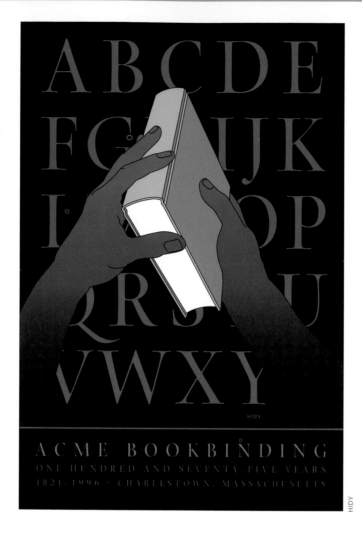

Lance Hidy
(Photoshop)

Illustrator Lance Hidy photographed hands holding a book several times until he had a "natural" pose. He scanned the photograph and, in Photoshop, lightened the shadows and other dark tones in the image before printing it. On this print, Hidy drew outlines of the hands directly, using a fine-tipped pen. Then he scanned the marked print and placed the resulting TIFF file in Illustrator as a tracing template. He was able to clearly follow the con-

tours and details of the hands as he manually traced with Illustrator's Pencil tool.

POUNDS

David Pounds
(Photoshop)

David Pounds used to do much of his creative work in Photoshop, but he can now work almost exclusively in Illustrator, due to recent improvements to the program. In this illustration, Pounds used Photoshop to make different versions of the photo in order to accentuate various details. For instance, he created a posterized version (Image > Adjustments > Posterize) to help him see the image as areas of color. He also created a few versions using Levels (Image > Adjustments > Levels) to accentuate specific details of the image. He opened his layered .psd file in Illustrator, then set up layers for hand-tracing the photo with closed paths. Using the Pen tool, he created closed shapes and used the Eyedropper tool, with the Shift key, to pick up color from various layered versions of the photograph in Photoshop (the Eyedropper tool in Illustrator now allows for greater range of color sampling options, much like Photoshop). Whenever he wanted to create another variation of his photo in order to accentuate a missing detail, he created that version in Photoshop (using Levels, for example). He then chose Select > All, and Copy. Moving back to Illustrator, he created a new layer for this version and used Paste in Front (⌘-F/ Ctrl-F), which placed the new version of the photo in perfect alignment with the previous variations of the same-sized Photoshop file.

YIP

Filip Yip
(Photoshop)

Filip Yip began by drawing Illustrator objects and organizing them on many separate layers (so each object would remain on its own layer when he later exported them to Photoshop). He decided on the overall color scheme, colored the shapes, and added blends. Yip then exported his Illustrator objects into Photoshop in order to add transparency, feathering, and lighting effects. The artwork (shown above right) was exported as a Photoshop PSD file. In Photoshop, Yip was able to easily manipulate the illustrator objects, since they were on separate layers. He enhanced the blends with the

Airbrush tool, adjusted the transparency, and applied the Add Noise filter. Blurring effects (such as Gaussian Blur) were used to highlight details of the image. To further soften the blends, Yip also applied the Fade Brush Tool (Edit > Fade Brush Tool > Fade > Dissolve) in the Dissolve mode.

JACKSON

Lance Jackson
(Photoshop)

Lance Jackson applied Distort & Transform effects to create this illustration for an annual music festival. Jackson began by typing a list of band names in a paragraph using one font with the Type Tool. He then drew paths to outline the shape of a head with specific features such as the cheeks, lips and nose. With the Type on a Path tool Jackson applied type to the paths that defined the face. Using groups of text from the original paragraph, Jackson filled in other areas of the face. Jackson selected the type, chose Object > Expand, and colored the text. He selected a group of type and applied Effect > Distort & Transform > Pucker & Bloat to abstract the text. He repeated this process to develop the head. Jackson placed the file into Photoshop to add more text and blocks of color to the background. In Photoshop he selected groups of type with the Magic Wand tool. He adjusted the opacity on layers of text to create depth. Jackson altered the text even further by choosing Edit > Transform to skew, scale or rotate. Finally, Jackson opened the Photoshop file in Illustrator to fill out the head with more distorted text.

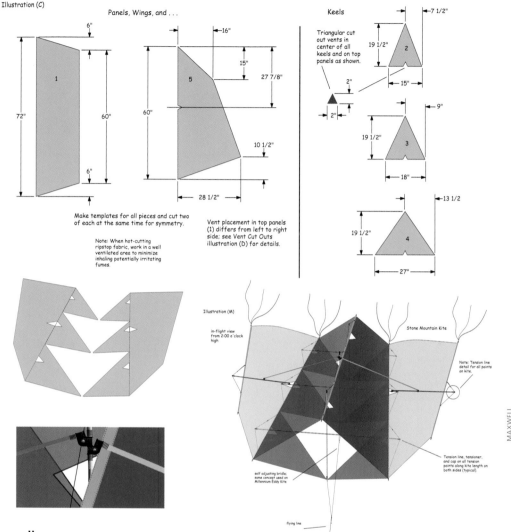

Illustration (C)

Panels, Wings, and . . .

Keels

Triangular cut out vents in center of all keels and on top panels as shown.

Make templates for all pieces and cut two of each at the same time for symmetry.

Note: When hot-cutting ripstop fabric, work in a well ventilated area to minimize inhaling potentially irritating fumes.

Vent placement in top panels (1) differs from left to right side; see Vent Cut Outs illustration (B) for details.

Illustration (M)

in-flight view from 2:00 o'clock high

Stone Mountain Kite

Note: Tension line detail for all points on kite.

Tension line, tensioner, and cap on all tension points along kite length on both sides (typical).

self adjusting bridle; same concept used on Millennium Eddy Kite

flying line

MAXWELL

Eden Maxwell
(Hot Door CADTools)

For his Stone Mountain Kite illustration (bottom right), Eden Maxwell started from part drawings (top) that he earlier drew to scale using a Wacom tablet and Hot Door CADTools (a third-party plug-in for Illustrator). To draw the kite with "in-flight" perspective, Maxwell manually adjusted the CADTools drawings by eye until they were oriented in the perspective he visualized. For example, he used the Rotate tool and the Direct Selection tool to edit wing and keel angles to achieve the desired perspective (middle left). After major components were in place, Maxwell drew smaller parts like eye loops, connectors, end caps, and tension lines (bottom left), right down to the stitching along the top sail. To simulate air under the wings during flight, Maxwell created a slight curve in the aft section of the wings for the final illustration.

Greg Maxson
(SketchUp)

To draw this arbor in perspective, Greg Maxson imported files he created in the SketchUp 3D modeling application (demo at sketchup.com) and combined the files in Illustrator. First, the client provided Maxson with 2D drawings. In SketchUp, Maxson used the drawings to create a 3D model of the arbor. From the set of viewing angles Maxson provided (bottom left), the client approved the final view (top). Maxson exported two 2D EPS files from the 3D model:

one filled and one outlined (bottom right). He used the outlined version to represent underground post segments. Maxson placed the two versions in Illustrator, aligned them, and applied the project's final stroke and fill specifications. To expedite editing, he used commands on the Select >Same submenu (such as Select >Same >Fill Color) to select objects with a common attribute. He could then change that attribute for all selected objects at once.

JONES

Joe Jones: Art Works Studio
(Ray Dream Studio, Bryce, Photoshop)

In this World War II tribute entitled "West Field Yardbird," Joe Jones used Illustrator artwork as components in building the 3D model in Ray Dream Studio, and as texture maps to cover the model in Bryce. To start the artwork that would serve as texture maps for the metal panel seams, window masks, rivets and other elements of the model, Jones drew objects on separate layers with the Pen tool. Then Jones brought the artwork into Photoshop where he applied edge treatments and simulated the effects of weathering by painting onto the art. Then he flattened and saved the files. In Bryce, Jones imported and mapped the images onto the modeled plane parts. In all, he filled the scene with nearly 3000 Illustrator objects.

Atrium
Hunziker Wing
Wightman Gym
Pool
Coach House
Hunziker Hall
Raubinger Hall
Shea Center for Performing Arts
Hobart Manor

WILLCOCKSON

Tom Willcockson / Mapcraft
(Bryce)

Cartographer Tom Willcockson visited the campus of William Paterson University to acquire photographs, building floor plans and other materials. Then in Illustrator, he built a base map of the campus roads, rivers, vegetation areas, building outlines and other features. After scanning a contour map, Willcockson drew closed contour lines, filling them with gray shades based on elevation. He exported two JPEG images to serve as source images in Bryce: the grayscale contour layer and the base map artwork. In Bryce, Willcockson imported the contour JPEG and generated a 3D terrain image. Then he imported the base map JPEG and draped it across the terrain. He rendered the image and exported it as a JPEG, which he placed on a template layer in Illustrator. He hand-traced the streets, building footprints and other features in Bryce-rendered perspective view. Willcockson drew the buildings, and then added trees and shrubs as Scatter brush objects from a brush library he had created for other maps. (See the *Brushes* chapter to learn about using scatter brushes for map symbols.)

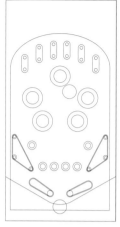

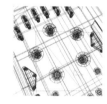

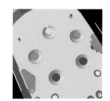

BERGMAN

Eliot Bergman
(Photoshop and Alias Sketch!)

Bergman created this illustration for a trade magazine advertisement with a combination of 2D and 3D programs. He took advantage of the precision possible with Illustrator to draft sections, plans and profiles of objects before importing them into Silicon Graphics Alias Sketch!, a 3D modeling program. He also made color and bump maps in Illustrator, then retouched them in Photoshop. For this illustration, the first step was to draft the layout of the pinball machine in Illustrator. The elements in this design served both as a template for 3D objects and as a basis for a color map. Bergman used the Gradient tool to create the background, and he used a combination of the Star tool (hidden within the Rectangle tool) and the Filter > Distort > Pucker and Bloat filter to create the starbursts. Bergman imported the artwork into Sketch! where he created 3D objects by extruding and lathing individual items. After rendering a rough preview image, Bergman added the final maps, colors and lights. He brought the finished rendered image into Photoshop for retouching.

Chris Spollen
(Photoshop)

Chris Spollen often creates his collage-like illustrations by weaving back and forth between Illustrator and Photoshop. He always starts with thumbnail pencil sketches (below right), which he scans and places as a template in Illustrator (see "Digitizing a Logo" in the *Layers & Appearances* chapter). He then creates his basic shapes and elements in Illustrator. While some of his illustrations do end up being assembled in Illustrator, this piece, "Hot Rod Rocket," was finalized in Photoshop, with many of the objects becoming "Illustrator/Photoshop hybrids" (such as his white clouds on an angle, which began as simple Illustrator shapes). In order to control his layers in Photoshop, Spollen moved one or more selected Illustrator objects at a time into a single layer in Photoshop using drag-and-drop. Spollen then reworked the shapes in Photoshop using the Paintbrush and Airbrush tools. He also adjusted the opacity. The 3D-looking rocket originated as a scanned toy "rocket gun," while the moon began as a scanned photo. "Hot Rod Rocket" received an Award of Merit in the Society of Illustrator's Show.

SPOLLEN

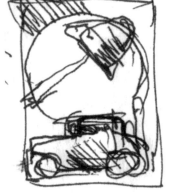

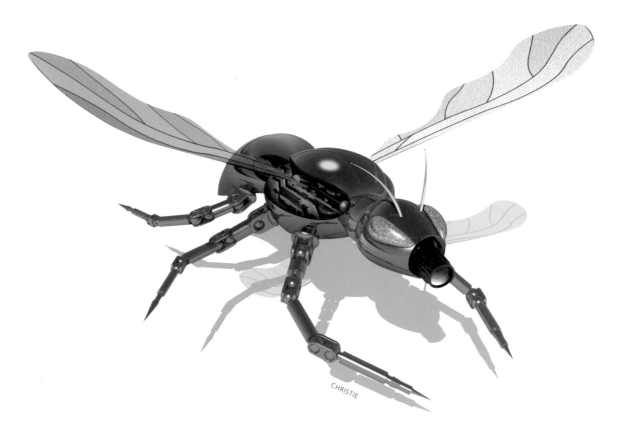

CHRISTIE

Bryan Christie
(Photoshop, MetaTools Infini-D)

Bryan Christie assembled this mechanical bug
with Illustrator and later integrated Photoshop
and Infini-D, a 3D modeling program. The 3D
shapes, such as the leg joints and circuit boards,
were first drawn in Illustrator as an outline
without detail or color, and then imported into
Infini-D and extruded into 3D shapes. To map
the color and the details of the circuit boards,
Christie drew and colored the circuitry in Illustrator. He then exported the artwork as a PICT
and mapped it onto the 3D shapes in Infini-D.
Christie created the transparency of the wing
by mapping a grayscale image that was origi-

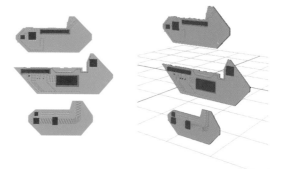

nally drawn in Illustrator onto the wing shape
in Infini-D. To complete the mechanical bug,
he rendered the artwork in Infini-D, opened
it in Photoshop to make minor touchups (such
as color correction and compositing separately
rendered elements), and finally converted the
entire image into CMYK.

Jason Taylor

CROUSE

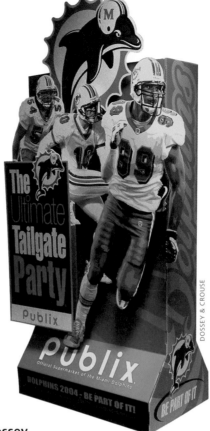

A. J. Feeley

DOSSEY & CROUSE

Scott Crouse and Warren Dossey (Photoshop)

Scott Crouse drew these illustrations for a promotion by Publix Super Markets and the National Football League's Miami Dolphins. Artist Warren Dossey used some of Crouse's drawings for a seven-foot-tall retail standee (center) created in Illustrator. Crouse hand-traced source images in Illustrator after first applying a process he developed to simplify source images for hand-tracing. In Photoshop, he lowered the number of colors by applying a Posterize adjustment layer set to about 3 levels, depending on the image. Crouse also applied the Noise: Median filter (typically with a Radius of 2 pixels) to the image's background layer to shift stray bits of color to a solid area, defining color edges more clearly. He then converted the image to Indexed Color with a Local Adaptive palette using 10 to 20 colors, again depending on the image. Crouse then placed the processed images in Illustrator as templates. He hand-traced the images using the Pen tool, following the clean color edges (detail, bottom right) resulting from his pre-processing method. (For variations on this method, see the "Trace Techniques" lesson in the *Beyond Basic Drawing & Coloring* chapter).

DesignTools™ Monthly

The Executive Summary of Graphic Design News

Every month, *Design Tools Monthly* publishes stories about the best plug-ins for Adobe Illustrator, InDesign, Photoshop, QuarkXPress and other applications. It also summarizes other important stories for graphic arts professionals — bug fixes, updates, new software and hardware, events, and valuable tips and tricks.

We've been reading *DTM* for many years and really appreciate being able to keep up with the changes in our industry and still have time to make a living. They've been publishing since 1992, with subscribers in 40 countries. Below are some of their stories.

We encourage you to explore the free sample issues on the *WOW! CD*. You can also get more information at **http://www.design-tools.com**.

Commercial Plug-ins for Illustrator

Use Multiple Pages in Illustrator

Hot Door MultiPage 2 ($79) fills a long-standing need in Adobe Illustrator: multiple pages. This plug-in for Illustrator CS lets you create as many pages as you'd like, using Master Pages if desired, and even export multiple-page PDF files. The previous version of MultiPage works with Illustrator 9 & 10 ($49).

http://www.hotdoor.com

Create Barcodes in Illustrator

Yin4Yang's Barcode Toolbox ($90) is a plug-in for Illustrator CS that provides an easy-to-use interface for creating barcodes of every common type. The result is a native Illustrator object.

http://www.yin4yang.com

Easier Logo Tracing

ComNet's LogoSpruce ($199) is a plug-in for Illustrator 8, 9, 10 and CS that intelligently helps you straighten up artwork from scanned logos and diagrams. Specialized tools let you quickly make perfect corners and curves, and create guides from any angled line. It was designed specifically to speed the creation of logo outlines from scanned artwork.

http://www.comnet-network.co.jp

Package Mockups in Illustrator

Comnet's FoldUP-3D ($379) is a plug-in for Illustrator 8, 9, 10 and CS that lets you preview package designs. You create die-lines or import them from a CAD system, apply your artwork, and then let FoldUP-3D create your carton. You can rotate the carton in 3D space, change background colors and lighting properties, reposition your artwork, show and hide layers, and export snapshots. A free viewer also allows clients to see your carton in 3D space

http://www.comnet-network.co.jp

Advanced Path-Editing

CValley's Xtream Path 1.1 ($139) is a plug-in for Adobe Illustrator CS that adds several features: You can click anywhere on a path and drag it to into a new shape, rather than adjusting anchor points (similar to the feature Macromedia FreeHand has had for six years). A new palette shows the numerical values of the position of anchor points, handles and the length of segments (a feature FreeHand has had for 12 years) and copy and paste the values onto another anchor point. You can symmetrically change a shape — pull on one side and the other side mirrors the change. A Smart Rounding effect changes sharp corners into rounded ones, even on editable type. A Multi-Line tool makes it easier to draw isometric shapes such as 3D boxes. You can copy paths and insert them into other paths. You can bevel or round corners and easily create arcs, and more.

http://www.cvalley.com

Much Sharper Bevels

Photoshop's Bevel feature is so smooth... it can be too smooth. That's when **Shinycore's Path Styler Pro** is valuable. This plug-in for Photoshop or Illustrator ($99 each or $129 for both) creates sharp, clean bevels, accurate reflections, and has multiple lighting options and advanced controls for these and a dozen other features. Photoshop uses pixels to create bevels, while Path Styler Pro uses multiple paths. The result is much more control and accuracy. You can apply multiple bevels to a path, and each bevel can have its own material, contour, textures, and procedural maps such as wood, metal, plastic, glass and others. Lights can be directional, omni, or tube. More than 100 presets are included. Have a look at their website to see the difference.

http://www.shinycore.com

Automate Illustrator

Zumedia's Automata 1.5 ($135) creates customized Illustrator CS documents based on data you provide in a text file. You create a template in Illustrator that includes variable fields (such as name, address, date of last purchase, etc.), then create layers whose visibility can be toggled, and add image placeholders. Your text file then instructs Illustrator to use This Text in That Field, the Picture in This Location on your hard drive or network in That Placeholder, and turn visibility of This Layer on and That Layer off. The result is a page with custom text, images and layout that can automatically be exported in several formats: PDF, EPS, Photoshop, Flash, JPG and GIF. Flash files can include hyperlinks provided by the text file. Some of Automata's uses include custom business cards, brochures, certificates, awards, static or animated Web graphics or ads, and any other repetitive layout project. Zumedia claims it can produce up to 1,500 files per hour.

http://www.zumedia.com

Import GIS Data into Illustrator

Avenza Software's MAPublisher 6.1 ($999) and MAPublisher Lt ($299) are powerful plug-ins for Illustrator 10 or CS that let you import CAD drawings and maps in geographic information systems (GIS) format, including shapes, boundaries, routes and elevations. MAPublisher also lets you automatically create legends and keys. It can import database tables, which can be linked to existing map layers, and can export to ArcView Shape files and SVG and dBASE formats. Their website shows examples of the beautiful, detailed maps made by customers.

http://www.avenza.com

Step-And-Repeat for Flexography

Wriston Development's FlexoStep ($299) is a plug-in for Illustrator or FreeHand that automates the process of distorting and arranging multiple copies of artwork for printing labels and containers using flexography.

http://www.flexostep.com

Instant Patterns

Artlandia SymmetryWorks 3 ($215) is a unique plug-in for Adobe Illustrator that lets you easily create and interactively edit seamless patterns and designs. You draw a simple shape, and SymmetryWorks rotates, reflects and spaces it to create a seamless pattern. As you edit the shape, the pattern updates in real time, encouraging you to experiment. You can also add additional shapes to the pattern and view the changes in real time. Their website shows good examples of how it works.

http://www.artlandia.com

Plug-ins That Integrate with Illustrator

Import Illustrator Files into Final Cut Pro

Ampede PDF ($10) is a plug-in for Final Cut Pro HD that renders vector content from Illustrator and PDF files, providing sharp images regardless of scale, movement or rotation. This is helpful if you don't want to use Adobe After Effects for rendering these files.

http://www.ampede.com

Math Expressions in InDesign

i.t.i.p.'s InMath 1.3 ($249–$595) is a plug-in for InDesign or InCopy that creates mathematical expressions using your input and InDesign's Styles palette. You enter text, click on a style, and InMath creates a correct expression using only InDesign's text-formatting abilities. You can also drag expressions from InDesign into Illustrator.

http://www.itip.biz

Link Illustrator Files to Motion

Ampede's LayerLink ($120) is a plug-in for Apple's powerful new Motion video application (see page 3) that lets you link to a native layered Illustrator file. Layers can be scaled, rotated, moved, filtered and animated in real time. And—get this—if the Illustrator file changes, the changes are reflected in Motion.

http://www.ampede.com

Free Catalog of Plug-ins

ThePowerXChange has a free downloadable catalog/database of plug-ins for Illustrator, InDesign, Photoshop, Acrobat and QuarkXPress. Download it at:
http://www.thepowerxchange.com/catalogue_download.html

The IAN Symbol Libraries include over 1000 Science / Nature / Ecology symbols. The complete collection, including an interactive tutorial is available completely free on the IAN website www.ian.umces.edu/symbols. The *Special WOW! Sampler Pack* includes a sampling of 100 symbols. (See the "IAN Wow Sampler" folder and .exe on the *Wow! CD*.)

Alfalfa	Banana Bunch	Banana Tree	Corn Cob	Hay
Hay Bales	Wheat Sheath	Effects; Insect attack	Mangrove Growth	*Avicennia marina* flower
Seagrass leaf with encrusting epiphytes	Seagrass Growth	*Enhalus acoroides*	*Halophila ovalis*	Water Lilly
Ecklonia radiata (brown)	*Myriophyllum spicatum* (Eurasian Watermilfoil)	*Phragmites australis* marsh	*Acrostichum speciosum*	*Spartina alterniflora*
Wetland	Eastern Hemlock (*Tsuga canadensis*)	Red Maple (*Acer rubrum*)	Chestnut Oak	Dinoflagellate cyst
Evapotranspiration	*Pfiesteria piscicida* (dinoflagellate)	Nauplii	*Akashiwo sanguinea* (dinoflagellate)	*Thalassiosira nordenskioeldii* (diatom)

The full collection is divided into 30 Illustrator (10 and CS) symbol libraries. The IAN symbols are designed primarily for creating conceptual diagrams of ecosystem processes to better communicate environmental issues. Using these symbols, diagrammatic representations of complex processes can be developed easily with minimal graphical skills.

Beaver	Grizzly Bear (*Ursus arctos*)	Coyote (*Canis* sp.)	Nutria (*Myocastor coypus*)	Walrus (*Odobenus* sp.)
Damselfish (*Chromis chromis*)	Sperm Whale (Family Physeteridae)	Orca (*Orcinus orca*)	Anemone Fish (*Amphiprion* sp.)	Hermit Crab
Moerisia (coelenterate)	Cow Bream (*Sarpa salpa*)	Striped Bass (*Morone saxatilis*)	Summer Flounder (*Paralichthys dentatus*)	Manta Ray (*Manta birostris*)
Dugong (*Dugong dugon*)	Mosquito (Family Culicidae)	Monarch Butterfly (*Danaus plexippus*)	Gypsy Moth (*Lymantria dispar*)	Pied Oyster Catcher (*Haematopus* sp.)
Red Cardinal (*Cardinalis* sp.)	Eurasian Wigeon (*Anas penelope*)	Water bird	Canada goose	Land clearing
Harvest	Helicopter Sprayer	Irrigation	Groundwater extraction & compression	Logging

The IAN Symbol Librariy provides a standard resource for scientists, resource managers, community groups and environmentalists worldwide. IAN Symbols are being used in over 140 countries.

Canal Estate	Aquaculture ponds	Water Treatment Plant	Refinery	Hydroelectric plant
Fisher	Dredge	Oil Spill	Port	Trawler
Jet Skiing	Inputs; sediments & nutrients	Salinity extremes	Low oxygen	Light; no light
Atmospheric Nitrogen	Weather; snow	Respiration	Vertical eddy diffusivity	Food webs; grazing
Mesocosm Cutaway	Aquarium from top 1	Sediment Incubator	Balance 1	CBOS Buoy
Auto Sampler	DNA	Satellite	Electron Microscope	Compound Microscope

The libraries include a series of landscape bases to allow easy construction of processes occurring within a variety of aquatic, marine and terrestrial environments. The IAN support forum offers a free 'Symbol Creation Service' where requests can be made for custom symbols .

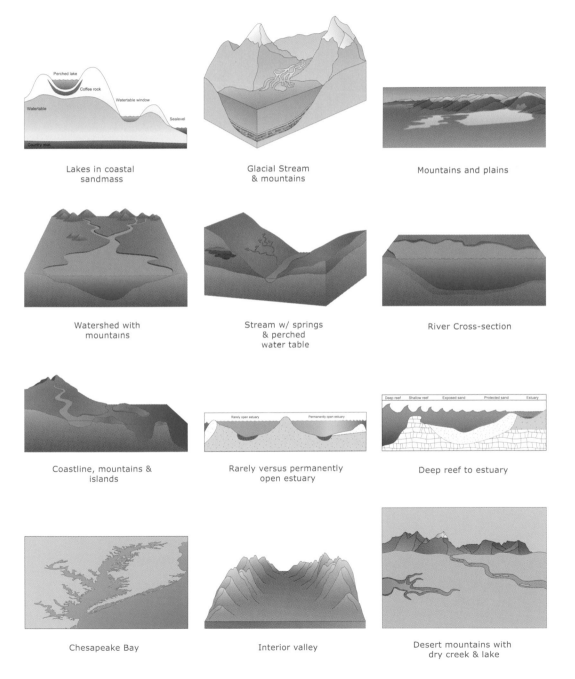

Lakes in coastal sandmass

Glacial Stream & mountains

Mountains and plains

Watershed with mountains

Stream w/ springs & perched water table

River Cross-section

Coastline, mountains & islands

Rarely versus permanently open estuary

Deep reef to estuary

Chesapeake Bay

Interior valley

Desert mountains with dry creek & lake

Artists

Agnew Moyer Smith, Inc.
503 Martindale Street
Pittsburgh, PA 15212
412-322-6333
rhenkel@amsite.com
www.amsite.com

Ted Alspach
Group Product Manager
Adobe Creative Suite
Adobe Systems, Incorporated
345 Park Ave., Mailstop W11
San Jose, CA 95110
talspach@adobe.com
www.adobe.com/creative suite

Kevan Atteberry
P.O. Box 40188
Bellevue, WA 98015-4188
206-550-6353
kevan@oddisgood.com
www.oddisgood.com

Kenneth Batelman
128 Birch Leaf Drive
Milford, PA 18337
888-532-0612
Kenneth@batelman.com
batelman.com

Christine Beauregard
2324 Sainte-Cunégonde
Montreal, Quebec H3V 2W3
514-935-6794
c.beauregard@videotron.ca
www.christinebeauregard.com

Russell Benafant
www.benfanti.com
represented by
www.mendolaart.com
212.986.5680

Eliot Bergman
362 West 20th Street
New York, NY 10011

Peter Cassell
1185 Design
411 High Street
Palo Alto, CA 94301
650-325-4804
peterc@1185design.com
www.1185design.com

David Cater
510-232-9420
adcater@aol.com

Ron Chan
24 Nelson Ave.
Mill Valley, CA 94941
415-389-6549

Conrad Chavez
design@conradchavez.com
www.conradchavez.com

Bryan Christie
www.bryanchristiedesign.com/

Sandee Cohen
33 Fifth Avenue, #10B
New York, NY 10003
212-677-7763
sandee@vectorbabe.com
www.vectorbabe.com

Scott B. Crouse
Lake Alfred, FL
scott@scottcrouse.com
scottcrouse.com

Shayne Davidson
Medical Illustration & Graphics
1301 Granger Ave.
Ann Arbor, MI 48104
734-994-6223 /
734-998-6140 ext133
sdmedill@umich.edu
www.medicalart.net

Rob Day & Virginia Evans
10 State Street, Suite 214
Newburyport, MA 01950
508-465-1386

Design Action Collective
369 15th Street
Oakland, CA 94612
510-452-1912
info@designaction.org
www.designaction.org

Timothy Donaldson
Domus Crossheads
Colwich Staffordshire ST180UG
England
01889 88 20 43
e@timothydonaldson.com
www.timothydonaldson.com

Virginia Evans, *see* Day & Evans

Gary Ferster
10 Karen Drive
Tinton Falls, NJ 07753
732-922-8903
Fax: 732-922-8970
gferster@comcast.net
www.garyferster.com/

Louis Fishauf
47 Lorne Ave.
Kettleby, Ontario
Canada L0G1J0
905-726-1597
fishauf@reactor.ca
www.fishauf.com

Mark Fox
415-258-9663
mfox@blackdogma.com

Ian Giblin
408-448-2614
n.giblin@comcast.net

Reggie Gilbert
Tech Vector
1454 Ashland St PMB#141
Ashland OR 97520
www.techvector.com

Mordy Golding
Design Responsibly LLC
320 Leroy Avenue
Cedarhurst, NY 11516
info@designresponsibly.com
www.designresponsibly.com

Janet Good
Industrial Illustrators, Inc.
P.O. Box 497
Harrison City, PA 15636-0497
800-683-9316
janet@ix3.com
jlgood524@earthlink.net
ix3.com

Steven H. Gordon
Cartagram, LLC
136 Mill Creek Crossing
Madison, AL 35758
wow@cartagram.com
www.cartagram.com

Caryl Gorska
1277 8th Avenue 105
San francisco, CA 94122
415-664-7721
408-910-6545
gorska@gorska.com
www.gorska.com

Laurie Grace
860-659-0748
lgrace@aol.com

April Greiman
620 MoultonAve. No. 211
Los Angeles, CA 90031
323-227-1222
info@madeinspace.la
ww.madeinspace.la

Brad Hamann
Brad Hamann Illustration &
Design
41 West Market Street
Red Hook, NY 12571
845-758-6186 studio
bhamann@hvc.rr.com
www.darkdesign.com

Michael Hamm
13555 Breton Ridge St. #426
Houston, TX 77070
281-451-6841
michael@pointsandpaths.com
www.pointsandpaths.com

Scott Hansen
scott@iso50.com
www.iso50.com

Pattie Belle Hastings
Ice House Press & Design
Pattie Belle Hastings
266 West Rock Ave.
New Haven, CT 06515
203-389-7334

Rick Henkel,
see Agnew Moyer Smith

Kurt Hess,
see Agnew Moyer Smith

Lance Hidy
2 Summer St.
Merrimac, MA 01860
978-346-0075

Kaoru Hollin
kaoruhollin@attbi.com

Gerard Huerta
Gerard Huerta Design, Inc.
54 Old Post Road
Southport, CT 06890
203-256-1625
gerard.huerta@sbcglobal.net
www.gerardhuerta.com

IAN Symbols (Integration and
Application Network)
University of Maryland Center
for Environmental Science
2020 Horns Point Rd
(PO Box 775)
Cambridge, MD 21613
410-228-9250 ext 254
ian@ca.umes.edu
http://ian.umces.edu/symbols

Lisa Jackmore
13603 Bluestone Court
Clifton, VA 20124
703-830-0985
ljackmore@cox.net

Lance Jackson
Lax Syntax Design
ljackson@sfchronicle.com

Jared Schneidman Design
16 Parkway
Katonah, NY 10536
914-232-1499

Dave Joly
15 King St.
Putnam, CT 06260
860-928-1042

Frank Jonen
Haupstrasse 15
65510 Idstein
Germany
49-6126 9581 81
Fax 49-6126 9581 83
getinfo@frankjonen.com
www.frankjonen.com

Joe Jones
Art Works Studio
802 Poplar St
Denver, CO 80220
303-377-7745
joejones@artworksstudio.com
www.artworksstudio.com

John Kanzler
424 Adams Road
Greenfield, Ma 01301
413-773-7368
800-210-0711
john@johnkanzler.com
www.johnkanzler.com

Andrea Kelley
Andrea Kelley Design
530 Menlo Oaks Drive
Menlo Park, CA 94025
650-326-1083
andrea@jevans.com

Marc LaMantia
64 Macdougal Street Apt 5
New York, NY 10012
212-677-6907
lamantia2003@yahoo.com

Tiffany Larsen
tiffany@uberpop.com
uberpop.com

Adam Z Lein
3 Woodlands Ave
Elmsford, NY 10523
914-347-1710
adamz@lein.com
www.adamlein.com

Joe Lertola
TIME / Editorial Art Dept
1271 Sixth Avenue / Rm 2442
New York, NY 10020
212-522-3721
www.joelertola.com

Vicki Loader
vickiloader@btopenworld.com

Terrance (Terry) Lush
info@tlush.net
www.tlush.net

Ma Zhi Liang
mazhiliangb@online.sh.cn

Todd Macadangdang
348 Arco St.
San Jose, CA 95123
408-536-6373
toddm@adobe.com
toddm@illustratorworld.com

Jacqueline Mahannah
Medical and Biological
Illustration
Mahannahj@aol.com

Rob Magiera
Noumena Digital
9636 Ruskin Circle
Salt Lake City, UT 84092
801-943-3650

Greg Maxson
116 W. Florida Ave
Urbana, IL 61801
217-337-6069
gmaxti@sbcglobal.net
gregmaxson.com
portsort.com

Eden Maxwell
artist@edensart.com
www.edensart.com

Nobuko Miyamoto
3-8 Matuba-cho
Tokorozawa-shi
Saitama-ken Japan/359-0044
04-2998-6631
venus@gol.com
http://venus.orracchi.com

Yukio Miyamoto
3-8 Matuba-cho
Tokorozawa-shi
Saitama-ken Japan/359-0044
04-2998-6631
yukio-m@ppp.bekkoame.ne.jp
www.bekkoame.ne.jp/~yukio-m

Bert Monroy
11 Latham Lane
Berkeley, CA 94708
510-524-9412
www.bertmonroy.com

Gary J. Moss
Moss Martin Graphic Design
319 Peck Street Box I-5
New Haven, CT 06513
203-785-8464
gm@mossmartin.net
mossmartin.net

Joachim Müller-Lancé
125 A Stillman St.
San Francisco, CA 94108
www.kamedesign.com

Innosanto Nagara
Design Action Collective
369 15th Street
Oakland, CA 94612
510-452-1912
info@designaction.org
www.designaction.org

Brad Neal
Thomas • Bradley Illustration
& Design
411 Center St. / P.O. Box 249
Gridley, IL 61744
309-747-3266
bradneal@thomas-bradley.com
www.thomasbradley.com

David Nelson
Mapping Services
721 Grape St.
Denver, CO 80220
303-333-1060

Gary Newman Design
2447 Burnside Rd
Sebastapol, CA 95472
gary@newmango.com
www.newmango.com

Chris D. Nielsen
714-323-1602
carartwork@comcast.net
htpp://home.comcast.
net~carartwork

Richard Ng, photographer
www.istockphoto/richard_ng

Ann Paidrick
5520 Virginia Ave.
St. Louis, MO 63111
314-351-1705
annpaid@attglobal.net
www.ebypaidrick.com

Ellen Papciak-Rose
In The Studio
inthestudio@mac.com
http://homepage.mac.com/
inthestudio

Tom Patterson
National Park Service
Media Development
Harpers Ferry Center
Harpers Ferry, WV 25425-0050
304-535-6020
t.patterson@nps.gov
www.nacis.org/cp/cp28/
resources.html

Daniel Pelavin
212-941-7418
daniel@pelavin.com
www.pelavin.com

John Pirman
johnpirman@aol.com
represented by
Gerald & Cullen Rapp
212-889-3337

David S. Pounds
7 Greenmoor
Irvine, CA 92614
949-733-0226
davidpounds@hisnet.org
www.hisnet.org/userpages/
davidpounds

Gary Powell
2417 SW Olson
Pendleton, OR 97801
541-276-6330
oil_artist@comcast.net

Tracey Saxby, *see* IAN Symbols

Jared Schneidman Design
155 Katonah Ave.
Katonah, NY 10536
914-232-1499
jared@jsdinfographics.com
jsdinfographics.com

Mike Schwabauer
Hallmark Cards, Inc.
2501 McGee, Box 419580, MD
142
Kansas City, MO 64141-6580
816-545-6948
mschwa2@hallmark.com

Robert Sharif
2791 Lexford Ave.
San Jose, CA 95124
rsharif@earthlink.net
sharifr@adobe.com

Joe Shoulak
joe@joeshoulak.com
joeshoulak.com.

Steve Spindler
Steve Spindler Cartography
1504 South St.
Philadelphia, PA 19146
215-985-2839
steve@bikemap.com
www.bikemap.com

Christopher Spollen
Moonlightpress Studio
362 Cromwell Ave.
Staten Island, NY 10305
718-979-9695
cjspollen@aol.com
spollen.com

Nancy Stahl
nancy@nancystahl.com
www.nancystahl.com

Steven Stankiewicz
artfromsteve@aol.com
www.porfolios.com/
stevenstankiewicz

Judy Stead
407-310-0051
judy@judystead.com
judystead.com

Sharon Steuer
c/o Peachpit Press
1249 Eighth St.
Berkeley, CA 94710
www.ssteuer.com

Barbara Sudick
California State University
Dept. of Communication
Design
Chico, CA 95929
530-898-5028

Clarke W. Tate
Tate Studio
P.O. Box 339 / 301 Woodford St.
Gridley, IL 61744-0339
312-453-0694
clarke@tatestudio.com
www.tatestudio.com

Kathleen Tinkel
MacPrePress
12 Burr Road
Westport, CT 06880
203-227-2357

Jack Tom
1042 Broad Street
Bridgeport, CT 06604
203-579-0889
jacktom@sbcglobal.net
jacktom.com

Ivan Torres
12933 Ternberry Ct.
Tustin, CA 92782
714-734-4356
ivanjessica@sbcglobal.net
ivanjessica2002@yahoo.com
www.meshsmith.com

Jean-Claude Tremblay
Illustrator Instructor & Prepress
Technician
7180 Des Erables
Montreal (Quebec)
Canada H2E 2R3

Trina Wai
5027 Silver Reef Dr.
Fremont, CA 94538

Timothy Webb
Tim Webb Illustration
305 W. Maywood
Wichita, KS 67217
316-524-3881
tim@timwebb.com
www.timwebb.com

Alan James Weimer
67 Bliss Street
Rehoboth, MA 0276-1932
508-252-9236
illustrator51@comcast.net

Ari M. Weinstein
ari@ariw.com
ariw.com

Hugh Whyte
Lehner & Whyte
8-10 South Fullerton Ave.
Montclair, NJ 07402
201-746-1335

Tom Willcockson
Mapcraft Cartography
731 Margaret Drive
Woodstock, IL 60098
815-337-7137

Filip Yip
877-463-4547
filip@yippe.com
www.yippe.com

Ma Zhiliang, Ma Zhi Liang
see alphabetized under Ma

Resources

Adobe Systems, Inc.
345 Park Avenue
San Jose, CA 95110-2704
408-536-6000
www.adobe.com

AGFA
prepress, production
Agfa Corp.
100 Challenger Road
Ridgefield Park, NJ 07660
201-440-2500
www.agfa.com

Ambrosia Software, Inc.
SnapzProX
PO BOX 23140
Rochester, NY 14692
800-231-1816
www.AmbrosiaSW.com

Apago, Inc.
*PDF Enhancer, Piktor,
PDF/X Checkup*
4080 McGinnis Ferry Road,
Suite 601
Alpharetta, GA 30005 USA
770 619-1884
www.apago.com

Apple Computer
ColorSync, QuickTime
800-767-2775
www.apple.com

Aridi Computer Graphics
Digital Art
P.O. Box 797702
Dallas, TX 75379
972-404-9171
www.aridi.com

Artlandia, Inc.
Artlandia SymmetryWorks
2015 Barberry Cr.
Champaign, IL 61821-5862
Toll-free: +1 (888) 972-6366
www.artlandia.com

@Last Software, Inc.
1433 Pearl Street, Suite 100
Boulder, CO 80302
303-245-0086
Fax: 303-245-8562
info@sketchup.com

Avenza Systems Inc.
MAPublisher
124 Merton Street Suite 400
Toronto, Ontario
Canada M4S 2Z2
416-487-5116
Fax: 416-487-7213
sales: 800-884-2555
www.avenza.com

Bare Bones Software, Inc.
BBEdit
P.O. Box 1048
Bedford, MA 01730
781-778-3100
www.barebones.com

Cartesia Software
Digital Maps
PO Box 757
Lambertville, NJ 08530
800-334-4291 (x3)
www.mapresources.com

CDS Documentation Services
printer of this book
2661 South Pacific Highway
Medford, OR 97501
541-773-7575

Comnet Co., Ltd.
*LogoSpruce FoldUP!3D
Professional design plug-ins
for Illustrator*
Sannomiya Grand Building 8F
2-2-21 Isogamidori, Chuo-ku
Kobe 651-0086 Japan
Fax: 1-877-804-2912 (US only)
www.comnet-network.co.jp

Corel Corporation
Painter
1600 Carling Ave.
Ottawa, ON Canada K1Z 8R7
800-772-6735
www.corel.com

CValley, Inc.
*FILTERiT4.1, CAD-COMPO,
Xtream Path*
212 Technology Dr. Suite N
Irvine, CA 92618
949-727-9161
www.cvalley.com

Dantz
Retrospect backup software
www.dantz.com

Design Tools Monthly
303-543-8400
Fax: 303-543-8300
info@design-tools.com
www.design-tools.com

Digital Wisdom, Inc.
*cartographic symbols & profes-
sional vector artwork for Illustrator, FreeHand, Corel Draw*
Tappahannock, Virginia
800-800-8560 / 804-443-9000
Fax: 804-443-3632
www.map-symbol.com/
info@map-symbol.com

Dynamic Graphics Inc.
clipart, etc.
6000 N. Forest Pk. Drive
Peoria, IL 61614
800-255-8800
www.dgusa.com

hot door
CADtools, Perspective, MultiPage
101 W. McKnight Way, Suite B
Grass Valley, CA 95949
1-888-236-9540
www.hotdoor.com

IAN Symbols
Integration and Application
Network
University of Maryland Center
for Environmental Science
Adrian Jones
2020 Horns Point Rd
(PO Box 775)
Cambridge, MD 21613
410-228-9250 ext 254
ian@ca.umes.edu
http://ian.umces.edu/symbols

Image Club Graphics
now available through:
www.fotosearch.com/image-
club/

iStockphoto
www.istockphoto

Macromedia
FreeHand, Dreamweaver, Flash
600 Townsend Street
San Francisco, CA 94103
800-989-3762
www.macromedia.com

Metafusion Training, LLC
25 NW 23rd Place/Suite 6-122
Portland, OR 97210-5599
Gabriel Powell
Senior Training Director
gabriel@metafusiontraining.com
www.metafusiontraining.com

Pantone, Inc.
color matching products
590 Commerce Blvd.
Carlstadt, NJ 07072
866-PANTONE
www.pantone.com

Photosphere
2272 Philip Avenue
North Vancouver, BC
Canada V7P 2W8
800-665-1496
604.924.5377
Fax: 604.904.3831
www.photosphere.com

SepPreview 2.0
Schawk, Inc.
Douglas Habben
Graphic Systems Analyst/
    Programmer
847-759-7091
Schawk IT Dept. 72a
1600 East Sherwin Avenue
Des Plaines, IL 60018
dept72a@schawk.com
dhabben@schawk.com

Steven Vincent
Illustrator plugins author
http://www.kagi.com/svincent/
default.html
svincent@kagi.com

TruMatch, Inc.
color matching software
50 East 72nd, Suite 15B
New York, NY 10021
800-878-9100
www.trumatch.com

Ultimate Symbol
Design Elements, clipart
31 Wilderness Drive
Stony Point, NY 10980
845-942-0003
www.ultimatesymbol.com

General Index

.ai file extension, 3, 31, 33, 380
.ait file extension, 3, 63, 122, 380
@Last Software, 416
2D artwork, 316–323
2D objects, 302, 303, 306
2D paths, 304, 314–315
3D bevel shapes, 303
3D effect dialog box, 302
3D effects, 302–323, See also live
    3D effects
    adding columns to create, 349
    applying multiple, 281
    creating basic paths, 310–311
    introduction of, 280
    programs for creating, 382
    and RAM, 305
    simple techniques, 308–309
    single-axes movements in, 308
3D Extrude & Bevel effect, 316–
    317, 319, 320
3D Extrude & Bevel Options
    dialog box, 303, 309, 313
"3D Logo Object" lesson, 312–313
3D modeling programs, 402, 404
3D objects, See also 3D effects
    applying surface shading to,
        305–306
    creating, 304, 314–315
    mapping artwork onto, 306, 317
    rotating, 304–305, 315
    smoothing, 305
    surface shading, 305–306
    transforming 2D objects into,
        302
3D packages, 316–323
3D programs, 378, 382
3D Revolve effect, 312–313, 320,
    322
3D StudioPro, 382
"3D–Three dialogs" Tip, 303
"9 Lives" cat symbol, 200–203
216-color palette, 30, 366
1185 Design, 265, 278, 412

A

Acrobat, 31, 258, 382, See also PDF
    format
Acrobat Distiller, 382
Acrobat PDF Maker, 277
Acrobat Reader, 31, 258
actions, 35–36, 77, 326, 358
Actions palette, 35–36, 358
AD Design & Consulting, 412
Add Anchor Point tool, 10, 11, 41,
    68, 243
Add Anchor Points command, 43,
    45, 177
Add Arrowheads command, 322
Add New Fill command, 128, 129,
    176
Add New Stroke command, 128,
    158
Add to Shape Area command, 203
Add to Shape Pathfinder
    command, 202, 203
Adobe Bridge, 36, 272
Adobe Color Picker, 29, 61, 362
Adobe Online, 35
Adobe Premier, 356
Adobe Stock Photos, 36
Adobe SVG Viewer, 362
Adobe Systems, 412, 416
"Africa" type treatment, 168–169
African Art exhibit, 182–184
After Effects, 356, 374–375
AGFA, 416
Agnew Moyer Smith (AMS),
    74–78, 412
AI files, 3, 379, 382
AICB (Adobe Illustrator
    Clipboard), 379, 381
"AICS2 images & files cropped!"
    warning, 2
Airbrush tool, 396, 403
airplanes, 395, 400
Alias Sketch!, 402
Align palette, 14–16
aligning
    to Artboard, 15
    meshes, 349
    objects, 12, 14–16
    relative to bounding box, 15
    by snapping to point, 12
    type, 150
Alspach, Ted, 288–289, 291, 412
Ambrosia Software, 416
AMS (Agnew Moyer Smith),
    74–78, 412
anchor points
    adding, 11, 68
changing to Pen tool, 9
converting, 10–11
creating, 7–8
defined, 7
deleting, 9, 11, 68, 216
non-printing, 8
selecting, 13
snapping objects to, 9
"Ancient 2000" CD-ROM, 73
Angle Threshold setting, 68
angles
    for Bézier curves, 8, 9
    constrain, 28, 77
    gradient, 223
"Animating Pieces" lesson,
    374–376
animation
    with After Effects, 374–375
    exporting, 360–363, 365,
        371–372
    Flash, 361–363
    Gallery pages, 373, 376
    and GoLive, 356
    lessons, 364–365, 370–372,
        374–376
    ordering, 375
    preparing artwork for, 370–371
    previewing, 370–372
    and Release to Layers command,
        359–360
    repurposing print artwork for,
        364
    robot character, 206–208
    tools for, 92, 356, 376
antialiasing, 25, 356, 366, 386
"Anti-antialiasing" Tip, 367
"Antiquing Type" lesson, 182–184
Apago, Inc., 416
appearance indicators, 127
Appearance palette, 127–129
    adding multiple fills/strokes
        with, 129
    and applied transparency,
        263–264
    designing intricate effects with,
        140
    editing warp effects in, 283
    stacking order for, 129
    targeting elements in, 128
    using with type, 155, 158–160
    working with, 258–259

F

fading masks, 332–335
Fairfield University poster, 162–163
Fall illustration, 239
feathered edges, 253–254
feathering, 114–115, 345, 354
Ferster, Gary, 73, 236–237, 338,
 contact information, 412
Fidelity option, 13, 91, 294
file formats, *See also specific formats*
 and exporting, 360–363
 Illustrator and other programs, 380–381
 for images, 32–33, 358, 360
 and linking, 378
 source of additional information on, 380
file-naming system, 24
files, *See also* documents; images
 bringing to front, 27
 controlling size of, 34–35, 35
 legacy, 258
 multi-version, 124
 naming, 24
 optimizing, 358
 printing, *See* printing
 reverting to earlier version of, 24
 saving, *See* saving
 templates for, *See* templates
"Fill Rules.pdf" file, 187
Fill/Stroke icon, 18
fills
 adding to appearances, 128–129
 adding to letters, 181, 182
 adding to objects, 60–61
 adding to paths, 287
 applying, 286
 color, 61, 196
 compound paths, 187
 copying, 18, 129
 creating multiple, 129
 default, 61
 deleting, 129
 described, 60
 gap detection, 197
 with Live Paint, 198, 207–208
 multiple, 129
 offset, 180–181
 patterns, 180–181, 305
 reapplying, 196

 redirecting, 234–235
 solid vs. patterns, 305
 strokes, 61
 swapping attributes for, 60
 using tints for, 71
 using transparency with, 233, 250, 276
Filter menu, 280, 283
FILTERiT4.1, 416
filters, *See also specific filters*
 for adding anchor points, 45
 color-modification, 68
 for distorting, 67–68
 setting measurement units for, 7
Final Cut video editing program, 263
Find Font command, 154–155
finding
 fonts, 154–155
 masks, 329
 objects, 75
finger dances, 39, 54, 56–58
fire station, 345
Fishauf, Louis, 175, 267, 412
fishing lure, 346
Fit Headline command, 155
flags, 292–295
Flare tool, 184, 281, 291
Flash
 animation, 361–363, 370–372, 376
 copying and pasting artwork into, 372
 importing symbols into, 371
 and Release to Layers command, 359–360
 using Illustrator files with, 361–363
Flash Export dialog box, 361
Flash files, 361–363
Flatten Artwork command, 123
Flatten Transparency command/ dialog box, 254–256
Flattener Preview palette, 34, 254–257, 256–257
flattening, 34, 254–259
Flip Horizontal/Vertical option, 22
flipping type, 150
"Floating Type" lesson, 268–269
Flood typeface, 174
flowers, 82–85, 224, 260–262, 352
Focoltone, 30

FoldUp!3D, 416
fonts, *See also* text; type
 embedded, 157
 finding, 154–155
 getting profession help with, 155
 for hand-rendered look, 299
 highlighting substituted, 154
 licenses, 157
 Linotype collections, 332–335
 missing, 154–155
 multinational, 156
 OpenType, 153
 replacing, 154
 Roman and Vertical Area Type, 160
 Yakima, 303
football player, 405
foreground images, 213, 214
foreign language, 157
formats, *See* file formats
formatting text, 157–158, *See also* styles
Fort Santiago illustration, 142–143
Fox, Mark, 199, 200–203, 412
fractions, 153
frames, layering, 364–365
Free Distort tool, 217
Free Transform tool
 adding energy/movement with, 80–81
 alternatives to, 20, 21
 creating perspective with, 81, 313
 described, 20–21
 distorting objects with, 67
 vs. bounding box, 20–21
"Free Transform variations" Tip, 21
FreeHand, 378, 416
French horn, 351
Friskets, 8
"From one swatch to another" Tip, 75
fruit, 330–331
Full Screen mode, 26

G

Gallery pages, xviii
Game Developer **cover art**, 216
gamut warning, 33

graphs, 277
grass, 116
grayscale images, 272–273
Great River Scenic Byway map, 138–139
"greeked" type, 156
"Green Tortoise" bus poster, 161
Greiman, April, 393, 413
grids, *See also* guides
    creating, 48–49
    creating typefaces from, 172–175
    customizing, 28, 250
    drawing, 13
    hiding/showing, 28
    making, 172
    purpose of, 172
    size, 172–173
    snap-to function for, 28
    working with, 27–28
Group Isolation Mode, xiv, 24, 186, 194–198, 208
Group layers, 125
Group Selection tool, 14, 205
groups
    assigning styles to, 141
    blending between, 222, 223
    changing arrows to, 322
    duplicating, 120
    layers, 125
    Live Paint, 194–198, 196
    objects, 13–14, 125, 194–195
    renaming, 125
    selecting all items in, 126–127
    targeting all items in, 128
    using transparency with, 250
guides, *See also* grids
    and blended objects, 143
    converting lines into, 142–143
    creating, 27
    customizing, 165
    lines as, 374–375
    locking/unlocking, 27, 142, 143
    preferences, 27, 28
    snapping to, 9, 143
    working with, 27–28
guitar, 162–163, 319
gzipped format, 362

H

Habben, Douglas, 417
Hallmark Cards, 318, 414
halos, 291
Hamann, Brad
    3D effects, 303, 304, 310–311
    contact information, 413
    "Crunching Type," 176–177, 283
    "E-MEN" cover title, 176–177, 283
    "Shape Shifting," 388–389
Hamm, Michael, 313, 413
Hand tool, 4, 25
handles, 8
hands, 394
Hansen, Scott, 216–217, 413
hard drive, 2
hardware calibration, 28
hardware requirements, 2
Hastings, Pattie Belle, xv, 413
hatch effects, 281, 282, 298
haze effects, 246–247
head tags, 368
headlines, 155, 176–177
Hebrew wedding certificate, 166–167
Help feature, viii, xiv, 34
Henkel, Rick, 74–78, 413
Herb Pharm logo, 312
Hess, Kurt, 76, 78, 413
hidden items, printing/viewing, 126
Hide command, 126
hiding/showing
    bounding box, 21, 28
    characters, 155
    edges, 22, 28, 297
    grids, 28
    layers, 97, 120, 122, 124, 139
    objects, 126
    page tiling, 4
    palettes, 21
    paragraph symbols, 155
    rulers, 26–27
    sublayers, 139
    text threads, 151
    tiling, 4
Hidy, Lance, 394, 413
Highlight Substituted Fonts option, 154
highlights
    creating, 71–72, 264–267

metallic, 236–237
objects, 28, 264
radial gradients, 239
with transparency, 264, 270–271
highway symbol, 141
hills, rolling, 242–243
holes, 187, 198, 204–205
holiday card, 296–297
Hollin, Kaoru, 110–112, 413
horizontal ruler, 302
hot door CADtools, 398, 416
"Hot Rod Rocket" image, 403
houses, 40–47
HSB color space, 30
HTML editors/files, 358, 368
Huerta, Gerard, 162–163, 413
hugerecords.com Web site, 374–375
hyphenation, 154

I

IAN Symbols, 114, 408–411, 413, 416
Ice House Press & Design, 413
iced tea, illustration, 353
illustrations, *See also* artwork; images
    lifelike, 347, 353
    magazine, 274–275
    product, 336–339
    realistic, 347, 353
Illustrator
    advanced techniques, 326–354
    basic techniques, 2–36
    flexibility of, 38
    glossary, 2
    and hand/eye coordination, 39
    Help feature, xiv, xviii, 34
    integration with other programs, 379–382
    keys to mastering, 38–39
    navigation techniques, 5–7
    older versions of, 123
    plug-ins, 406–407
    preferences, 3
    as stand-alone layout tool, 164–165
    status line in, 24
    system requirements, 2
    User Guide for, xiv
    as Web design tool, 366–367

Welcome screen, 2, 3
Illustrator CS2 Wow! Course Outline, xv
Illustrator Options dialog box, 258
Image Club Graphics, 416
image formats, 32–33, 358, 360
image maps, 358, 369
ImageReady, 359
images, *See also* artwork; files; illustrations
    creating new, 2–3
    dimmed, 122
    displaying different aspects of, 24–28
    embedded, 379
    file formats for, 32–33, 358, 360
    foreground, 213
    importing, 114
    linked vs embedded, 32, 378, 379
    masking, *See* masking
    modifying, 168
    naming, 24
    opening existing, 3
    perspective, *See* perspective
    placing, 165, 168
    printing, *See* printing
    saving, *See* saving
    scanned, 130–131, 210, 272–273
    templates for, *See* templates
    tracing, *See* tracing
importing
    artwork/images, 96, 114, 361–362
    existing layer/sublayer, 134
    symbols, 371
    as template layers, 96
in-betweens, 220
in port, 148, 149, 151
In The Studio, 414
InDesign, 153, 381–382
InDesign CS Visual QuickStart Guide, 153
indexed color, 215
Industrial Illustrators, 230, 413
Infini-D, 404
Info palette, 235
Inner Glow effect, 140, 271, 274–275
instances, 93–94
Intensity option, 94
"**Interactive Print Preview**" Tip, 4

interlaced GIF, 360
Intersect Pathfinder command, 201–202
"**Intricate Patterns**" lesson, 86–87
Invert Wrap command, 151
isometric formulas, 76–79
"**Isometric Systems**" lesson, 76–79
iStockphoto, 416

J

Jackmore, Lisa, xv, 100–101, 413
Jackson, Lance, 161, 209, 232, 397, 413
Jacoby, Frank, 263
Japanese fonts, 156
JavaScript, 363
Jeep, 338
Jenkins, George, 212–214
Jerusalem map, 136
Join function, 16–17, 44–45
Join styles, 67
joining
    curves, 201
    endpoints, 16–17
    error message, 16
    objects, 44–45, 45
    paths, 203
    while averaging, 16–17, 17, 44–45
Joly, Dave, 194, 206–208, 234–235, 413
Jonen, Frank, 332–335, 413
Jones, Adrian, 416
Jones, Joe, 400, 413
JPEG format, 209, 358, 360
justification, 154

K

Kanzler, John, 80–81, 413
Kelley, Andrea, 70–72, 270–271, 413
kerning, 163, 299
Ketubah, 166–167
"**KevanAtteberry-blends.ai**" file, 222
Keyboard Increment settings, 43, 367
keyboard shortcuts, xvi, 5–6, *See also* power-keys

keyframes, 364–365
kiosk, 263
kite, 276, 398
Knife tool, 12, 374
knockouts, 253–254
Korean fonts, 156

L

labels, 74–75, 75, 306, 321
LaMantia, Marc, 344, 413
Larsen, Tiffany, 69, 266, 413
Lasso tool, 13, 77, 243
Last Color proxy, 61
@Last Software, 416
Lax Syntax Design, 413
layer-based slices, 359
layer masks, 251, 331
Layer Options dialog box, 120, 121–122
"**Layering Frames**" lesson, 364–365
layers, 120–143, *See also* sublayers and Layers palette
    activating, 124
    adding to Layers palette, 120
    assigning appearance attributes to, 141
    blending modes, 262
    color, 121
    contiguous, 120
    converting sublayers to, 139
    copying objects between, 135
    custom, 97, 132–137
    deleting, 120, 134
    described, 120
    dimmed images, 122
    distributing artwork/objects to, 92, 359–360
    duplicating, 120, 213
    exporting CSS, 363
    grouping, 125
    hiding/showing, 97, 120, 122, 124, 139
    importing art into, 134
    lessons on, 130–143
    locking/unlocking, 97, 120, 121, 122, 125–126, 139, 213
    moving, 139
    naming, 121, 133
    nested, 138–139
    non-printing, 122

end cap styles, 66
refining with Pencil tool, 131
tangent, 202
linked images
applying transparency to, 378
and file size, 35, 378
vs. embedded, 32, 378–379, 379
"Links are manageable" Tip, 32
Links palette, 32
Linotype font collections, 332–335
Liquify tools, 67
live 3D effects, 302–323, *See also*
3D effects
described, 302
extruding objects, 302, 303
revolving/rotating objects,
304–305, 312
shading 3D objects, 305–306
simple techniques, 308–309
live effects, 257, 280, 282, 299
Live Paint Bucket tool, 64, 157,
190, 194–198, 208
Live Paint command, 186
Live Paint feature, 194–198, *See
also* painting
coloring paths with, 195–196
editing paths with, 198
filling areas with, 198, 207–208
Group Isolation Mode and, xiv,
186, 194–198
groups in, 194–198, 207, 208
using Live Trace with, 190, 192,
193
Live Paint objects, 47, 190, 193,
221
Live Paint Selection tool, 198
Live Trace command, 114, 186
Live Trace feature, 190–193
assembling composition, 211
Gallery pages, 209–211
global swatches, 213
JPEG images, 209
options, 207, 215
scanning sketches for, 210
tracing images with, 114, 190–
191, 207, 215, 216
using swatch libraries with,
192–193
using with Live Paint, 190, 192,
193
Live Trace objects, 191–192, 207,
214
Loader, Vicki, 94, 129, 280, 413

Locate Layer command, 123, 139
Locate Object command, 123, 139
Lock All Layers/Others command,
124
Lock command, 125–126
Lock Guides command, 142, 143
locking/unlocking
all items, 125–126
guides, 27, 142, 143
layers, 97, 120–122, 125–126,
139, 213
objects, 125–126
sublayers, 139
template layers, 121
logos
basketball, 228–229
Craik Consulting, Inc., 48–49
digitizing, 130–131
Herb Pharm, 312
QuickBooks, 236–239
"Rivers For Life," 178–179
ungrouping objects in, 194–195
LogoSpruce, 416
Louveaux, Pierre, 128, 187, 224,
250
Lurd illustrations, 193, 210–211
Lush, Terry, 374–375, 413

M

Ma, Zhiliang, 248, 413
Mac OS X, 258
Macadangdang, Todd, 298, 413
Macintosh
keyboard shortcuts, xvi
and Page Setup button, 4–5
preferences, 3
rendering engine, 258
system requirements, 2
MacPrePress, 415
Macromedia, contact information,
416
Macromedia Flash (SWF) export,
361–363
magazine advertisements, 402
magazine illustrations, 274–275
Magiera, Rob, 384–386, 413
magnification percentages, 27
Mah, Derek, tip, 220
Mahannah, Jacqueline, 107, 413
Make command, 165
Make Guides command, 143

Make Opacity Mask command,
252, 278
"Make Time" illustration, 204–205
Make With Warp command, 177
"Making a Typeface" lesson,
172–175
Map Art feature, 306, 311, 317
map symbol artwork, 308–309
Mapcraft Cartography, 401, 415
mapping artwork, 317
Mapping Services, 414
mapping symbols, 306
maps
backdrops for, 227
Boston, 170–171
Chicago, 140–142
color in, 227
creating layer structure for,
138–139
Great River Scenic Byway,
138–139
image, 358, 369
Jerusalem, 136
Sonoran Desert, 322
sources of, 414, 416
various examples of, 106, 323,
401
William Patterson University,
401
MAPublisher, 416
Mardi Gras illustration, 266
market illustration, 347
mask-editing mode, 275
mask error message, 329
"Mask Upon Mask" lesson,
332–339
masking
advanced techniques, 326–329
lessons on, 330–335
with letter forms, 168–169
RAM considerations, 329
raster shapes, 386
"Masking Details" lesson, 330–331
"Masking Words" lesson, 168–169
masks
blending, 332–335
clipping, 326–328
details, 330–331
editing, 251, 275
fading, 332–335
finding, 329
identifying, 329
inserting objects in, 328

masks, *continued*
  layer, 251, 331
  and legacy documents, 329
  multiple objects as, 329
  opacity, *See* opacity masks
  problem-solving strategies,
      328–329
  Quick Masks, 384
  RAM considerations, 329
  shadows, 330–331
  troubleshooting, 329
  using compound masks as,
      328–329, 330–331
  using multiple objects as, 326
  using type as, 328–329
Maxson, Greg, 95, 399, 414
Maxwell, Eden, 276, 398, 414
McDonald's packaging design,
    142–143
McHugh, Joshua, 204
measurement units, 7, 17, 146
mechanical objects, 70–73, 404
medallion designs, 342–343
Median filter, 215
Medical and Biological
    Illustration, 413
Medical Illustration & Graphics,
    412
medical illustrations, 105, 118,
    412, 413
memory, *See* RAM
menus, *See also specific menus*
  context-sensitive, 7, 26
  Illustrator CS, 5–6, 7
  restaurant, 364–365
Merge Graphic Styles command,
    285
Merge Pathfinder command, 189
Merge Selected command, 123
Mesh tool, *See also* gradient mesh
    224, 243, 265, 351, 352
meshes, *See* gradient meshes, mesh
    tool
"Meshsmith" art piece, 348–350
meta tags, 368
Metafusion Training, 417
metallic surfaces, 236–239
MetaTools Infini-D, 404
Miami Dolphins illustrations,
    215, 405
Microsoft Excel, 277

"Millard and the Pear" animation,
    370–372
Mini Cooper, 337
Minus Back Pathfinder, 187, 189
mist effect, 278
Miter joins, 67
Miter limits, 67
Miyamoto, Nobuko, 226, 244, 414
Miyamoto, Yukio
  cat image, 252, 354
  contact information, 414
  French horn image, 351
  "Molding Mesh," 244–245, 354
mobile media, 363
"Modeling Mesh" lesson, 348–354
modifier keys, 40
"Molding Mesh" lesson, 244–245,
    354
monitors, 2, 357
Monroy, Bert, 102–104, 383, 414
Moonlightpress Studio, 415
morphing, 220
Moss, Gary, 316–317, 414
mouse, drawing freehand with, 13
Müller-Lancé, Joachim, 174, 414
"Multinational font support" Tip,
    156
multinational fonts, 156
MultiPage, 416
Multiply blending mode, 253, 254,
    271
mural, 393
Murphy, Mark, 364–365

N

Nagara, Innosanto, 178–179, 414
naming
  brushes, 90
  files, 24
  groups, 125
  images, 24
  layers, 121, 133
  styles, 152
  symbols, 115
  views, 25
National Park Service, 322, 414
navigation techniques, 5–7
Navigator palette, 26
"Navigator palette & views" Tip,
    26
Neal, Brad, 336, 414

negative space, 205
Nelson, David, xiv, 91, 414
Nelson, Jay, xiv
neon sign, 383
"Nested Layers" lesson, 138–139
New Art Has Basic Appearance
    option, xvii, 128, 261, 304
New Character Style command,
    152
New Paragraph Style command,
    152
New Style button, 152
New View command, 25
Newman, Gary, 187, 414
Ng, Richard, 114, 414
Nielsen, Chris, 339, 414
"Not enough steps..." Tip, 305
Noumena Digital, 413

O

Object Highlighting preferences,
    28
Object menu command, 328
"Objective Colors" lesson, 74–75
objects
  adding to groups, 194–195
  aligning, *See* aligning
  appearance attributes for, 19
  applying effects to, 281
  applying gradients to, 223,
      234–237
  applying graphic styles to, 19
  assigning URLs to, 358–359
  base, 228–229
  beveled edges, 303
  bringing to front, 126, 311
  combining, 186–189
  constructing, 201–202
  controlling stacking order,
      124–126
  copying between layers, 135
  creating, 53, 186–189
  creating custom guides from, 28
  deleting stray points from, 11
  deselecting, 58
  distributing to layers, 359–360
  dividing, 204–205
  extruding, 302, 303, 309, 319
  filling, 18, 60–61
  finding, 75
  geometric, 12–13

VectorBabe, 180, *See also* Cohen, Sandee
vectors, working with, 194
Vertical Area type, 148
Vertical Area Type tool, 146, 160
Vertical Path Type tool, 146
vertical ruler, 302
Vertical Type tool, 146, 147
"Victory Climb" illustrations, 225
View menu, 26, 27
views, 24–28
vignettes, 273
Vincent, Steven, 417

W

Wai, Trina, 320, 415
wall mural, 393
warp effects, 176–177
   applying, 282–283, 292–293, 318
   deleting, 293
   editing, 283
   grouping clip art for use with, 292
   lesson on, 292–295
   saving as graphic styles, 293
   and Smart Guides, 285
   transforming type with, 176–177
   vs. envelope effects, 282
Warp Effects tool, 282
"Warps & Envelopes" lesson, 292–295
washes, 98
Watanabe, Andrew T., 362
water effect, 340
water glass, 246–247
watercolor effect, 260, 263
wave shapes, 178–179
Web
   printing from, 34
   saving files for, 356–361, 365, 368
   templates for, 4
Web graphics, 356–357, 356–376, *See also* artwork
   color considerations, 356–357, 359, 361, 362, 366
   export file formats, 360–363
   exporting, 360–361
   Gallery pages, 369, 373, 376
   lessons on, 364–368, 370–372
   optimizing, 356, 358, 359

   rasterizing artwork for, 357
   tools for working with, 356
Web safe colors, 356–357, 359, 361, 362, 366
Web slices, 358–359
Web Swatches library, 357
Webb, Tim, 225, 415
"Webward Ho!" lesson, 366–369
Weimer, Alan James, 86, 342, 343, 415
Weinstein, Ari M., 166–167, 182–183, 282, 415
Welcome screen, 2, 3
"West Field Yardbird" image, 400
West Nile virus map, 323
Western European language fonts, 156
Whyte, Hugh, 364–365, 415
Willcockson, Tom, 401, 415
William Patterson University, 401
Window menu, xvi, 17
windows, working with, 25, 26, 27
Windows (Microsoft)
   keyboard shortcuts, xvi
   preferences, 3
   system requirements, 2
wine bottle, 306, 321
wine goblet, 232
Winter Olympics mascots, 384–386
Wireframe option, 305
woodcut effect, 225
Woodstock, 142
words, 156–157, 173
"Working with Live Paint and Group Isolation Mode", xiv, 186, 194–198
workspaces, managing, 19–20
Worldstudio Foundation, 203–204
worms, 116
Wow! Actions folder, 326
Wow! CD
   artwork on, xv, xvii
   Bézier curves, 131
   brushes on, 94, 95, 286
   Creating Vector Content: Using Live Trace, 190
   "creating_vector_content.pdf" file, 190
   Design Tools Monthly, xiv, 406–407
   "Fill Rules.pdf" file, 187
   IAN Sampler Pack, 114, 408–411

   isometric formula demo, 77
   "KevanAtteberry-blends.ai" file, 222
   material on, xiv–xv
   "Moving from FreeHand to Illustrator," 378
   "OpenType_Guide.pdf" file, 153
   Paste commands exercises, 125
   "Prepress and Printing" PDF, 29, 34
   Real World Adobe Illustrator CS excerpt, xiv
   symbol libraries, 114
   Wow! Actions folder, 326
   "Zen" practice lessons, xv, xviii, 40, 50–52
wrap object, 151
wrapping text, 151
Write Slices option, 359

X

X axis, 28, 302, 304, 308
XML, 363
Xtream Path, 416

Y

Y axis, 28, 302, 304, 308
Yamaha French horn, 351
Yip, Filip, 130–131, 396, 415

Z

Z axis, 302, 304, 308
Zen, 38, 39
Zen lessons, xv, xviii, 40–58
"Zen of the Pen", xv
"Zen Rotation" lesson, 52
"Zen Scaling" lesson, 50–51
"zenhouse.ai" file, 40
Zig Zag effect, 161
"Zippy Zooming" tip, 67
Zimmerman, Neal, 199
Zion National Park label, 184
zoom percentages, 27
Zoom tool, 26
zooming in/out, 25–27

WOW! BOOK PRODUCTION NOTES:

Interior Book Design and Production

This book was produced in InDesign CS using primarily Adobe's Minion Pro and Frutiger OpenType fonts. Barbara Sudick is the artist behind the original *Illustrator Wow!* design and typography; using Jill Davis's layout of *The Photoshop Wow! Book* as a starting point, she designed the first edition in QuarkXPress.

Hardware and Software

With the exception of some of the testers and tech editors, all of the *Wow!* team uses Macintosh computers. We used Adobe Illlustrator CS2, Photoshop CS, and Ambrosia Software's Snapz Pro X for the screenshots. We used Adobe Acrobat 5, 6, and 7 for distribution of the book pages to testers, the indexer, Peachpit and the proofreaders. Adam Z Lein created an online *Wow!* database for us so the team could track the details of the book production. Many of the team members use Dantz Retrospect for backups of our computers. CDS Documentation Services printed this book. See the *Resources* appendix for company contact information.

How to contact the author

If you've created artwork using the newer features of Illustrator that you'd like to submit for consideration in future *Wow!* books, please send printed samples to: Sharon Steuer, c/o Peachpit Press, 1249 Eighth Street, Berkeley, CA 94710.

Real World Adobe® Illustrator® CS2

is the definitive guide to learning industrial-strength techniques using Adobe Illustrator.

- Completely revised from the ground up, by leading Illustrator expert Mordy Golding.

- Focuses on workflow, best-practices, and techniques that can be used immediately in the work environment and for individual projects.

- Doubles as a detailed reference to Illustrator topics and an "insider" guide to important concepts and features.

Real World Adobe Illustrator CS2
ISBN 0-321-33702-6
Mordy Golding
$44.99, 616 pages

Peachpit

Windows Finger Dance Summary *from "The Zen of Illustrator"*

Object Creation	*Hold down keys until AFTER mouse button is released.*
⇧ Shift	Constrains objects horizontally, vertically or proportionally.
Alt	Objects will be drawn from centers.
Alt click	Opens dialog boxes with transformation tools.
[ ]	Spacebar turns into the grabber Hand.
Ctrl [ ]	Turns cursor into the Zoom-in tool. Click or marquee around an area to Zoom in.
Ctrl Alt [ ]	Turns cursor into the Zoom-out tool. Click to Zoom out.
Caps lock	Turns your cursor into a cross-hair.

Object Selection	*Watch your cursor to see that you've pressed the correct keys.*
Ctrl	The current tool becomes the last chosen Selection tool.
Ctrl Alt	Current tool becomes Group Selection to select entire object. Click again to select next level of grouping. To move selection release Alt key, then Grab.
Ctrl Tab	Toggles whether Direct Selection or regular Selection tool is accessed by the Ctrl key.
⇧ Shift click	Toggles whether an object, path or point is selected or deselected.
⇧ Shift click ▷	With Direct Selection tool, click on or marquee around an object, path or point to toggle selection/deselection. **Note:** *Clicking inside a filled object may select the entire object.*
⇧ Shift click ▸ ▸₊	Clicking on, or marqueeing over objects with Selection tool or Group Selection tool, toggles selection/deselection (Group Selection tool chooses objects within a group).

Object Transformation	*Hold down keys until AFTER mouse button is released.*
⇧ Shift	Constrains transformation proportionally, vertically and horizontally.
Alt	Leaves the original object and transforms a copy.
Ctrl Z	Undo. Use Shift-Ctrl-Z for Redo.

90°
−30°   30°
30°   −30°
−90°

To move or transform a selection predictably from within dialog boxes, use this diagram to determine if you need a positive or negative number and which angle is required. (*Diagram from Kurt Hess / Agnew Moyer Smith*)

Windows Wow! Glossary of Terms

Ctrl **Alt**	**Ctrl** will always refer to the Ctrl (Control) key. **Alt** will always refer to the Alt key, and is used to modify many of the tools.
←↑→↓	The keyboard Arrow keys: Left, Up, Right, Down.
Toggle	Menu selection acts as a switch: choosing once turns on, again turns it off.
Marquee	With any Selection tool, click-drag from your page over object(s) to select.
Hinged curve	A Bézier curve that meets a line or another curve at a corner.
Direct Selection tool **Group Selection tool** **Selection tool**	Direct Selection tool selects points and paths. Group Selection tool. The first click always selects the entire object, subsequent clicks select "next group-up" in the grouping order. Selection tool (selects the biggest grouping which includes that object— if an object is ungrouped, then only that object is selected). **Note:** *See the* Basics *chapter for more on selection tools.*
Select object(s)	Click on or marquee with Group Selection tool to select entire object. Click on or marquee with the regular Selection tool to select grouped objects.
Deselect object(s)	To Deselect *one* object, Shift-click (or Shift-marquee) with Group Selection tool. To Deselect *all* selected objects, with any selection tool, click outside of all objects (but within your document), or press Shift-Ctrl-A.
Select a path	Click on a path with the Direct Selection tool to select it. **Note:** *If objects are selected, Deselect first, then click with Direct Selection tool.*
Select anchor points	Click on path with Direct Selection tool to see anchor points. Then, Direct-select marquee around the points you want selected. Or, with Direct Selection tool, Shift-click on points you want selected. **Note**: *Clicking on a selected point with Shift key down deselects that point.*
Grab an object or point	After selecting objects or points, use Direct Selection tool to click and hold down mouse button and drag to transform entire selection. **Note:** *If you click by mistake (instead of click-and-hold), Undo and try again.*
Delete an object	Group-Select the object and press the Delete (or Backspace) key. To delete grouped objects, use the Selection tool, then Delete.
Delete a path	Direct-Select a path and press the Delete (or Backspace) key. If you delete an anchor point, both paths attached to that anchor point will be deleted. **Note:** *After deleting part of an object the entire remaining object will become selected; therefore, deleting twice will always delete the entire object!*
Copy or Cut a path	Click on a path with Direct Selection tool, then Copy (Ctrl-C) or Cut (Ctrl-X). **Note:** *See the "Windows Finger Dance Summary" for more ways to copy paths.*
Copy or Cut an object	Click on an object with Group Selection tool, then Copy (Ctrl-C) or Cut (Ctrl-X). For grouped objects, Click on one of the objects with the Selection tool, then Copy (Ctrl-C) or Cut (Ctrl-X).